Alice Kehl

GREGG SPEED STUDIES

By

JOHN ROBERT GREGG, S.C.D.

Third Edition

THE GREGG PUBLISHING COMPANY

NEW YORK CHICAGO BOSTON SAN FRANCISCO
TORONTO LONDON SYDNEY

G-68-NP-20

SHORTHAND PLATES WRITTEN BY
ASTRID F. RAMSEY
CHARLES E. ZOUBEK
CHARLES RADER

Printed in the United States of America

PREFACE

When *Gregg Speed Studies* first appeared in 1917, it revolutionized the teaching of shorthand by welding shorthand theory and speed practice from the first lesson. Among the outstanding features of the book that have done much to improve results and raise the standards of accomplishment are: first, the presentation of practice matter in shorthand instead of in print; second, the development of a large and varied vocabulary through a unique plan of incorporating vocabulary drills with the work in dictation; third, a series of systematic shorthand penmanship studies for the purpose of establishing correct form and control of the basic strokes and combinations.

All these good features have been retained in the present edition, but many improvements in detail and in the material used have been effected. The emphasis on the importance of reading shorthand for the purpose of enabling a student to get a correct visual impression of the shorthand forms that has been one of the features of the previous editions is retained. The amount of shorthand material has been substantially increased, and even greater emphasis has been placed on establishing correct writing habits in the beginning. When the student is trained to write the basic forms for the alphabetic characters and combinations accurately and fluently, he will soon gain an automatic control of the hand in writing the forms that will eliminate the need for remedial drills later. The experienced teacher knows that it is comparatively easy to establish correct writing habits at the *beginning,* but difficult to correct bad writing habits later. Every one of the distinguished reporters and shorthand champions whose work is illustrated in this book devoted a great deal of time in the beginning of his study to learning to write the forms easily and fluently. Then with the sense of proportion, "style," and hand control thus firmly established, his notes were not wholly shattered under the pressure of high-speed writing.

This principle of making the right start is applicable to all arts and sports in which *skill* and rapidity are essential to high achievement. To gain the best results from the studies in shorthand penmanship, however, the drills should be given with animation. If the student understands the important influence that these drills will have upon his future progress, he will become more interested and enthusiastic about them.

A factor often overlooked is the necessity for establishing early association between *sound* and *sign*. Without this association, the response of the hand to the sound will naturally be slow; when this association is well established, the execution of the form becomes almost automatic. Therefore, the drills should be given as much as possible from dictation.

The following is the general plan of this new and revised edition of *Gregg Speed Studies*.

SPEED STUDIES I–XII

1. The instructional material and the reading and dictation practice in Speed Studies I–XII are divided into units corresponding to those of the Manual. When the principles in a unit in the Gregg Shorthand Manual have been presented, they are then reinforced by supplementary lists and shorthand plates in the corresponding unit in *Gregg Speed Studies*. Many illustrations of the principles, the brief forms, and the phrases in that unit are carefully worked into the reading and dictation practice.

2. A penmanship drill is given in each unit of Speed Studies I–VII. In these drills, all the alphabetic strokes in Gregg Shorthand are introduced. The drill in each unit consists of enlarged models of the strokes introduced in that unit, a brief explanation of what to look for in those models, and several sentences in shorthand containing a number of words involving the application of the penmanship problems presented.

3. Each unit in Speed Studies I–VI contains either a brief-form derivative drill or a brief-form phrase drill, or a combination of both.

4. The principles in each unit are supplemented by word drills selected from a list of 6,000 words taken from the "Horn List of 10,000 Words Most Commonly Used in Writing." [1] Practice on these lists will do much to build up an automatic vocabulary of the most frequently used words of the language.

5. Five or six hundred words of printed shorthand follow the instructional material of each unit. This shorthand material consists of business letters and articles chosen for their literary and informational merit. A feature that greatly adds to the interest value of the material is the number of complete "transactions" given throughout the book. The student reads and writes a letter from one firm to another; he then reads and writes the answer to that letter, and so on until the transaction is closed.

6. After a few prefixes or suffixes have been presented to the student, his readiness in using them is developed in *Gregg Speed Studies* by a supplementary list and one or more letters and articles in which those prefixes or suffixes are employed.

7. The short vocabulary in Unit 36 of the Manual has been divided into thirteen groups. Each group contains a derivative drill that is followed by letters and articles in which the words of the short vocabulary (or their derivatives) are used. This division will enable the student to learn these forms a few at a time.

[1] *Basic Writing Vocabulary*, Ernest Horn, Ph.D., University of Iowa Monograph in Education.

SPEED STUDIES XIII–XVIII

1. The material in Speed Studies XIII–XVIII also consists of business letters and articles of inspirational and informational value.

2. The material has been carefully chosen so that each Speed Study reviews the major principles presented in the Manual. For example, the letters and articles in Speed Study XIII review the principles in Chapter VII of the Manual; in Speed Study XIV, Chapter VIII, etc. The automatic review that this material provides is one of the outstanding features of Part II of this text.

The attention given in *Gregg Speed Studies* to the development of the student's understanding of the principles and his ability to construct with facility the forms for any words that he may be called upon to write will do much toward enriching his writing vocabulary and increasing his technical skill.

The author has received many suggestions from teachers all over the country that have been of great assistance in the preparation of this book, and he desires to make grateful acknowledgment to these teachers for their co-operation. He also wishes to make acknowledgment to the editorial staff of the Gregg Publishing Company for the assistance he has received in the preparation of the book for the press; to Mr. Charles L. Swem, Mr. Albert Schneider, and Mr. Martin J. Dupraw for posing for the photographs of themselves at work, which add so much to the interest and value of the book; to Mr. Charles E. Zoubek for writing the penmanship drills; and to Mrs. Astrid F. Ramsey and Mr. Charles Rader for writing the shorthand plates.

With the exception of the Manual, *Gregg Speed Studies* has been the most popular shorthand book ever published. I hope that the present edition will be of greater service to teachers and students of the fascinating art of shorthand writing.

JOHN ROBERT GREGG

SPEED STUDY I

Speed and accuracy in shorthand writing begin with the very first lesson. They depend almost wholly upon two things: first, the clearness of the mental picture that the student has of each form; and, second, his ability to execute correctly and rapidly the movements necessary to reproduce the picture. A good shorthand style depends eventually, not upon what the writer has in mind, but upon what he can put on paper. It demands clear vision plus *mastery of movement.*

An analysis of Gregg Shorthand shows certain elementary combinations that are repeated, with slight variations, over and over again—even in the most advanced writing. A mastery of these combinations will therefore give the writer a firm foundation upon which to build his superstructure of speed and accuracy.

In studying the drills, aim first at obtaining a *clear mental picture* of the form to be executed; analyze carefully the movement necessary to make it rapidly; and then repeat the movement until facility is acquired and all hesitation is removed.

At the beginning a careful comparison of the written notes with the correct forms in the text is essential. Such comparison should be carried on until the habit of correct movement has been established. The characters are to be *written,* not drawn. Two important features to be constantly watched are: first, comparative length of consonant strokes; and, second, relative size of vowels.

UNDERWOOD & UNDERWOOD STUDIOS

MR. CHARLES L. SWEM

The writing position of Mr. Charles L. Swem, formerly personal stenographer and official reporter to President Woodrow Wilson. Winner of the World's Shorthand Championship in 1923 and 1924; official reporter, New York State Supreme Court.

UNIT 1

PENMANSHIP

The most effective way to get a sharp, clear mental picture of a shorthand character is to study an enlarged model of it. The study of an enlarged model will very often bring to your notice points that might have escaped you in the outline written in its normal size. Therefore, in these lessons you will find enlarged models of many strokes and joinings, together with a brief explanation of what to look for in the models.

In practicing these drills, compare each outline you write with the enlarged model before you write the outline again.

1. K, G, R, L

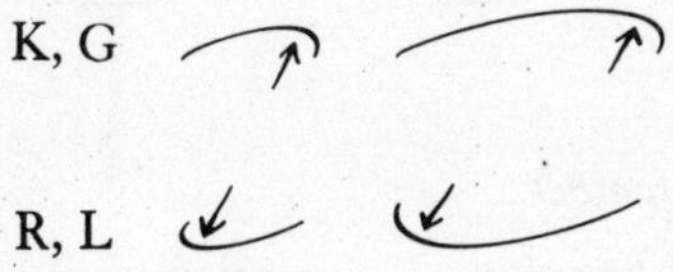

Points to Remember:

a. Each of these strokes begins and ends on the same plane. The beginning and the end of *k* and *g* rest on the line of writing. *R* and *l* rest on the line of writing as a saucer would rest on a table.

b. The deep part of the curve in *k* and in *g* is at the end; in *r* and *l*, at the beginning, as indicated by the arrows.

c. *K* and *r* are the same size, as are *g* and *l*.

d. Correctly written, *r* and *l* look like *k* and *g* when the paper is turned upside down.

Practice:

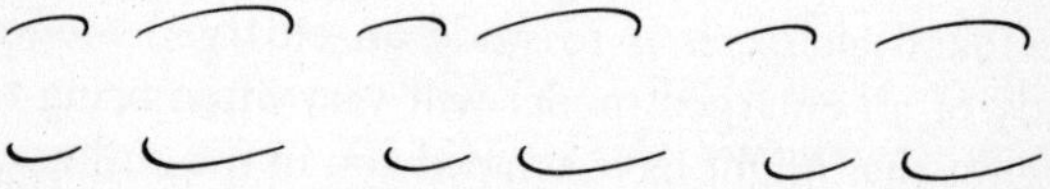

2. Circles Joined to Curves

Ak, Ag

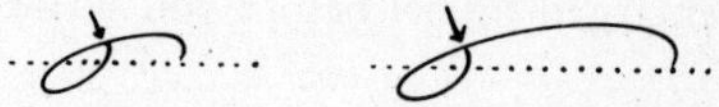

Ra, La

Points to Remember:

a. The dotted line shows the position of the circle in relation to the curve. (Remember, the dotted line in *ra* and *la* does *not* represent the line of writing. The *base* of the *r* and of the *l* rests on the line of writing.)

b. The circle joins the curve at a right angle.

Practice:

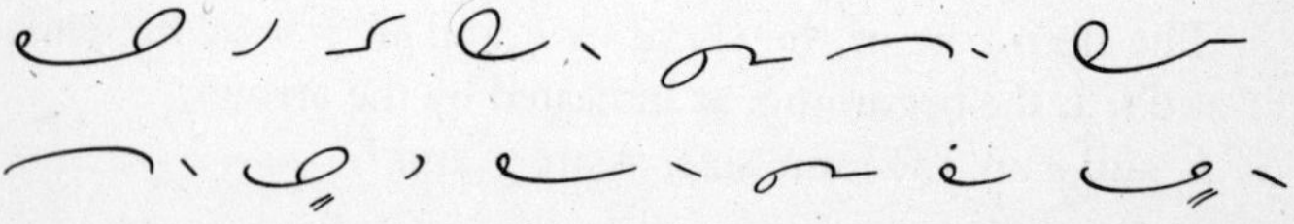

3. Circles Joined to Straight Strokes

Ad, Da, Am, Ma

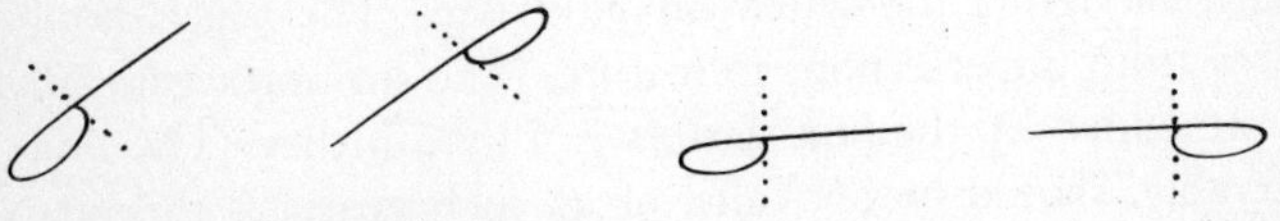

Points to Remember:

a. In joining the circle to a straight line, start and finish as shown by the dotted lines.

b. Keep straight lines absolutely straight.

Practice:

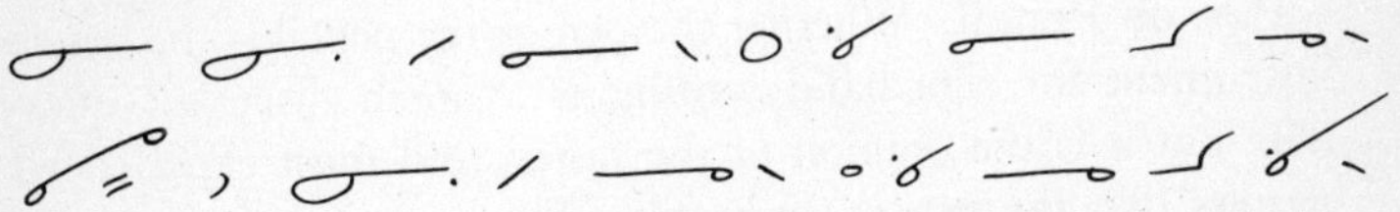

MOST-USED WORDS AND PHRASES

4. Frequently Used Words

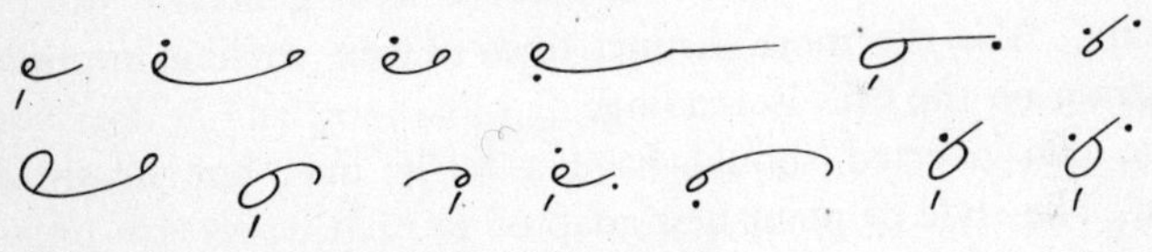

5. Frequently Used Phrases

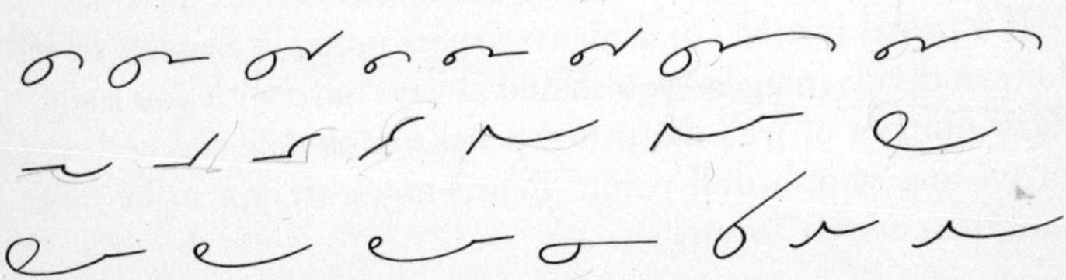

SPEED POINTERS

Notebooks. The notebook is especially important. The surface of the paper should be firm and smooth so that a light touch—the lighter the better—may be used. The paper should be free from imperfections in texture. The size most generally recommended by the best writers is 6 by 9 inches. The lines, preferably, should be one-third of an inch apart, as this spacing will tend to develop a more compact style of writing. The page should have a vertical ruling down the middle, so as to provide two columns for writing on each page. A column 3 inches wide enables you to write across the line of writing without shifting the arm to any appreciable degree.

Pen or Pencil. Whether the pen or the pencil is the better instrument for shorthand writing is a much discussed question, but it is the opinion of the fastest and most experienced writers that the pen is preferable. The pen gives a firm, distinct, easily recognized outline. The small circles and the hooks, especially, can be much more readily and accurately executed with the pen than with the pencil. Pen writing is also very much easier to read, because it is generally more accurate. Also the more distinct lines of pen writing impose less strain on the eyes in reading.

The pen selected should have a fairly fine, but smooth, point. The style of point best adapted to each writer can only be ascertained by experimentation. The fountain pen has so many advantages that it is to be recommended in all cases.

If a pencil is used—and many writers prefer it in spite of its known disadvantages—you should always have with you a sufficient number of well-sharpened pencils to obviate the necessity of writing with a dull point. Pencil notes are apt to be large and inaccurately formed.

6. READING AND DICTATION PRACTICE

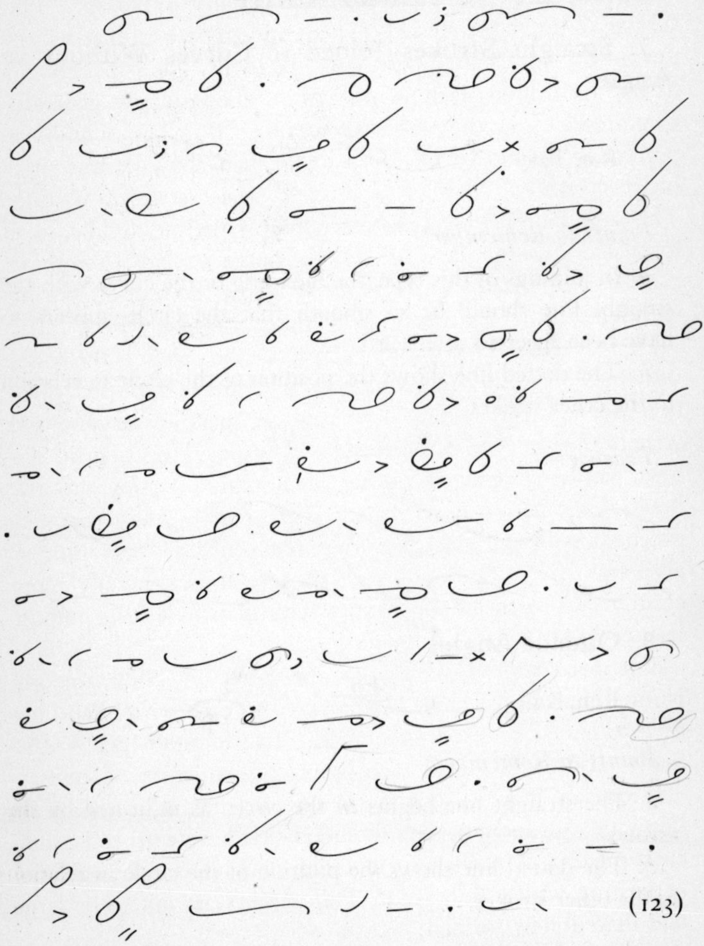

(123)

UNIT 2

PENMANSHIP

7. Straight Strokes Joined to Curves Without an Angle

Rat, Tak 

Points to Remember:

a. In joinings of this type, the blending ot the curve with the straight line should be so smooth that the circle appears to have been inserted afterward.

b. The dotted line shows the position of the circle in relation to the other strokes.

Practice:

8. Outside Angles

Ran, Kan 

Points to Remember:

a. The straight line begins *in* the circle, as indicated by the arrows.

b. The dotted line shows the position of the circle in relation to the other strokes.

c. If the page is turned upside down, the word *ran* will become the word *knack*.

Nal, Mel 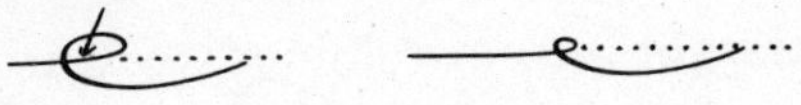

Points to Remember:

a. To accommodate the circle in these joinings, the *n* and the *m* are written slightly longer than they would normally be written. The arrow shows how the *n* is extended in the word *nail*.

b. The dotted line indicates the position of the circle in relation to the other strokes.

Practice:

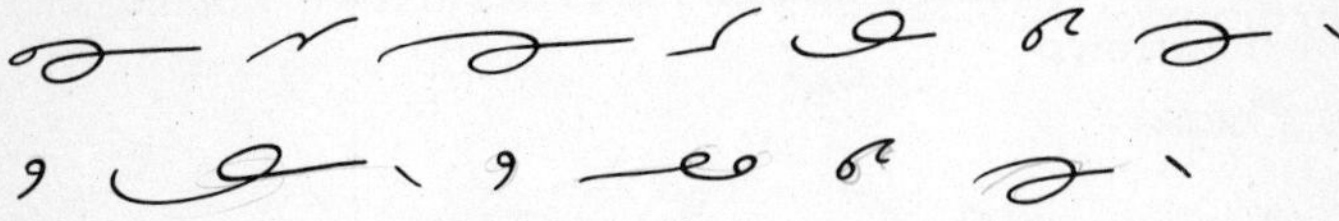

9. Circles Between Strokes in the Same Direction

Mam, Ded 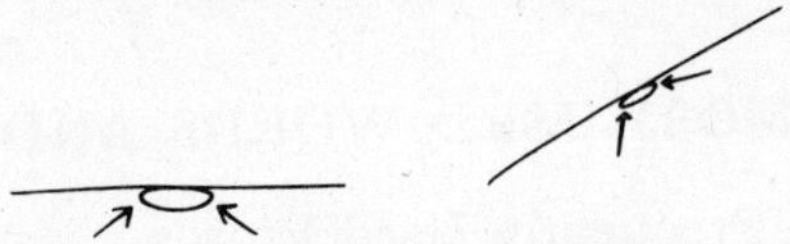

Points to Remember:

a. The joining should be so smooth and snug that, if the circle were eliminated, the two straight lines would blend into one stroke.

b. Avoid forming points on the circles in the places indicated by the arrows.

Practice:

10. Circles Between Opposite Curves

Gal, Lag 

Points to Remember:

a. If the circle were erased, the curves should blend into a continuous stroke.

b. Avoid forming points on the circles in the places indicated by the arrows.

Practice:

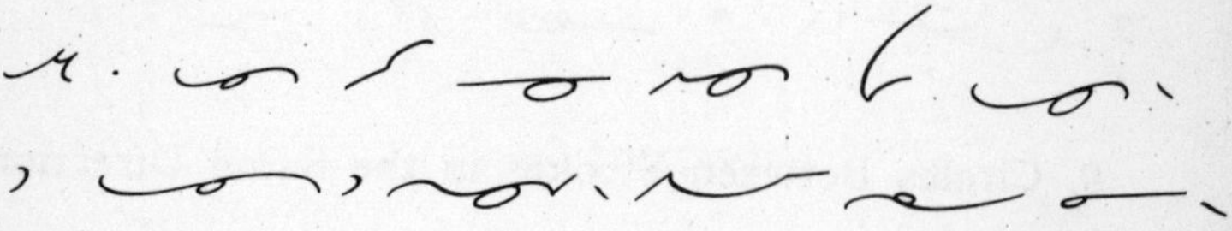

MOST-USED WORDS AND PHRASES

11. Frequently Used Words

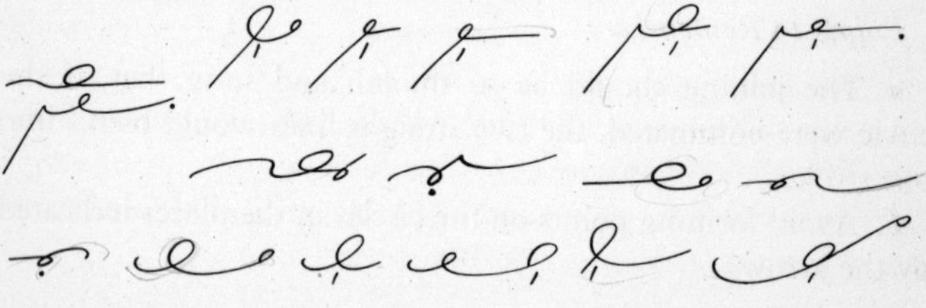

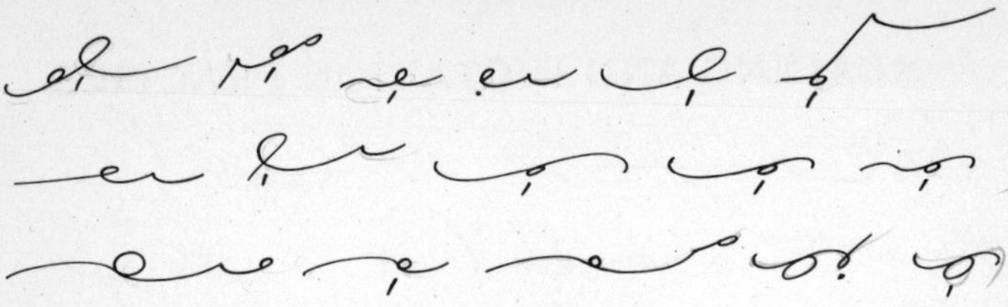

12. Frequently Used Phrases

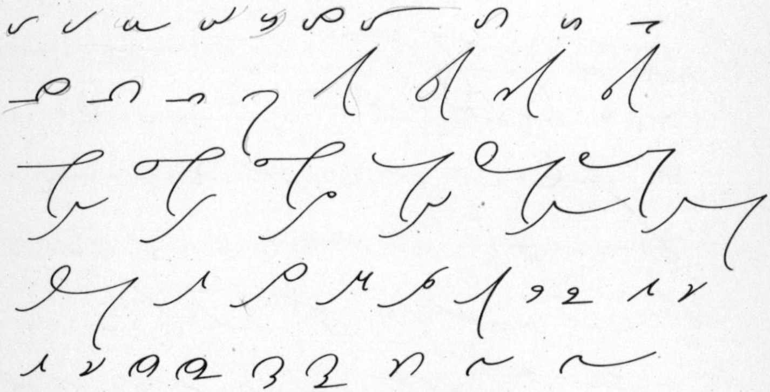

SPEED POINTER

Size of Notes. Adopt a size of notes that seems natural to you. The characters given in this text and in *The Gregg Writer* are a good standard to follow. As a general thing, students make characters too large; and, as this tendency is magnified in rapid writing, much is to be gained by starting with notes that are rather small. The size of notes, however, is a point that must be determined largely by the writer himself. You should consult with your teacher and aim to adopt a size best suited to your hand. The size should be such as to give a natural freedom of movement.

READING AND DICTATION PRACTICE

13.

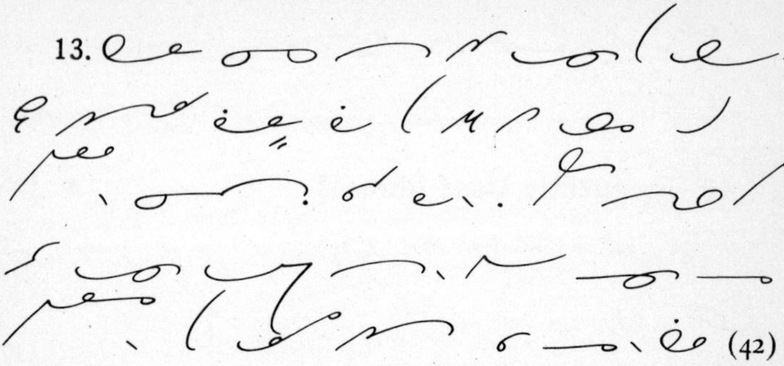

(42)

14.

(73)

15.

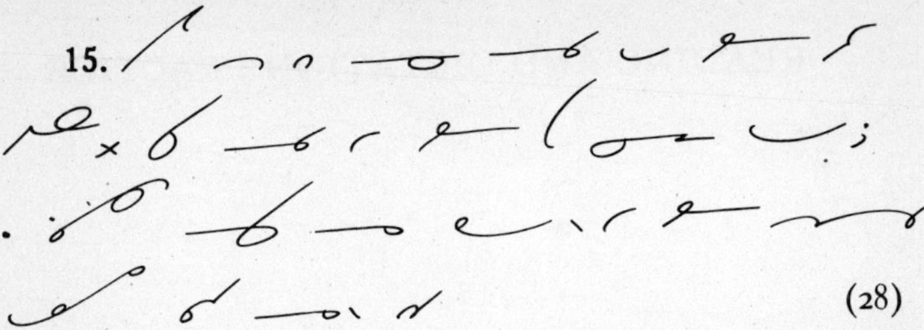

(28)

16.

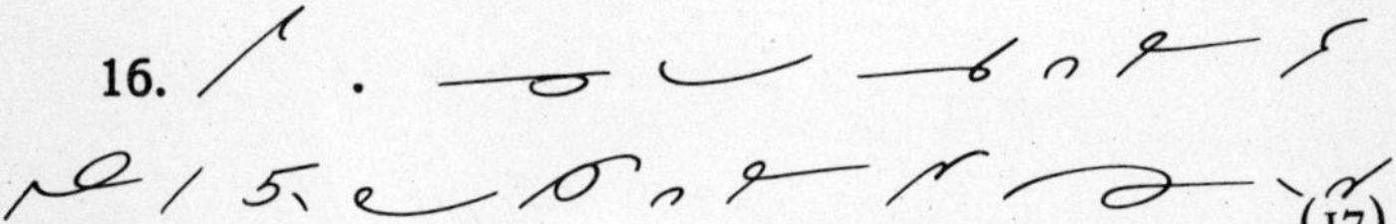

(17)

17.

(31)

18.

(41)

UNDERWOOD & UNDERWOOD STUDIOS

MR. MARTIN J. DUPRAW

At the age of nineteen, Mr. Dupraw won the World's Shorthand Championship in 1925. By repeating his victories in 1926 and 1927, Mr. Dupraw won permanent possession of the World's Championship Trophy. He is now official reporter in the New York State Supreme Court.

UNIT 3

PENMANSHIP

19. Joining of Equal Curves

Kr, Gl, Rk 

Points to Remember:

a. In these combinations, the curves are rather shallow. They have a wavelike appearance and are very fluent.

b. Kr (or *rk*) is slightly shorter than the combined length of *r* and *k* when standing alone. The same is true of *gl* (or *lg*).

Practice:

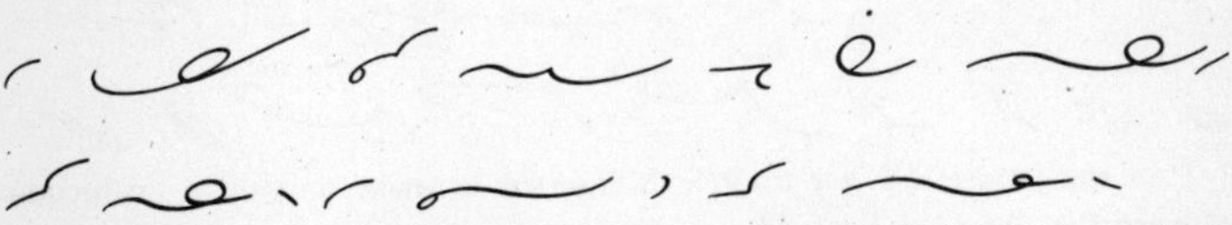

20. Joining of Curves of Unequal Length

Gr, Kl 

Point to Remember:

The horizontal dotted lines show the relation of the strokes to each other.

Practice:

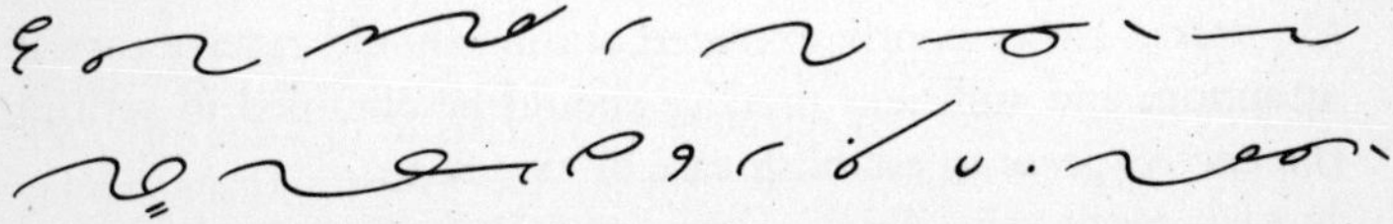

MOST-USED WORDS AND PHRASES

21. Frequently Used Words

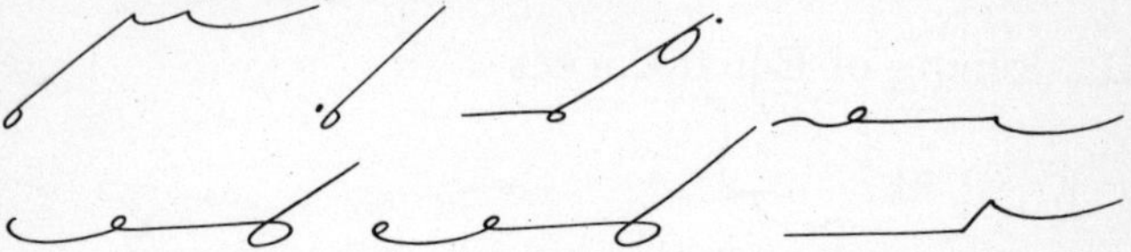

22. Frequently Used Phrases

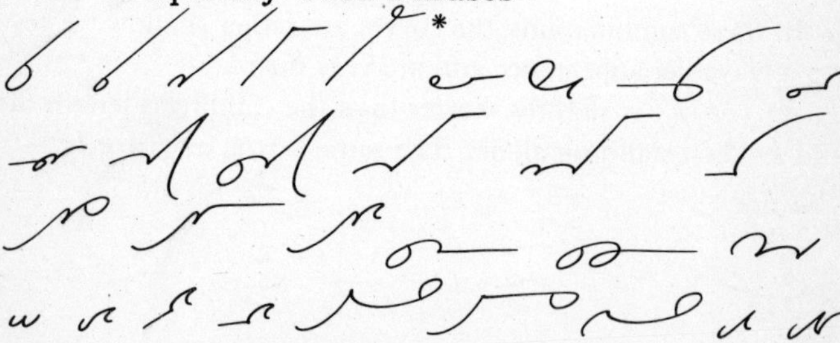

* In the phrase *did not* a circle is inserted to make a positive distinction between this phrase and *would not.*

SPEED POINTER

Correcting Outlines. When practicing for speed and accuracy or when taking dictation, you should never, under any circumstances, *correct or change word forms while writing.* The loss of time in crossing out words incorrectly written is equivalent to that of writing several words correctly, to say nothing of the mental disturbance it causes. The time to make corrections in outlines is *while reading or transcribing the notes.* Every poorly executed outline should receive careful attention, and sufficient practice should be obtained in writing the *correct form* to establish ease of execution.

READING AND DICTATION PRACTICE

23. A Wreck

(147)

24.

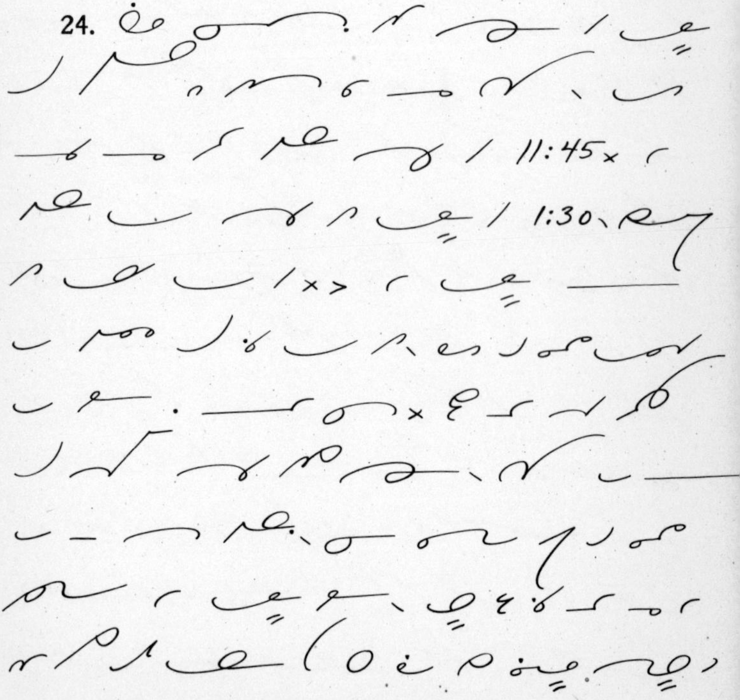

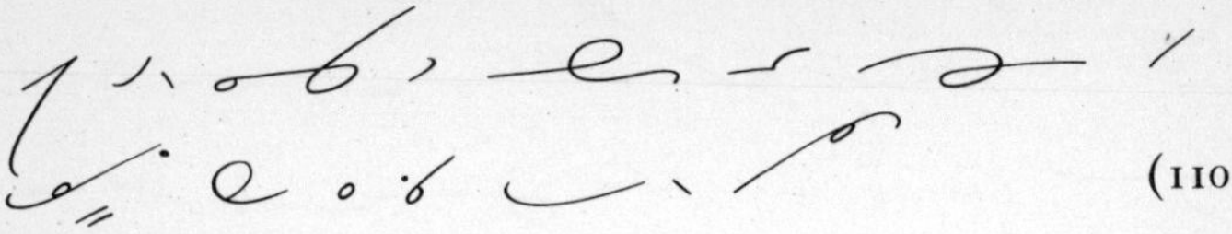

(110)

25.

(71)

26.

(39)

27.

(42)

28. Ned and the Cattle

(84)

29. 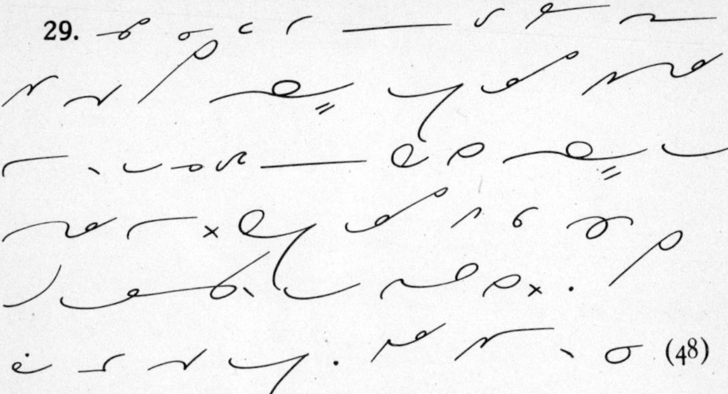 (48)

30.  (27)

31. 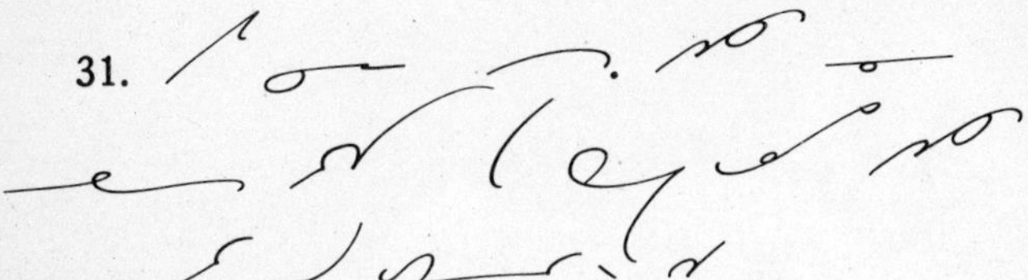 (24)

32. 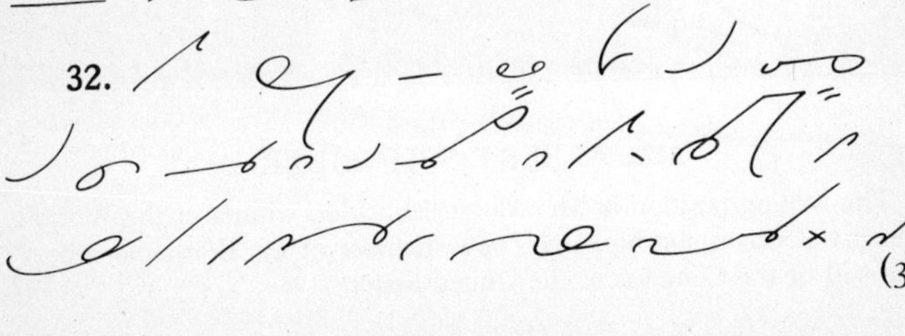 (31)

HARRIS & EWING

MR. ALBERT SCHNEIDER

The writing position of Mr. Albert Schneider, winner of the World's Shorthand Championship, 1921, now member of the shorthand reporting staff of the Congress of the United States.

SPEED STUDY II

UNIT 4

PENMANSHIP

In practicing the following drills, be sure to compare each outline that you write with the enlarged model.

33. S, P, B; S, F, V

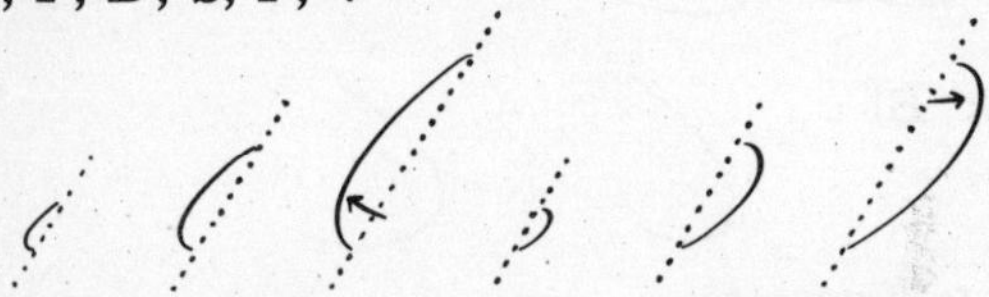

Points to Remember:

a. The dotted line shows the slant of the strokes as well as the relation of the beginning of the outline to the end.

b. The deep part of the curve comes at the end of left-*s, p,* and *b*; at the beginning of right-*s, f,* and *v* as indicated by the arrows.

c. In your writing, observe carefully the proportion of these strokes.

Practice:

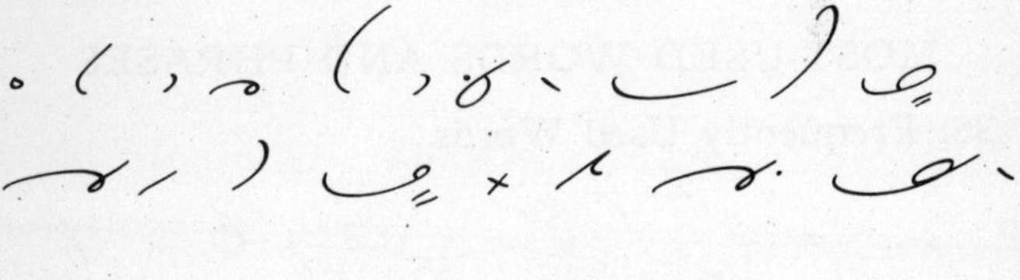

34. Pr, Pl 

Points to Remember:

a. These combinations are written with one sweep of the pen.

b. At the beginning of these combinations, the hand moves from the right to the left; it does not move immediately down.

Practice:

35. Br, Bl

Points to Remember:

a. These combinations are written with one sweep of the pen.

b. At the beginning of these combinations, the hand starts immediately *down* instead of to the left as in *pr* and *pl.*

Practice:

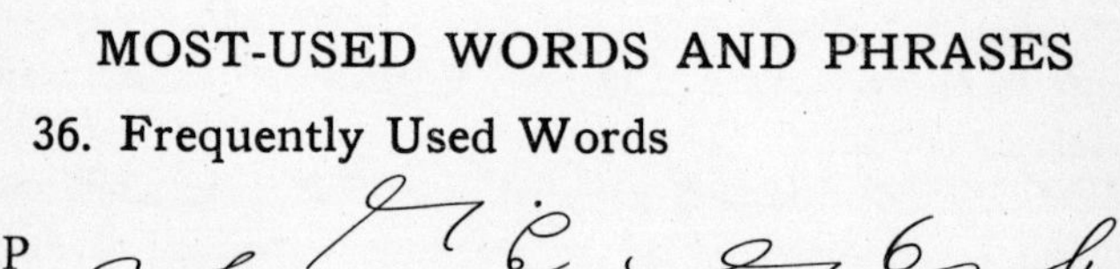

MOST-USED WORDS AND PHRASES

36. Frequently Used Words

P

B

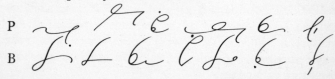

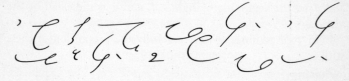

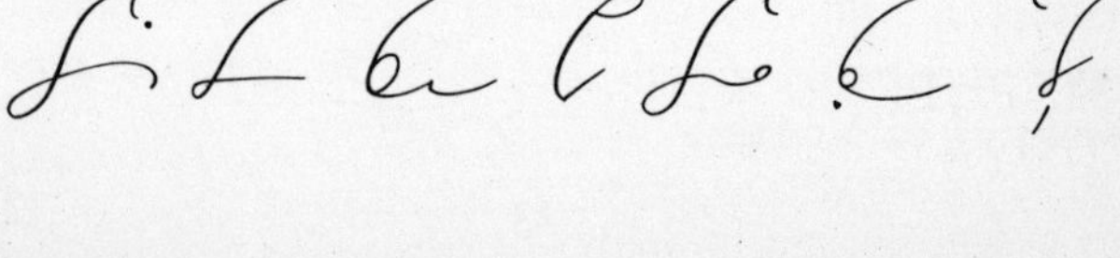

F

V

CH

J

SH

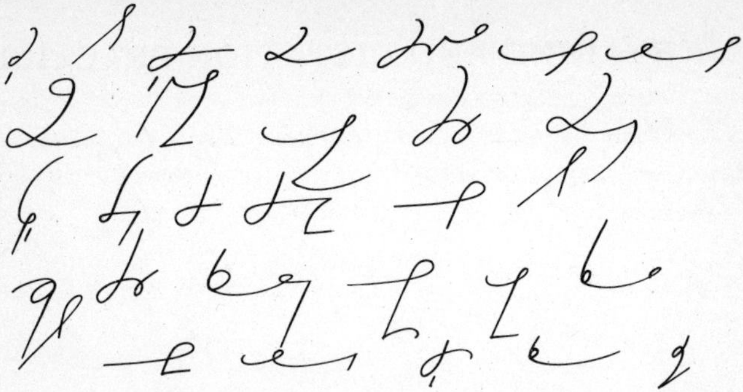

37. Frequently Used Phrases

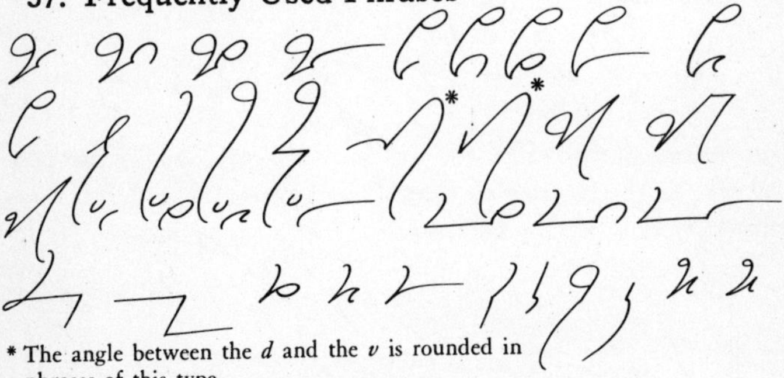

* The angle between the *d* and the *v* is rounded in phrases of this type.

SPEED POINTER

Passing from One Outline to Another. The shorthand writer should cultivate from the start the habit of passing directly from one outline to another without any preliminary or useless movements. The best time to acquire this habit is while taking dictation that has been practiced, as the attention can then be concentrated on the movement used in passing from one word to another. Poorly trained writers often make several unnecessary movements in the air with the pen after completing each outline.

READING AND DICTATION PRACTICE

38.

(64)

39.

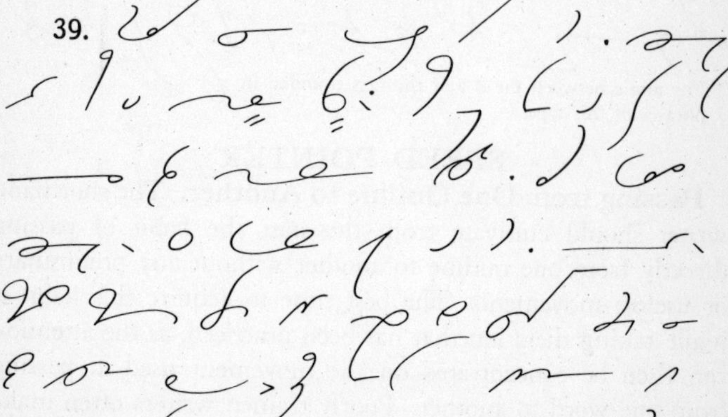

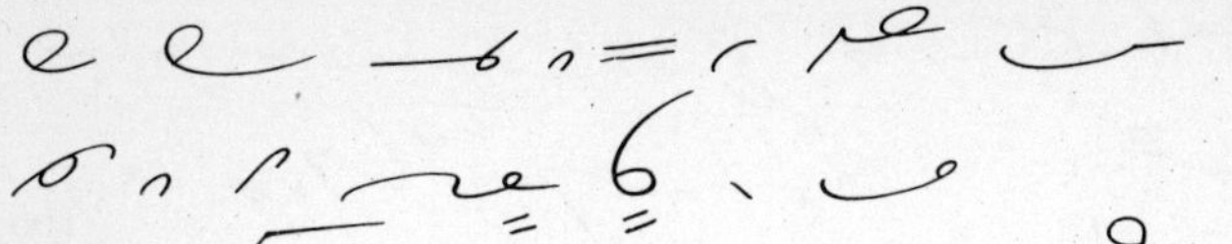

(73)

40.

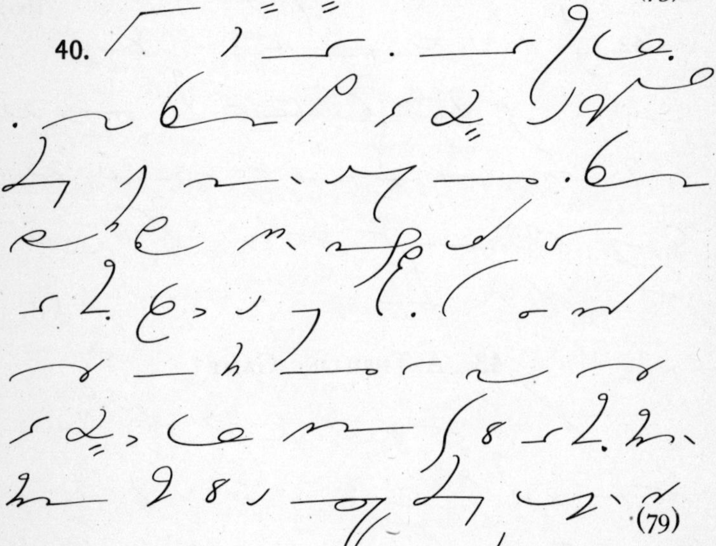

(79)

41.

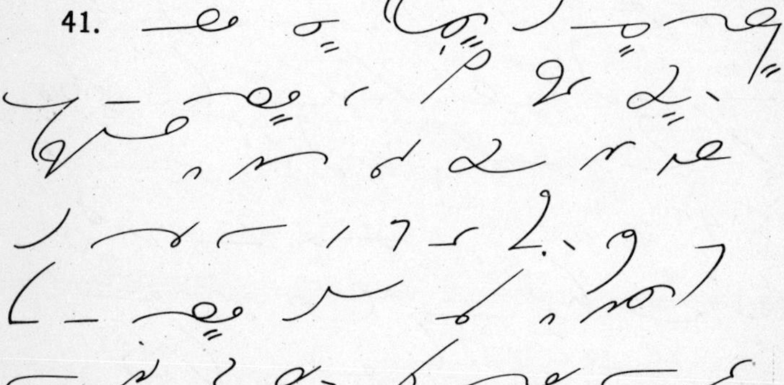

(66)

42.

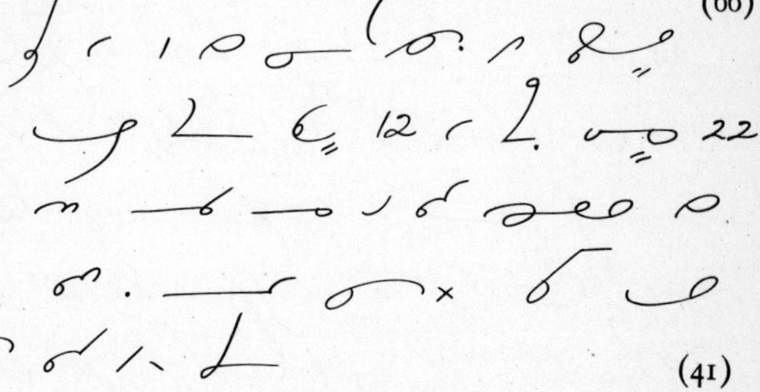

(41)

43. A Thrilling Game

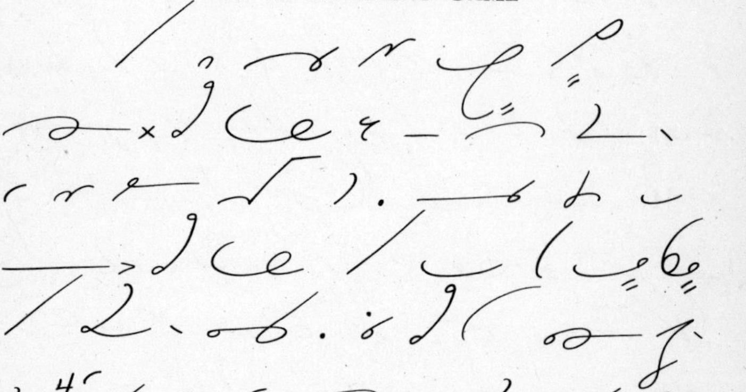

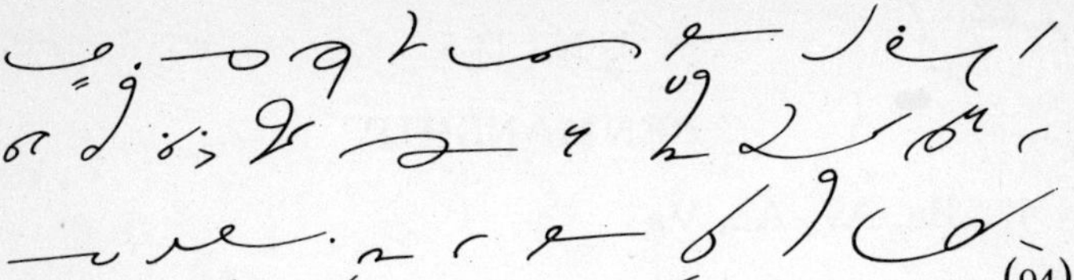

(94)

44. 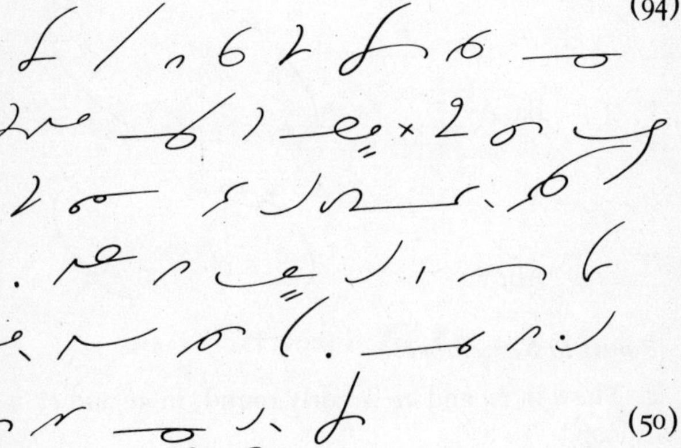

(50)

45. 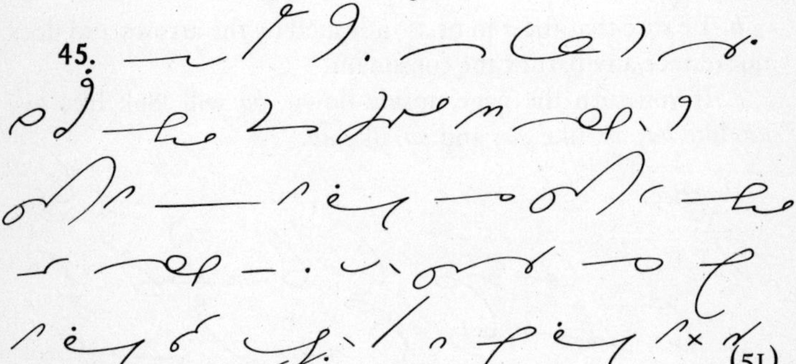

(51)

46. 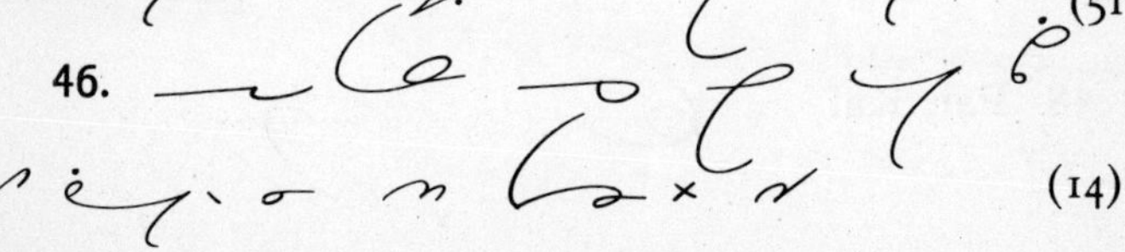

(14)

UNIT 5

PENMANSHIP

47. Ba, Av; Ab, Va

Ba, Av

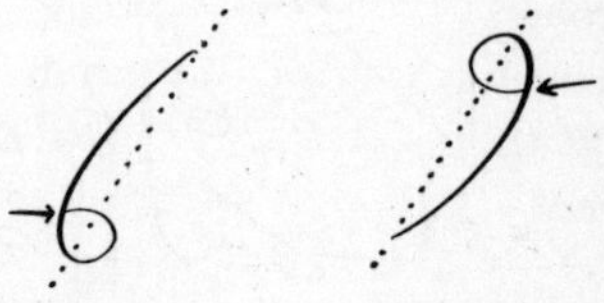

Ab, Va

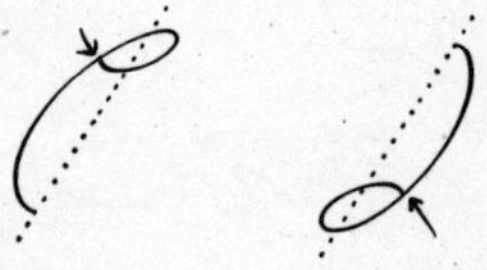

Points to Remember:

a. The *a* in *ba* and *av* is fairly round; in *ab* and *va* it is more of a loop.

b. Be sure that the *a* joins as indicated by the arrows and does not retrace any part of the consonant.

c. If you turn the page upside down, *ba* will look like *av*; *av*, like *ba*; *ab*, like *va*; and *va*, like *ab*.

Practice:

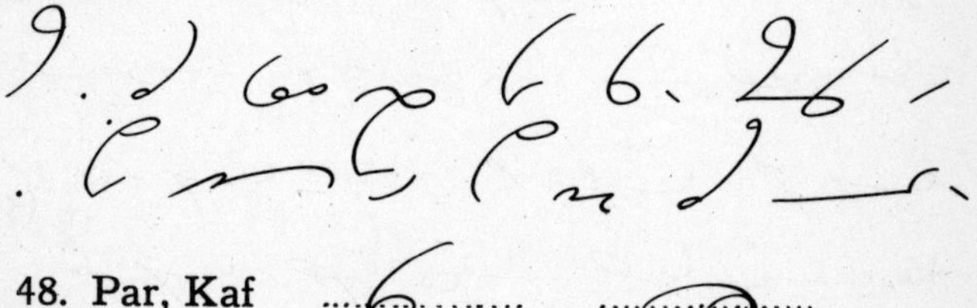

48. Par, Kaf

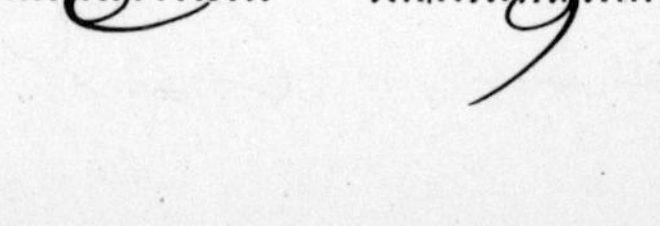

Points to Remember:

a. The circle should join so smoothly that if it were removed, the consonants would form a continuous curve.

b. The dotted line indicates the relation of the circle to the other strokes.

c. If you have written an accurate outline, when you turn your page upside down, *kaf* will look like *par*; *par*, like *kaf*.

Practice:

49. Far, Fal

Point to Remember:

As the *a* is being completed, it should start to come *down* before it reaches the *f*. In other words, the *r* or *l* should be started before the circle is completed.

Practice:

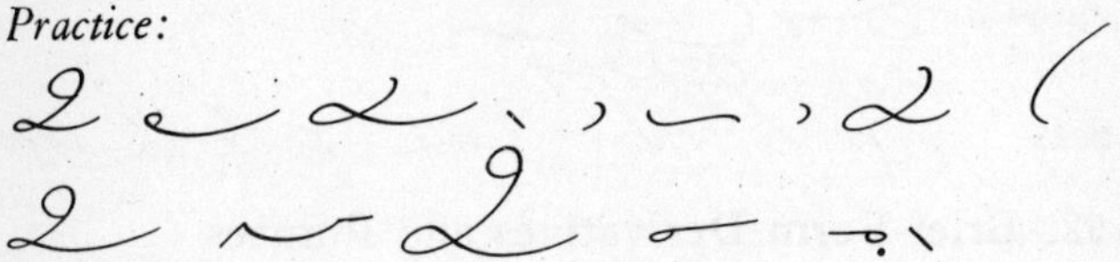

50. Dash, Shad

Points to Remember:

a. The vowel becomes a loop.

b. Both the *sh* and *d* are slightly extended in order to accommodate the loop.

c. If you were to turn these outlines upside down, *shade* would become a perfect copy of *dash*; *dash*, a perfect copy of *shade*.

Practice:

MOST-USED WORDS AND PHRASES

51. Frequently Used Words

Right-motion *s*:

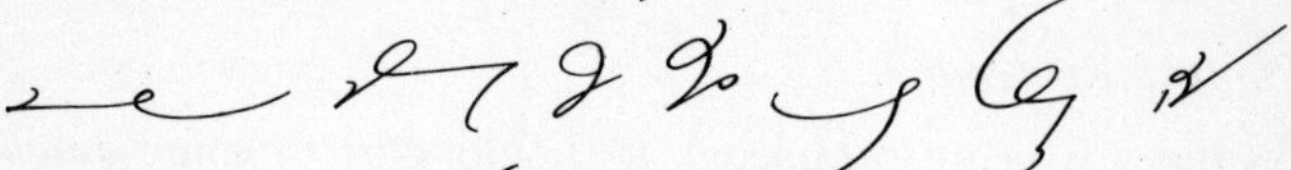

Left-motion *s*:

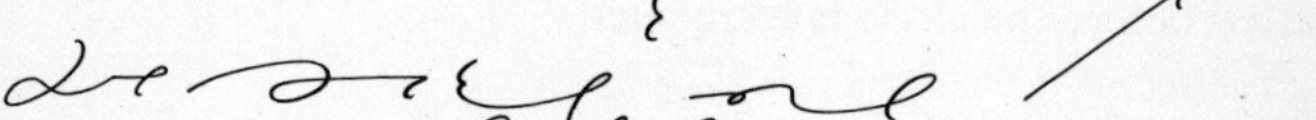

Ses:

52. Brief-Form Derivatives and Phrases

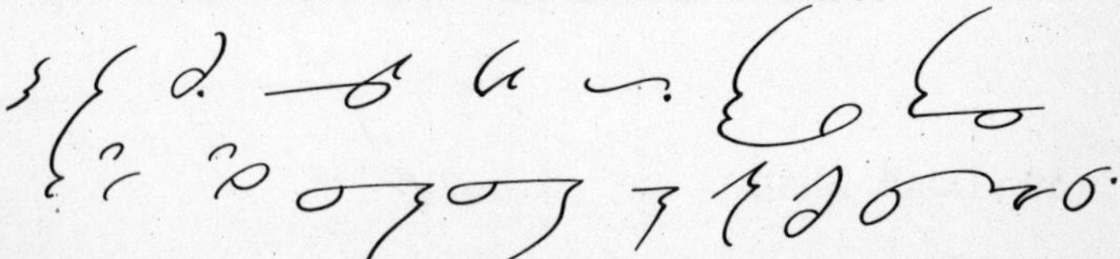

READING AND DICTATION PRACTICE

53. Autobiography of a Penny

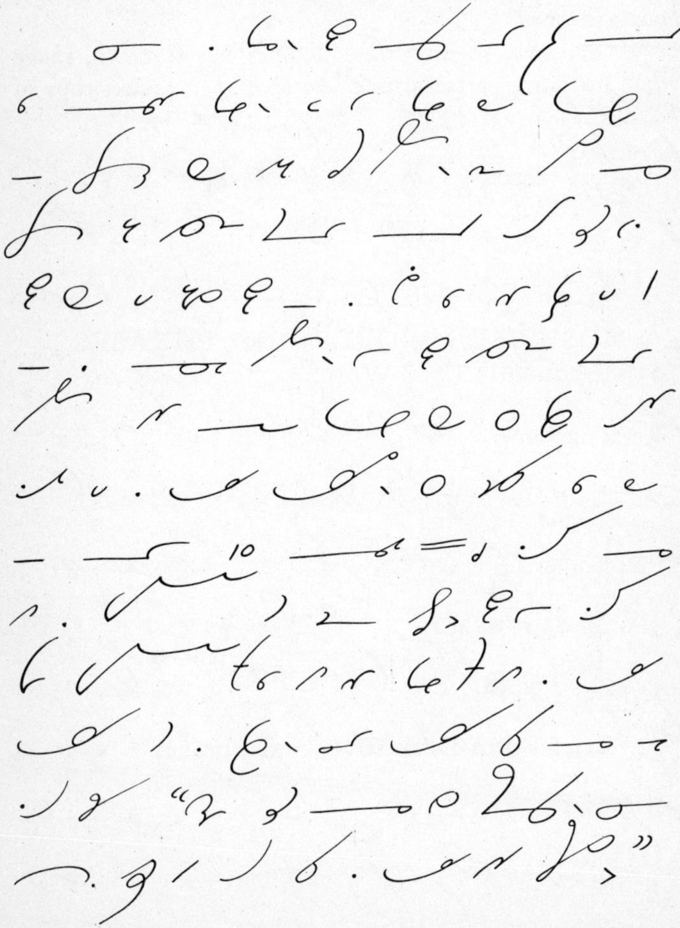

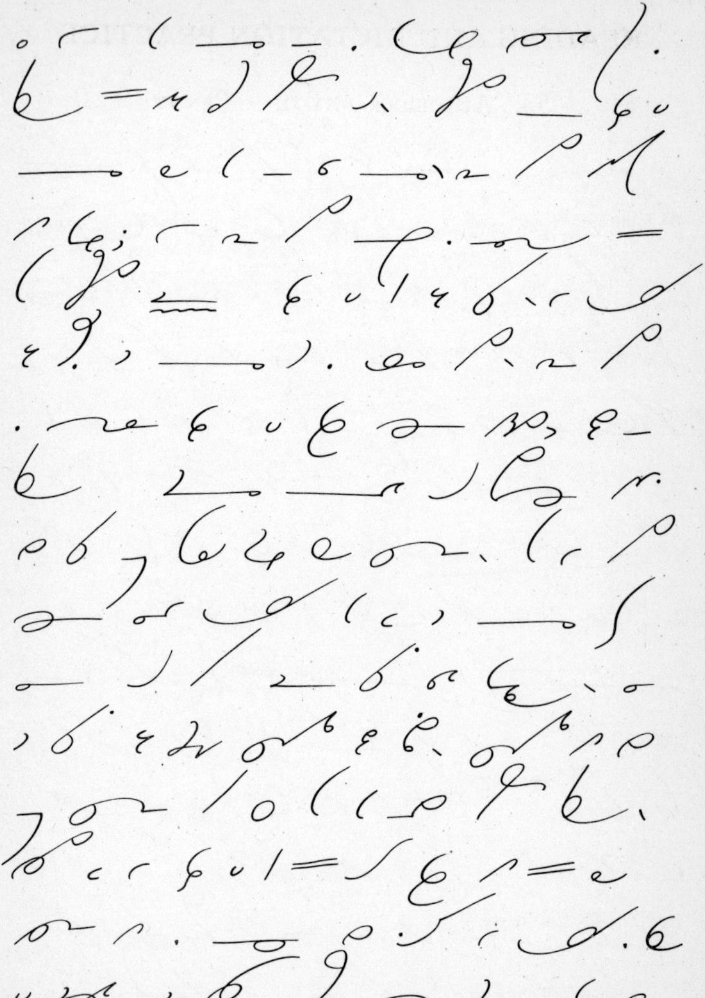

(282)

54.

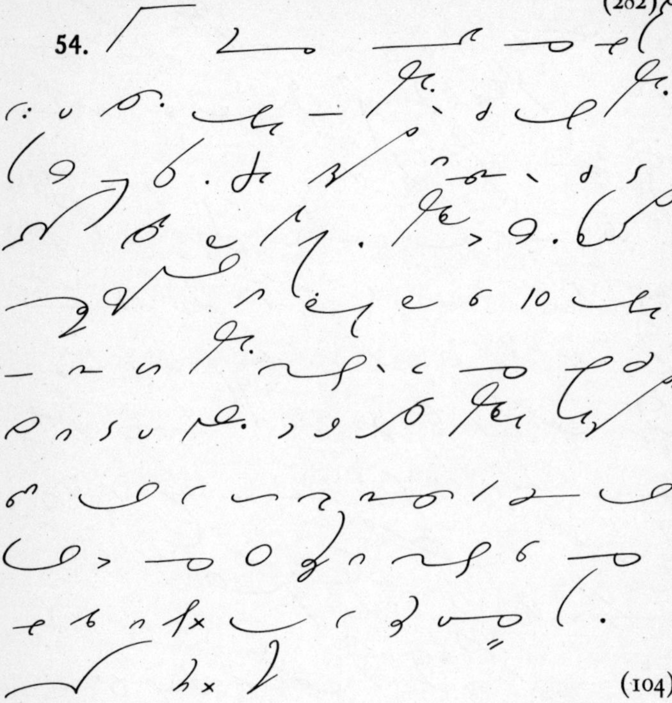

(104)

55.

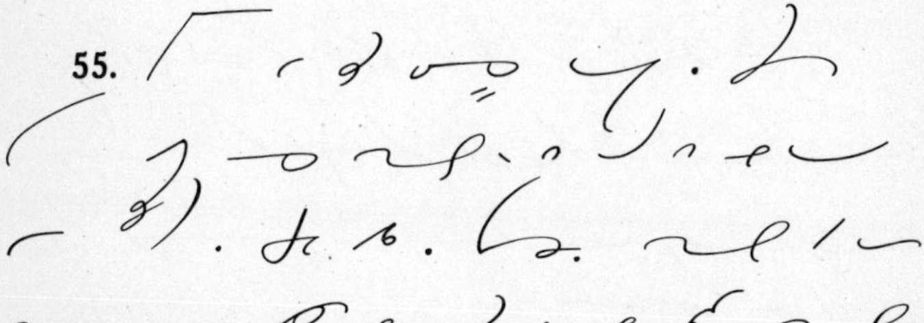

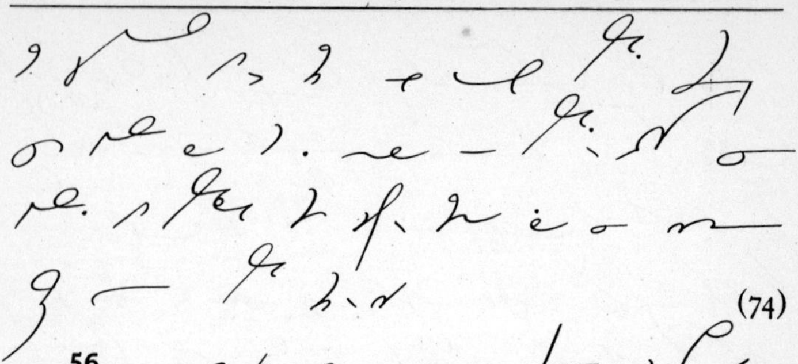

(74)

56.

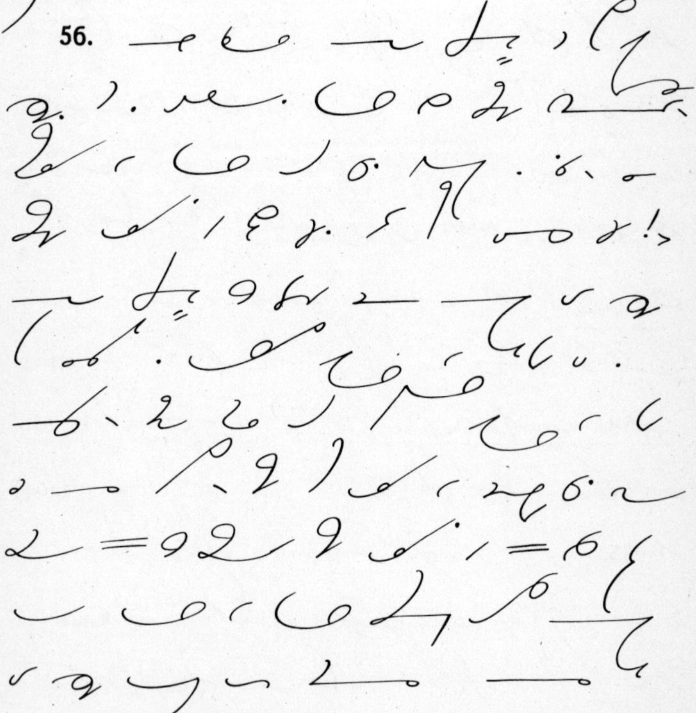

(104)

57.

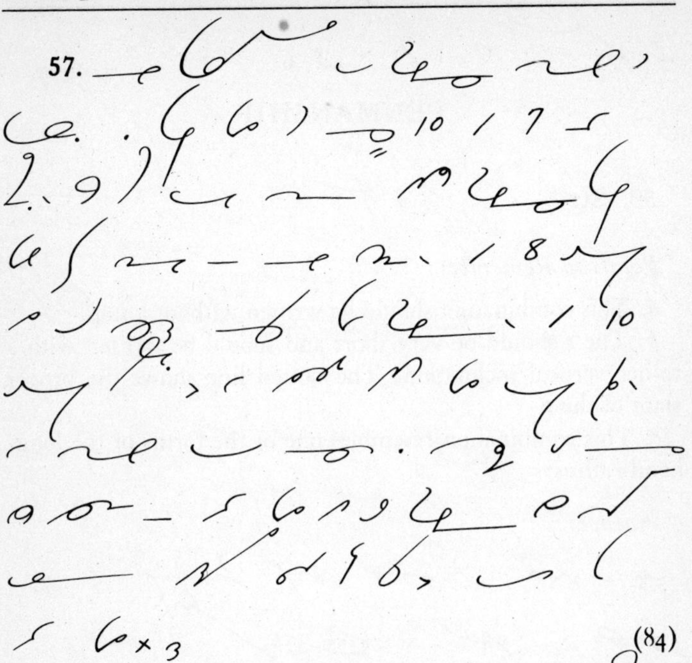

(84)

58.

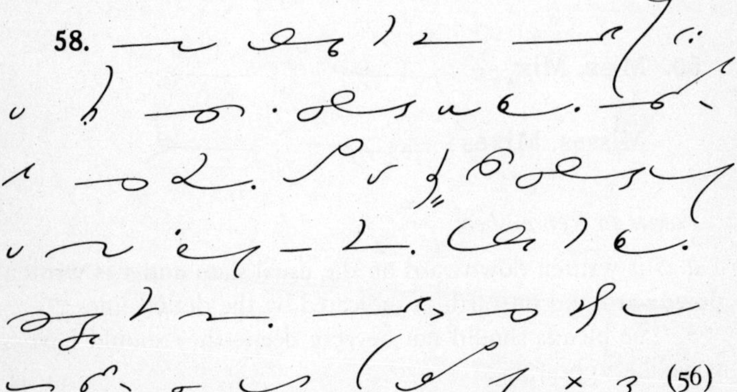

(56)

UNIT 6

PENMANSHIP

59. Str 

Points to Remember:

a. This combination should be written without a stop.

b. The *t* should be very short and should be written with a rather vertical inclination. The dotted line shows the proper slant of the *t*.

c. This combination resembles one of the forms of the long-hand *r*, thus: 

Practice:

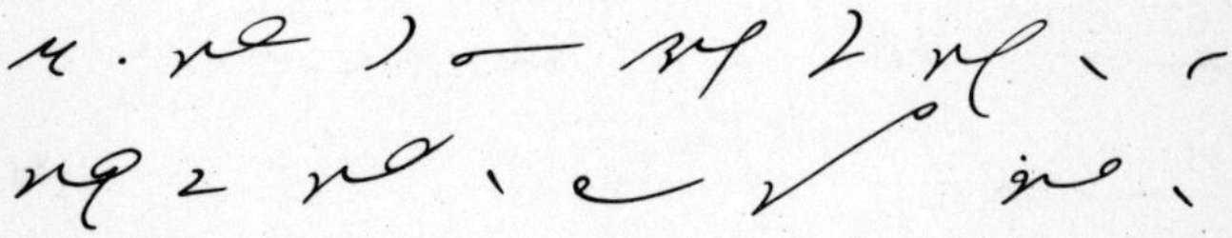

60. Miss, Mix 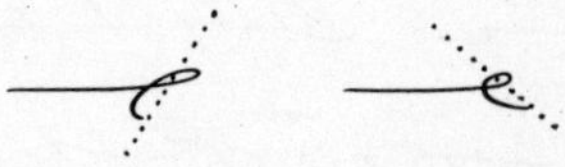

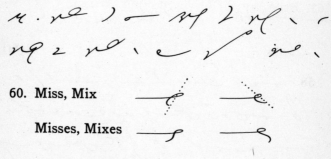

Misses, Mixes 

Points to Remember:

a. S is written downward on the usual slant and *x* is written downward and onward, as indicated by the dotted lines.

b. The blends should not be very deep—they should have a wavelike appearance.

Practice:

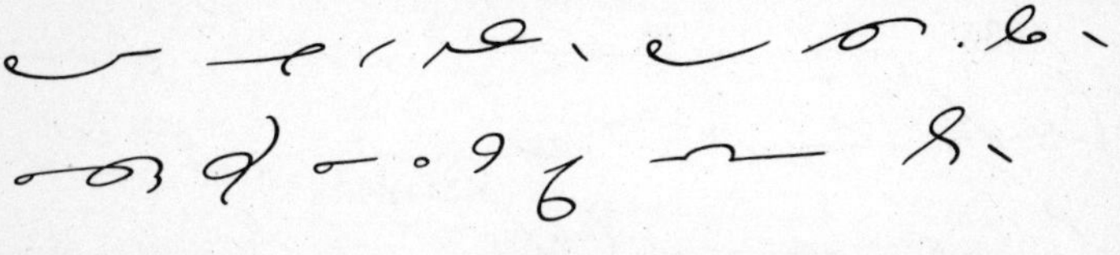

MOST-USED WORDS AND PHRASES

61. Frequently Used Words

X, Xes 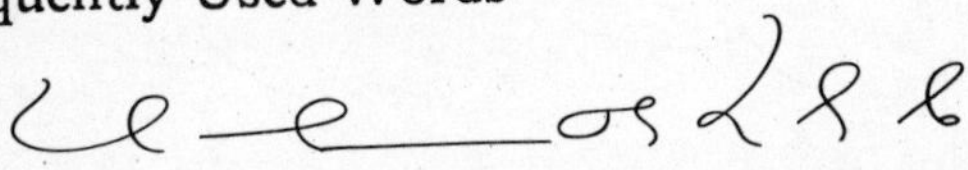

Shun 

62. Brief-Form Derivatives and Phrases

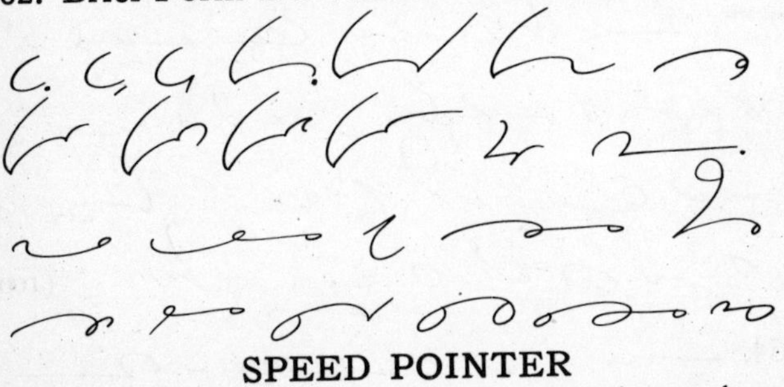

SPEED POINTER

Light Touch. A light touch of pen or pencil upon the paper is necessary to high speed. No more pressure should be exerted than is necessary to make a clear, definite outline. Using a heavy touch means gripping the pen, thus destroying all flexibility of movement, retarding the development of speed, and leading to inaccuracy—all results to be avoided.

READING AND DICTATION PRACTICE

63.

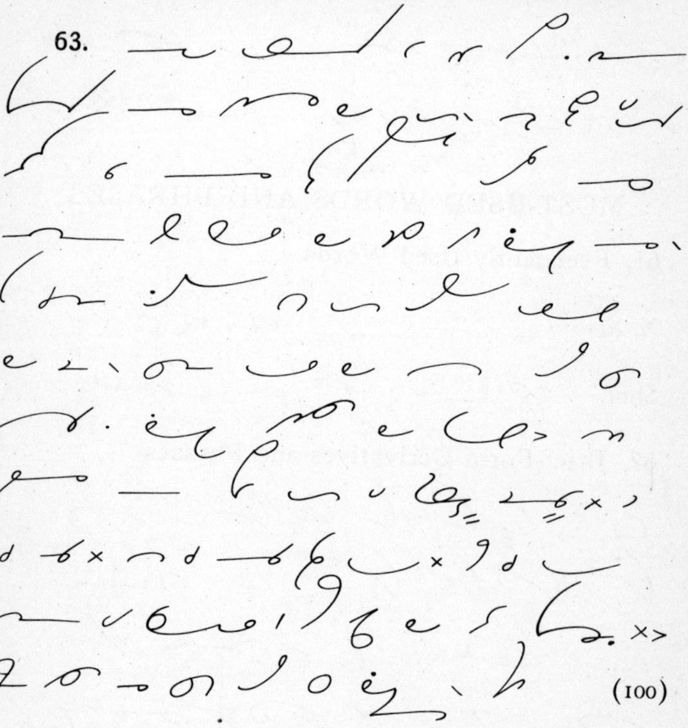

(100)

64.

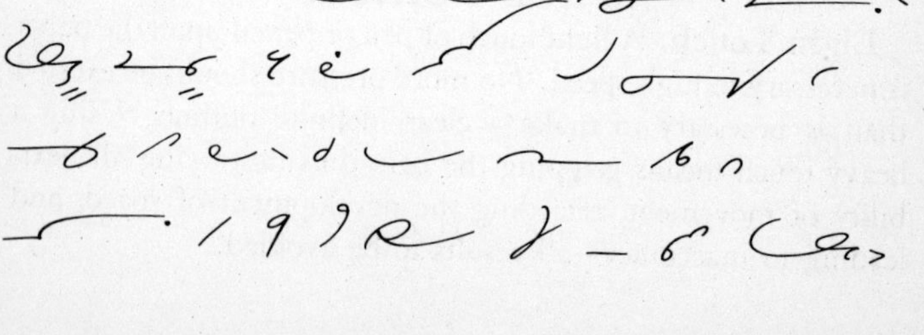

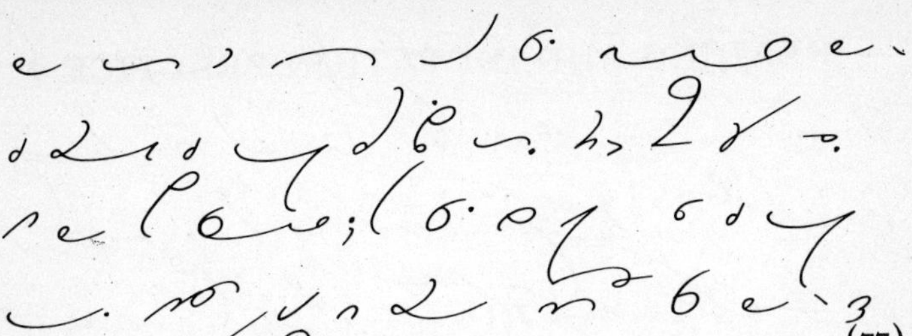

(77)

65.

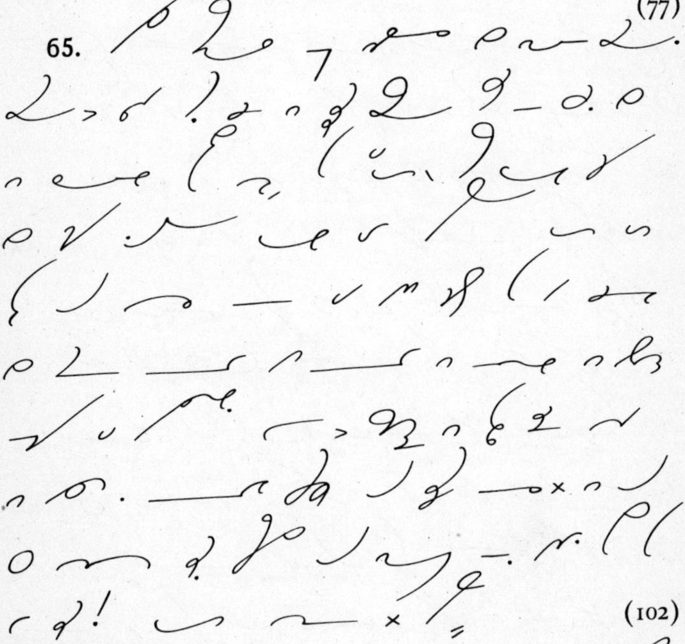

(102)

66.

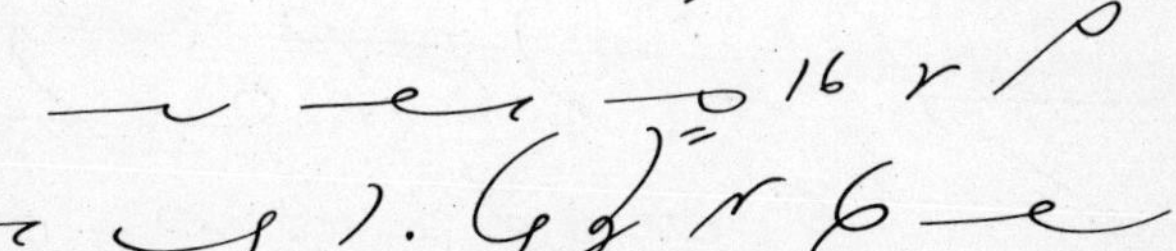

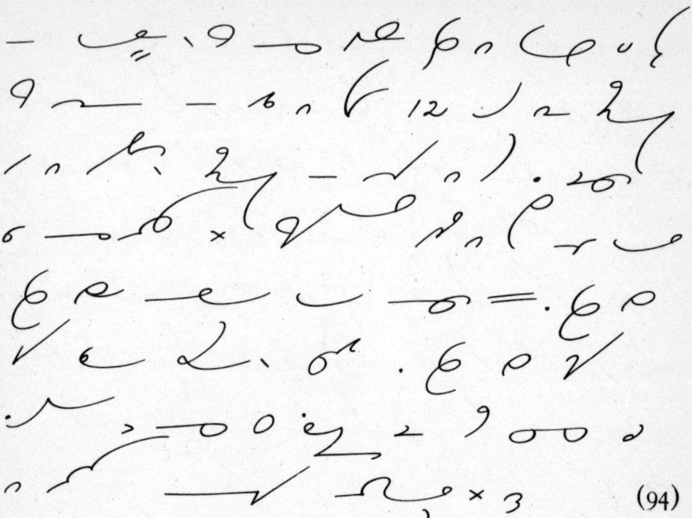

(94)

67.

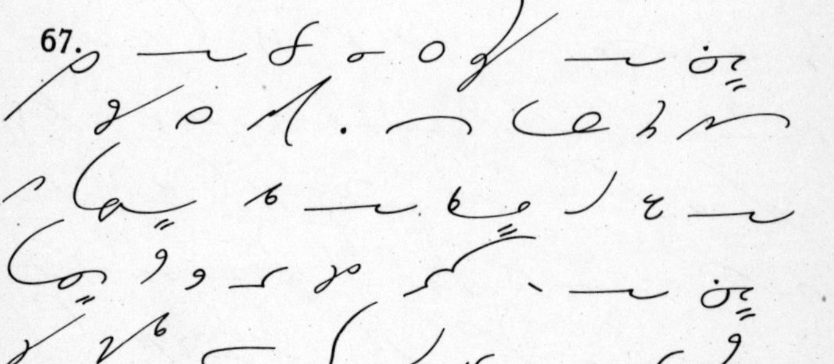

(88)

68.

(106)

69.

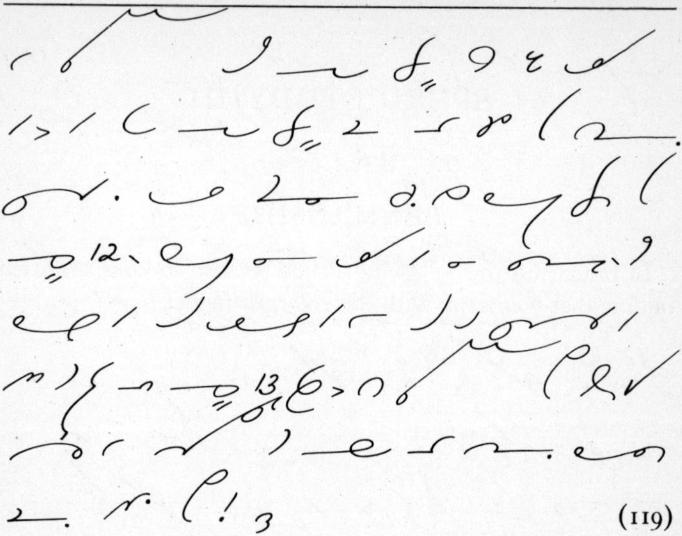

(119)

70.

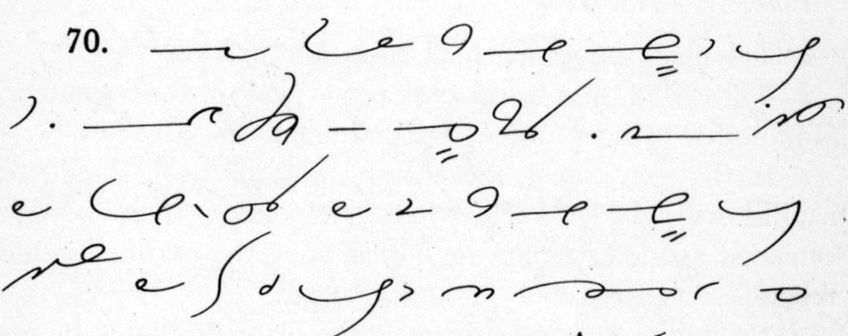

(47)

71.

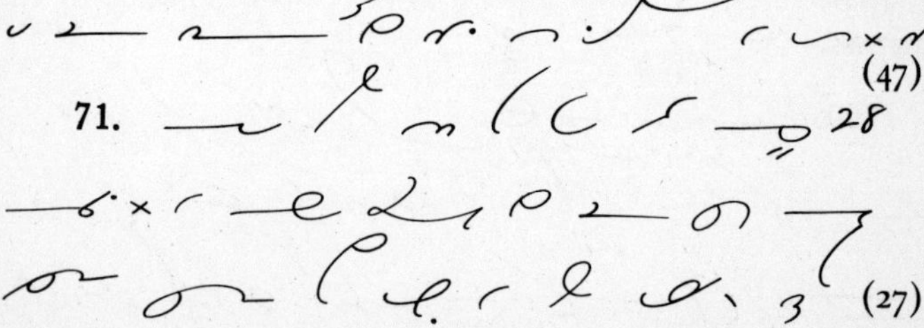

(27)

SPEED STUDY III

UNIT 7

PENMANSHIP

In practicing the following drills, be sure to compare each outline that you write with the enlarged model.

72. O, On, Ot, Sho

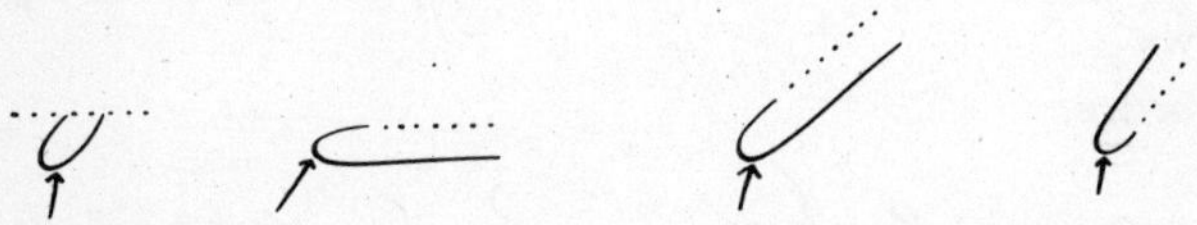

Points to Remember:

a. The hook should be small, deep, and narrow.

b. The end of the *o* comes back to the plane of the beginning, as indicated by the horizontal dotted line in the *o*.

c. In the words *own*, *what*, and *show*, the hook should be parallel with the stroke to which it is joined. If the *o* were extended as indicated by the dotted lines, the outlines would resemble a hairpin.

d. Be careful to avoid a point at the places indicated by the arrows.

Practice:

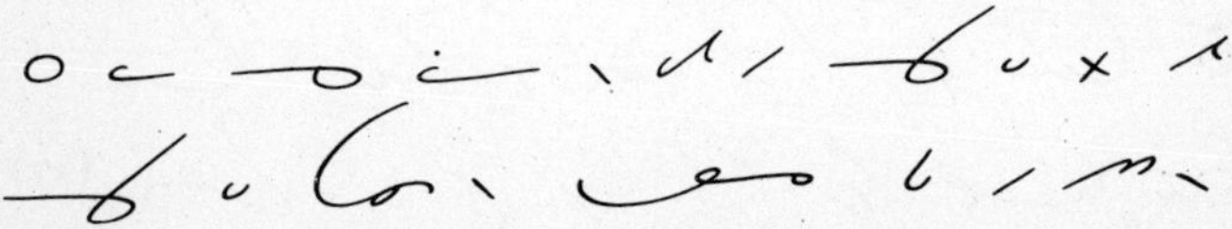

73. Kor, Non, Tot

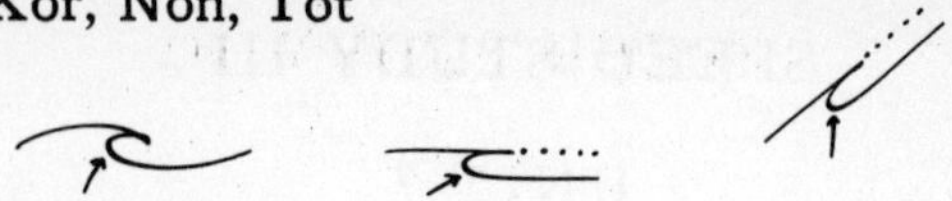

Points to Remember:

a. In these joinings, the first part of the *o* retraces the preceding stroke.

b. In *non* and *tot*, the beginning and the end of the *o* are parallel with the straight strokes.

c. Be careful to avoid a point at the places indicated by the arrows.

Practice:

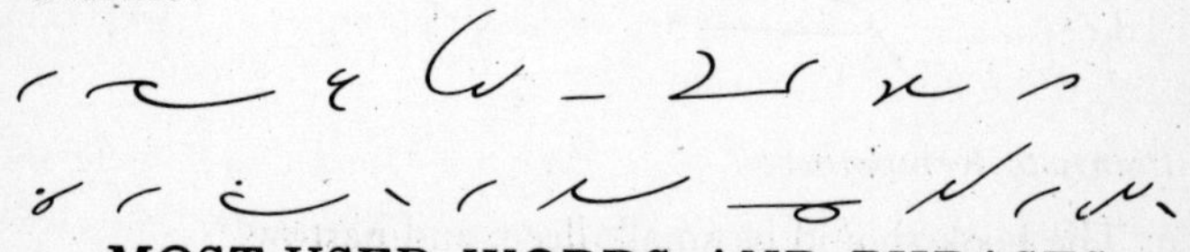

MOST-USED WORDS AND PHRASES

74. Frequently Used Words

Ŏ

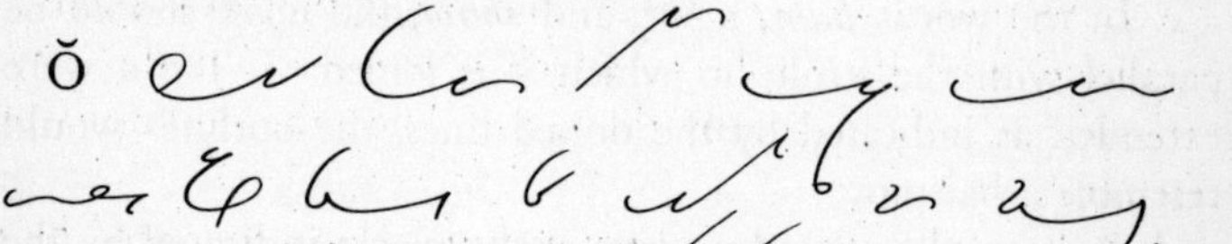

Aw

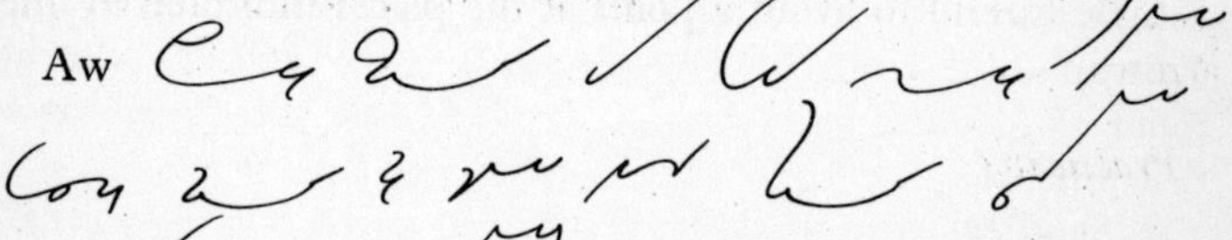

Ō

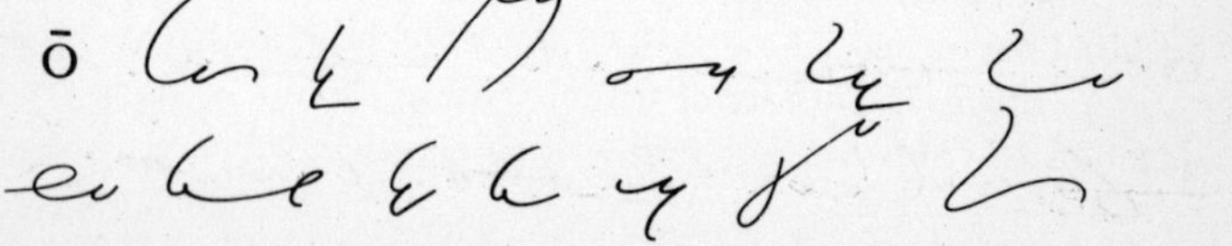

75. Brief-Form Derivatives and Phrases

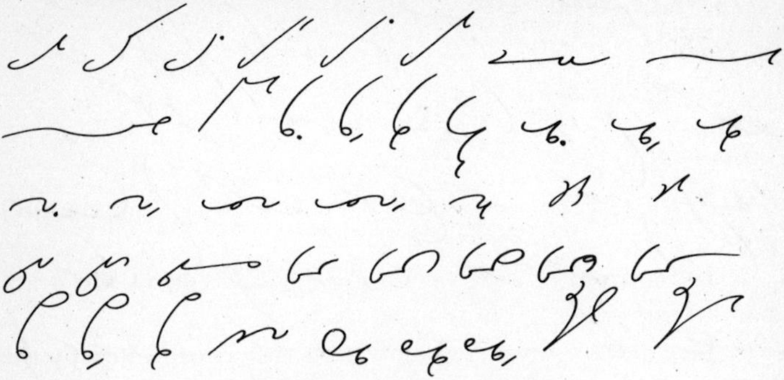

SPEED POINTERS

To become expert in writing and in reading shorthand, keep in mind the following principles:

1. The principles of the system must be applied accurately and intelligently in order to write the correct shorthand outline at high speeds.

2. The proportion of the characters must be constantly observed; that is, a careful distinction must be made between the different lengths of strokes and sizes of circles.

3. Everything written must be read.

4. Frequent and thorough reviews are essential to rapid and sure progress. The review should not be confined solely to "mental" review, but should be accompanied by much practice in writing. Each time the writer goes over a principle thoughtfully with his mind concentrated on it, the deeper will become the impression of that principle.

5. Shorthand writing skill is based upon correct habits; habits are acquired not by doing a thing once, but by repetition with attention.

6. As much as possible of actual writing should be done from dictation or from copying well-written shorthand.

READING AND DICTATION PRACTICE

76.

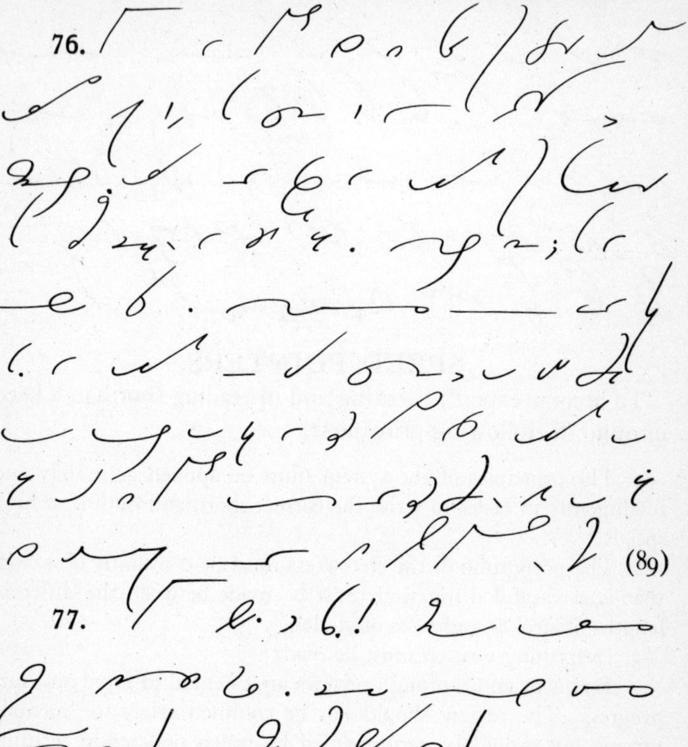

(89)

77.

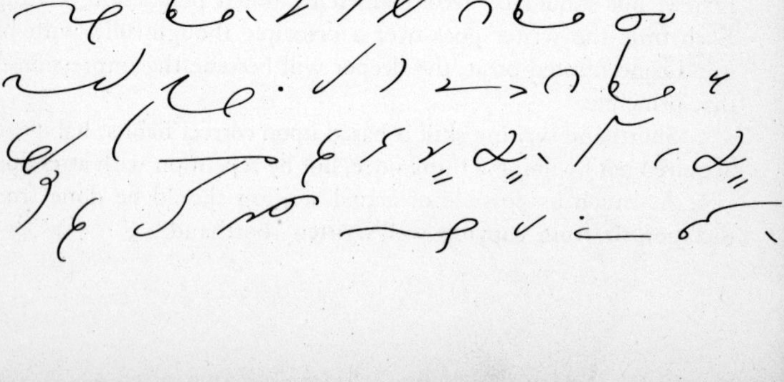

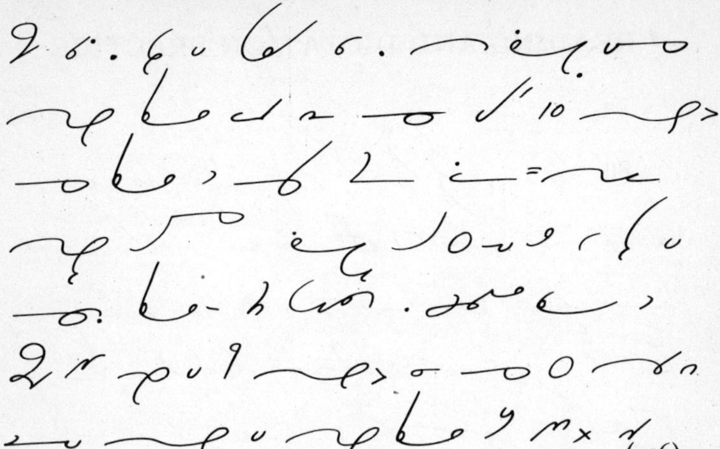

(126)

78.

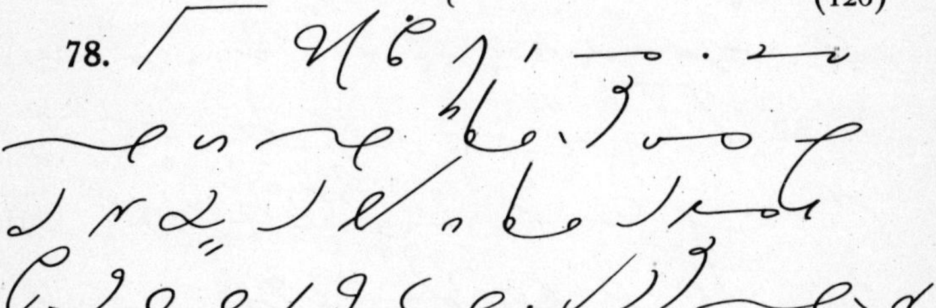

(45)

79.

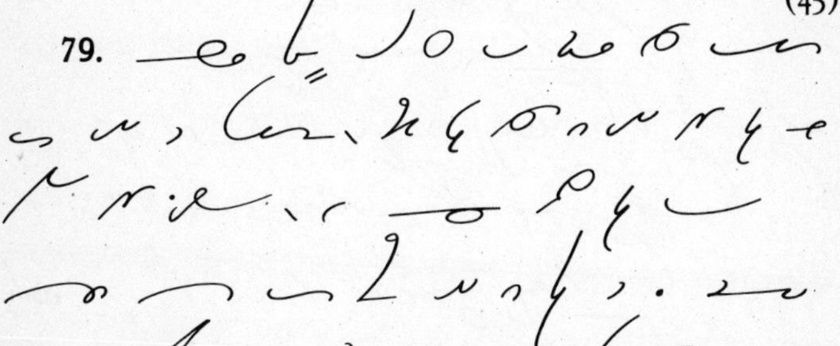

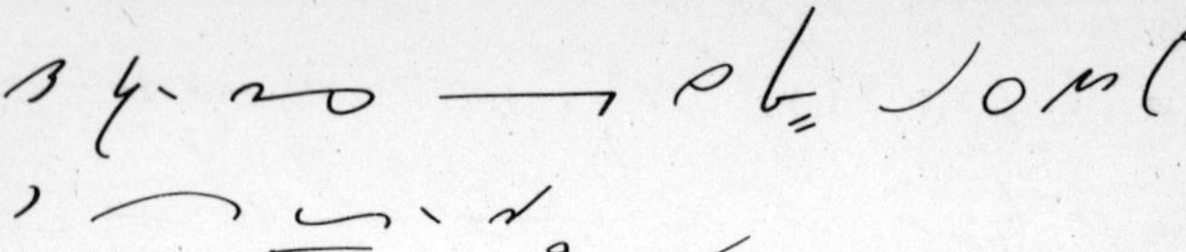

(66)

80.

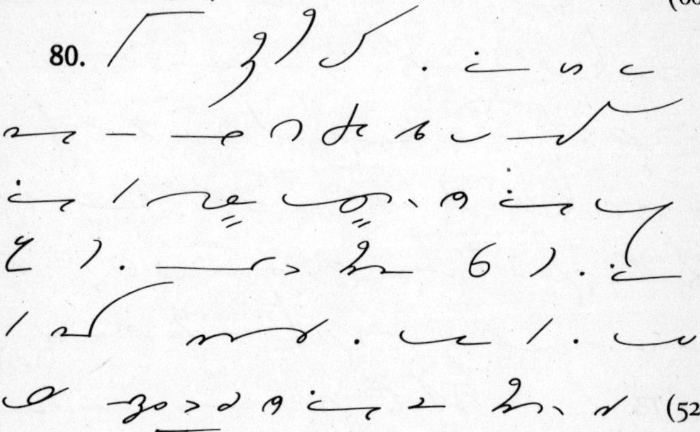

(52)

81.

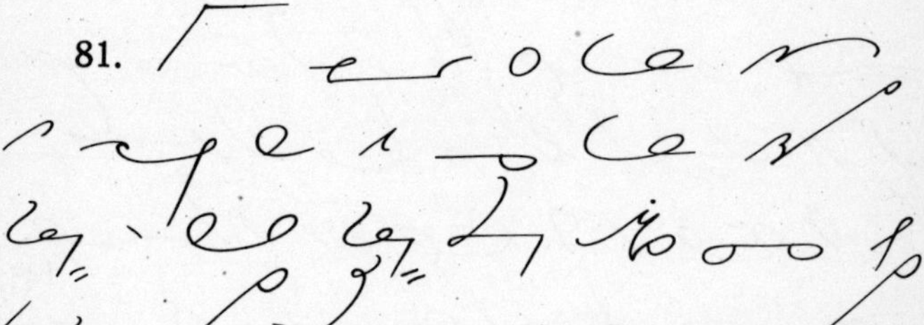

(61)

82.

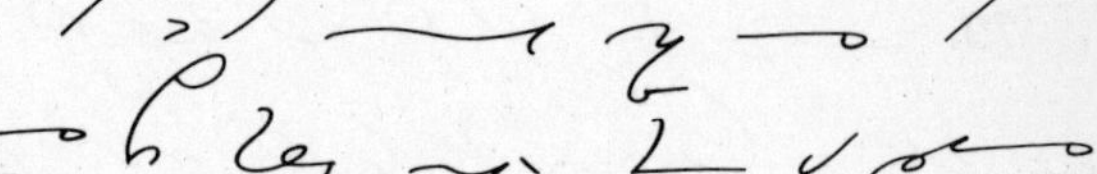

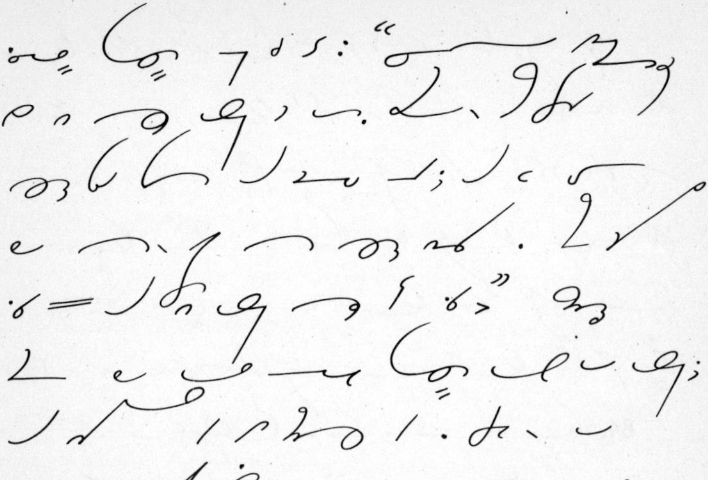

(136)

83.

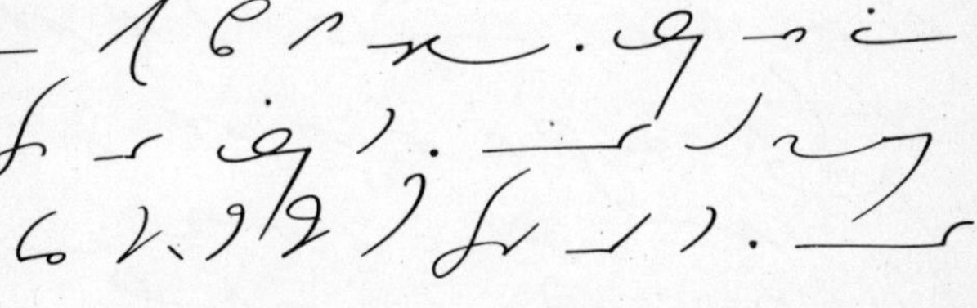

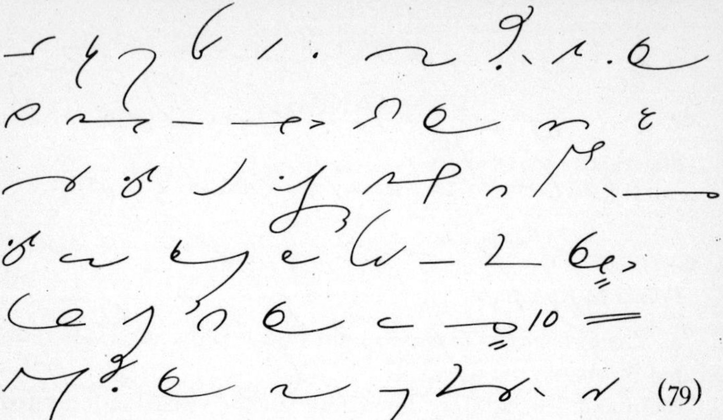

(79)

84.

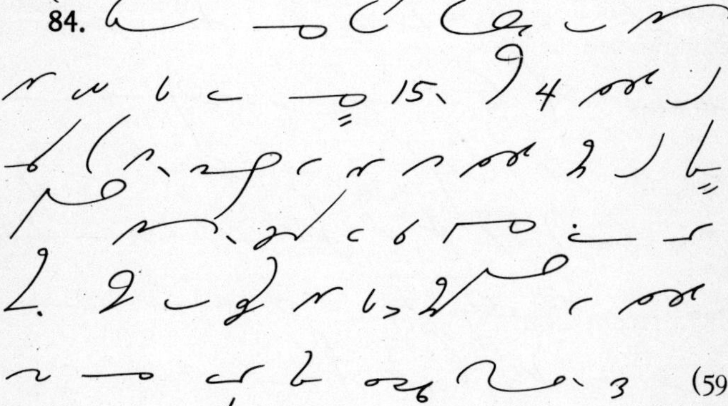

(59)

85.

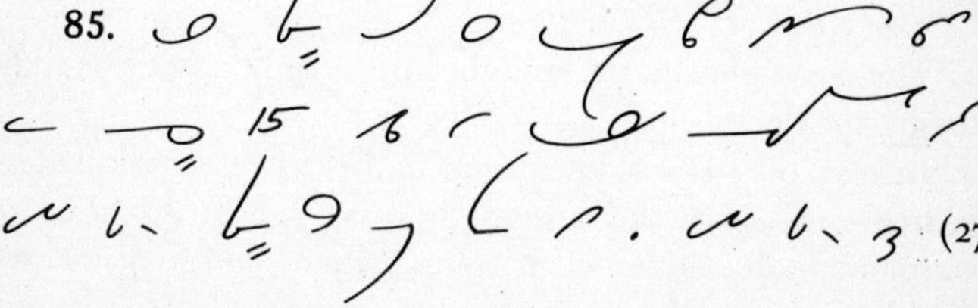

(27)

UNIT 8

PENMANSHIP

86. Arm, Dare

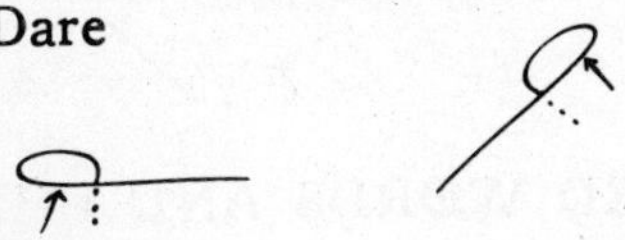

Points to Remember:

a. The circle joins to the straight line at right angles, as indicated by the dotted lines.

b. In *arm,* the straight line begins in the circle, as indicated by the arrow; in *dare,* the straight line is slightly extended to accommodate the circle.

Practice:

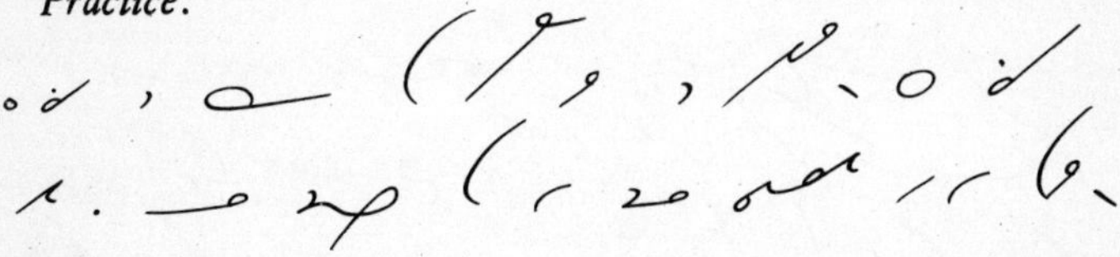

87. Arch, Char

Points to Remember:

a. The circle joins to the straight line at right angles, as indicated by the dotted lines.

b. In *arch*, the straight line begins in the circle, as indicated by the arrow; in *char*, the straight line is slightly extended to accommodate the circle. (If it were written the usual size, we would have the word *share.*)

Practice:

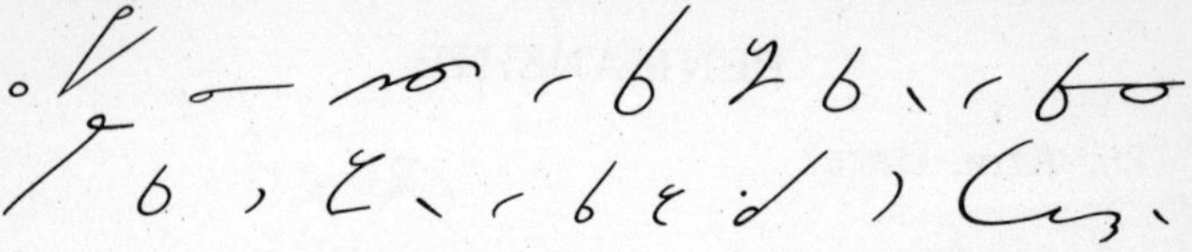

MOST-USED WORDS AND PHRASES

88. Frequently Used Words

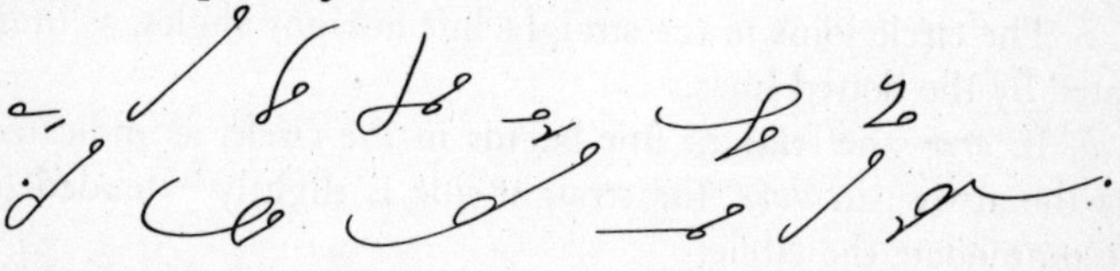

89. Brief-Form Derivatives and Phrases

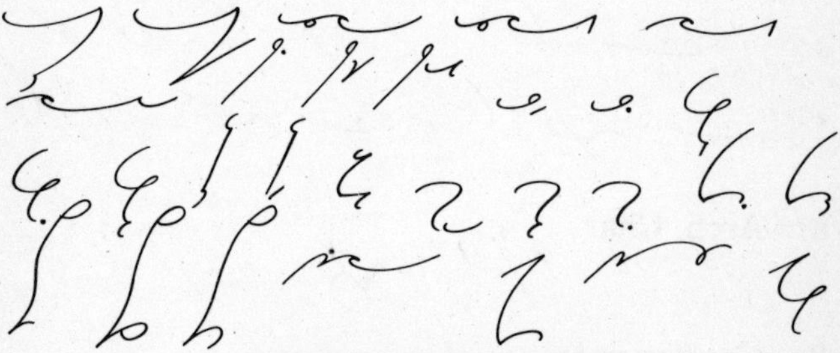

SPEED POINTER

Substitute Shorthand for Longhand. Even though you cannot at this stage write all the words with which you come in contact, you should have at your finger tips the outlines for many of the commonest words of the language. In writing down your homework assignments and in making your personal notes, write in shorthand as many words as you can.

READING AND DICTATION PRACTICE

90.

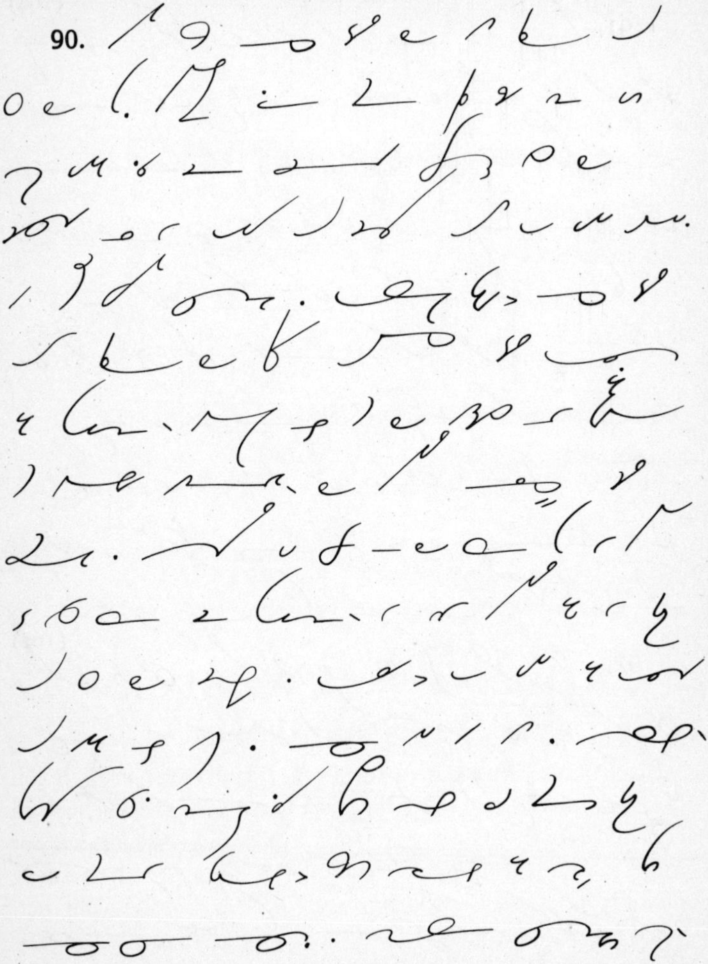

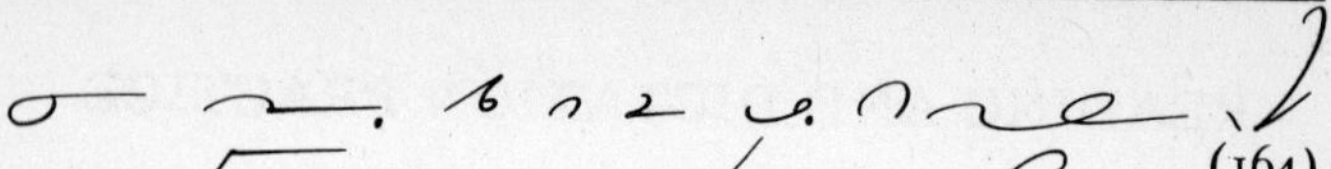

(164)

91.

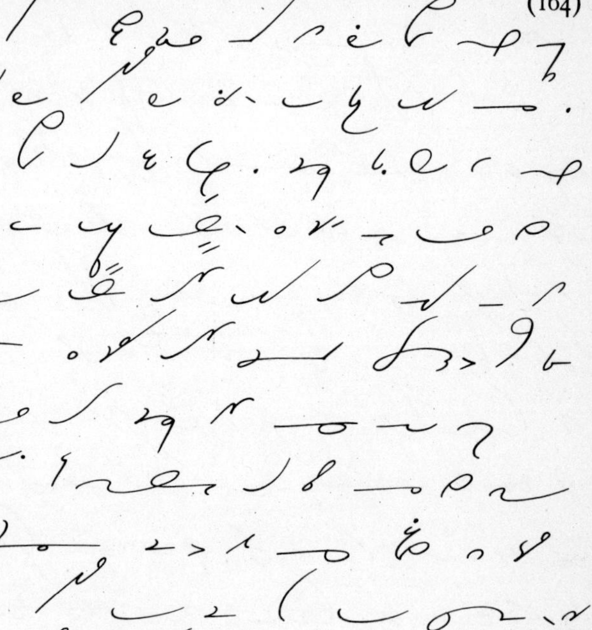

(101)

92.

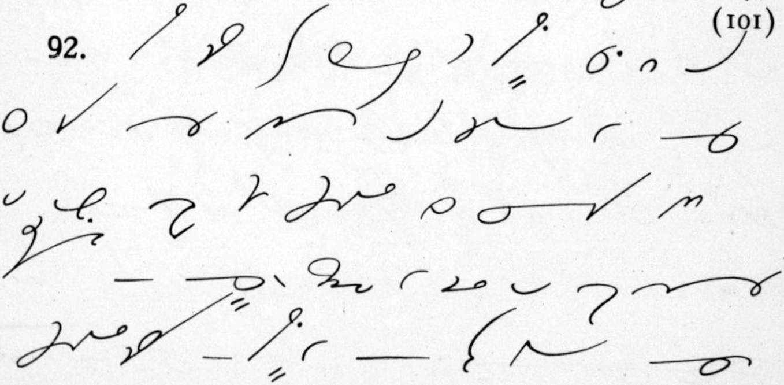

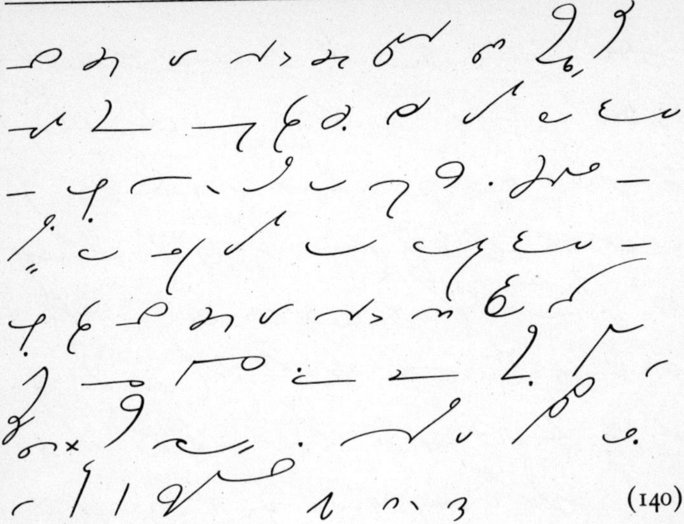

(140)

93.

(86)

94.

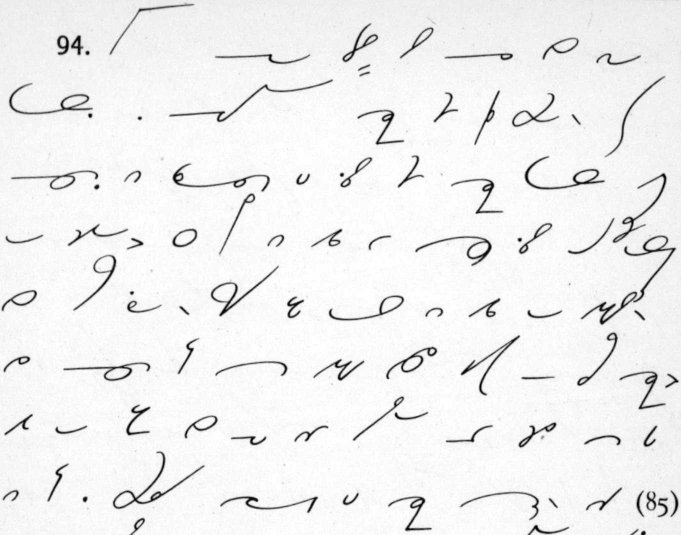

(85)

95.

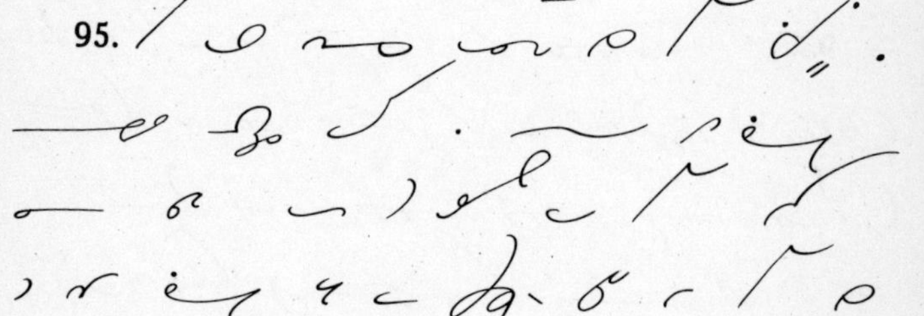

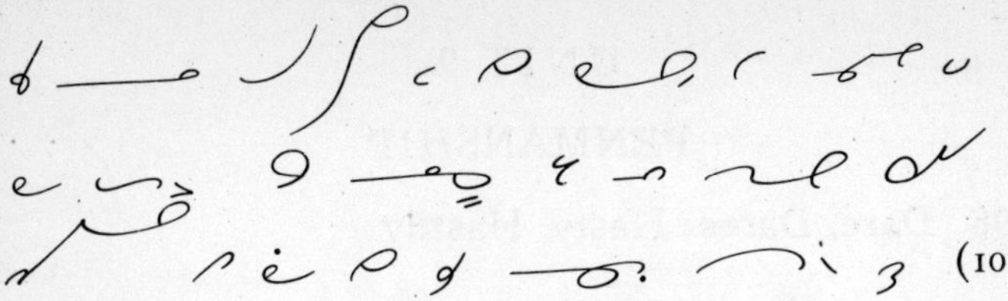

(101)

96.

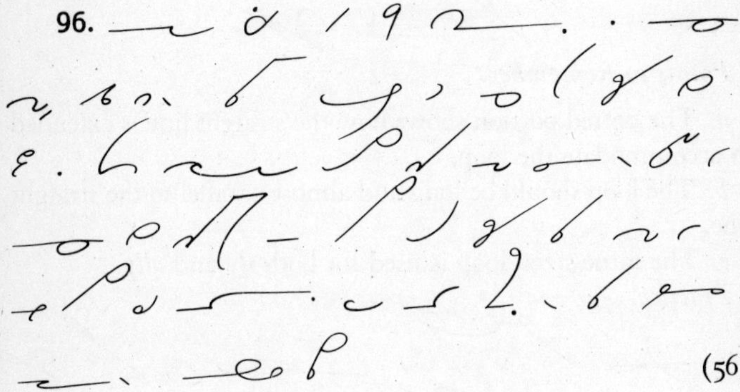

(56)

97.

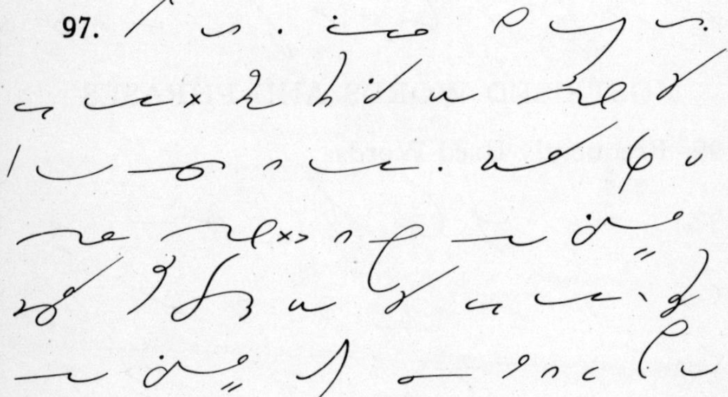

(59)

UNIT 9

PENMANSHIP

98. Dare, Dares; Hasty, Hastily

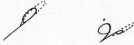

Points to Remember:

a. The dotted portion shows how the straight line is extended to accommodate the loop.

b. The loop should be long and almost parallel to the straight line.

c. The same-sized loop is used for both *ily* and *ally.*

Practice:

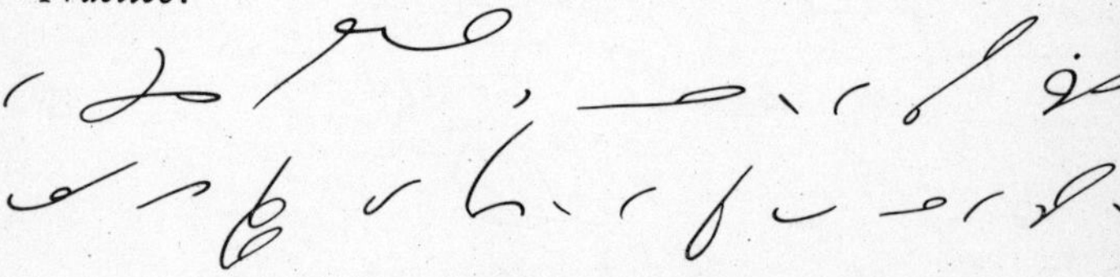

MOST-USED WORDS AND PHRASES

99. Frequently Used Words

Th 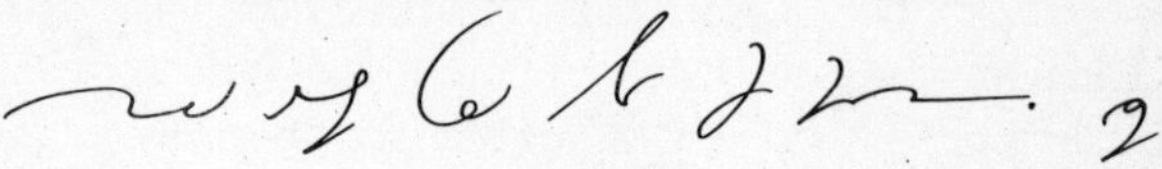

Con 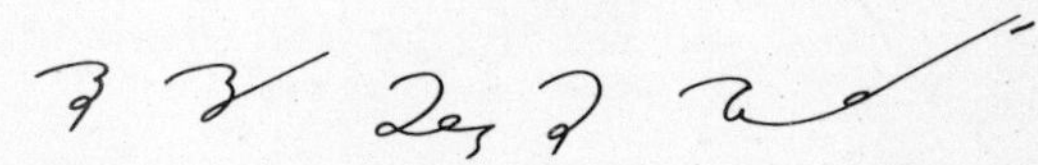

Com 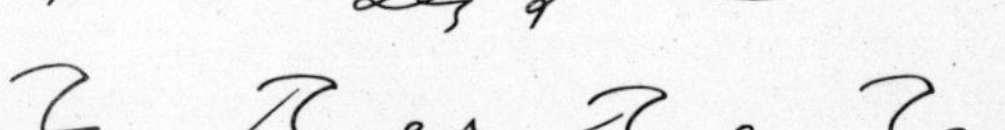

Can, Coun 

Ly 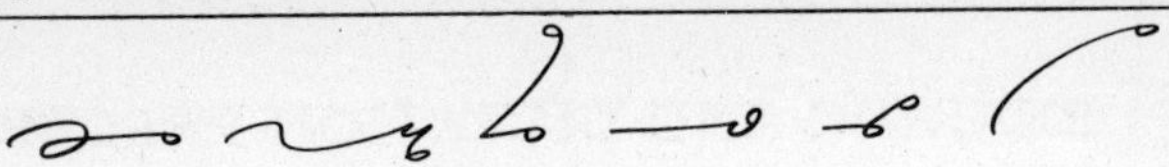

100. Final Loop

Ily, ally 

Ers, ars 

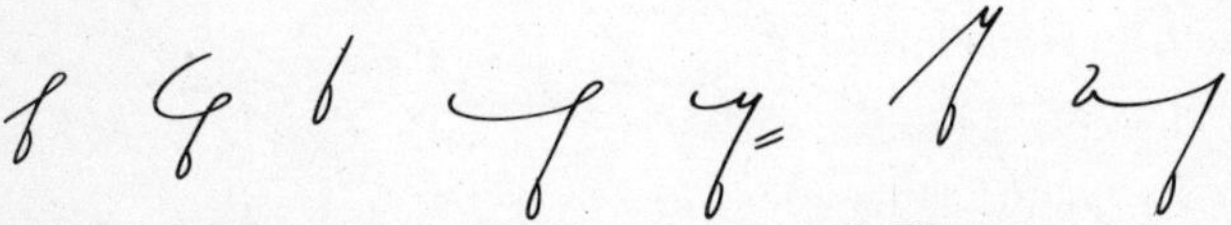

101. Brief-Form Derivatives and Phrases

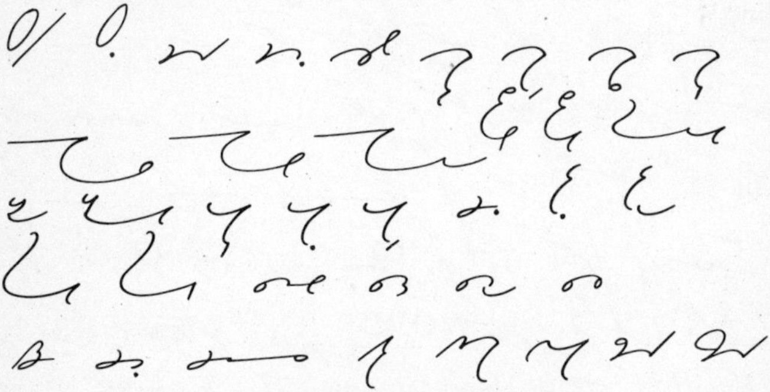

SPEED POINTER

Left-handed Writers. Left-handed writers will usually find it more satisfactory to reverse the columns in the book, writing in the second column first and in the first column second.

Those left-handed writers who write from above the line of writing will find it more satisfactory to write from the very top of the entire notebook down to the binding. This prevents the usual inconvenience that comes from writing across the binding.

READING AND DICTATION PRACTICE

102. Hard Workers

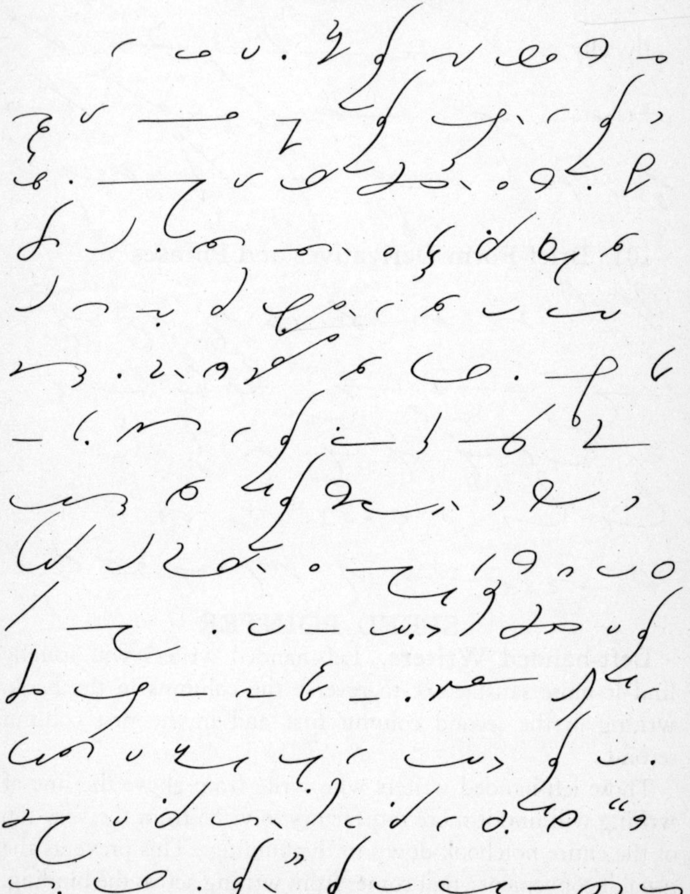

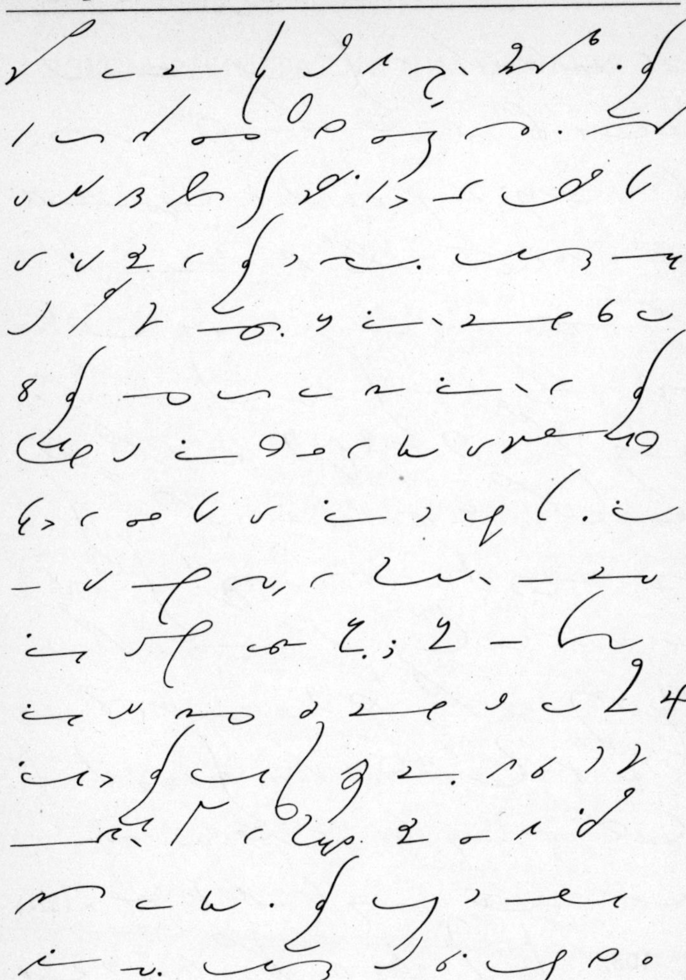

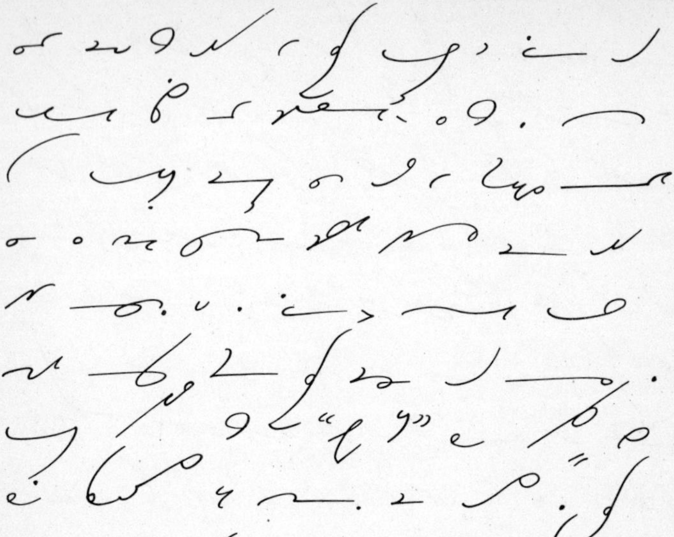

(423)

103.

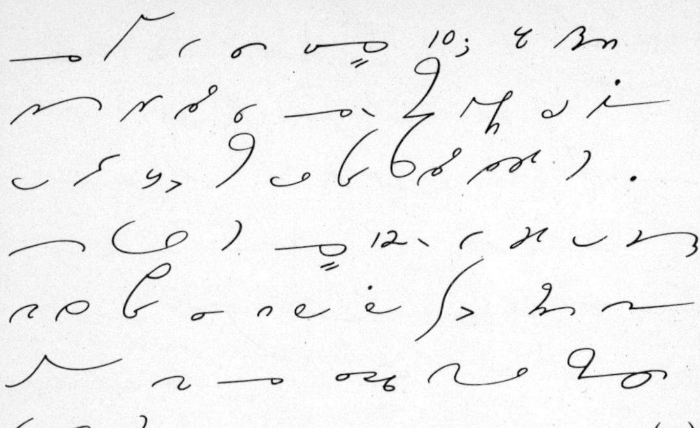

(94)

104.

(96)

105.

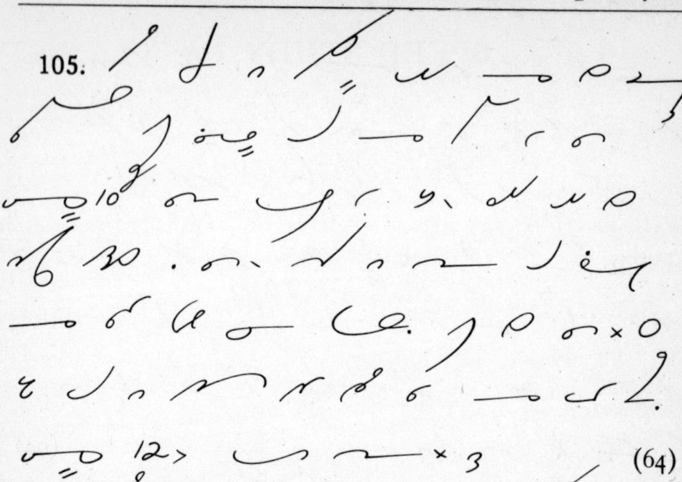

(64)

106.

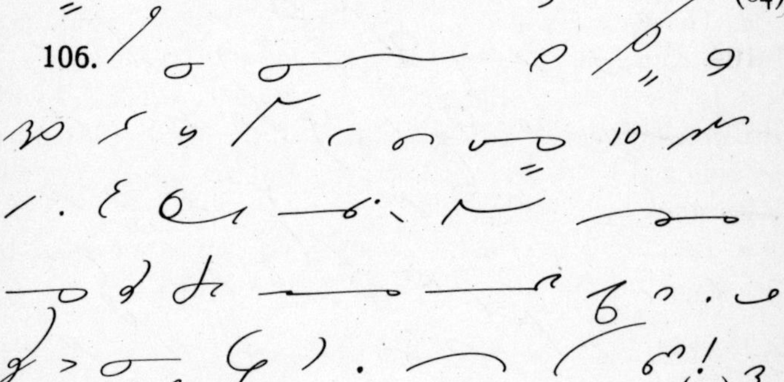

(43)

107.

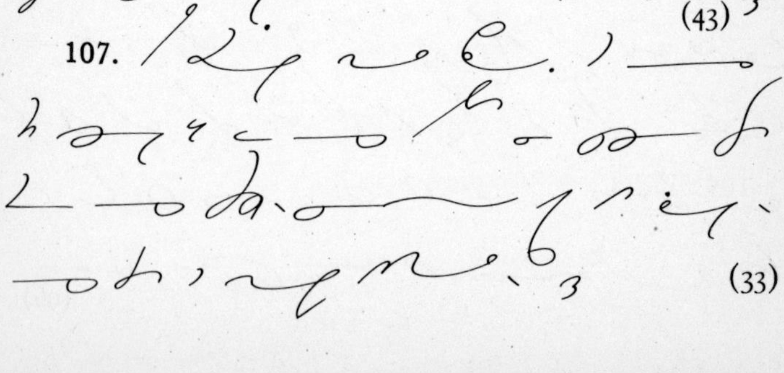

(33)

SPEED STUDY IV

UNIT 10

PENMANSHIP

In practicing the following drills, be sure to compare each outline that you write with the enlarged model.

108. O͞O, No͞o, To͞o

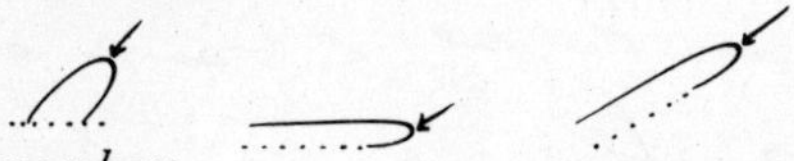

Points to Remember:

a. The hook should be small, deep, and narrow.

b. The o͞o-hook comes back to the line of writing, as indicated by the dotted line.

c. In the last two enlarged forms, the hook is parallel with the straight line to which it is joined. If the o͞o were extended as indicated by the dotted lines, the outlines would resemble a hairpin.

d. Be careful to avoid a point at the places indicated by arrows.

Practice:

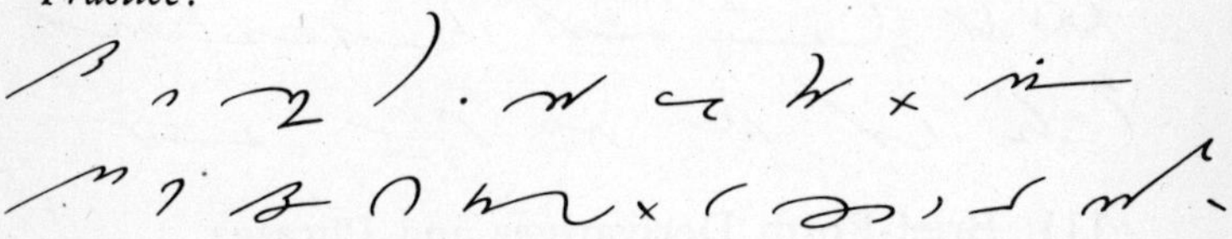

109. Ko͞ol, No͞on, To͞ot

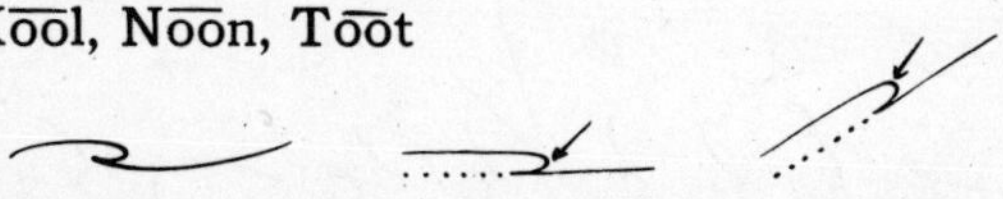

Points to Remember:

a. In these joinings, the strokes following the o͞o-hook retrace the end of the hook.

b. In the last two enlarged forms, the beginning and the end of the hook are parallel with the straight lines.

c. Be careful to avoid a point at the places indicated by arrows.

Practice:

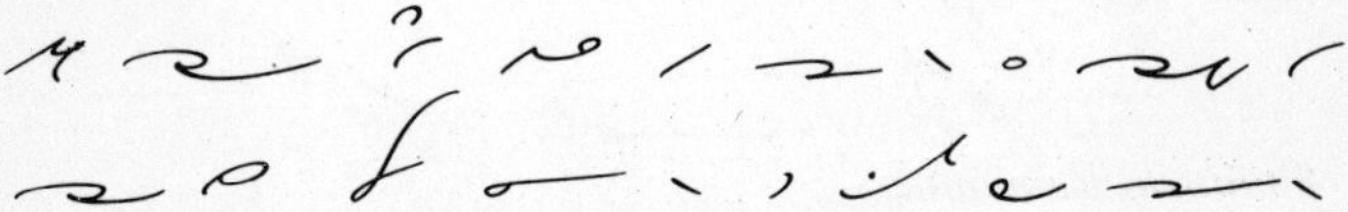

MOST-USED WORDS AND PHRASES

110. Frequently Used Words

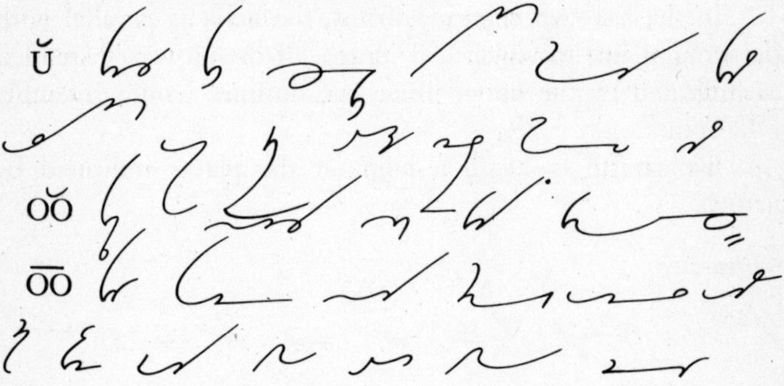

111. Brief-Form Derivatives and Phrases

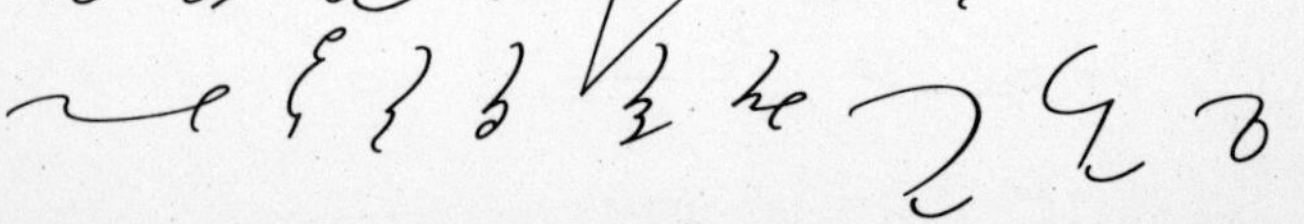

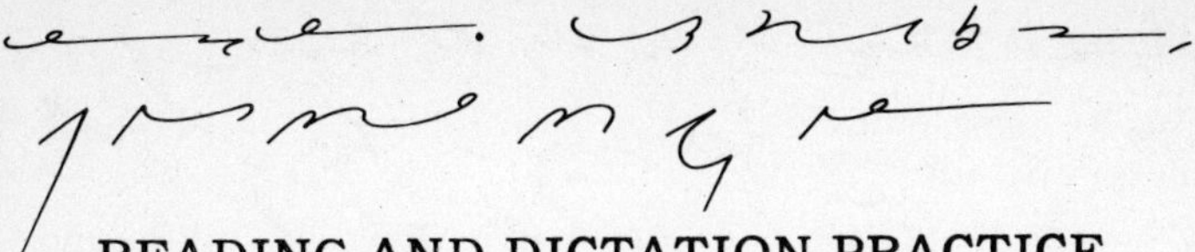

READING AND DICTATION PRACTICE

112. Honey

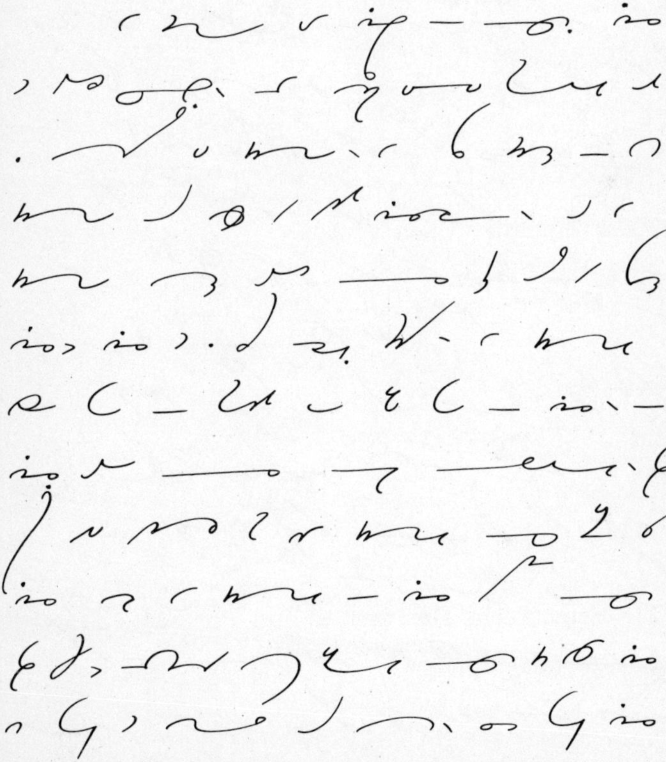

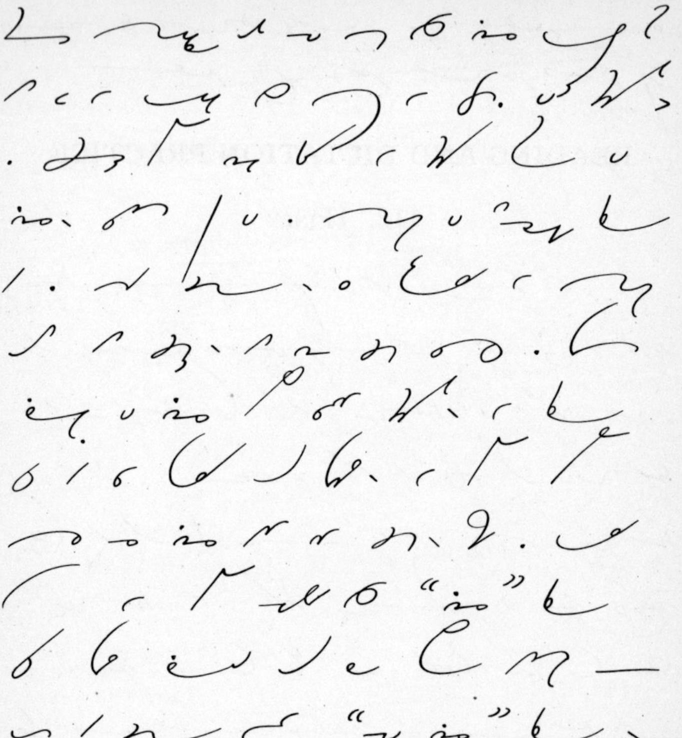

(229)

113.

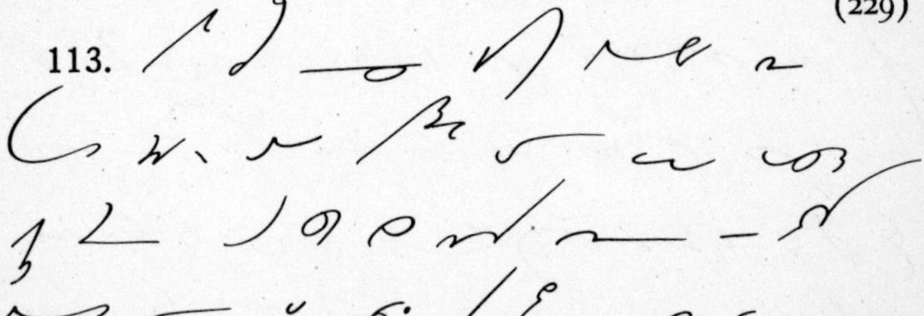

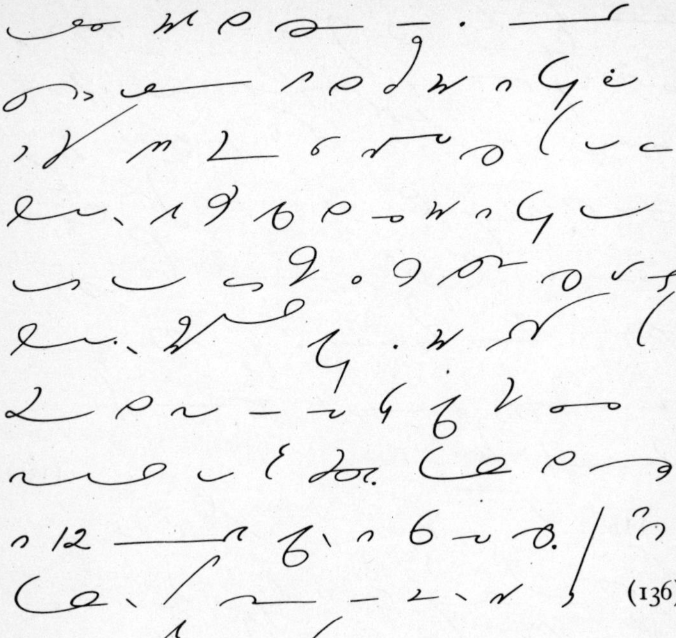

(136)

114.

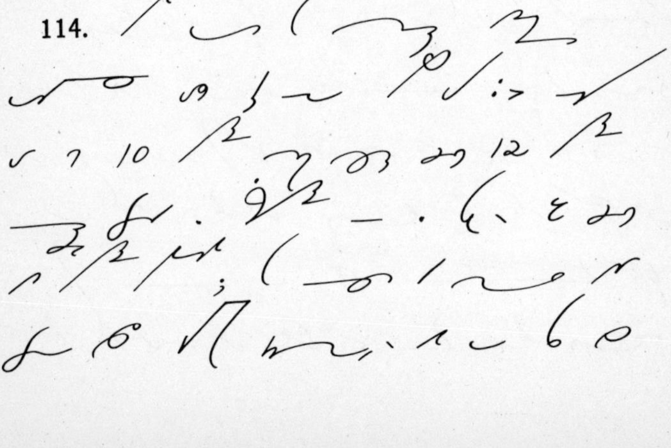

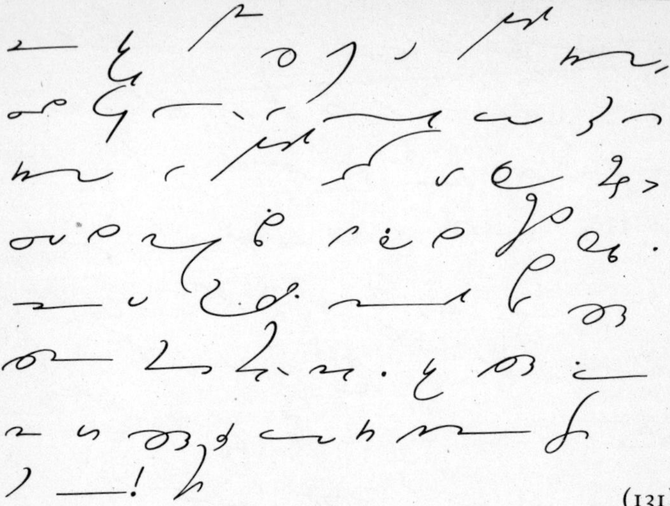

(131)

115.

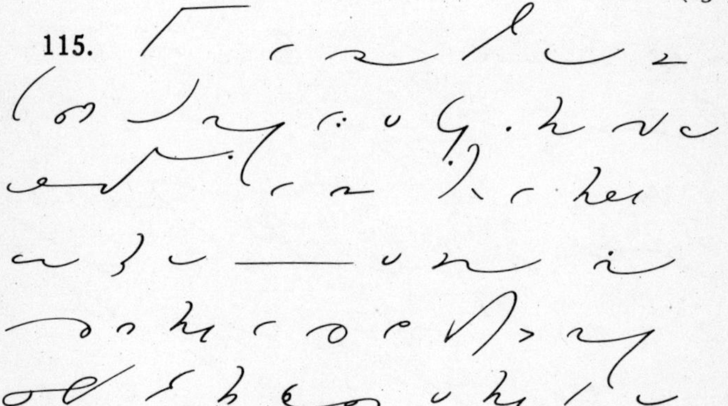

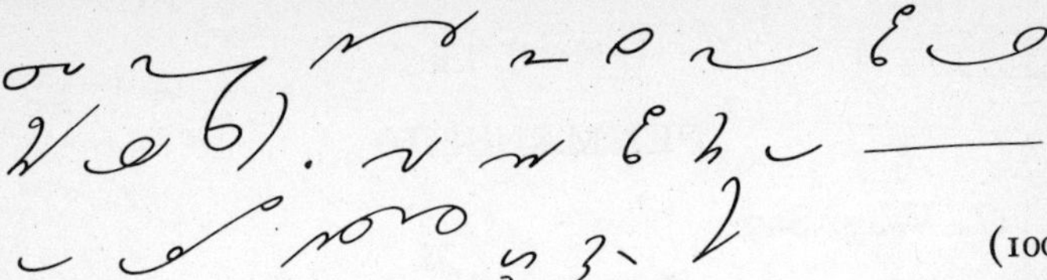

(100)

116.

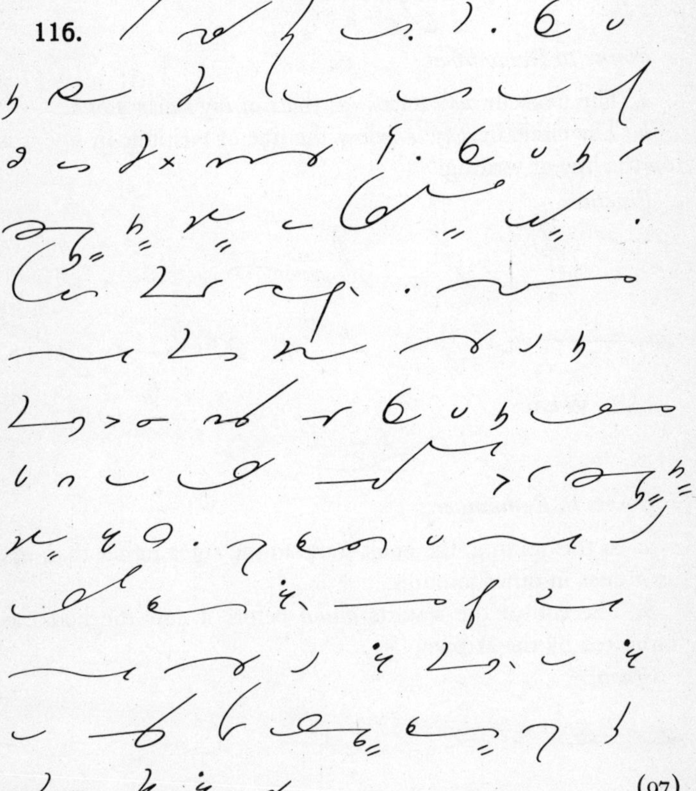

(97)

UNIT 11

PENMANSHIP

117. Way, Say

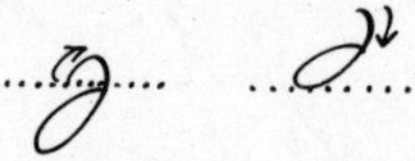

Points to Remember:

a. The hook in *way* starts *up*; the *s* in *say* starts *down.*

b. The circle in *way* is below the line of writing; in *say*, it is *on* the line of writing.

Practice:

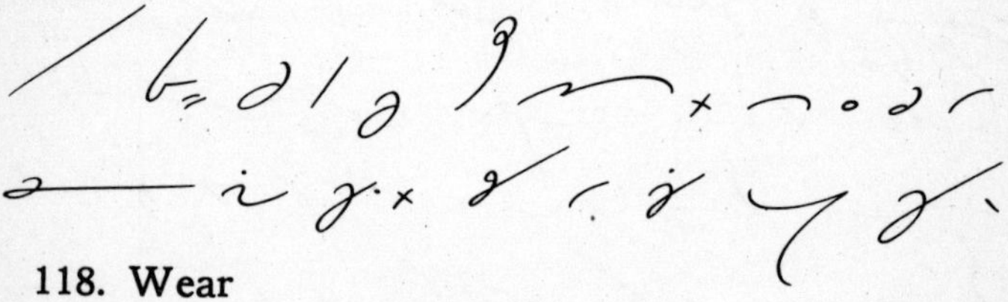

118. Wear

Points to Remember:

a. In this joining, the hook starts to the *right* rather than *up*, as it does in other joinings.

b. The end of the *a* starts *down* before it cuts the hook, as indicated by the arrow.

Practice:

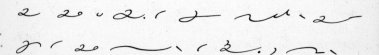

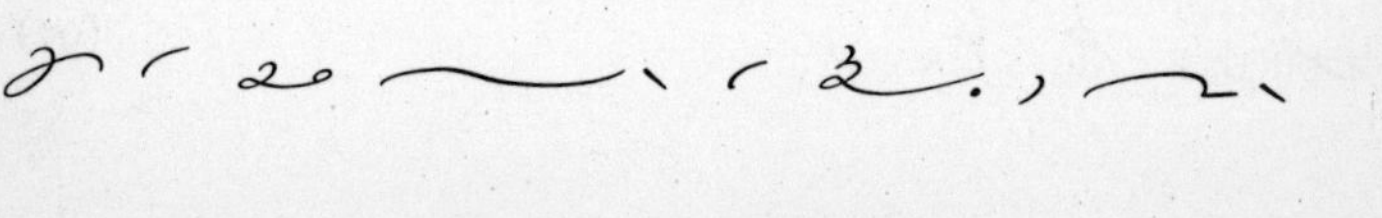

MOST-USED WORDS AND PHRASES

119. Frequently Used Words

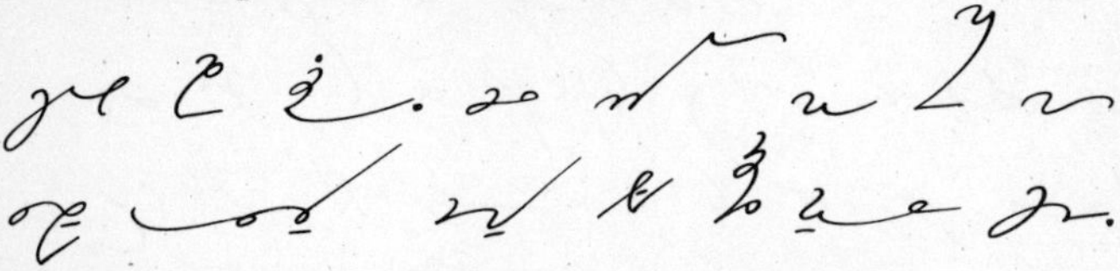

120. Brief-Form Derivatives and Phrases

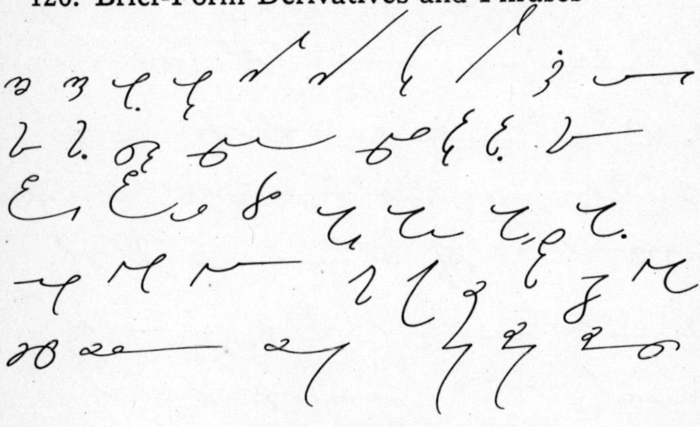

SPEED POINTER

Concentrating. Facility in writing reaches the highest point only when the writer can give his undivided attention to the work in hand. The writer should never let his attention be diverted if he can possibly avoid it. He should even accustom himself to continue his writing when the most startling causes for interruption appear. Holding command of the attention is a habit that cannot be overvalued.

READING AND DICTATION PRACTICE

121.

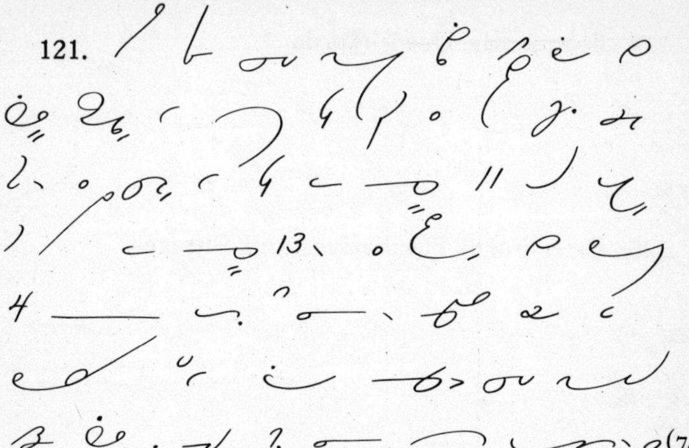

(74)

122.

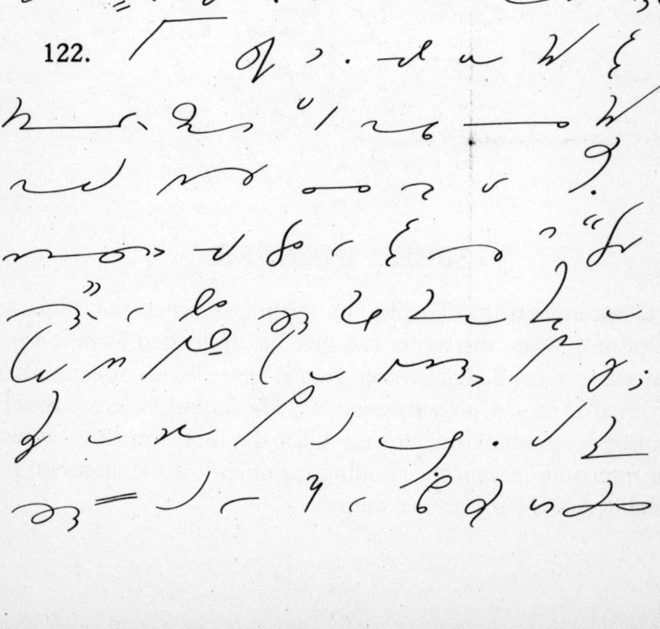

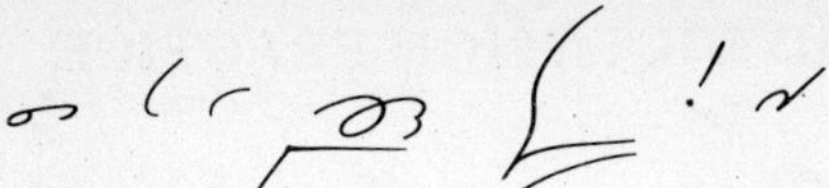

(87)

123.

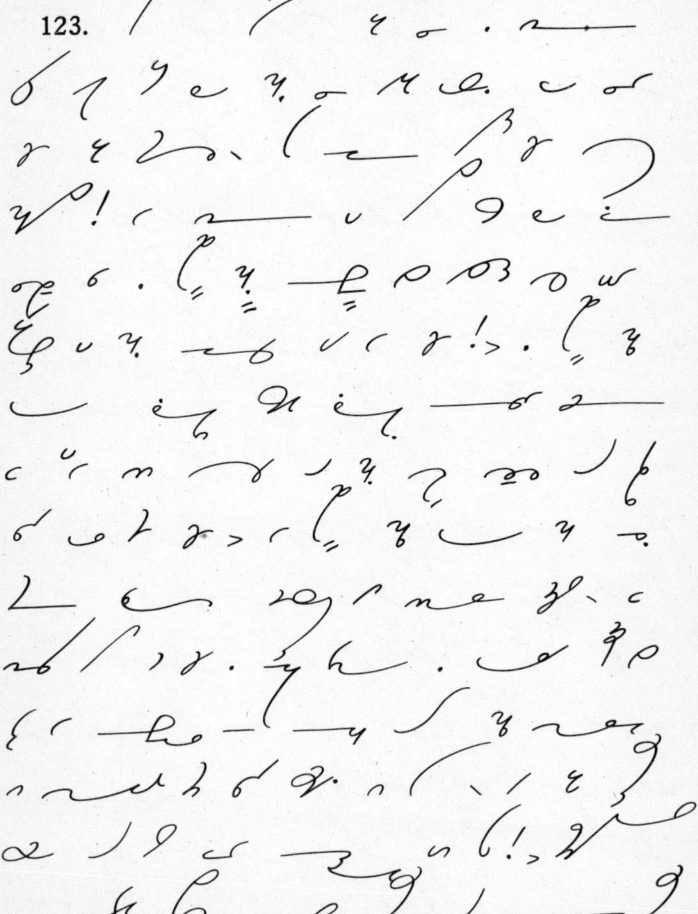

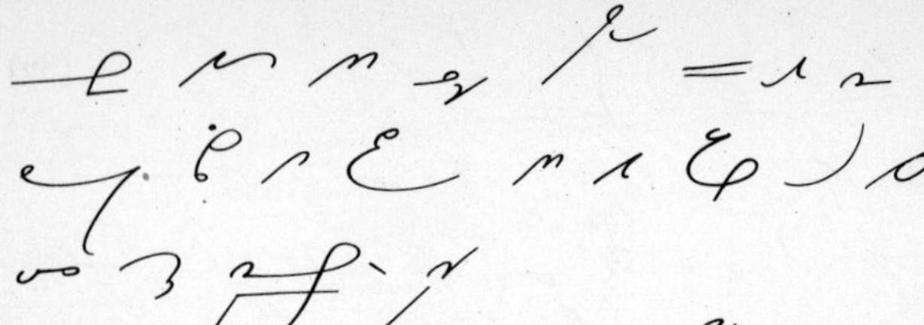

(183)

124.

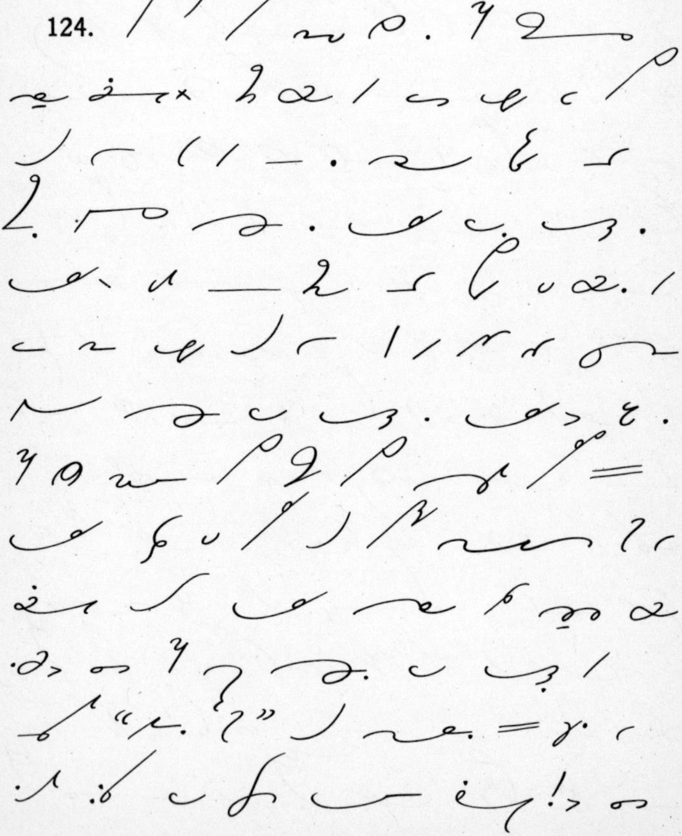

[Gregg shorthand outlines]

(153)

125. *[Gregg shorthand outlines]*

28 *[shorthand outlines]*

[shorthand] 120 (140

10 *[shorthand]* 46 *[shorthand]*

[shorthand]

1 42 *[shorthand]* 898 *[shorthand]*

[shorthand] 105 (

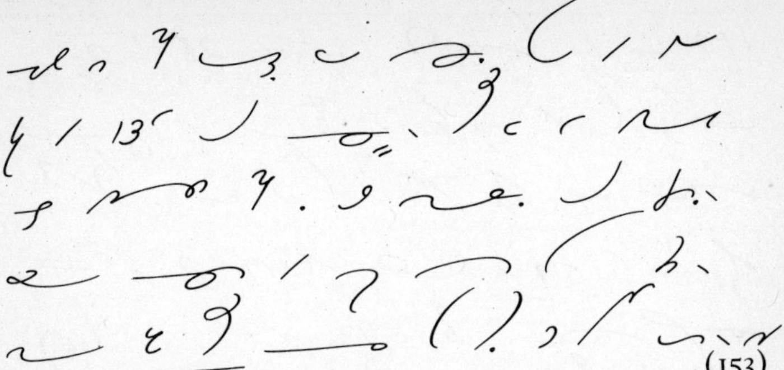

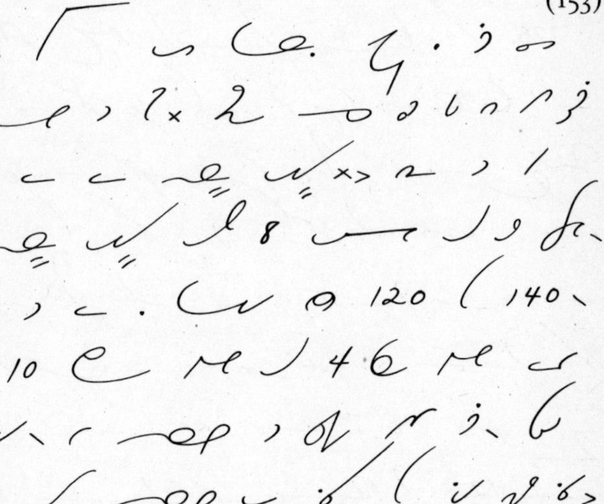

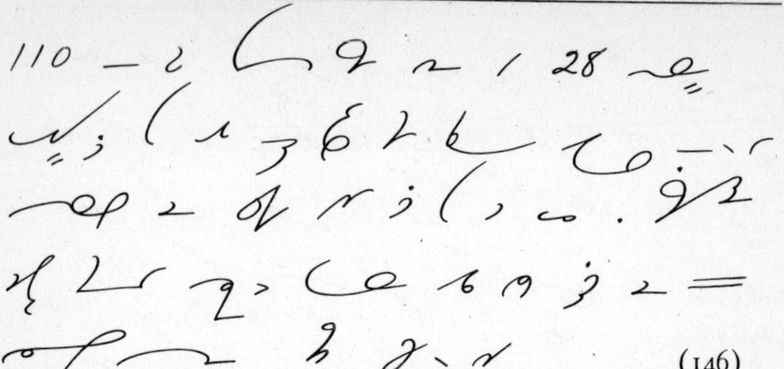

(146)

126.

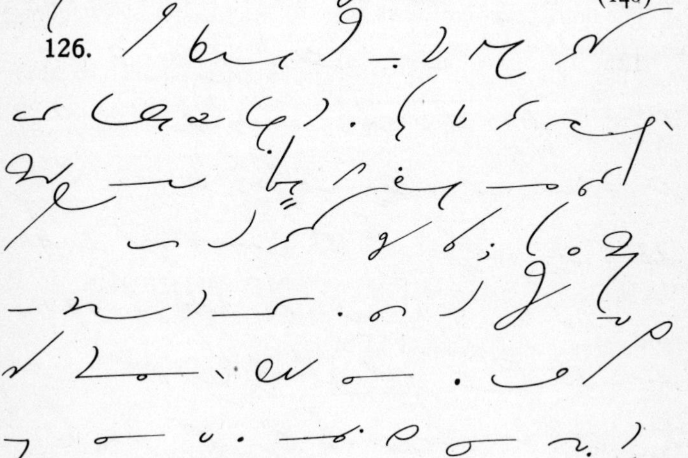

(93)

UNIT 12

PENMANSHIP

127. Hard, Yard

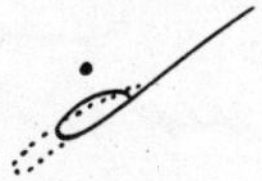

Points to Remember:

a. The dotted portion shows how the straight line is extended to accommodate the loop.

b. The loop should be long and almost parallel to the straight line.

Practice:

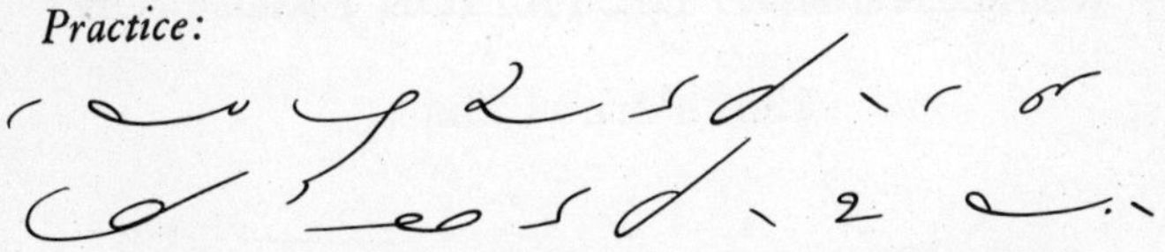

MOST-USED WORDS AND PHRASES

128. Frequently Used Words

Ng

Nk

En, In, Un

Em, Im

Ex

Ings, Ingly

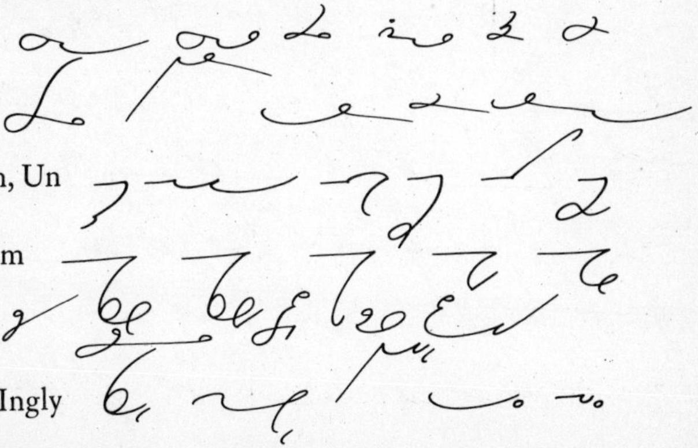

129. Brief-Form Derivatives and Phrases

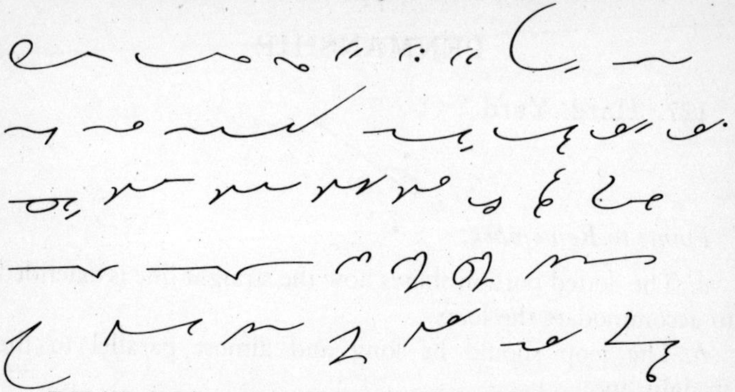

READING AND DICTATION PRACTICE

130. Pull vs. Skill

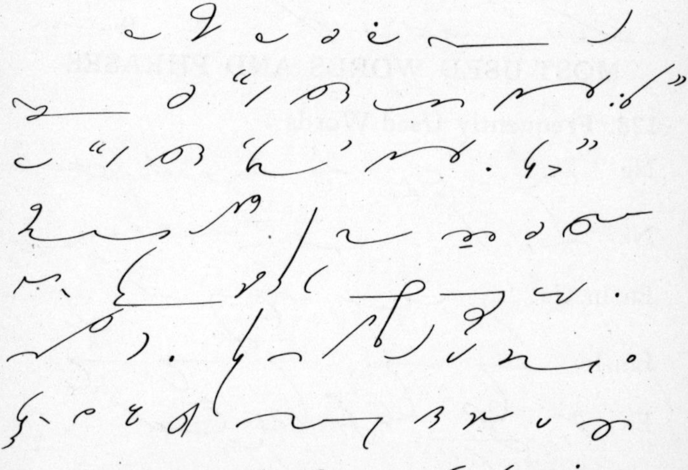

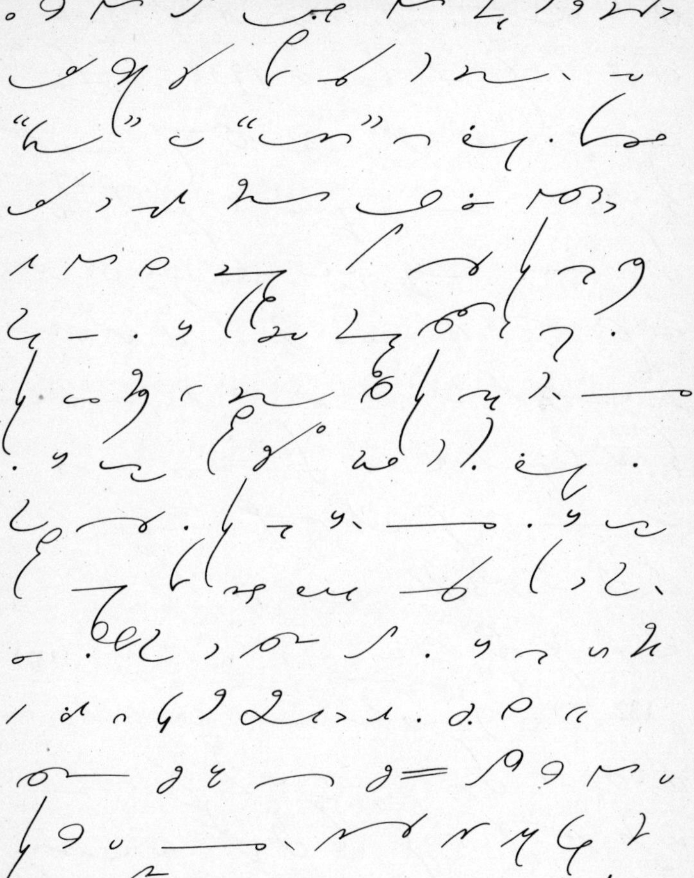

(234)

131.

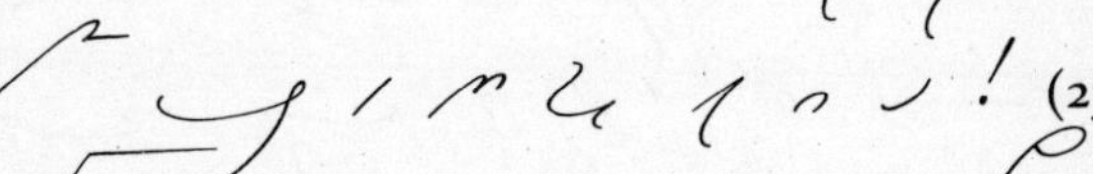

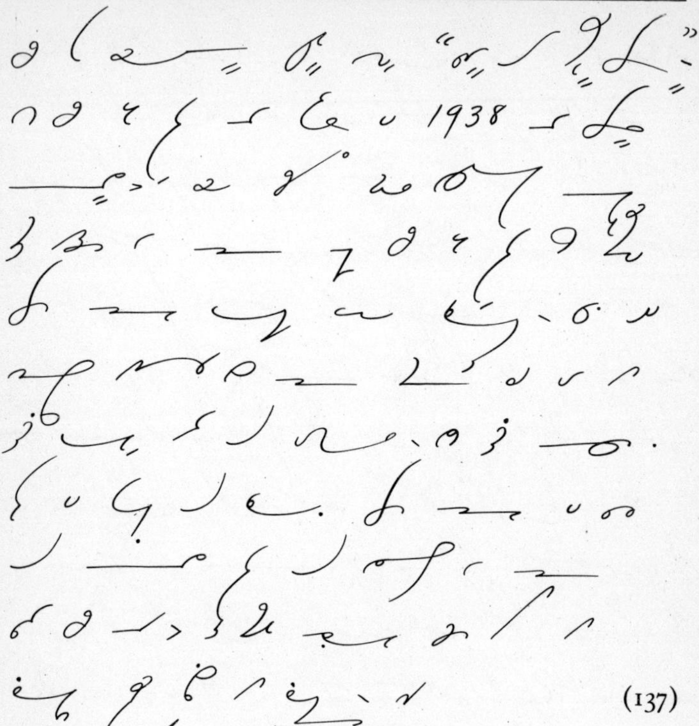

(137)

132.

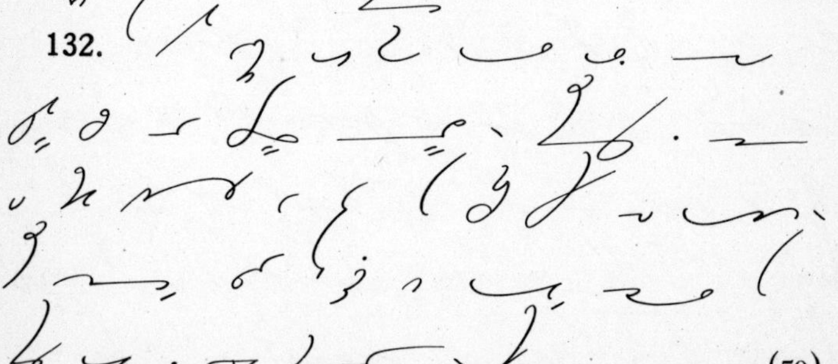

(59)

133.

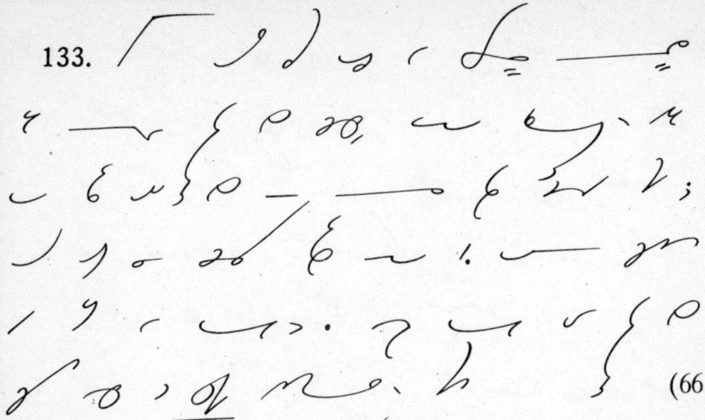

(66)

134.

(108)

135.

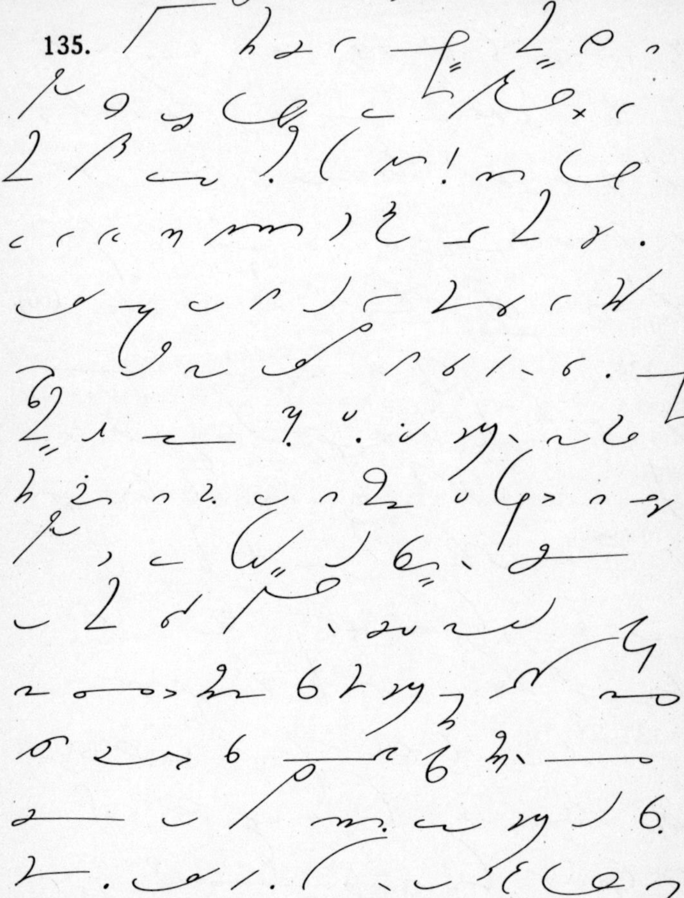

(151)

SPEED STUDY V

UNIT 13

PENMANSHIP

In practicing the following drills, be sure to compare each outline that you write with the enlarged model.

136. Ow, Oi

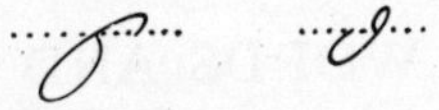

Points to Remember:

a. The vowel should be placed *outside* the hook as indicated by the dotted lines. (The dotted line in *oi* does *not* represent the line of writing—the base of the *o* rests on the line of writing.)

b. The hooks should remain deep and narrow.

Practice:

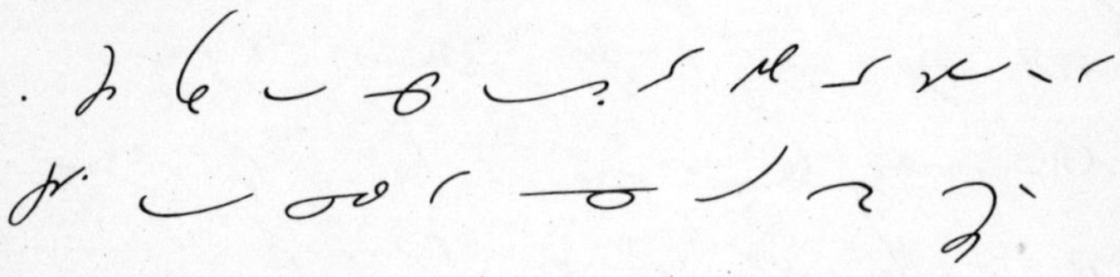

137. Di, Li, Fi

Points to Remember:

a. I is written with the same motion as *a* except that the end is curled back.

b. Be sure that the circle touches the consonant before it is curled back.

c. Be careful to avoid a point at the places indicated by arrows.

Practice:

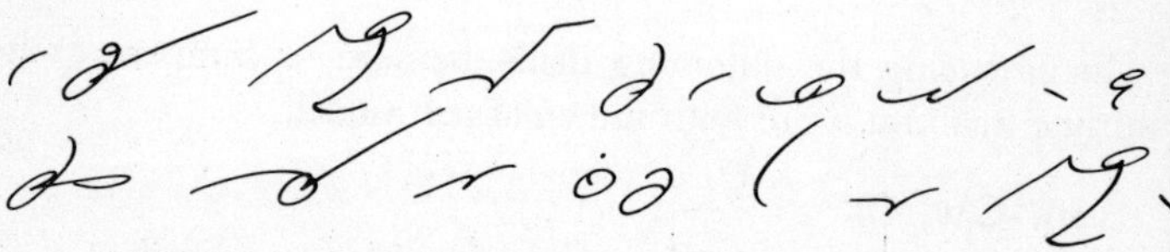

MOST-USED WORDS AND PHRASES

138. Frequently Used Words

Ū

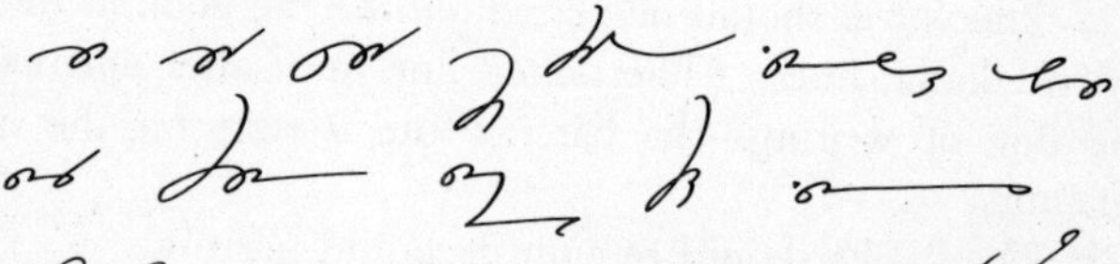

Ow

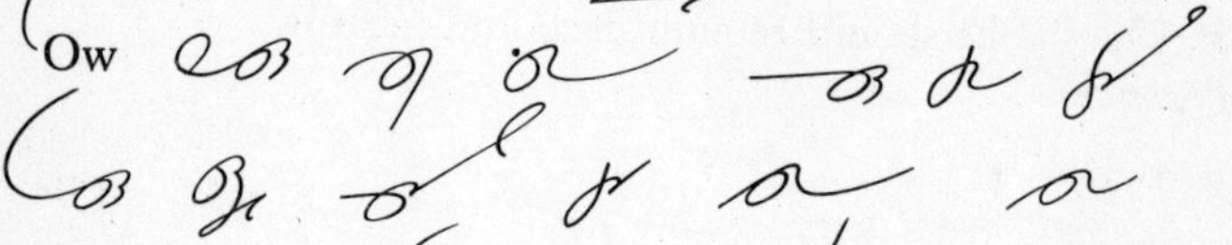

Oi

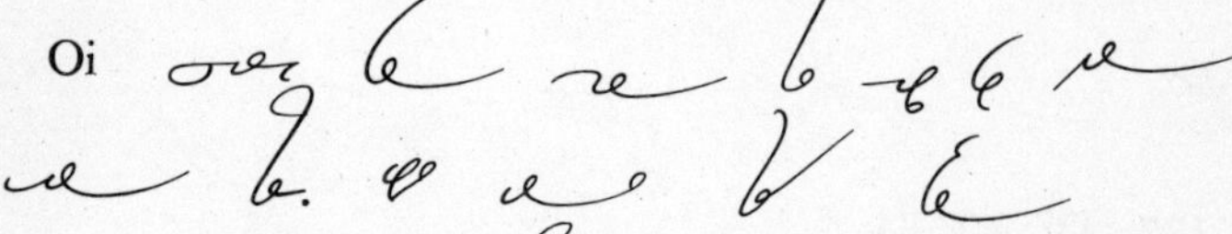

Ī

139. Brief-Form Derivatives and Phrases

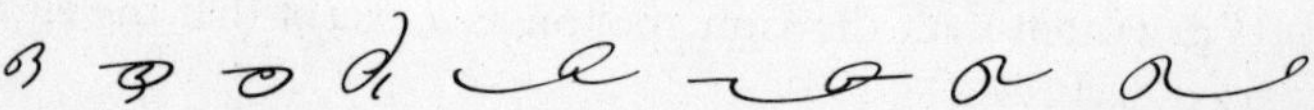

READING AND DICTATION PRACTICE

140. Tea

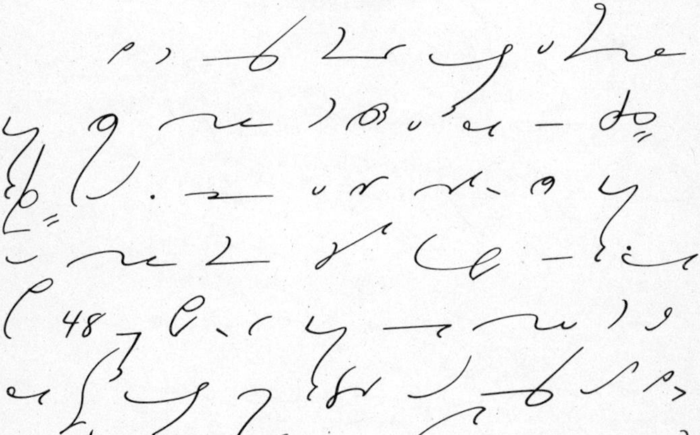

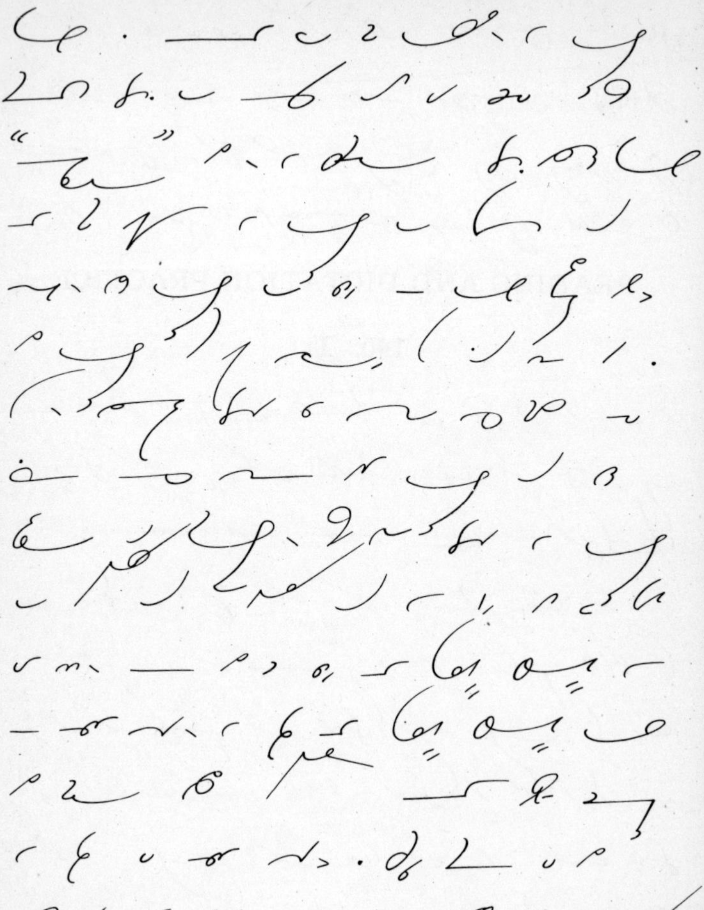

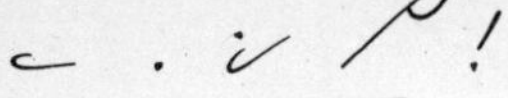

(224)

141.

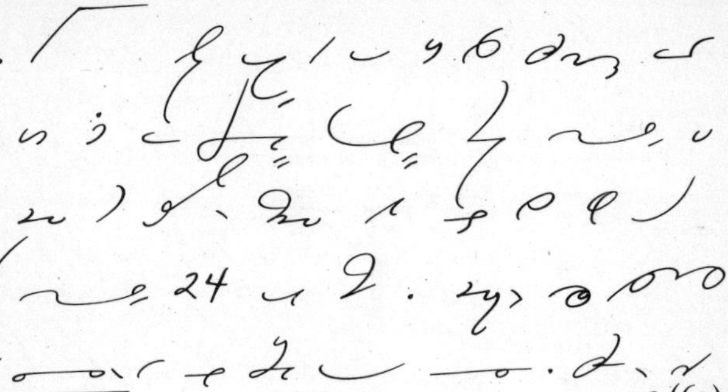

(62)

142.

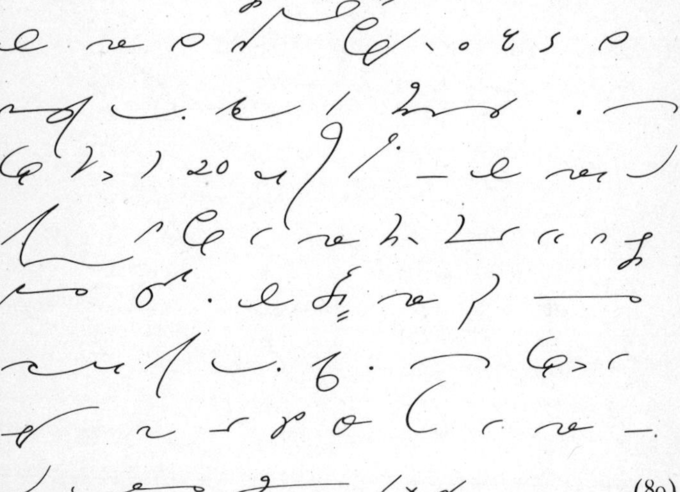

(89)

143.

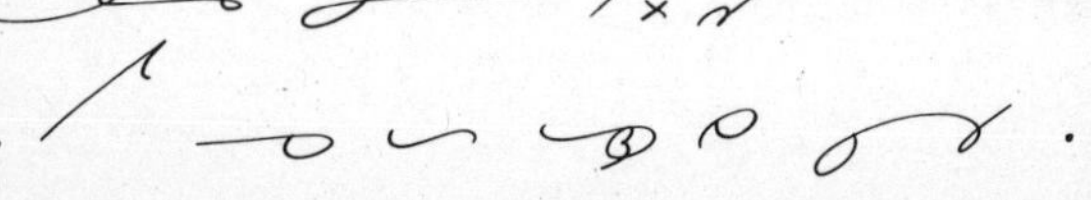

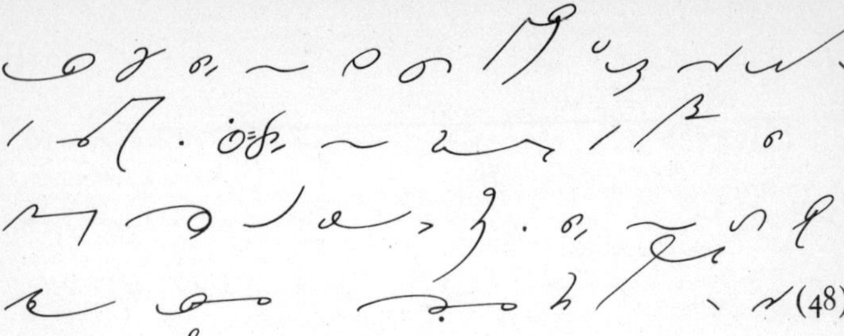

(48)

144.

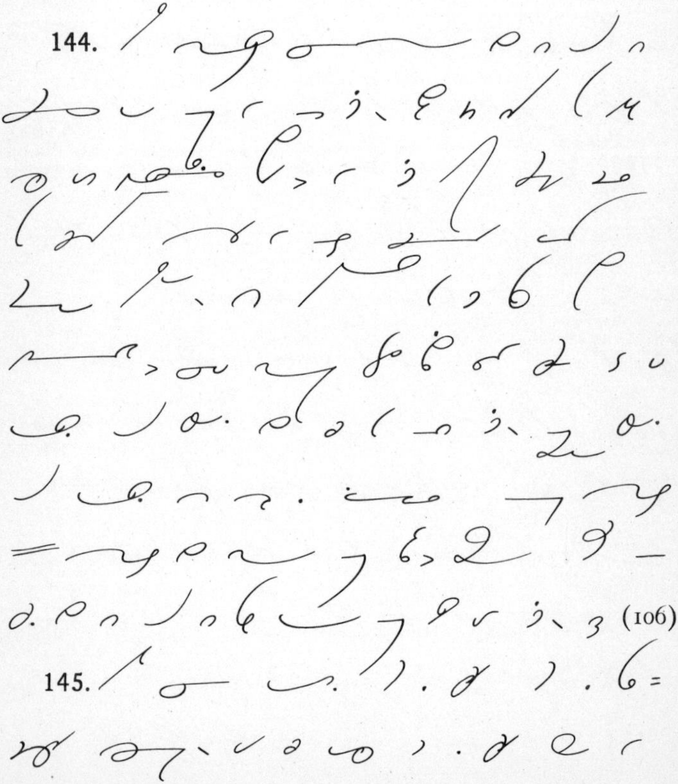

(106)

145.

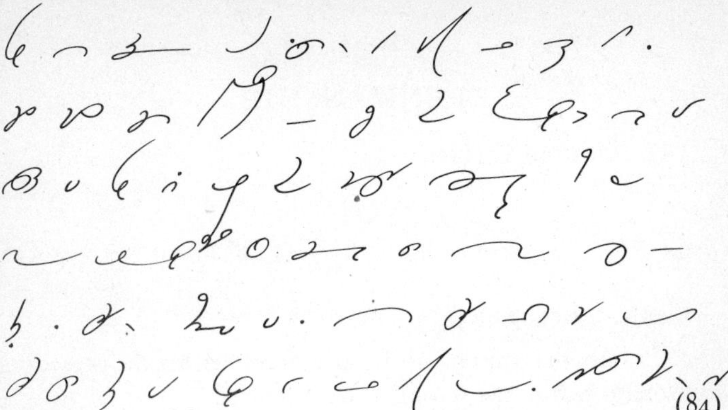

(84)

146.

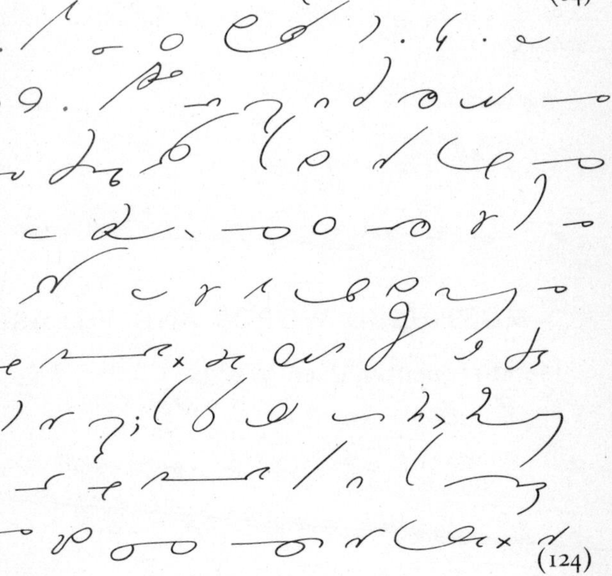

(124)

UNIT 14

PENMANSHIP

147. Double Circles

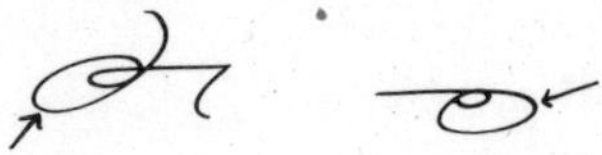

Points to Remember:

a. Be sure that the end of the first circle touches the preceding consonant before the second circle is started.

b. Be careful to avoid a point at the places indicated by arrows.

Practice:

MOST-USED WORDS AND PHRASES

148. Frequently Used Words

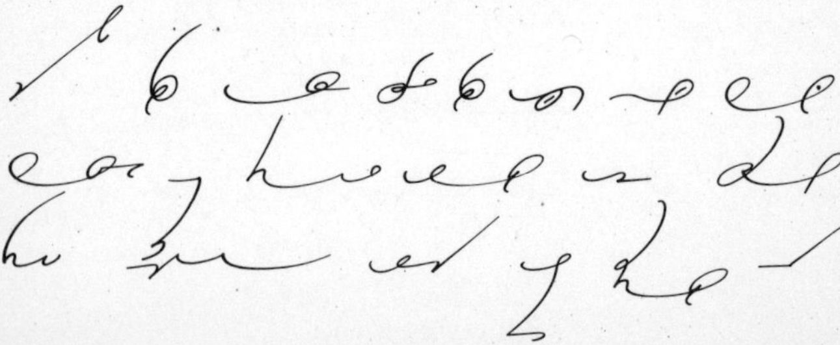

149. Brief-Form Derivatives and Phrases

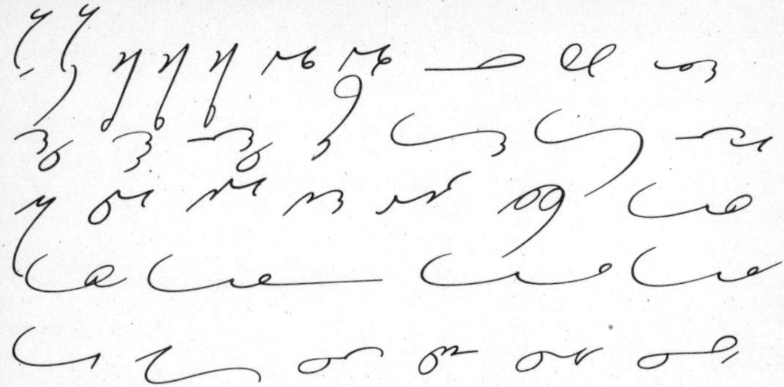

READING AND DICTATION PRACTICE

150. The Story of Flying

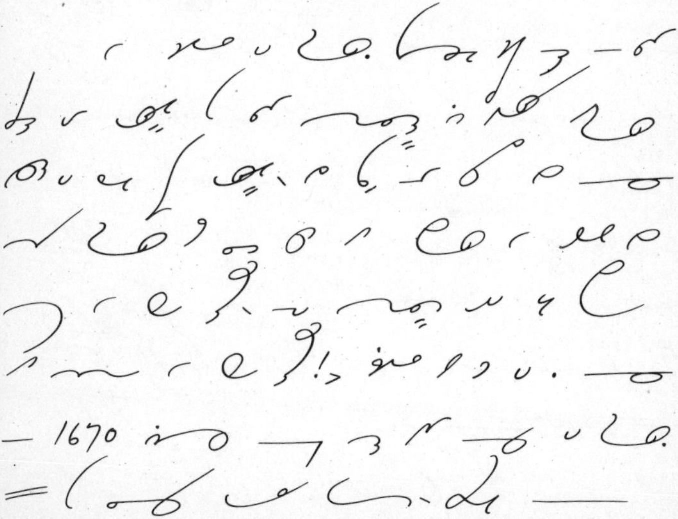

(242)

151.

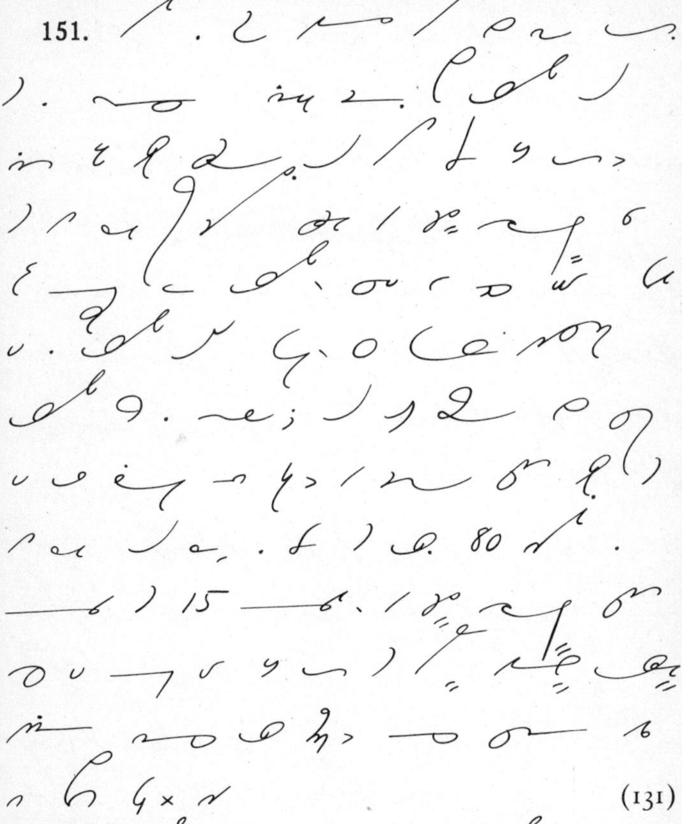

(131)

152.

(66)

153.

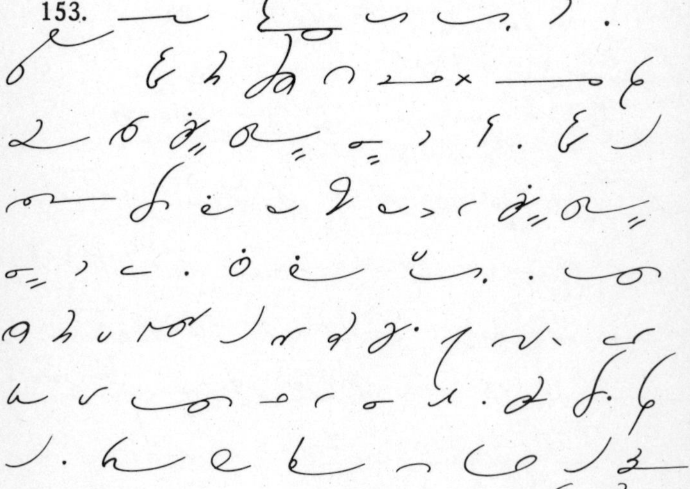

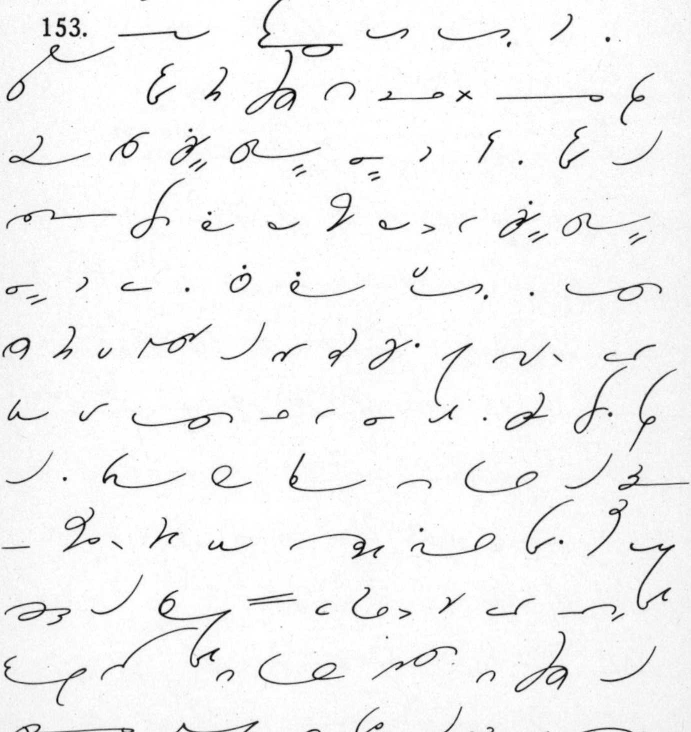

(122)

154.

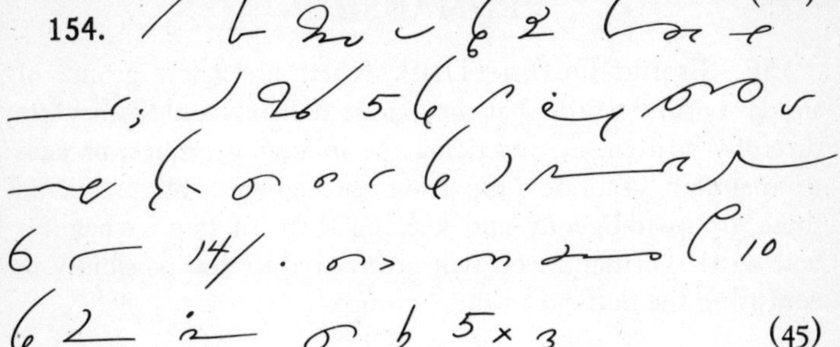

(45)

155.

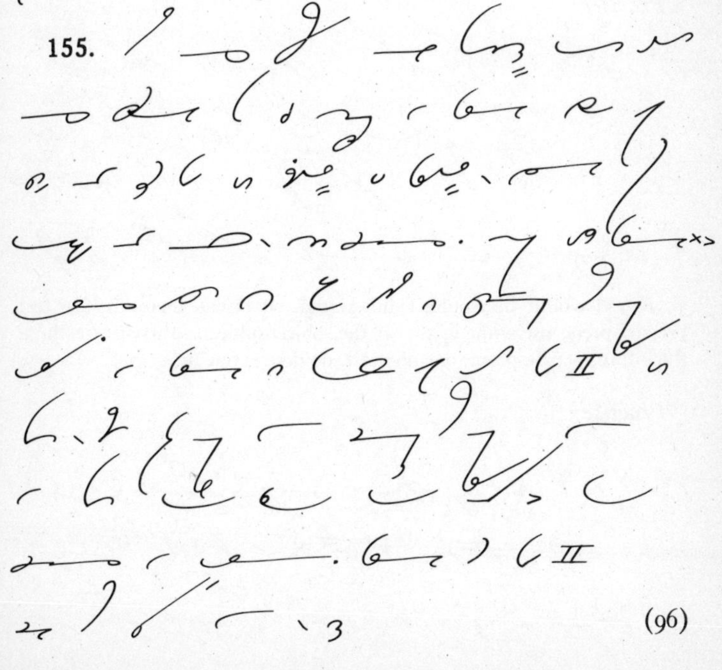

(96)

UNIT 15

PENMANSHIP

156. Similar-Outline Drill. There are a few groups of similar-outline words that may cause difficulty unless they are carefully written. In practicing the following groups, be sure to maintain accurate proportion throughout. By practicing these groups diligently and keeping them in mind whenever you write shorthand, you will greatly reduce the possibility of confusing the outlines in these groups.

Practice:

Key: I would–he would, I did–he did, vital-final, their-our, fear-feel, prepare-press, use-with, in the–at the, object-subject, satisfy-fit, its-those, thick-thin, person-proof, one-no-most, do-desire, few-first.

Practice:

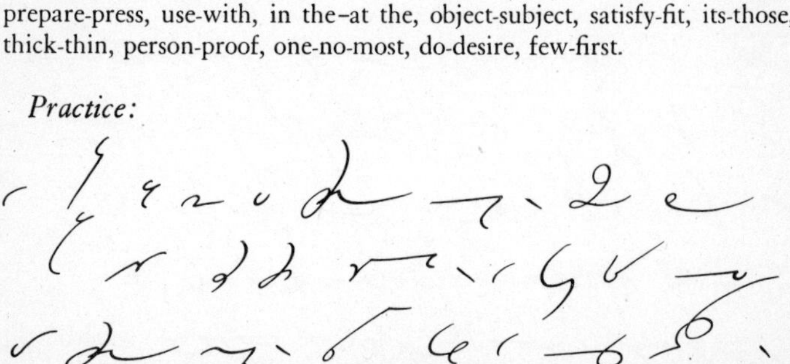

MOST-USED WORDS AND PHRASES

157. Freqently Used Words

Ŭ *and* Ow *omitted*

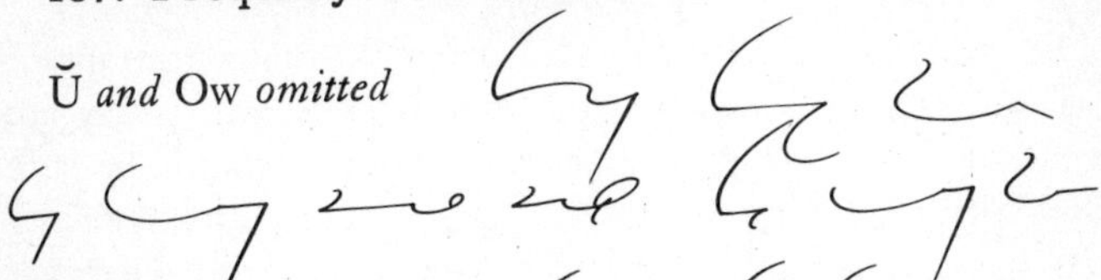

Per, Pur

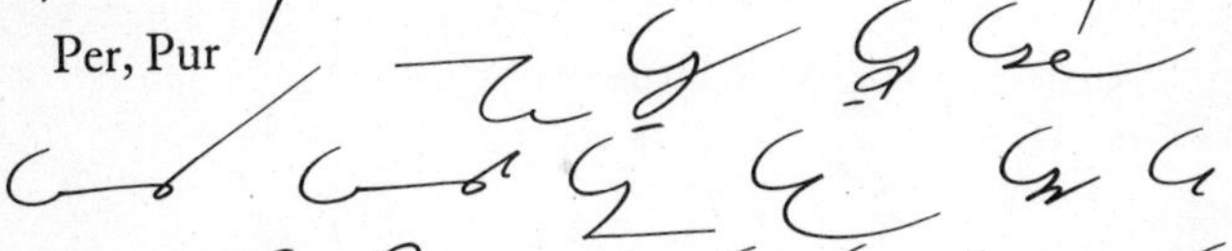

Pro

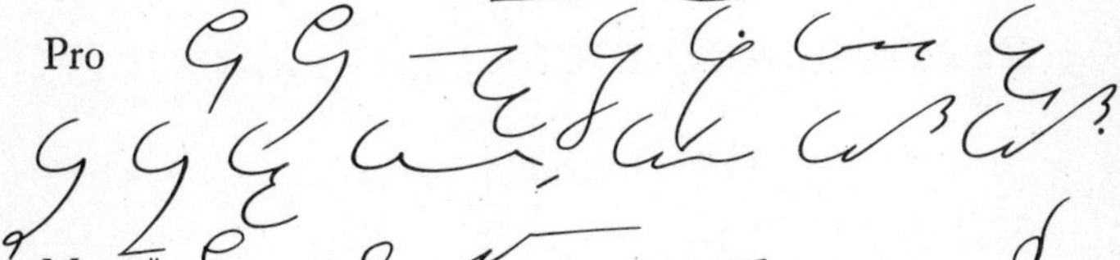

Ment *

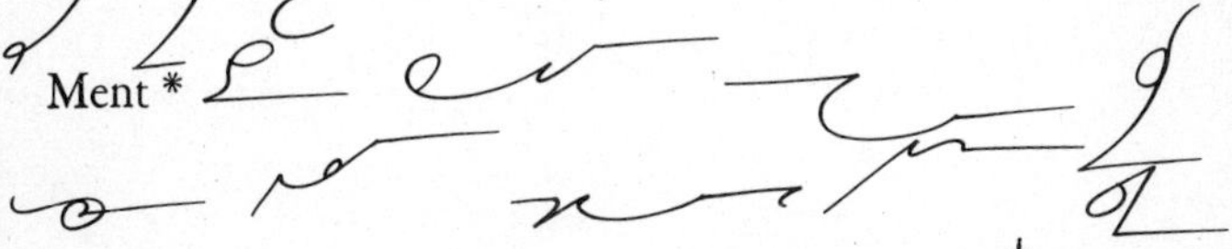

Sume

Ple

Ble

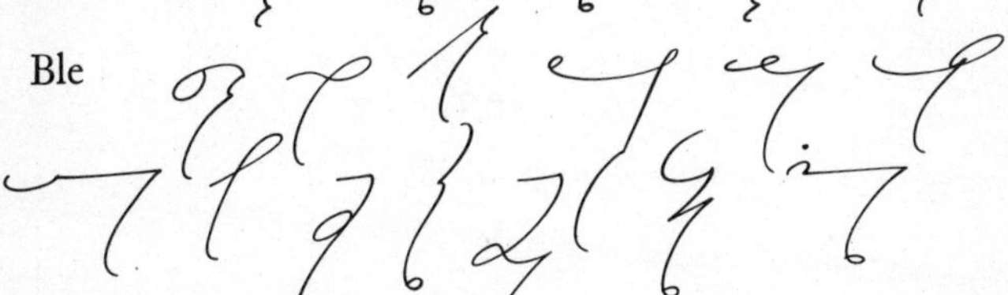

* The four words *cement, raiment, lament,* and *comment* are written in full.
† *Pre* is always written in full except in *presume* and its derivatives.

158. Brief-Form Derivatives and Phrases

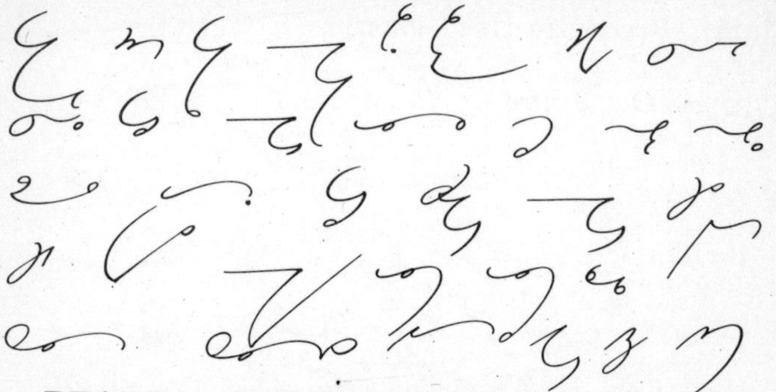

READING AND DICTATION PRACTICE

159. Elizabeth Fry

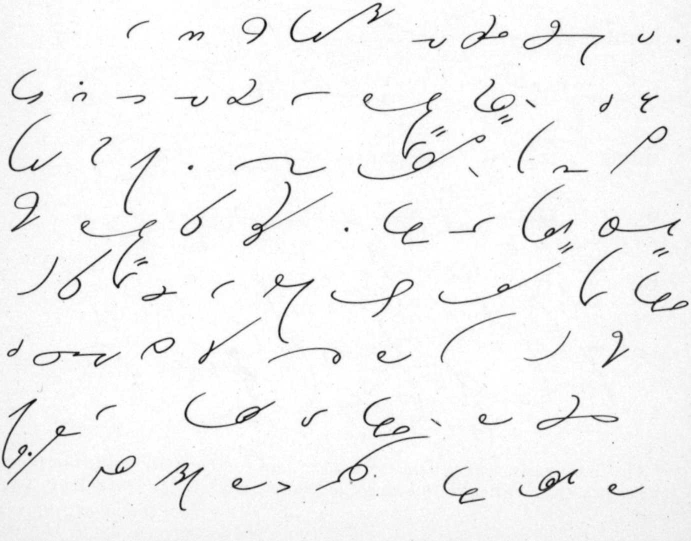

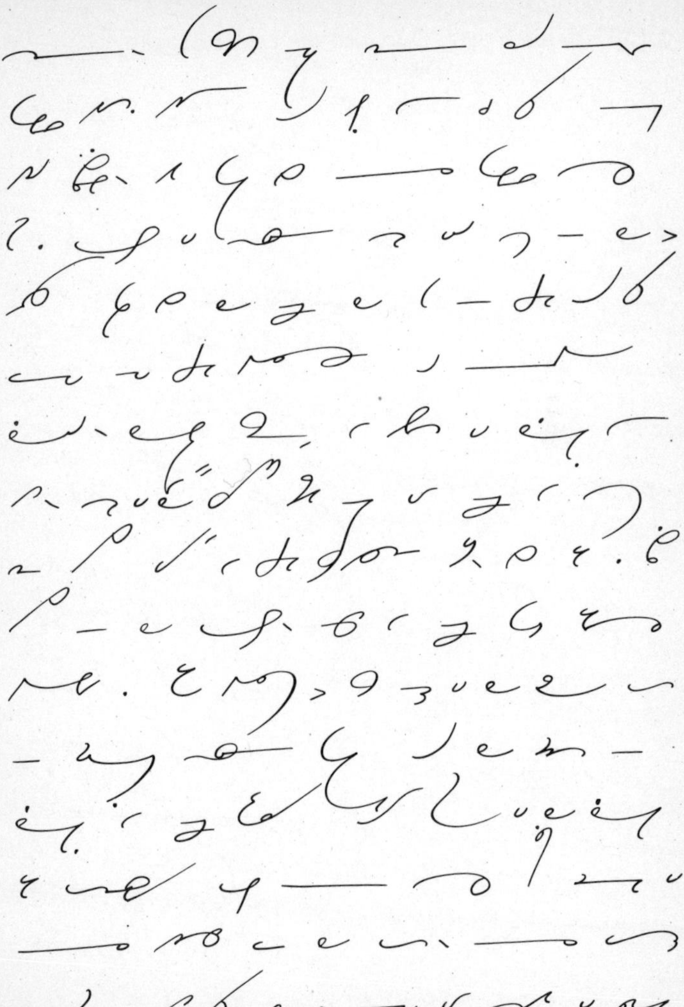

(332)

160.

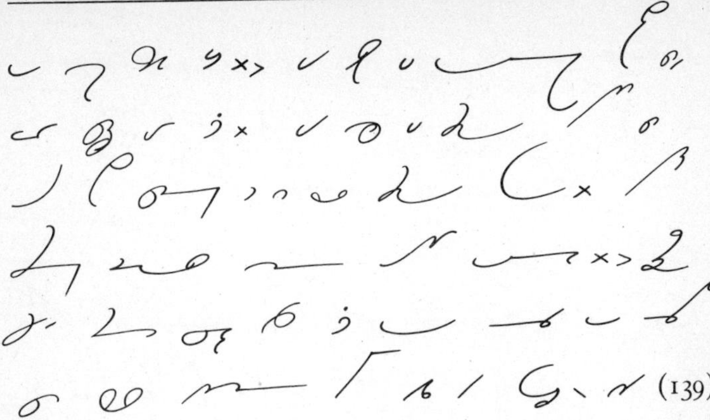

(139)

161.

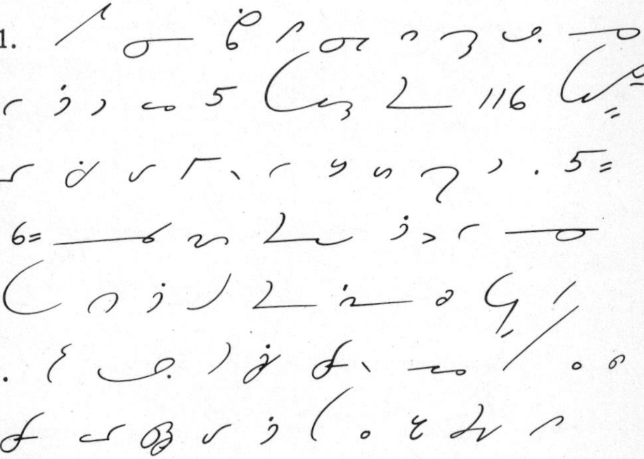

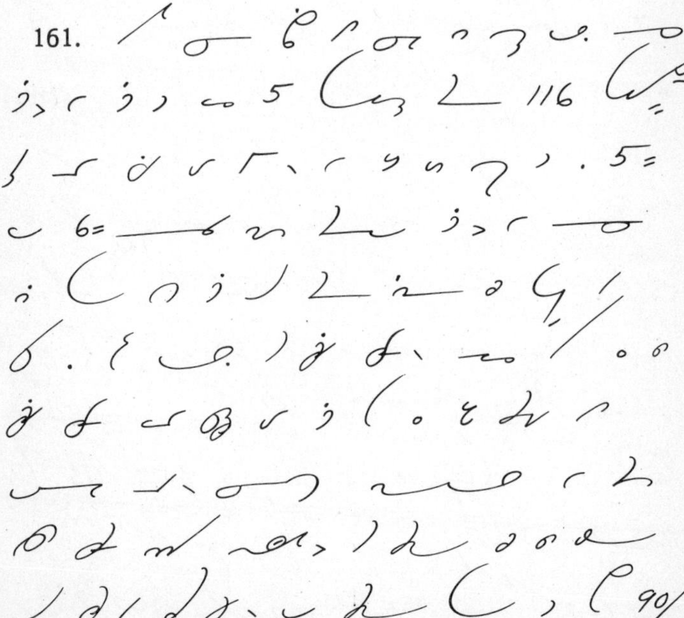

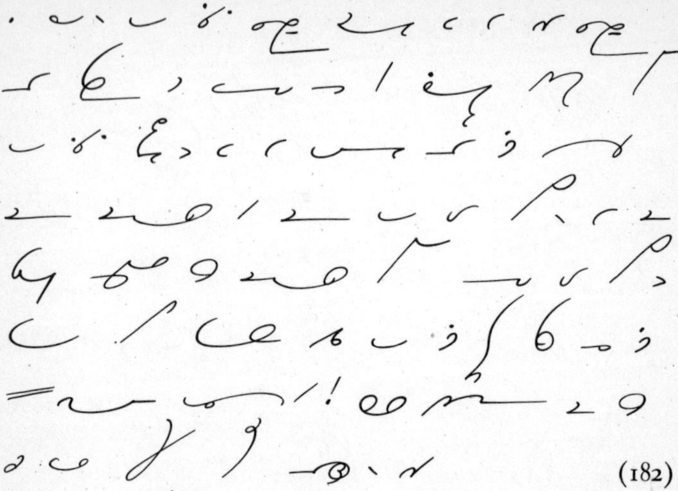

(182)

162.

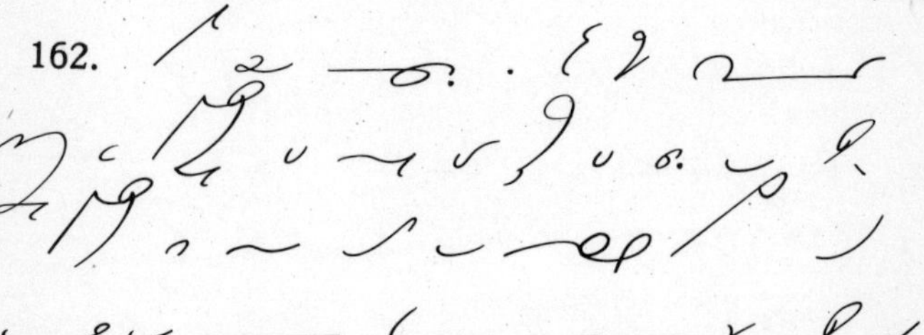

(42)

163.

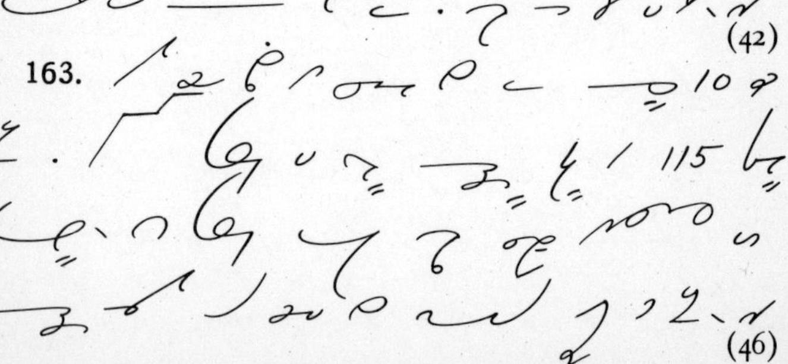

(46)

SPEED STUDY VI

UNIT 16

PENMANSHIP

In practicing the following drills, be sure to compare each outline that you write with the enlarged model.

164. Th, Ent, Emt

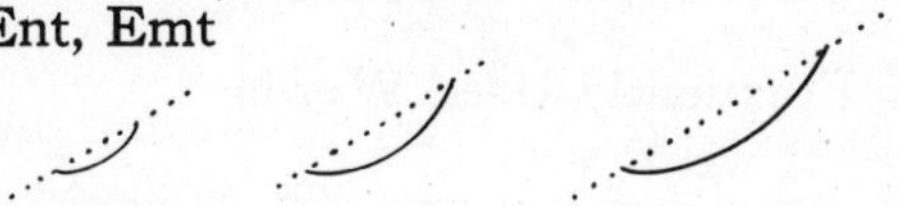

Points to Remember:

a. These curves start to the right and then swing upward. There should be no hook at the beginning or at the end.

b. The dotted line shows the slant of the strokes.

Compare: 

Practice:

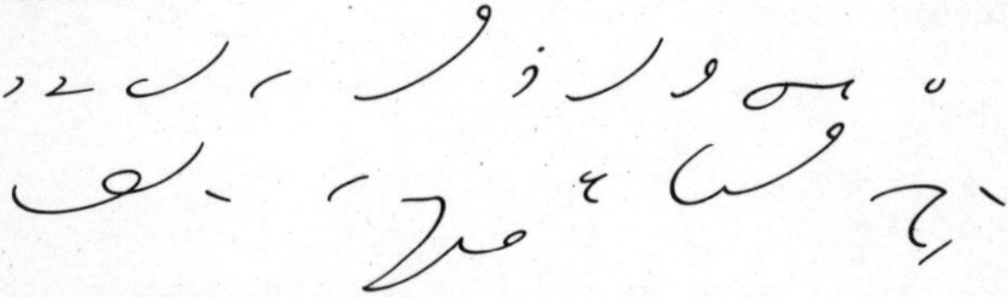

165. Held

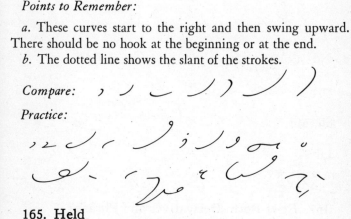

Points to Remember:

a. In this combination, the *l* should maintain its general shape, except that it is given a swing upward at the end.

b. Be careful not to raise the *l* too soon or the stroke will look like *emt.*

Practice:

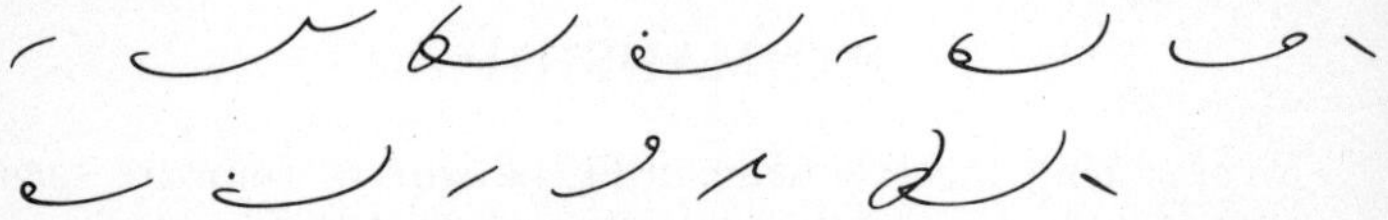

MOST-USED WORDS AND PHRASES

166. Frequently Used Words

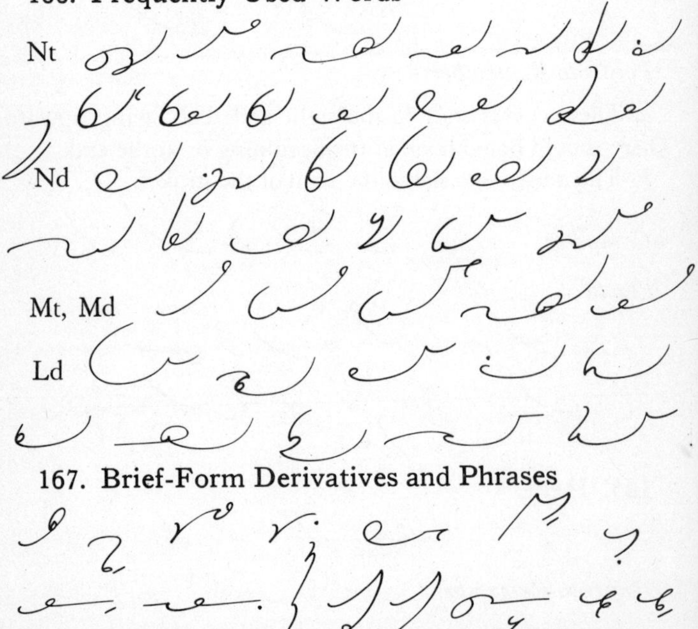

167. Brief-Form Derivatives and Phrases

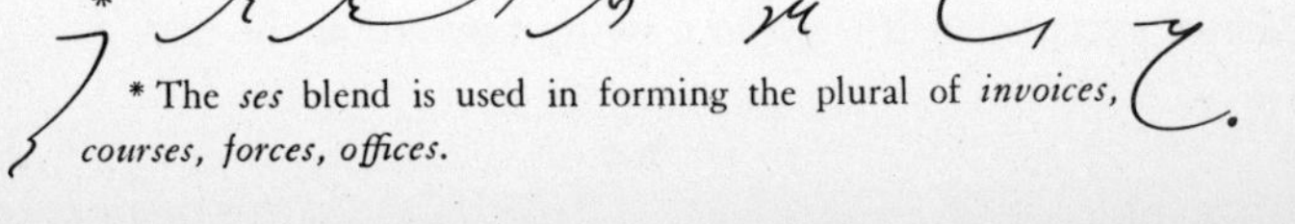

* The *ses* blend is used in forming the plural of *invoices, courses, forces, offices.*

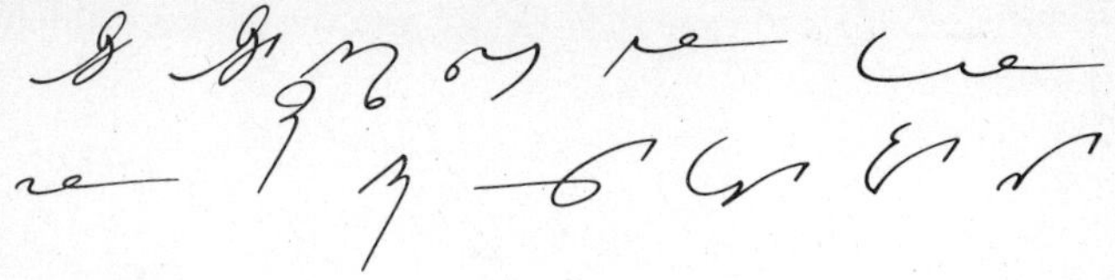

READING AND DICTATION PRACTICE

168. Fishing

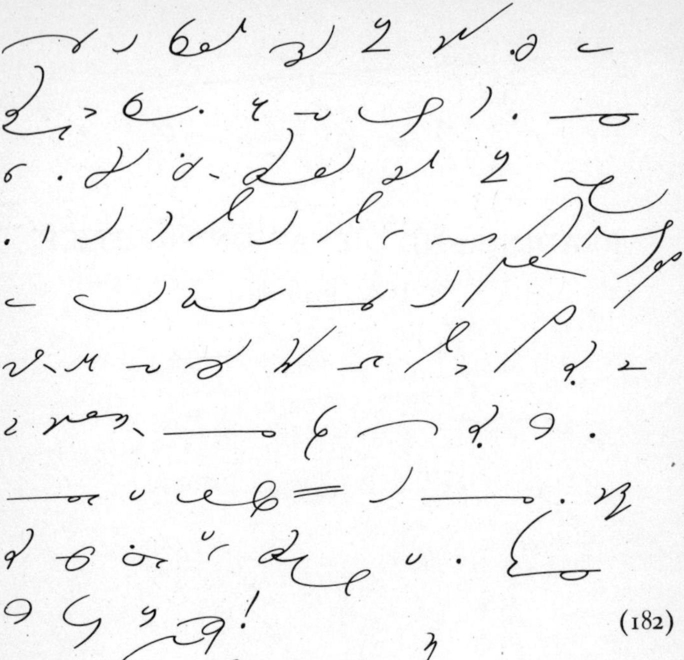

(182)

169.

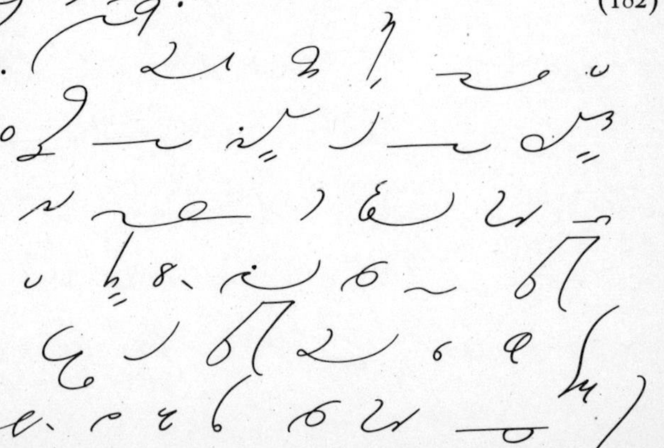

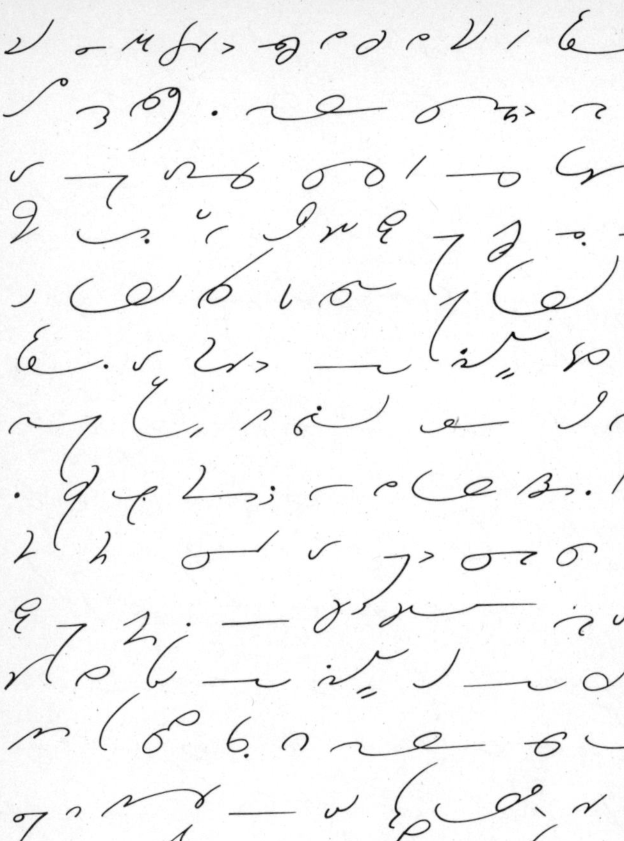

(204)

170.

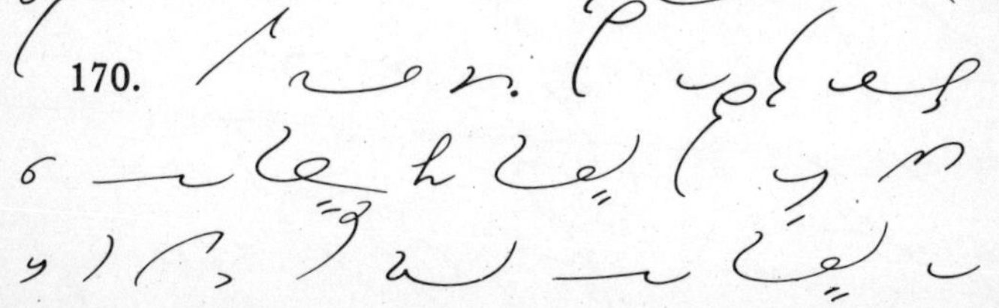

(82)

171.

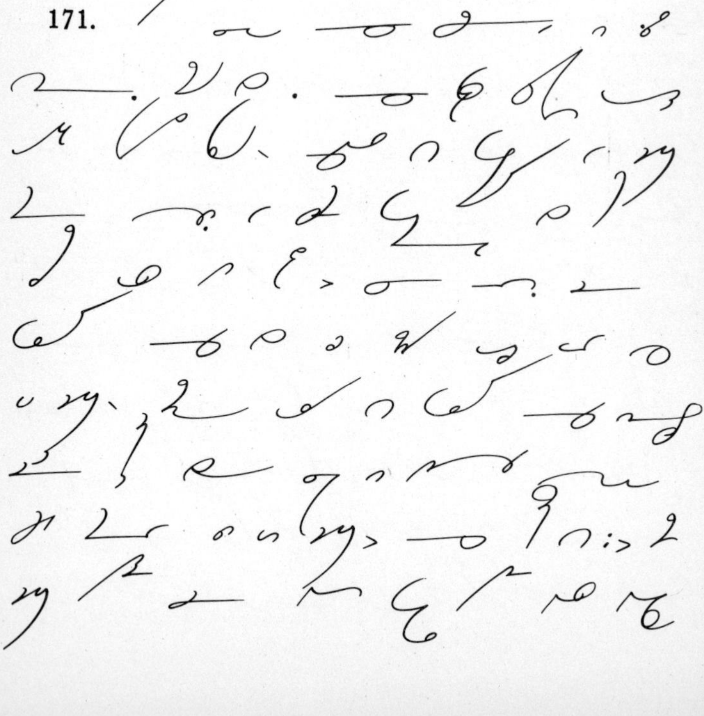

(106)

172.

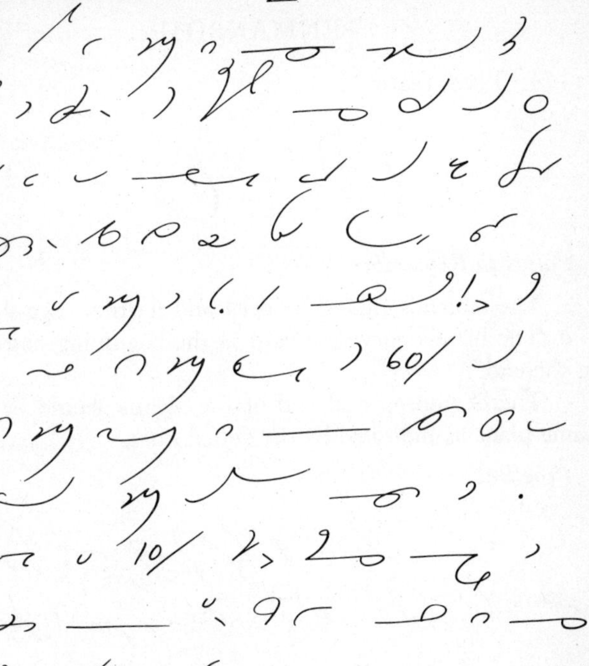

(96)

173.

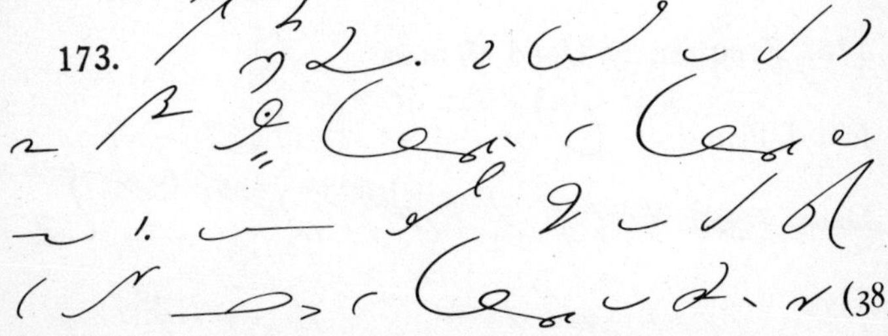

(38)

UNIT 17

PENMANSHIP

174. Tive, Gent

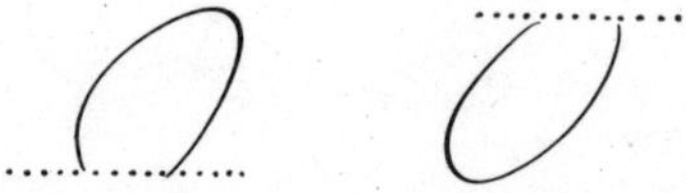

Points to Remember:

a. These blends should be deep and narrow—egg-shaped.

b. The blends curve outward at the beginning and inward at the end.

c. The beginning and end of the blends should be on the same plane as indicated by the dotted lines.

Practice:

MOST-USED WORDS AND PHRASES

175. Frequently Used Words

Jent-d, Pent-d 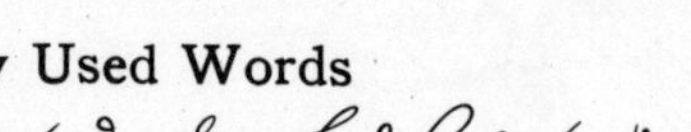

Def-v 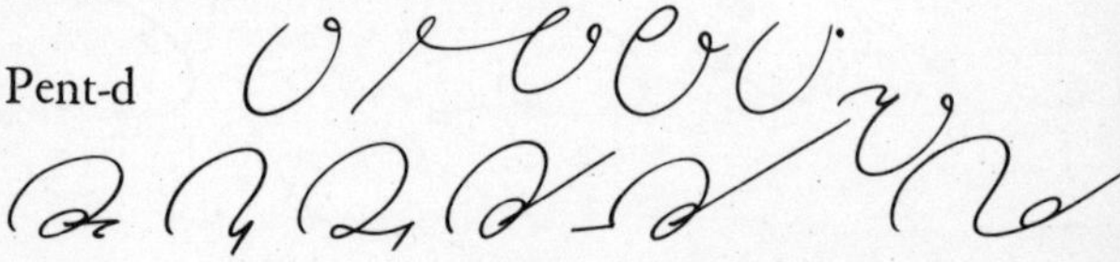

Tive 

176. "Morning," "Night" Phrases

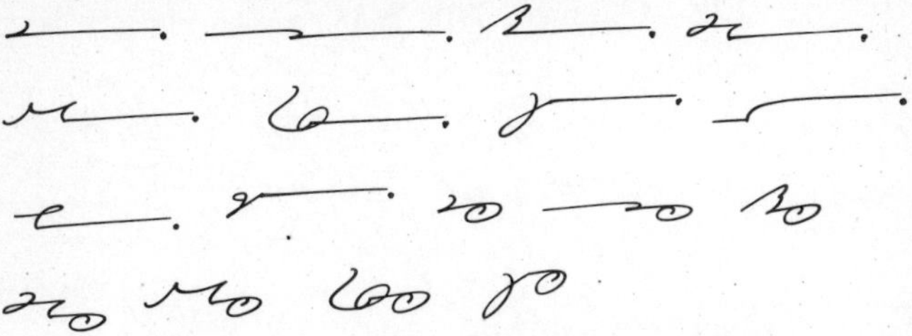

177. Brief-Form Derivatives and Phrases

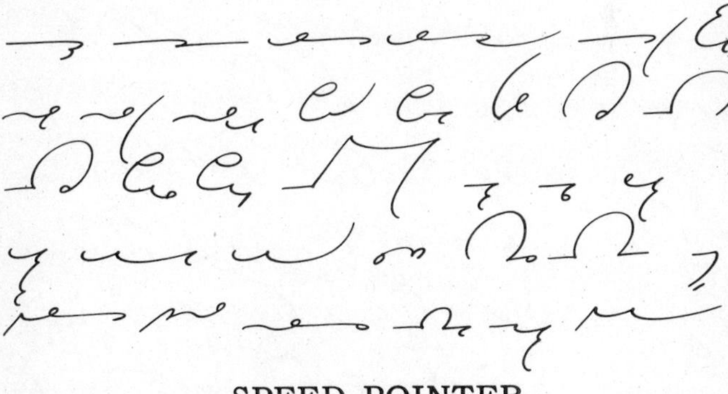

SPEED POINTER

Mental Pictures. It is well to have a mental picture of the entire shorthand form of a word or phrase before writing it. If you write the word form with a jerky movement the first time you attempt it, keep on practicing it until you can write it fluently. That is one of the most important of the "speed secrets." Acquire the habit of fluent writing early; it will help you immensely throughout your training.

READING AND DICTATION PRACTICE

178. Galileo, the Star Gazer

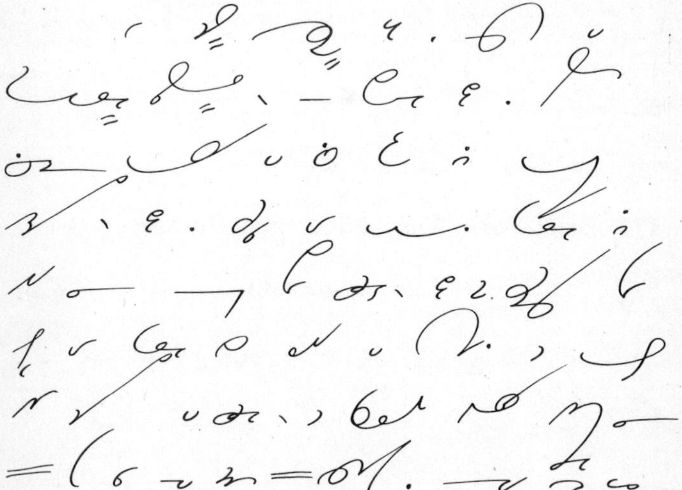

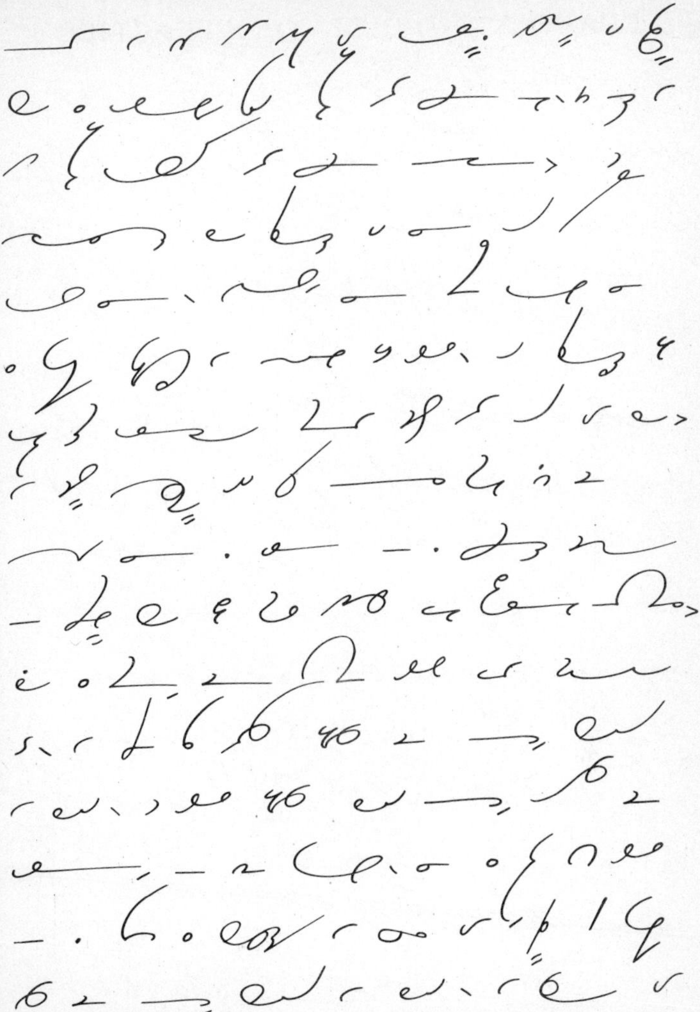

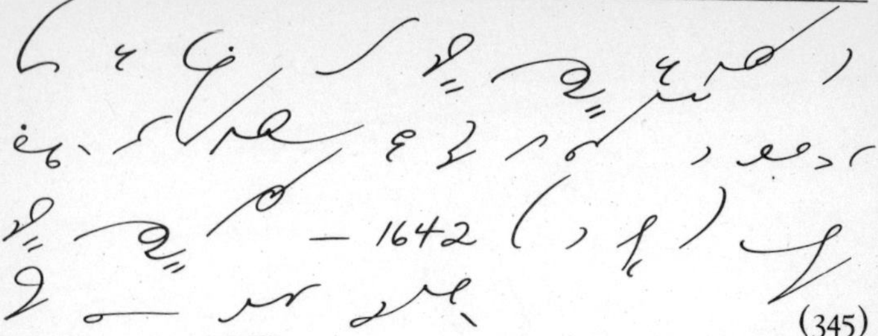

(345)

179.

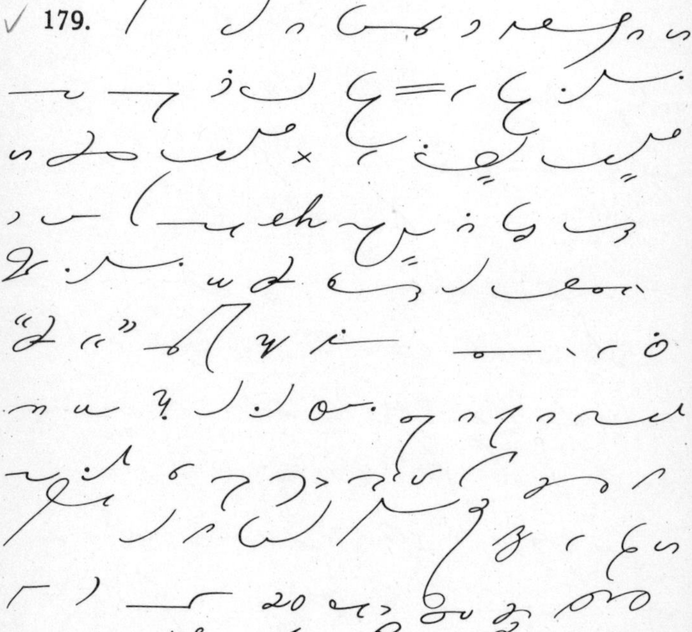

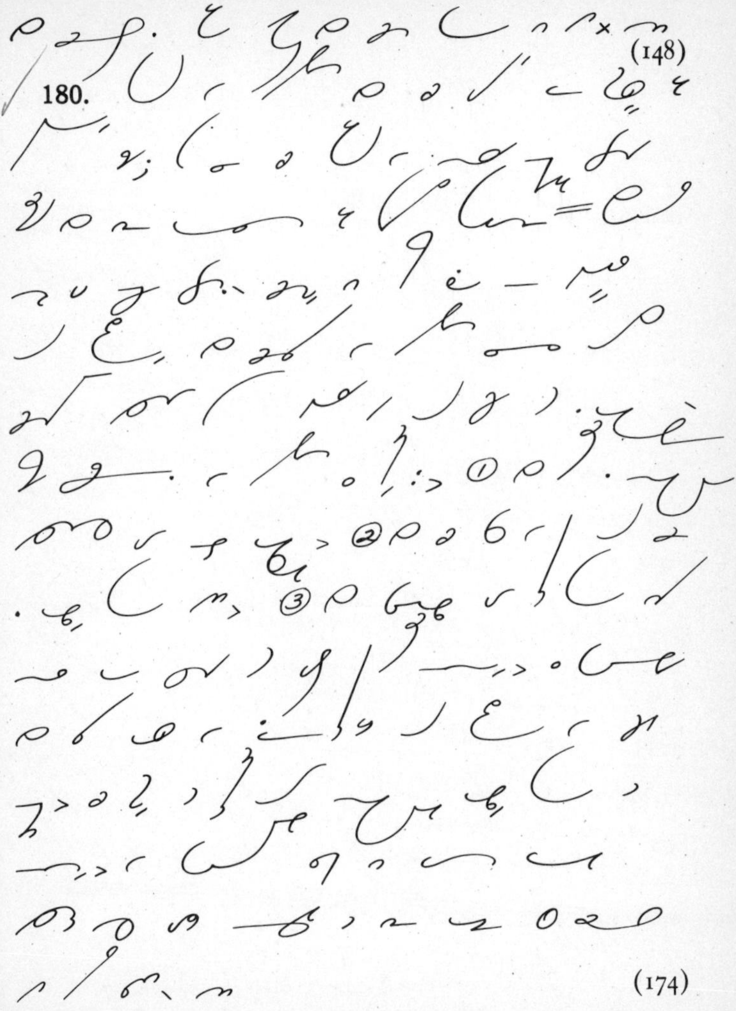

(148)

180.

(174)

181.

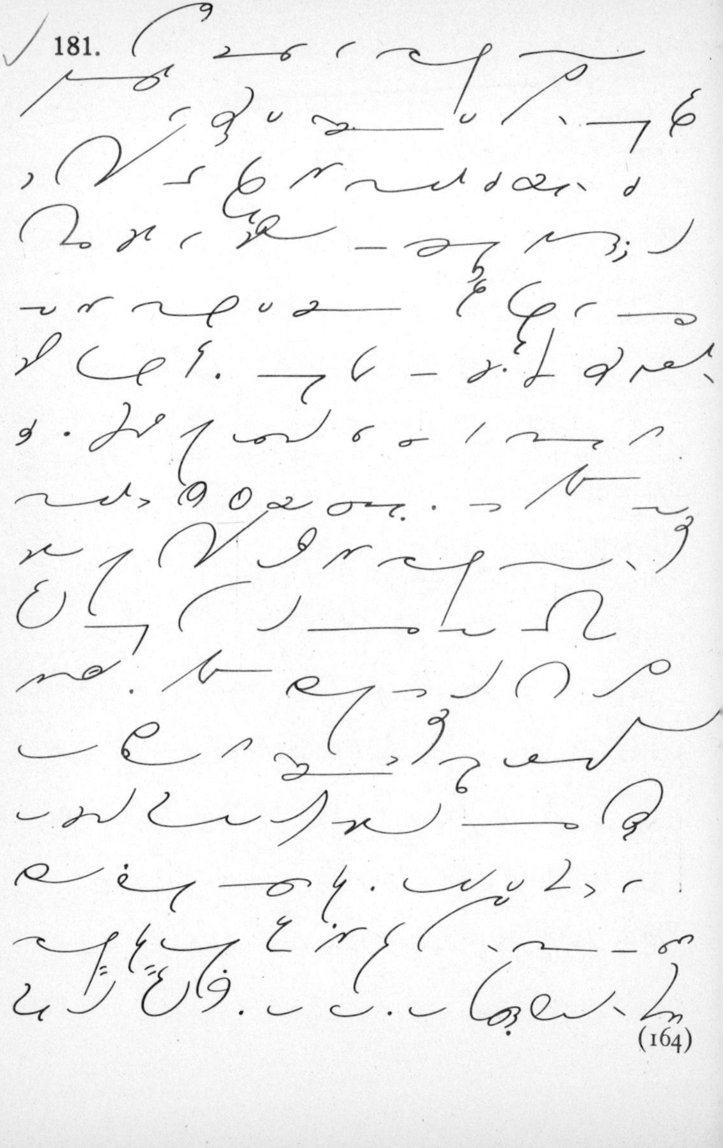

(164)

UNIT 18

PENMANSHIP

182. I Had, We Had

Points to Remember:

a. The phrase *I had* begins with a right motion. When the circle has been completed, it is broken and the *d* added.

b. In *we had,* we have a small broken circle. Be sure that the end of the circle touches the o͞o-hook before the circle is broken and the *d* added.

Practice:

MOST-USED WORDS AND PHRASES

183. Frequently Used Words

Be

Mis

De

Dis

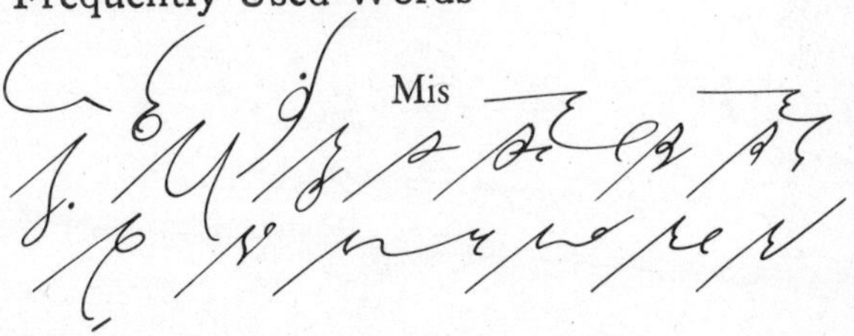

Re

184. Brief-Form Derivatives and Phrases

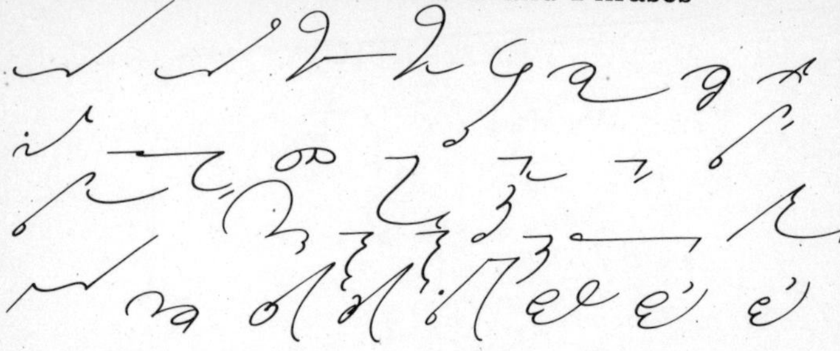

READING AND DICTATION PRACTICE

185. Advertising

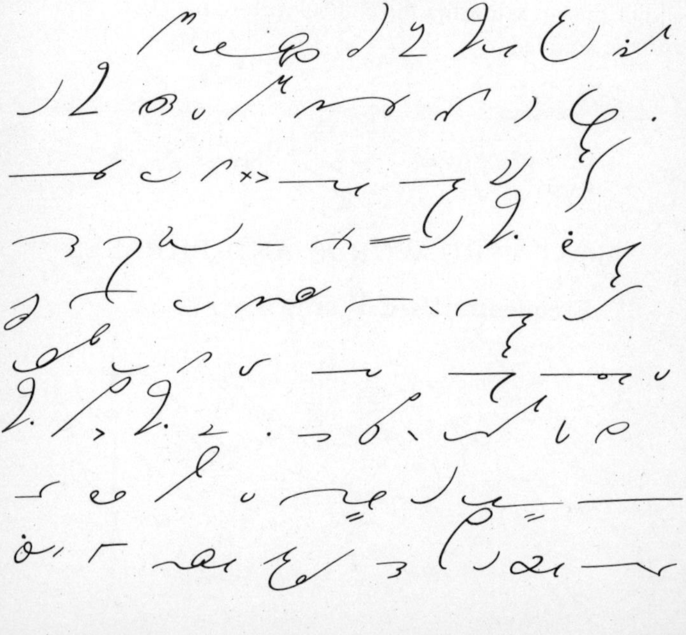

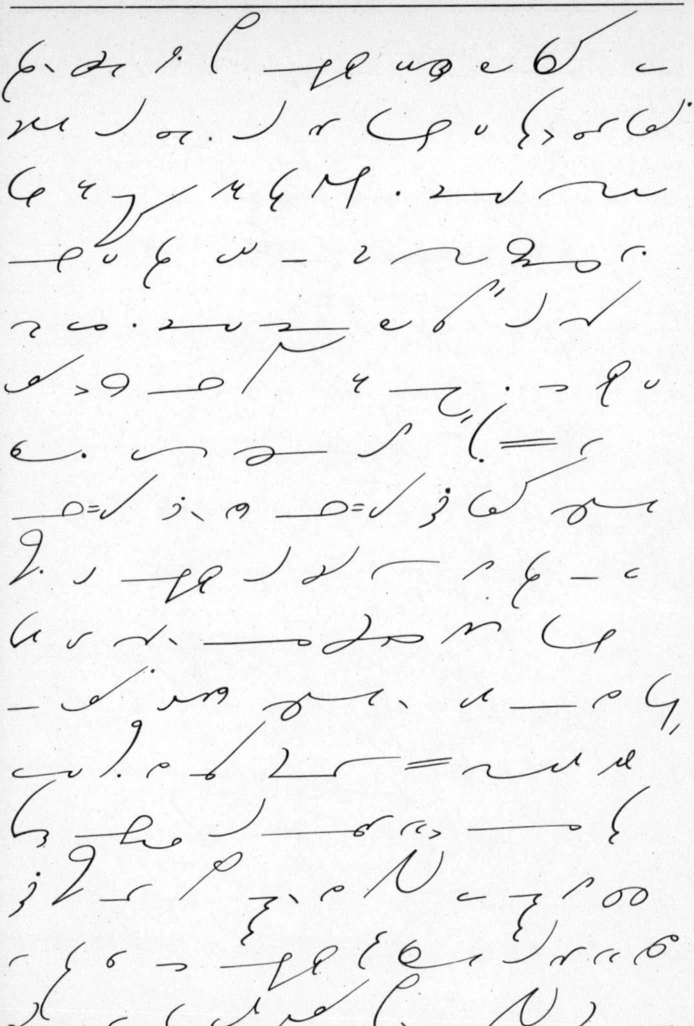

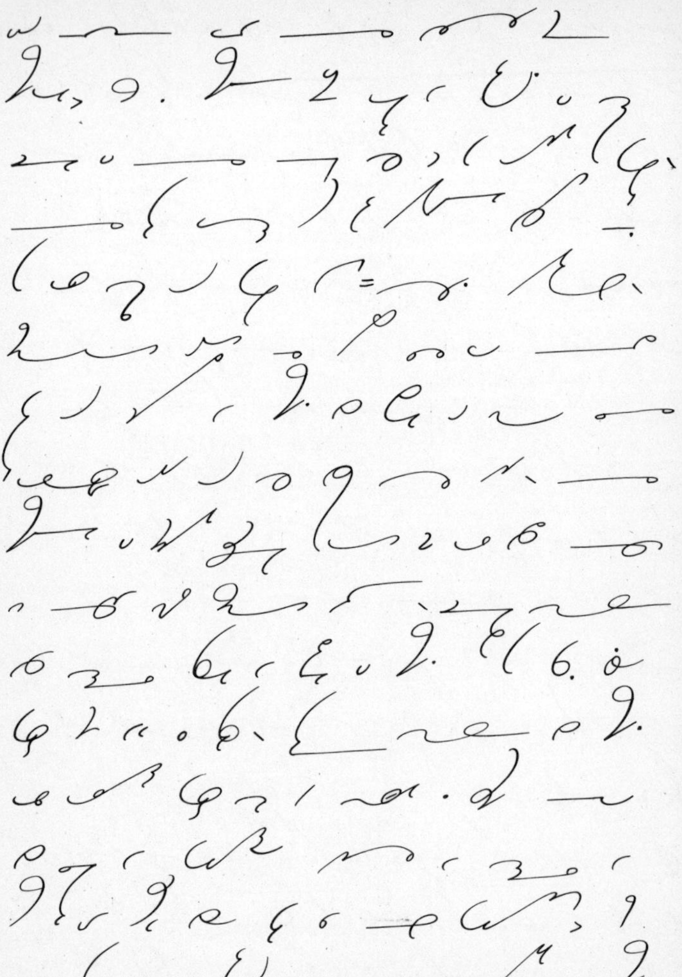

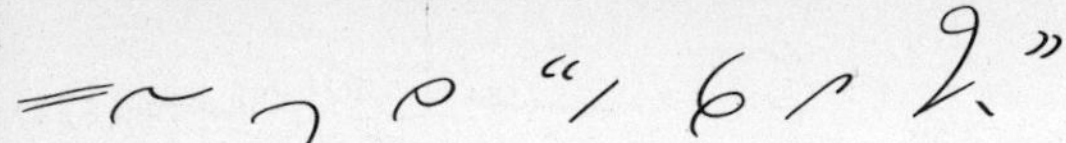

(466)

186.

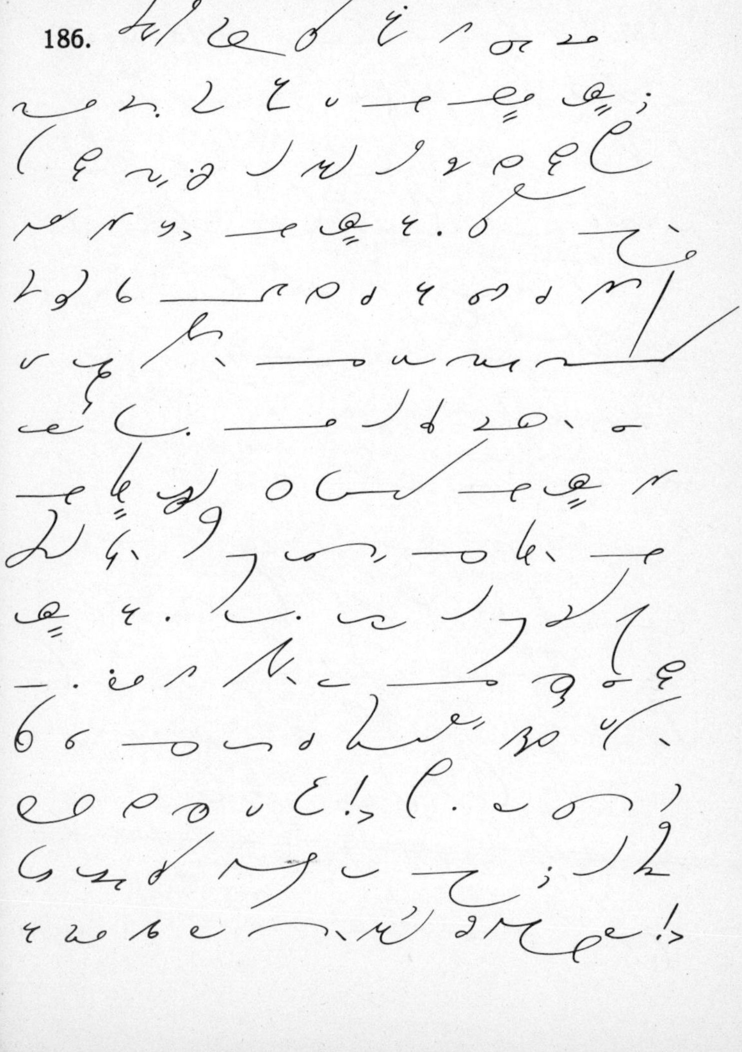

(173)

187.

(159)

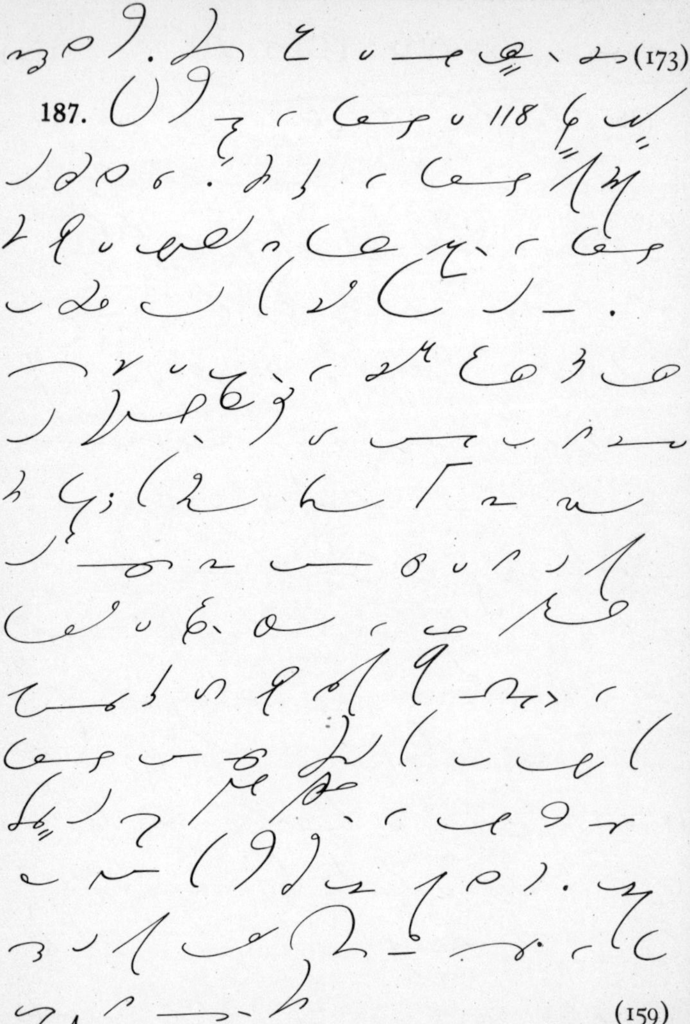

SPEED STUDY VII

UNIT 19

PENMANSHIP

188. Th, Ten, Tem

Points to Remember:

a. These curves start *outward* at the beginning. Consequently, the curve is deep at the beginning and flattens out toward the end.

b. The dotted line indicates the slant of the blends.

Practice:

MOST-USED WORDS AND PHRASES

189. Frequently Used Words

Ten

Den

Tem

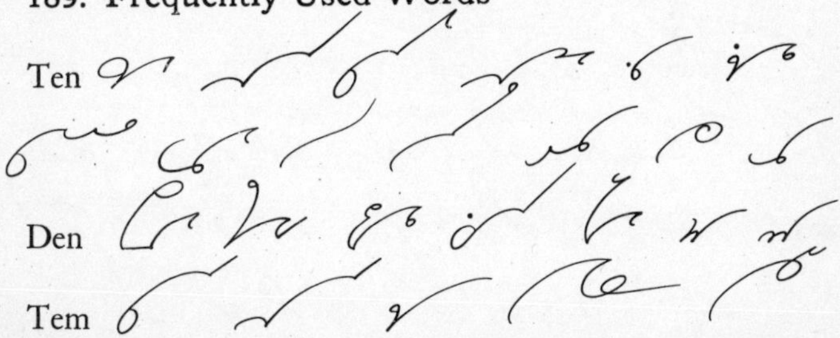

Dem 

190. Frequently Used Phrases

READING AND DICTATION PRACTICE

191. A Camping Trip

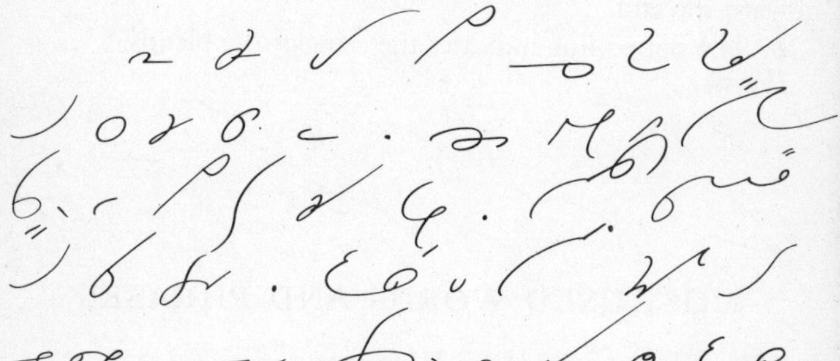

(237)

192.

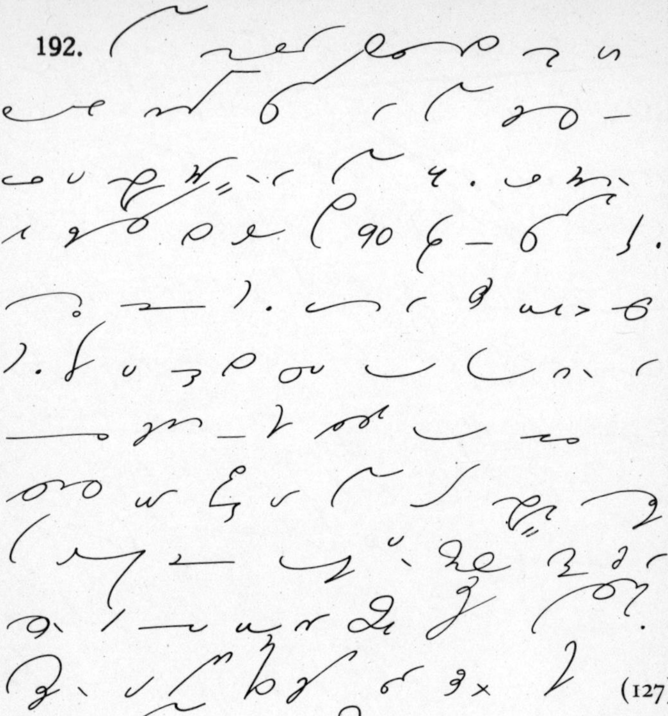

(127)

193.

(142)

194.

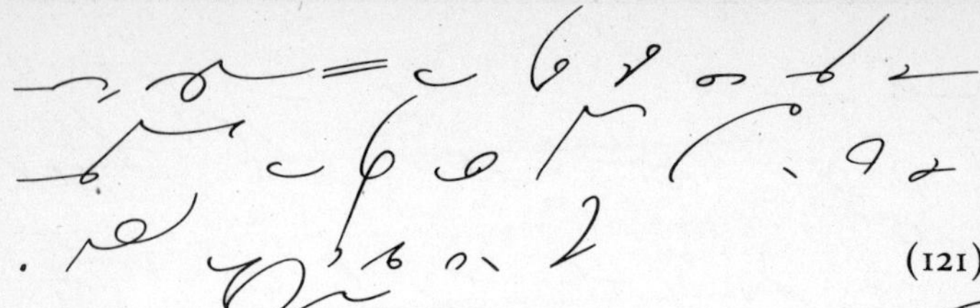

(121)

195.

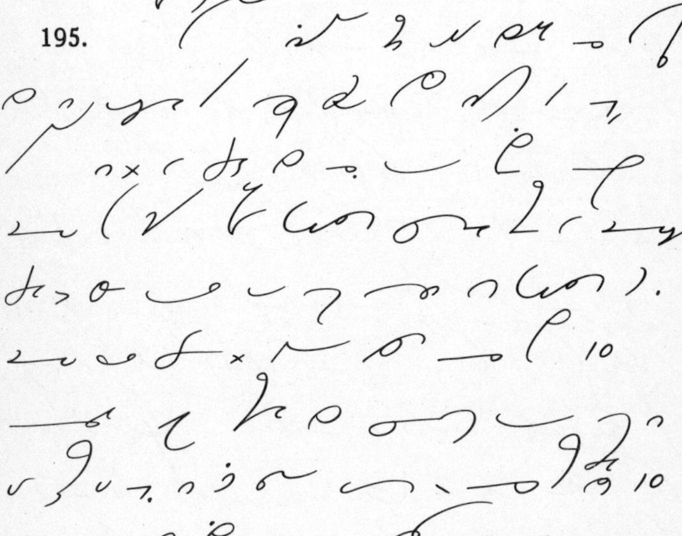

(111)

196.

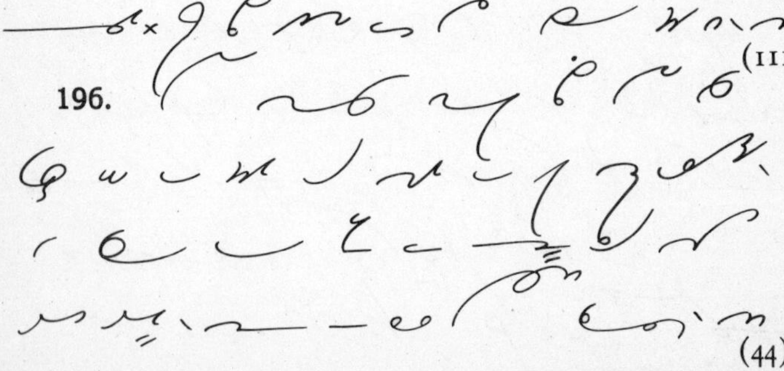

(44)

UNIT 20

PENMANSHIP

197. Barn, Period

Point to Remember:

The circle should fit snugly so that, if it were erased, the consonants would join smoothly. In the word *period*, be careful not to curve the *d*.

Practice:

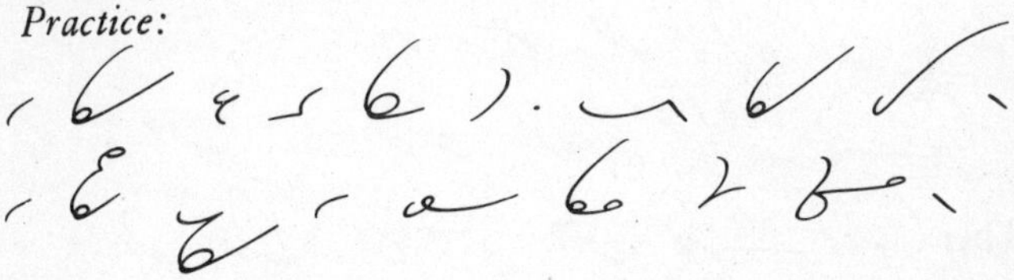

198. Mart, Card

Points to Remember:

a. In these joinings, the reversed circle retraces the preceding consonant.

b. Be sure that the consonants meet at the top of the reversed circle.

Practice:

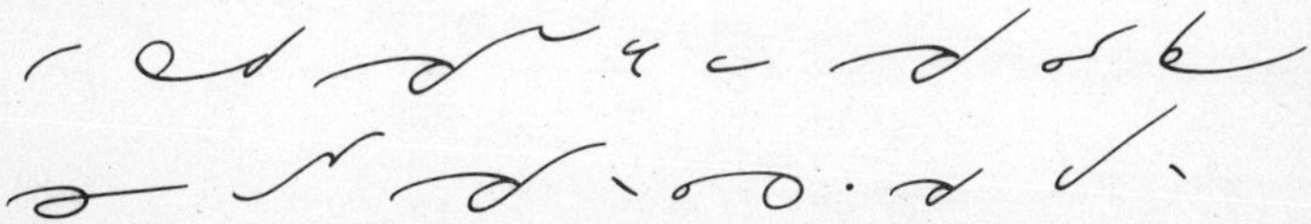

MOST-USED WORDS AND PHRASES

199. Frequently Used Words

Er, Ar

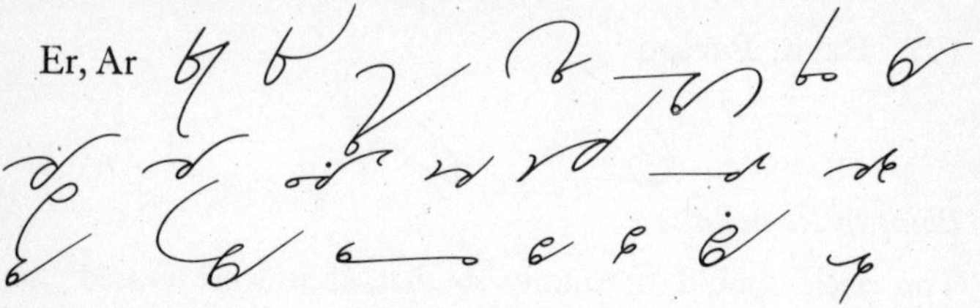

R *omitted*

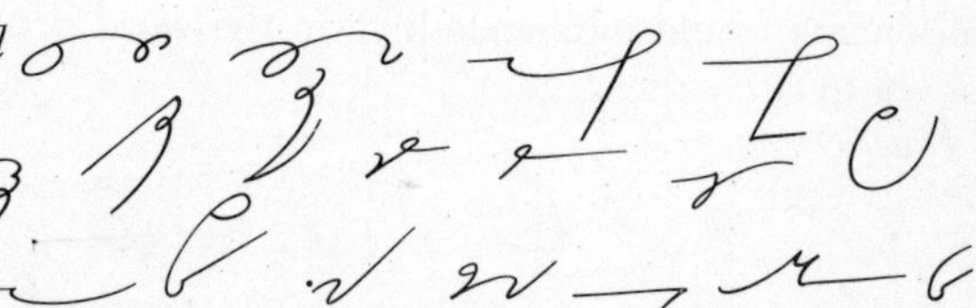

Ther

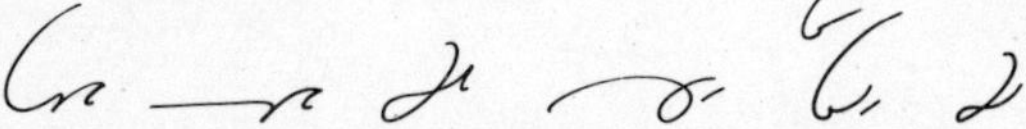

200. Frequently Used Phrases

Were

Early

Year

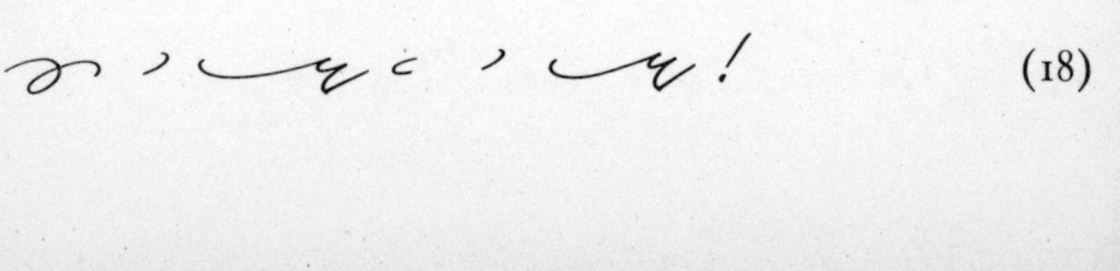

(18)

READING AND DICTATION PRACTICE

201. The Farmer and the Larks

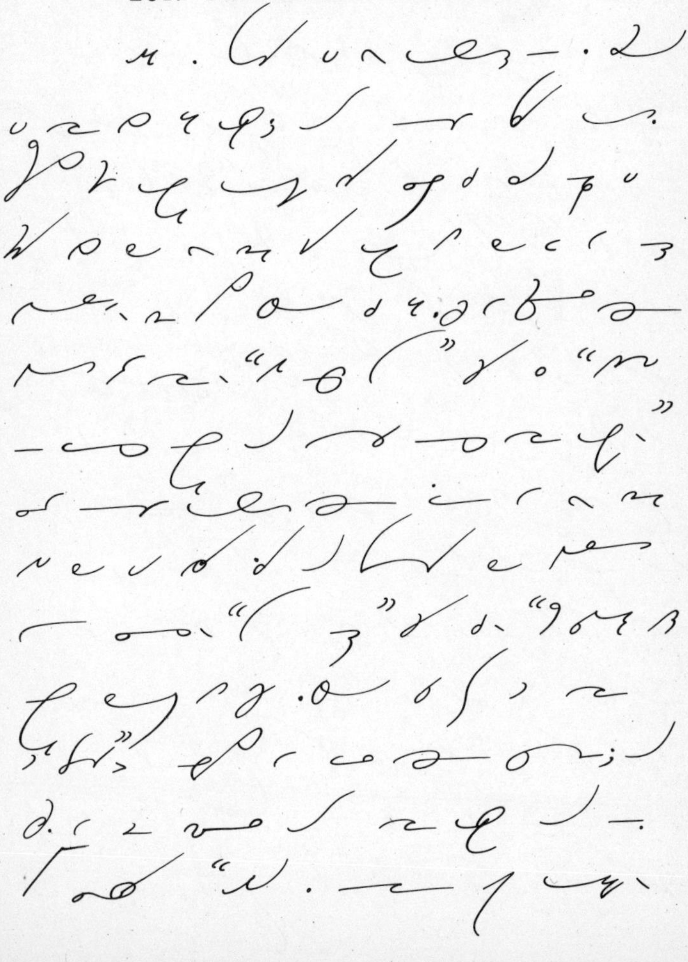

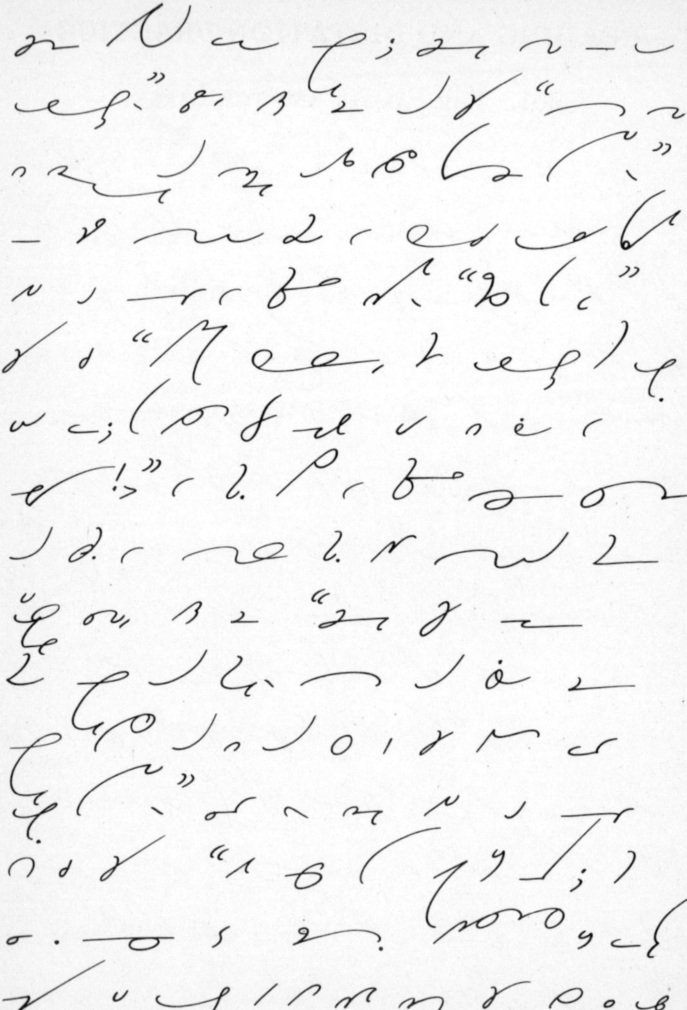

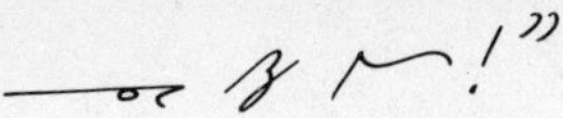 *—Adapted from Aesop's Fables*

(286)

202. The Fisherman

 *—Adapted from Aesop's Fables* (85)

203. 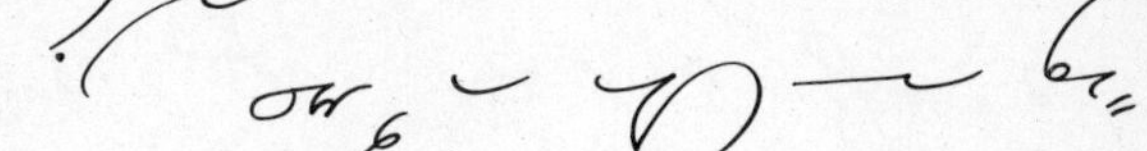

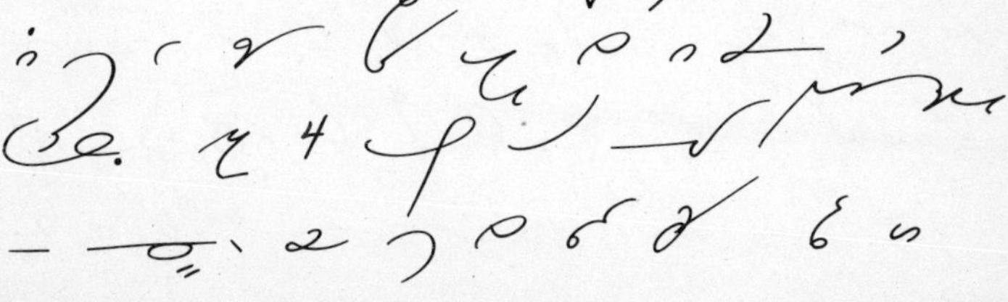

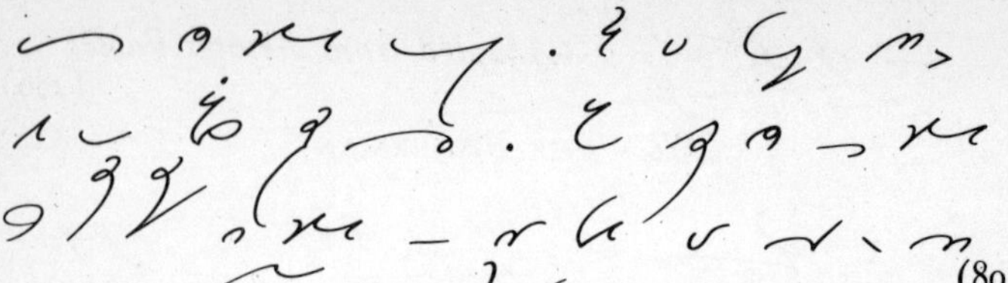

(80)

204.

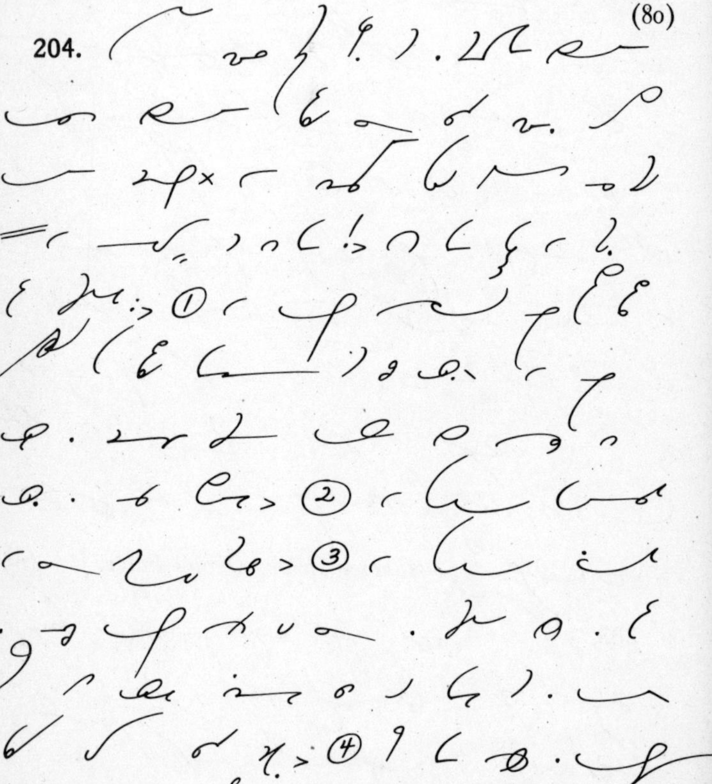

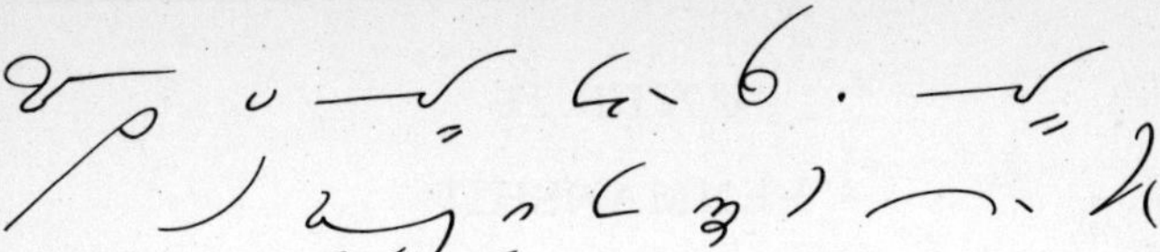

(151)

205.

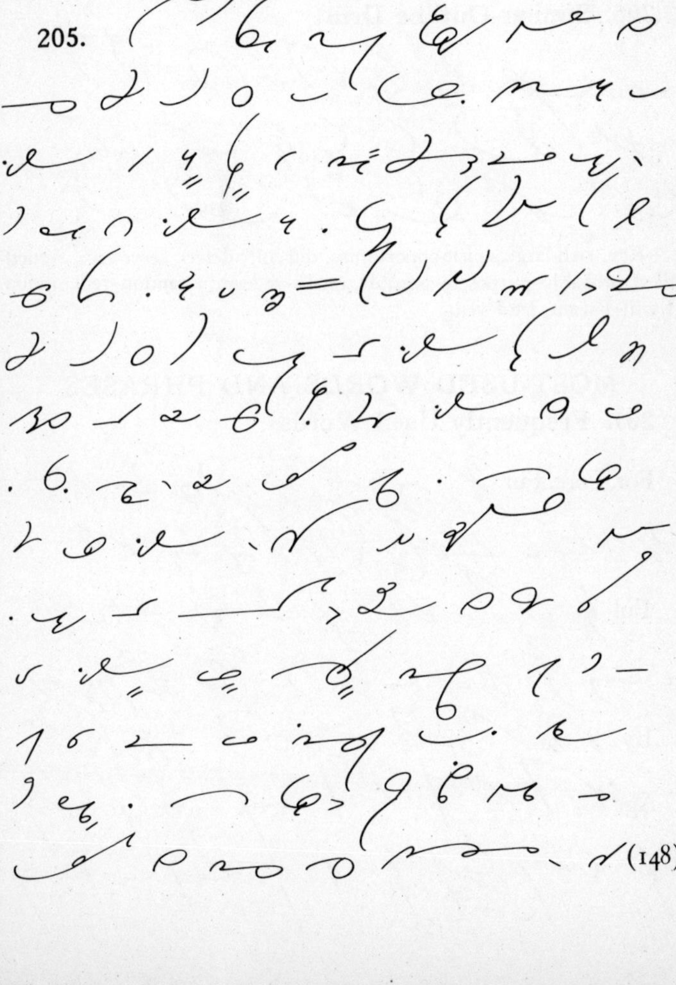

(148)

UNIT 21

PENMANSHIP

206. Similar-Outline Drill

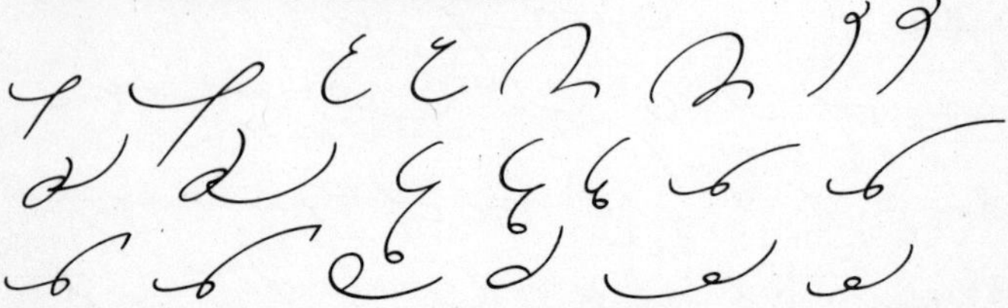

Key: rich-large, spirit-opportunity, difficulty-defect, serve-save, signed-filed, probably–purposely–possibly, retain–redeem, retention–redemption, I will–I want, lend–rent.

MOST-USED WORDS AND PHRASES

207. Frequently Used Words

For, Fore, Fur

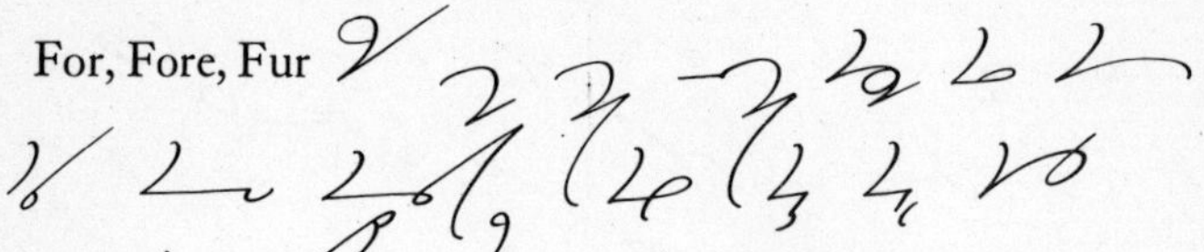

Ful

Ify

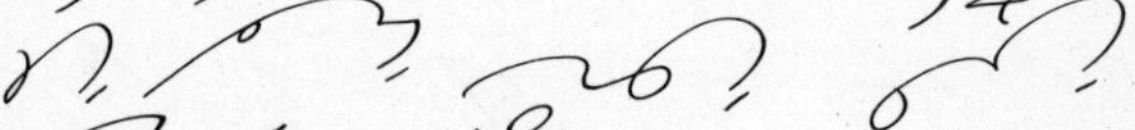

Age

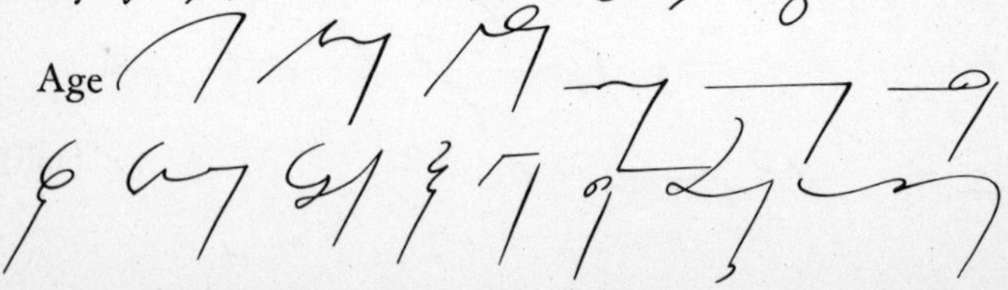

208. Frequently Used Phrases

Him

Hope

Sorry

Want

Ago

Possible

Few

Sure

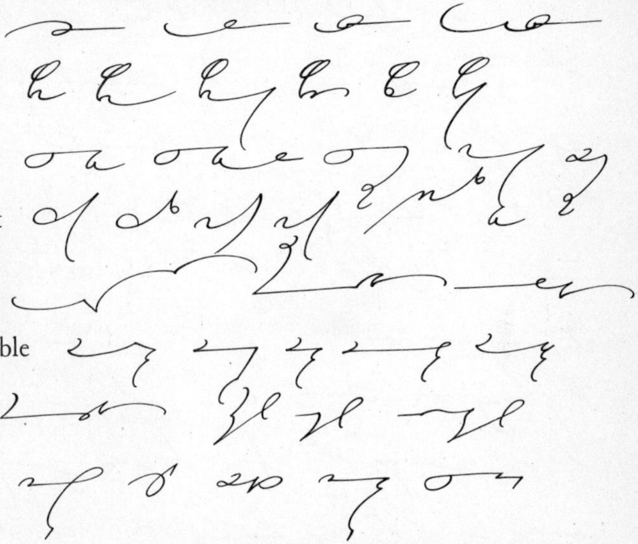

READING AND DICTATION PRACTICE

209. Columbus

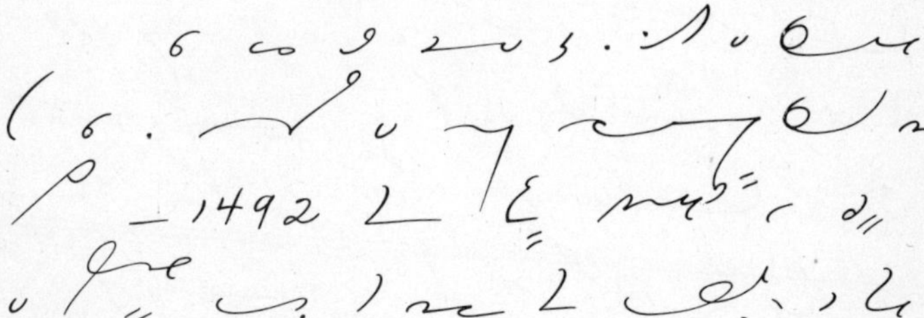

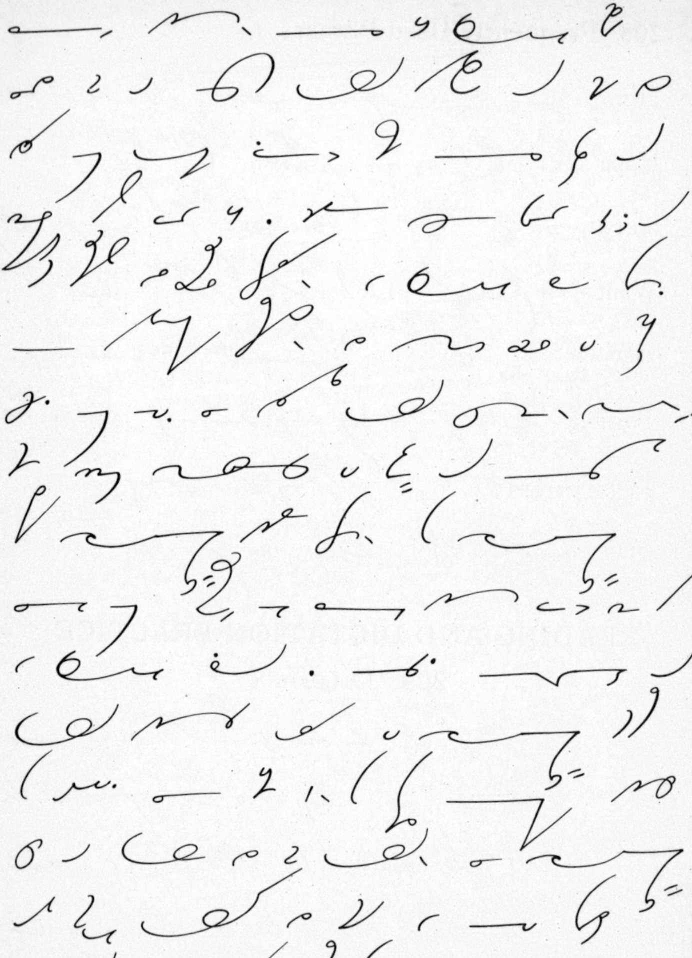

(270)

210.

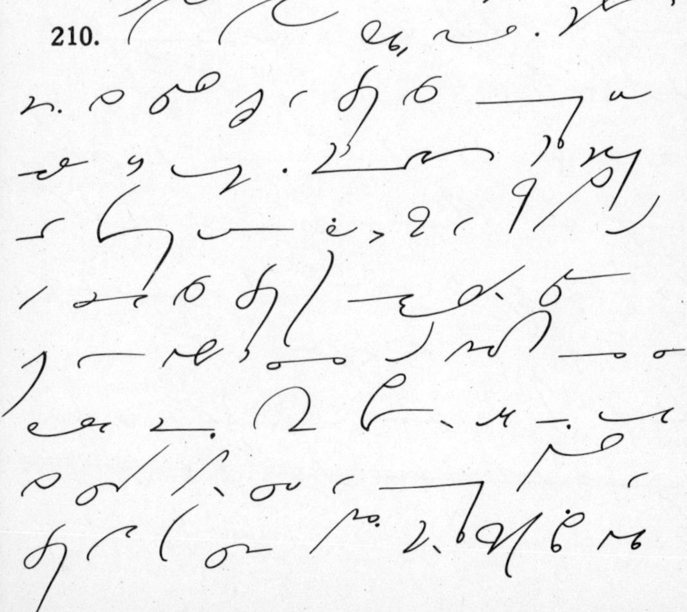

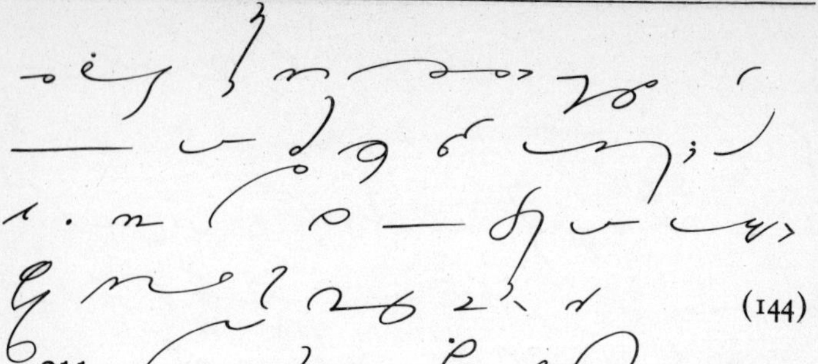

(144)

211.

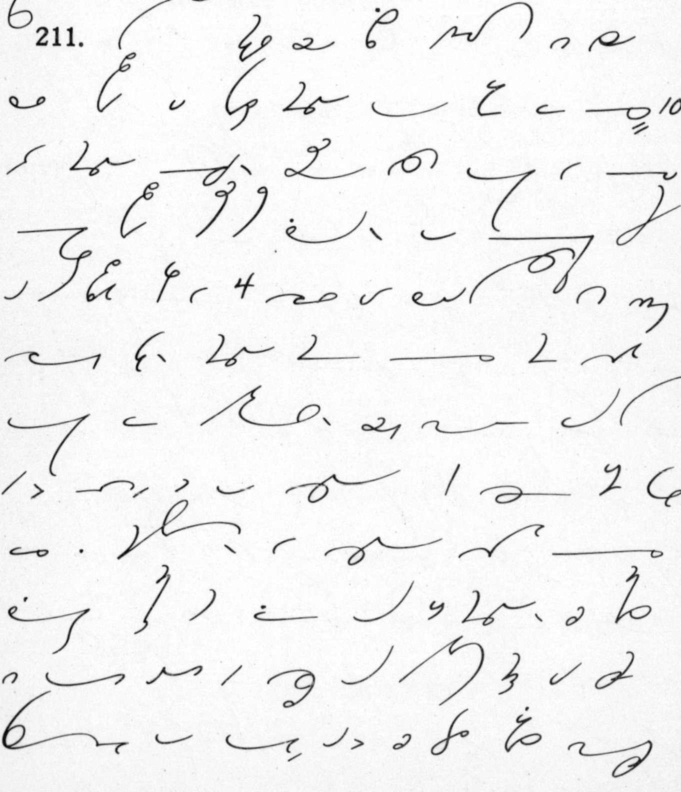

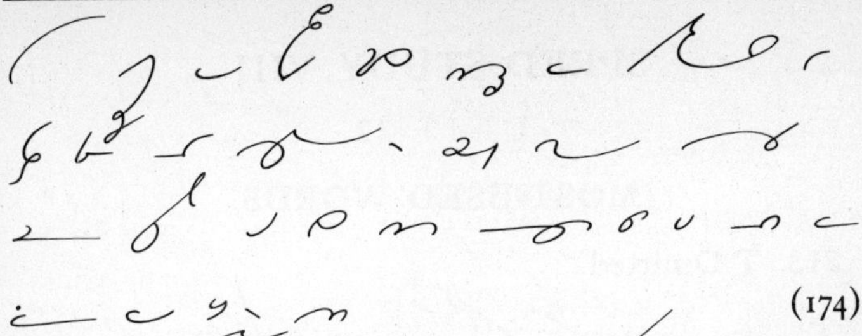

(174)

212.

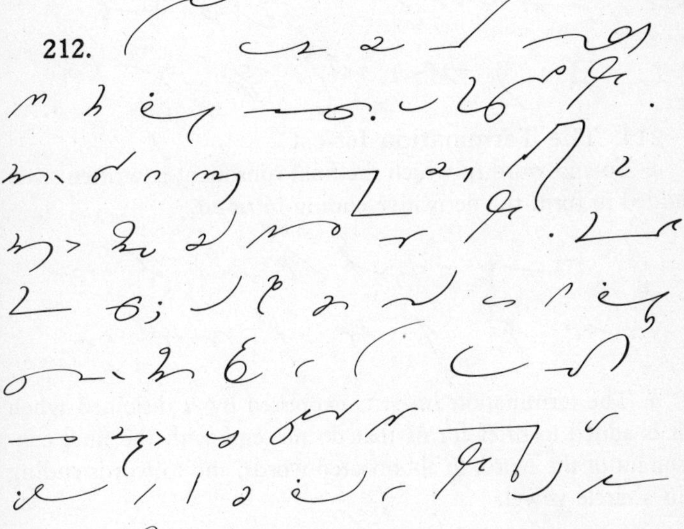

(119)

SPEED STUDY VIII

UNIT 22

MOST-USED WORDS

213. T Omitted

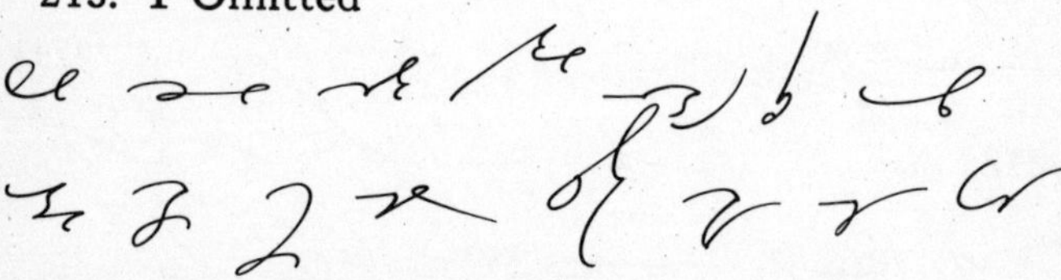

214. The Termination Ist-est

a. To any word in which the final consonant is written, *es* is added to form the derivative ending in *ist-est.*

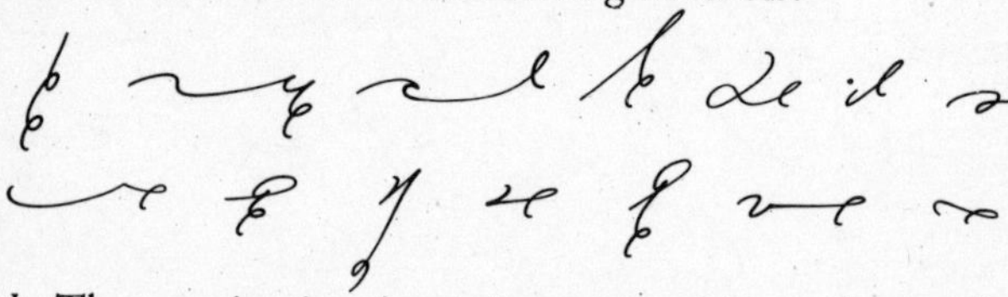

b. The termination *ist-est* is expressed by *st* disjoined when it is added to brief forms that do not end with the final consonant of the word, to abbreviated words, and to words ending in a circle vowel.

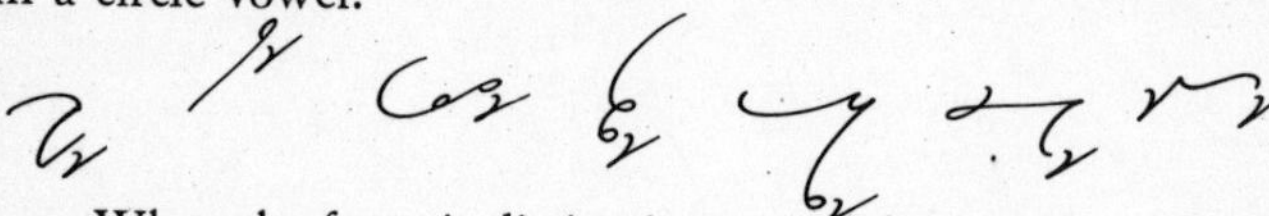

c. When the form is distinctive, *st* may be joined.

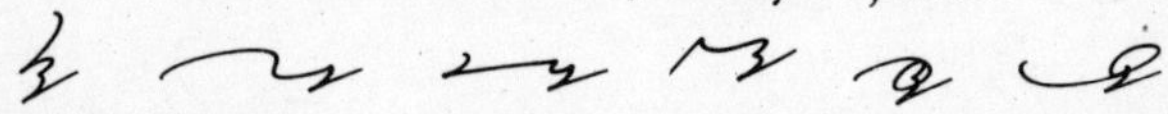

d. Special forms.

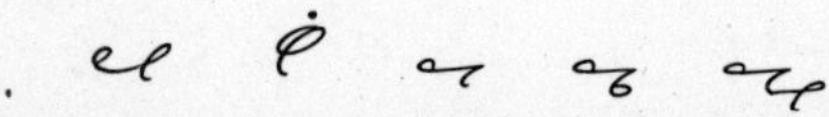

READING AND DICTATION PRACTICE

215. Plan to Reach Enough Prospects

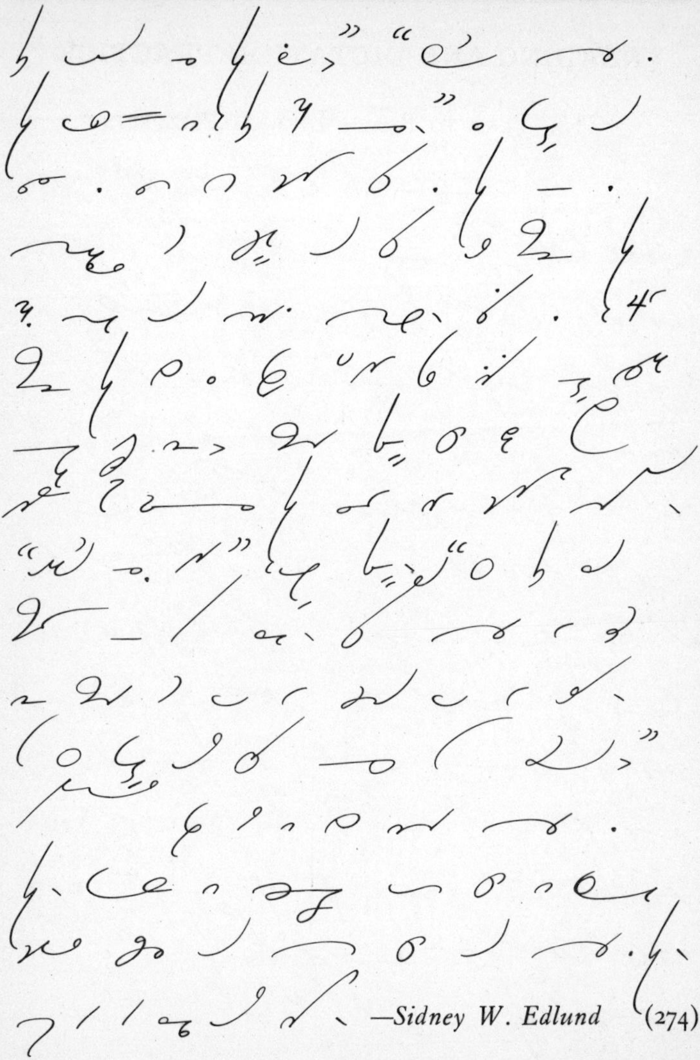

—*Sidney W. Edlund* (274)

216.

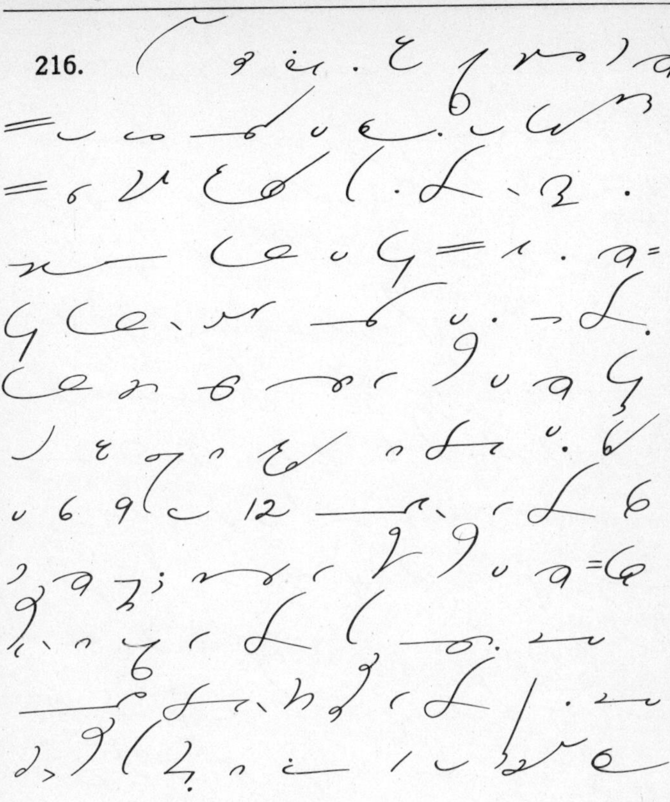

(124)

217.

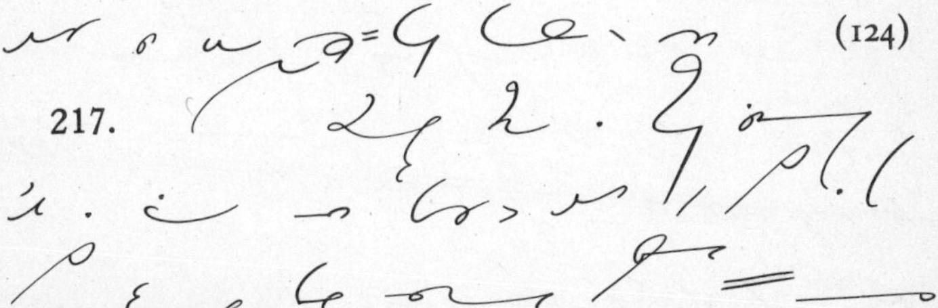

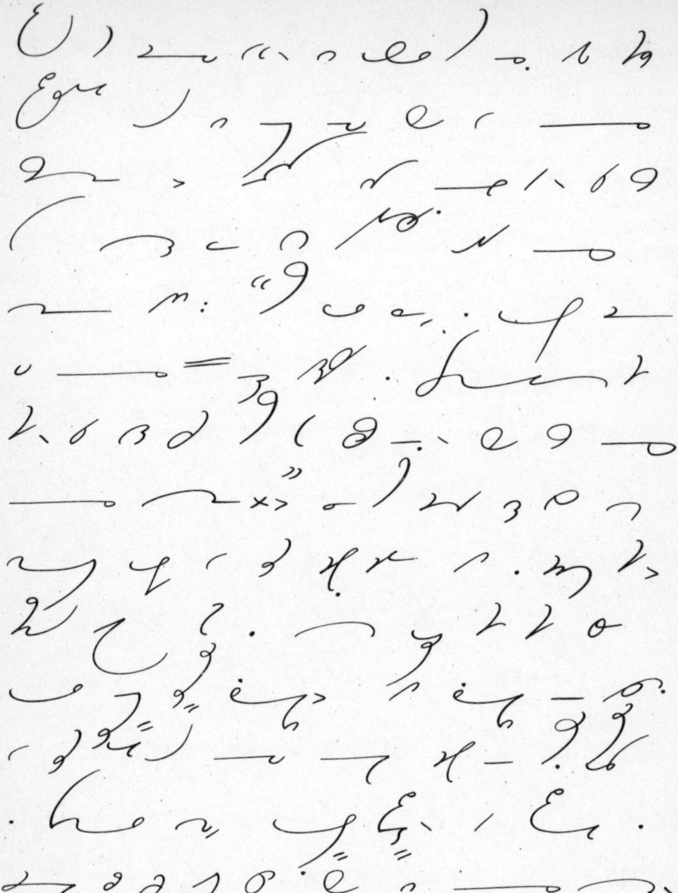

(183)

218.

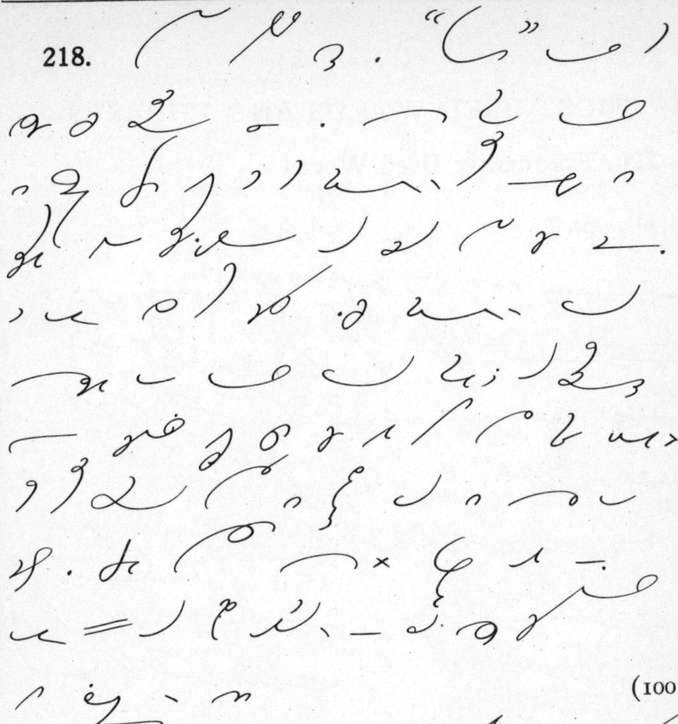

(100)

219.

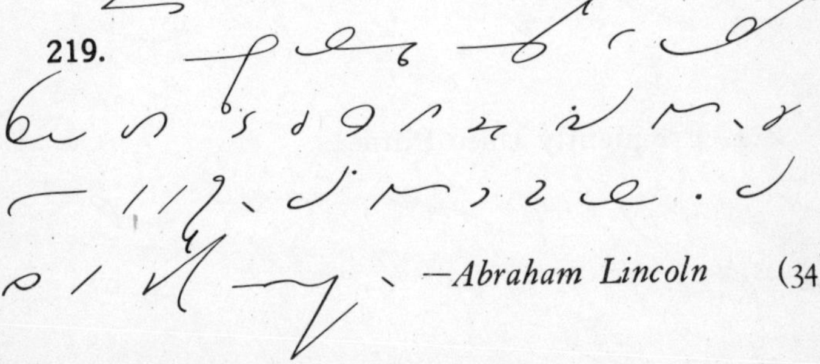

—*Abraham Lincoln* (34)

UNIT 23

MOST-USED WORDS AND PHRASES

220. Frequently Used Words

D *omitted*

Al Ul

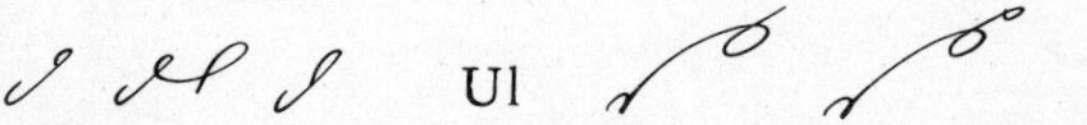

Less

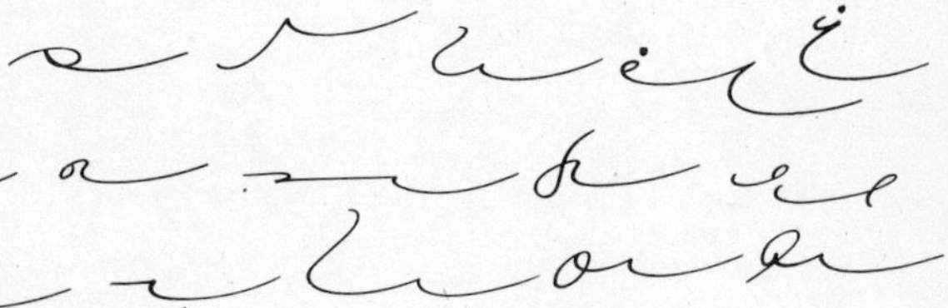

Sub

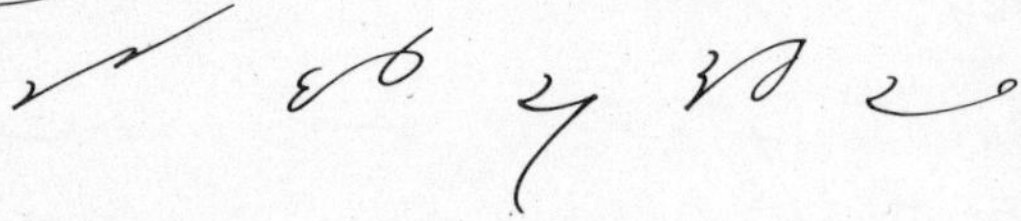

221. Frequently Used Phrases

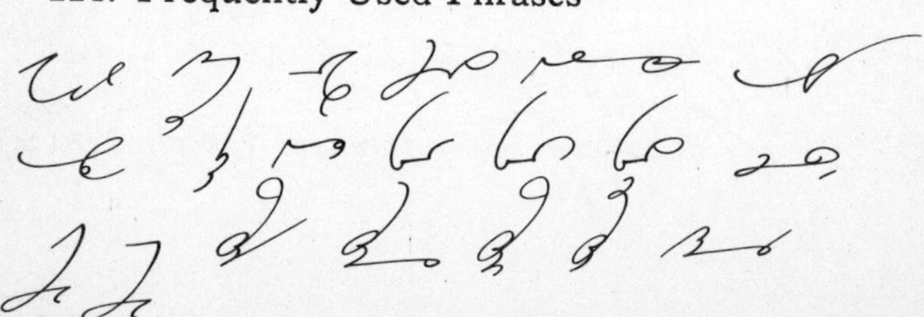

READING AND DICTATION PRACTICE

222. Diamonds

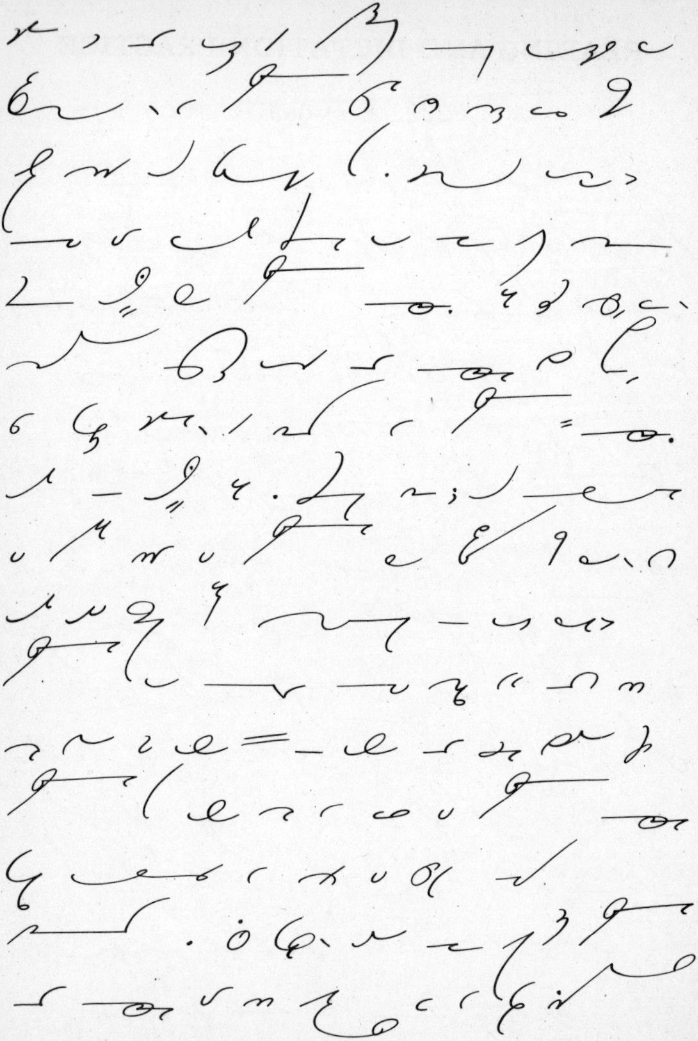

(335)

223.

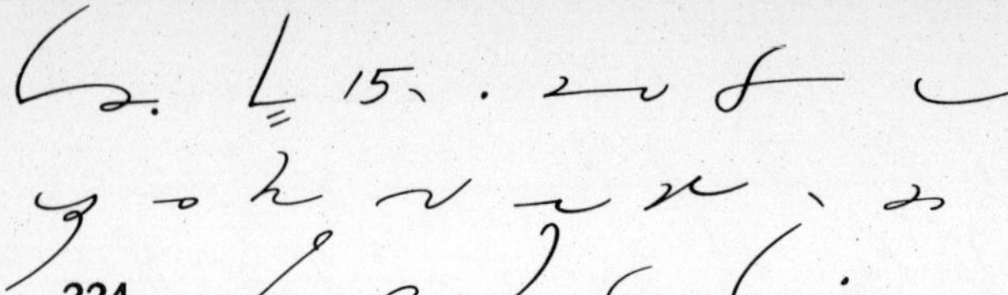

(134)

224.

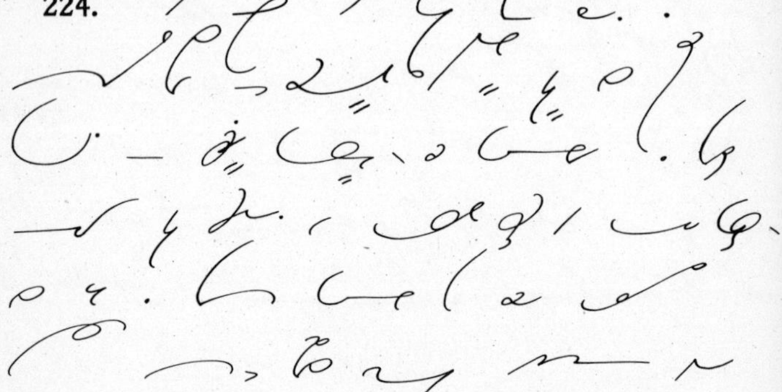

(119)

225.

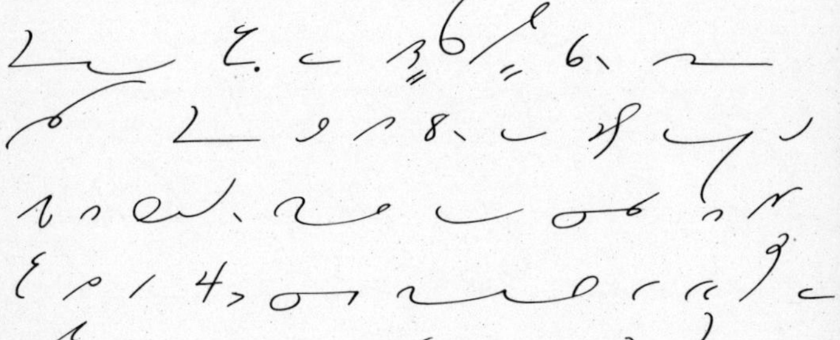

(184)

UNIT 24

226. Frequently Used Phrases—Words Omitted

The *omitted* 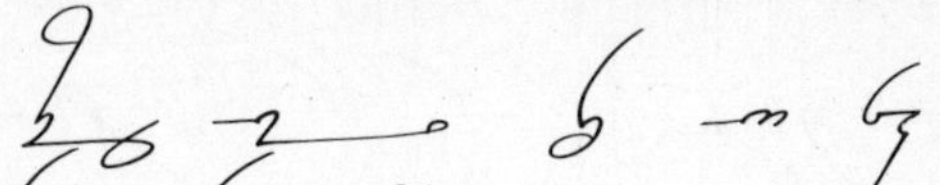

Of *omitted* 

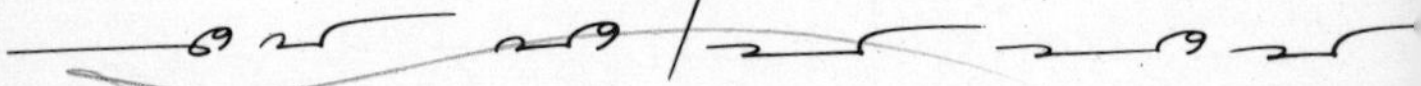

To *omitted* 

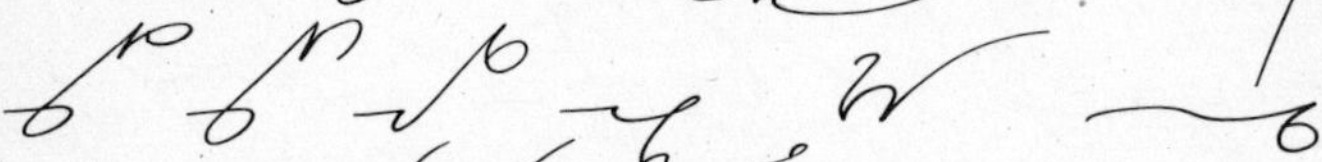

And *omitted* 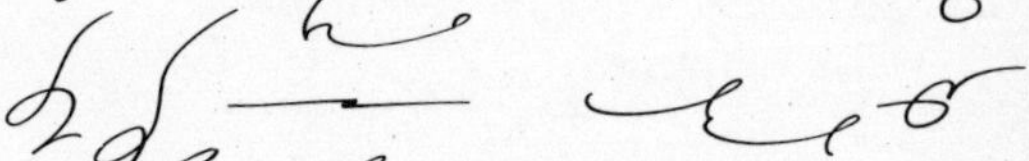

A *omitted* 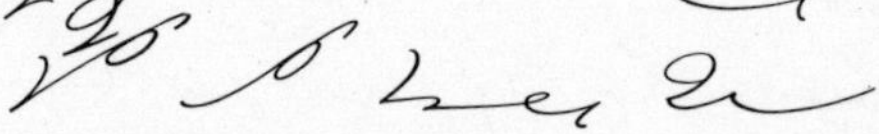

Or *omitted* 

In *omitted* 

227. Brief-Form Derivative Drill

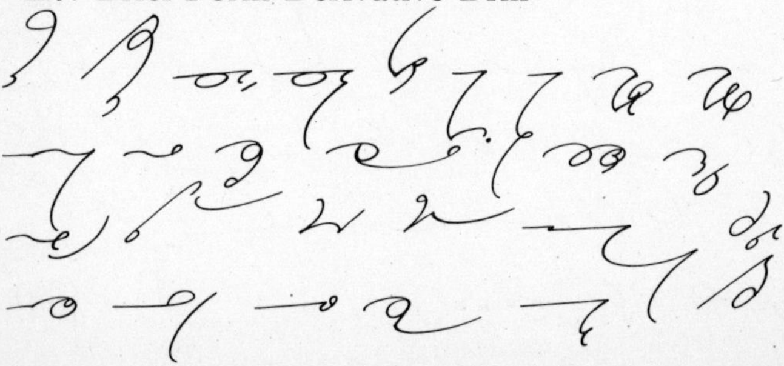

READING AND DICTATION PRACTICE

228. The Wild West

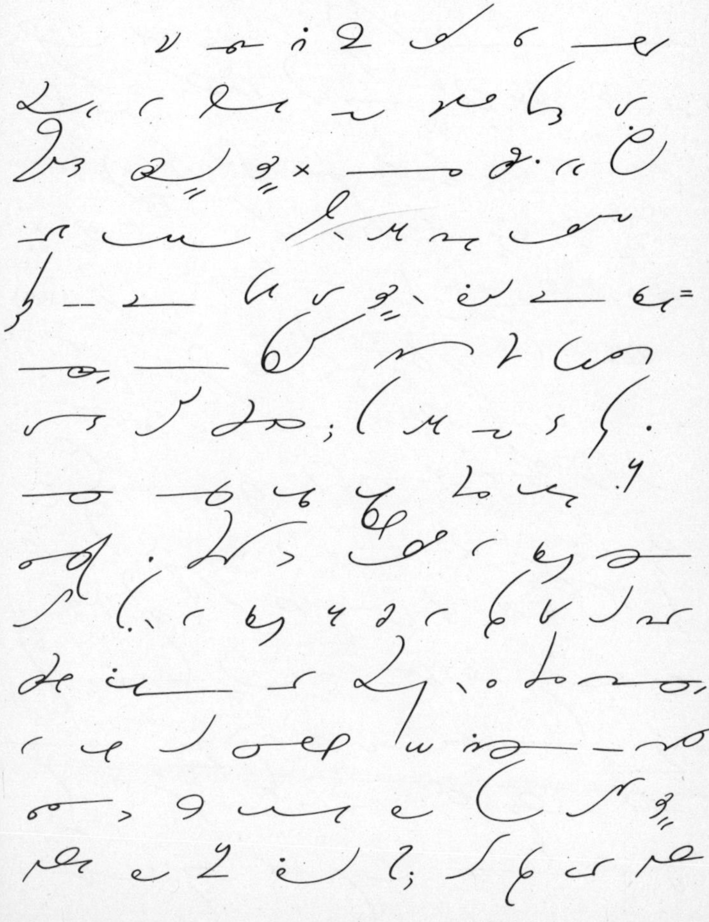

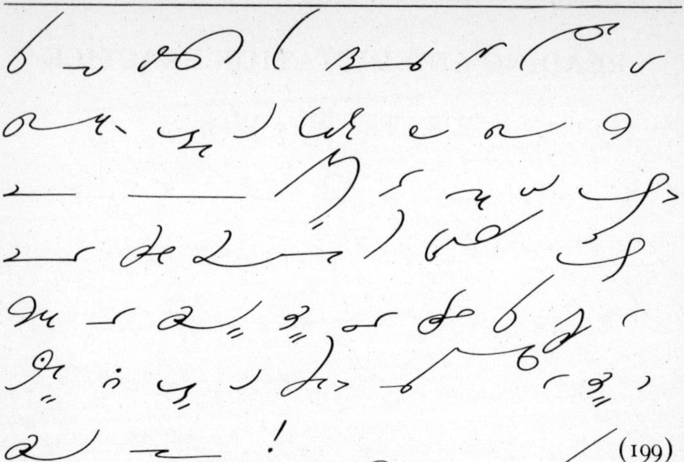

(199)

229.

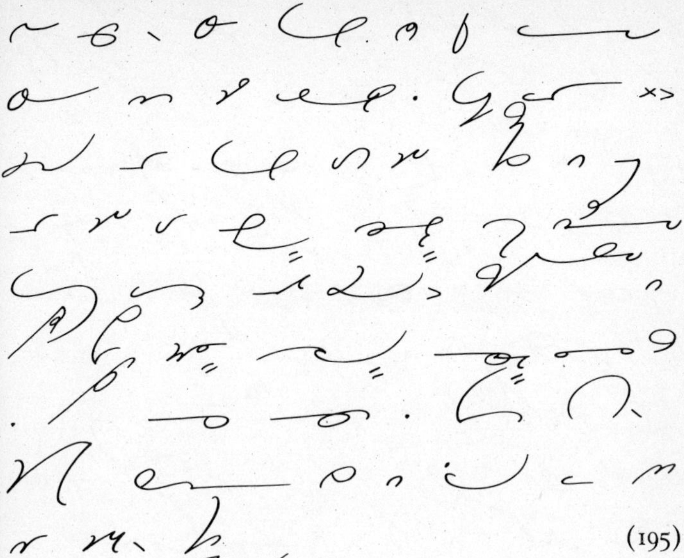

(195)

230.

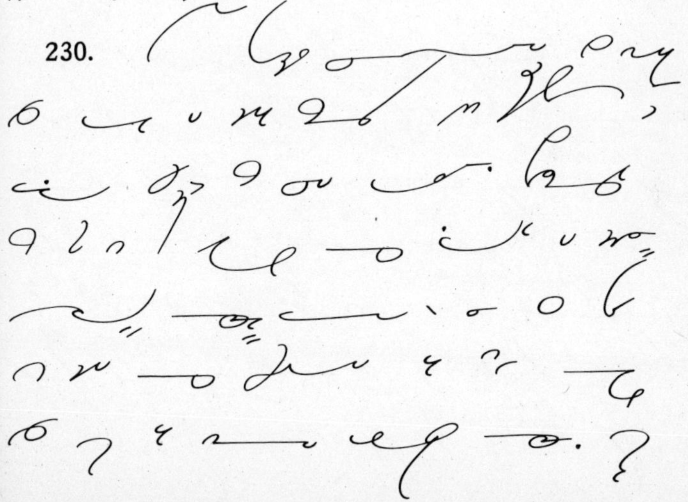

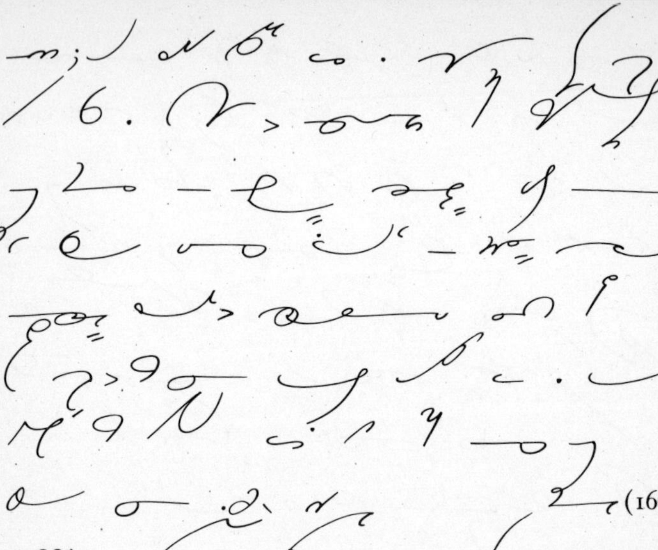

(166)

231.

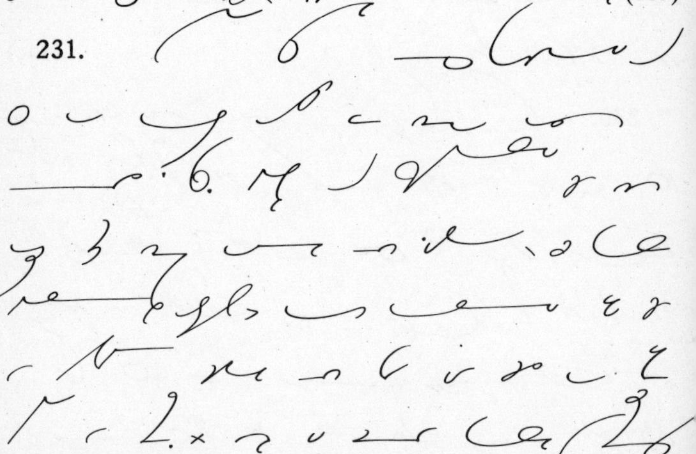

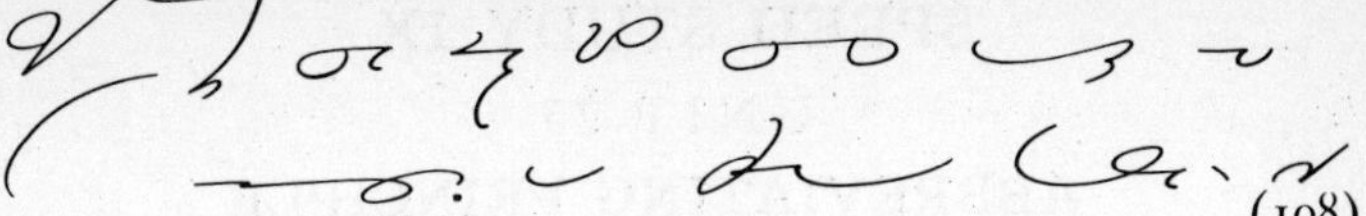

(108)

232.

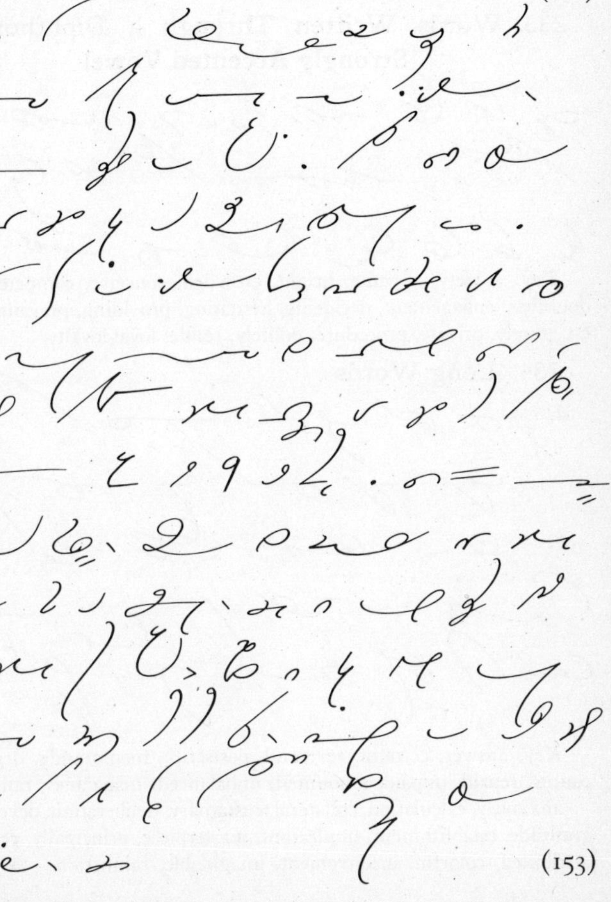

(153)

SPEED STUDY IX

UNIT 25

ABBREVIATING PRINCIPLE

233. Words Written Through a Diphthong or Strongly Accented Vowel

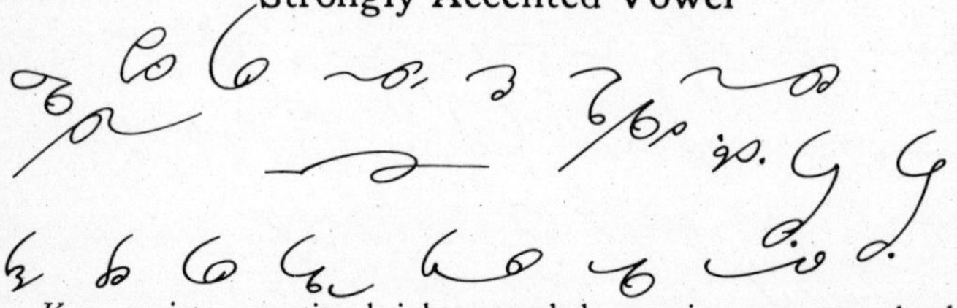

Key: anxiety, appetite, bright, crowded, conceive, compete, cloudy, doubtless, engagement, decidedly, hesitating, providing, prevailing, poorest, purely, private, procedure, politely, reside, loyal-loyalty.

234. Long Words

a. *b.*

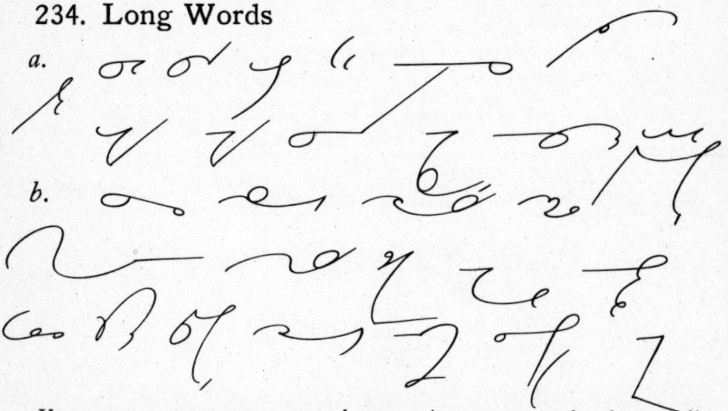

Key: answer, account, reverend, postscript, memoranda, degree, discounts, repaid, unpaid, amounted, unbalanced, magazines, railroads.

anxiously, calculation, collateral, customary, deliberation, development, gratitude, establishment, unpleasant, masterpiece, principally, certificates, attributed, colorful, inconvenient, imaginable, injunction.

READING AND DICTATION PRACTICE

235.

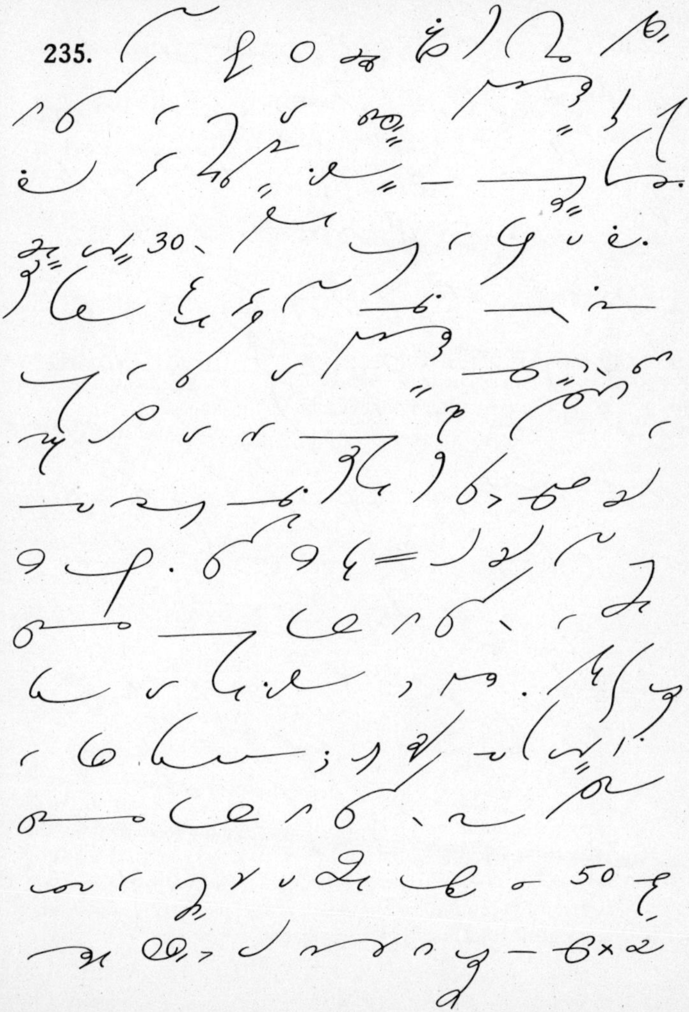

[shorthand outlines]   (184)

236.   *[shorthand outlines]*

30 *[shorthand outlines]*

[shorthand outlines]

[shorthand outlines]

[shorthand outlines]

[shorthand outlines]

[shorthand outlines]

[shorthand outlines]

[shorthand outlines]

[shorthand outlines]   (121)

237.   *[shorthand outlines]*

[shorthand outlines]

[shorthand outlines]

[shorthand outlines] 30 *[shorthand outlines]* 31 *[shorthand outlines]*

[shorthand outlines]

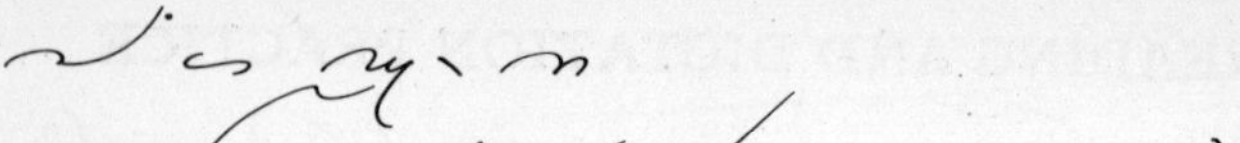

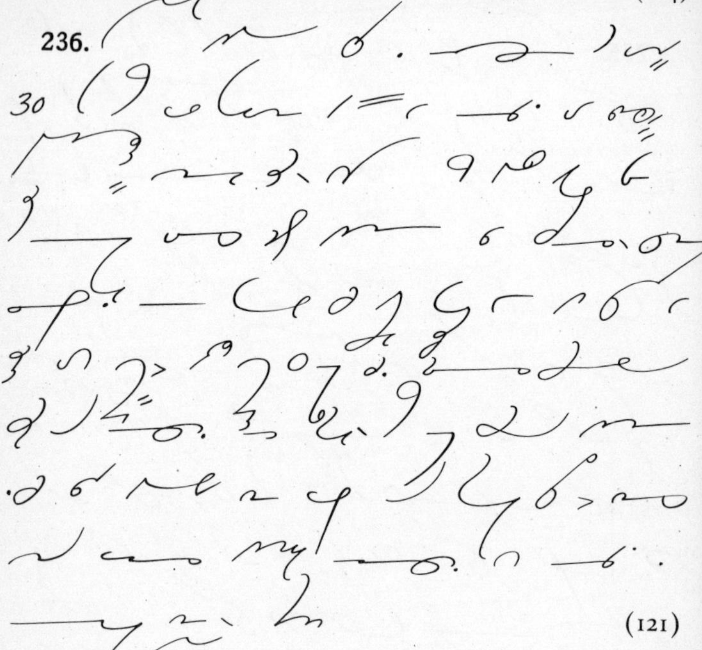

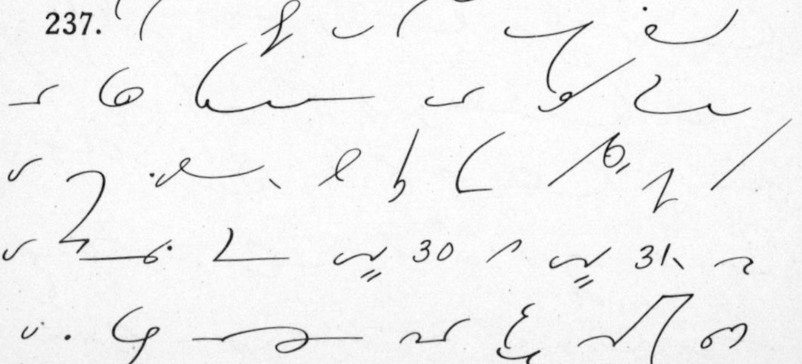

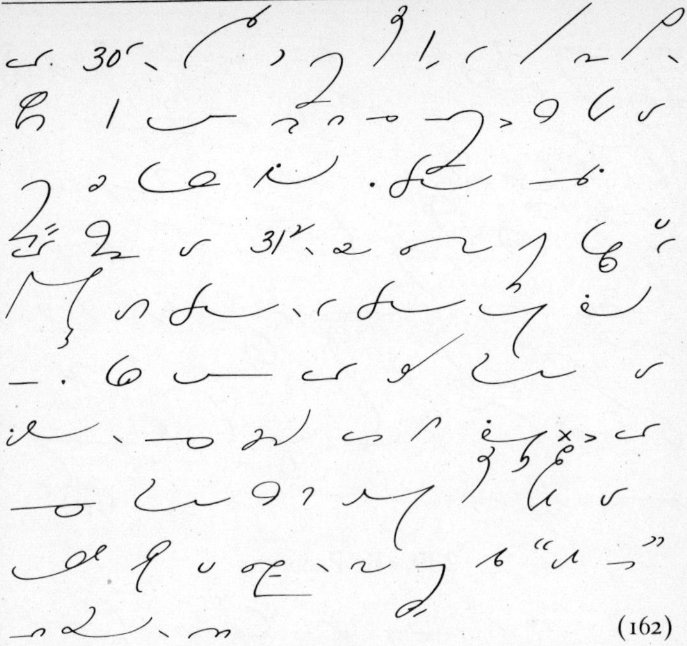

(162)

238.

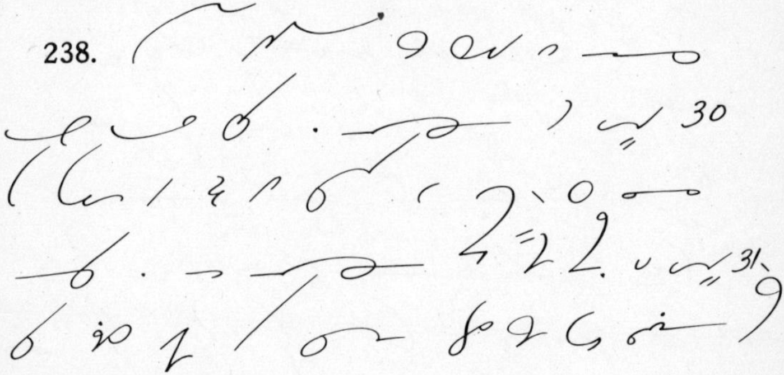

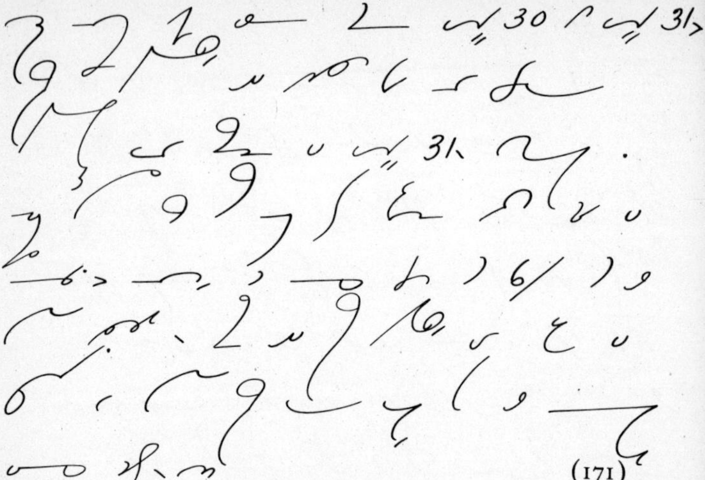

(171)

239. By-Products

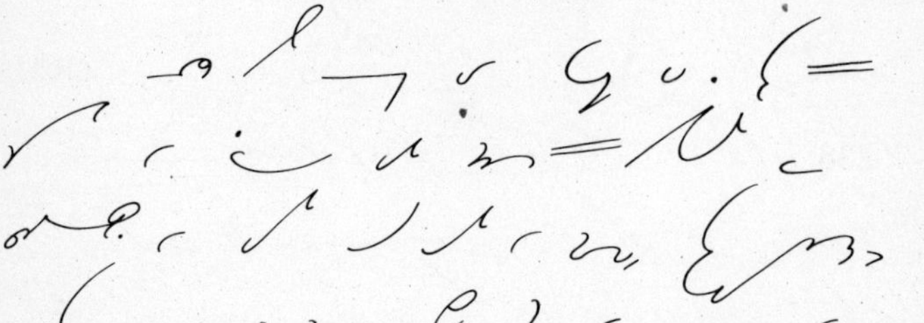

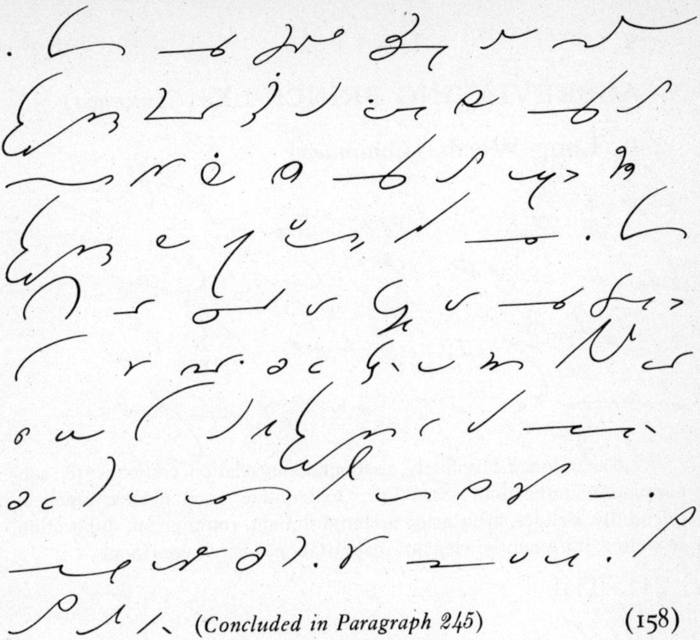

(Concluded in Paragraph 245) (158)

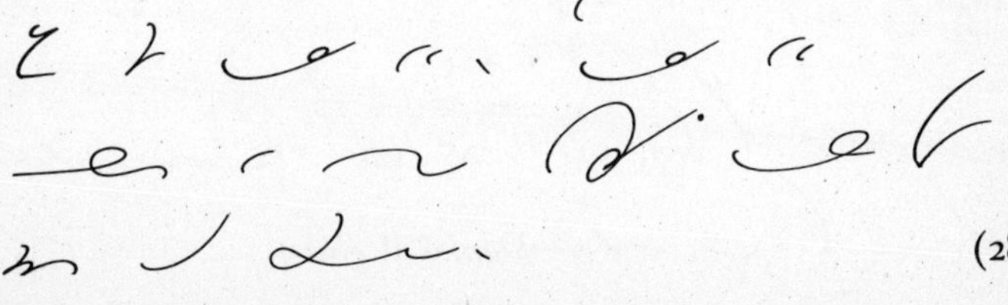

(28)

UNIT 26

ABBREVIATING PRINCIPLE (*Continued*)

240. Long Words (*Continued*)

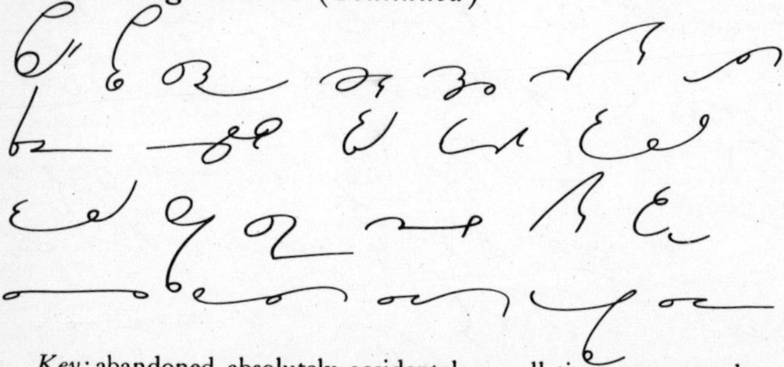

Key: abandoned, absolutely, accidental, cancellation, consequently, contemplation, indication, journalism, materialize, spontaneous, practices, splendidly, slender, arbitrarily, accomplishment, commercial, duplication, separator, imminently, elegant, inauguration, liberal, enormous.

241. Tial

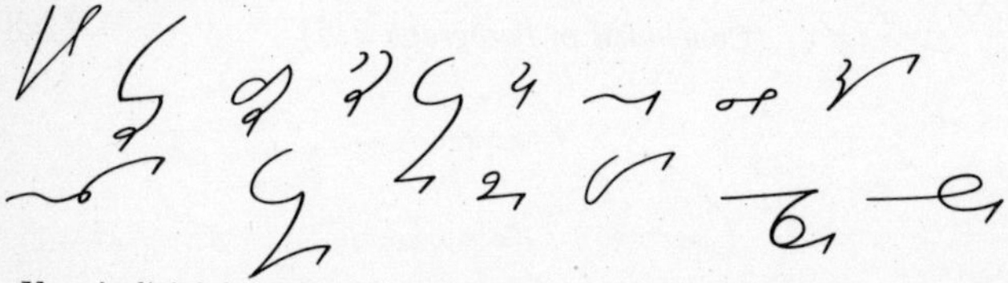

Key: judicial, beneficial, artificial, superficial, provincial, social, crucial, initial, substantial, credential, providential, essential, potential, impartial, martial.

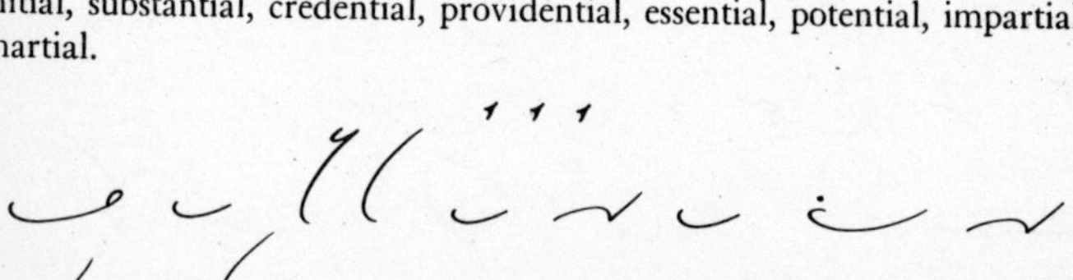

—*Daniel Webster* (14)

READING AND DICTATION PRACTICE

242.

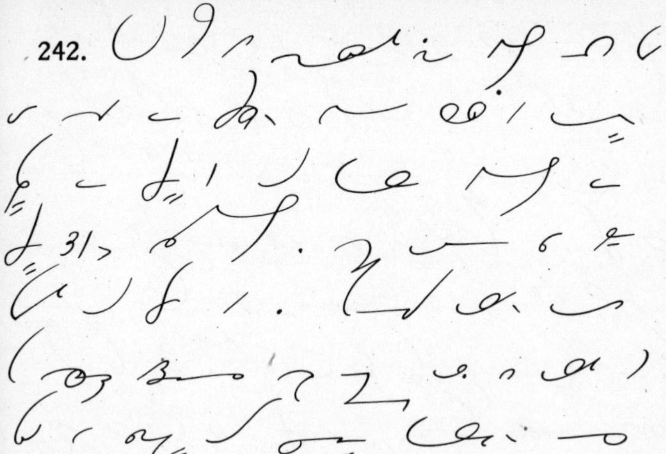

(144)

243.

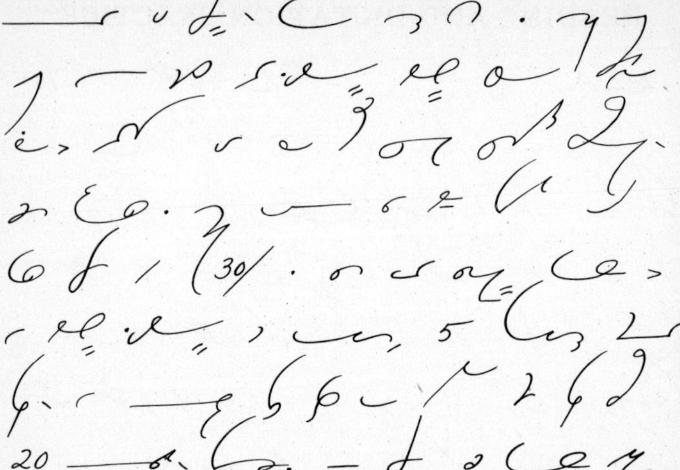

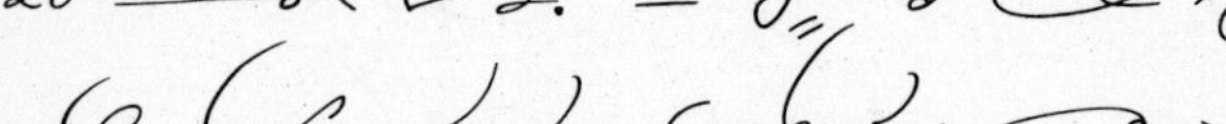

(179)

244. 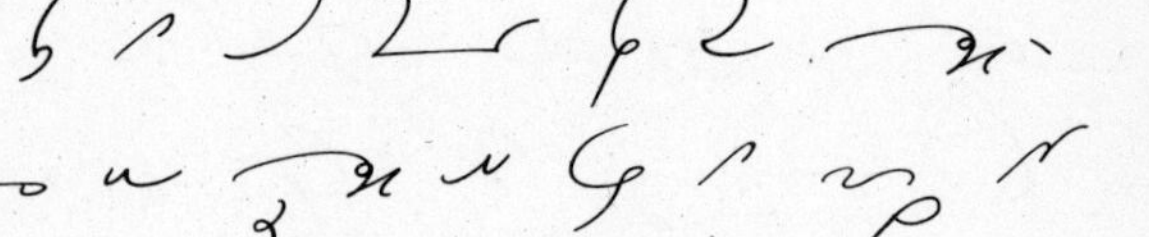

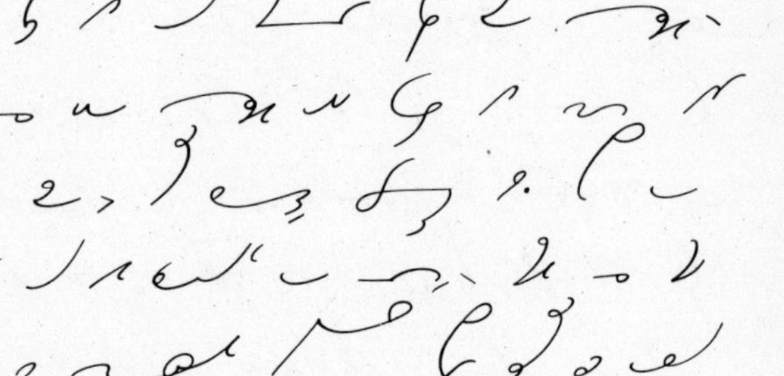

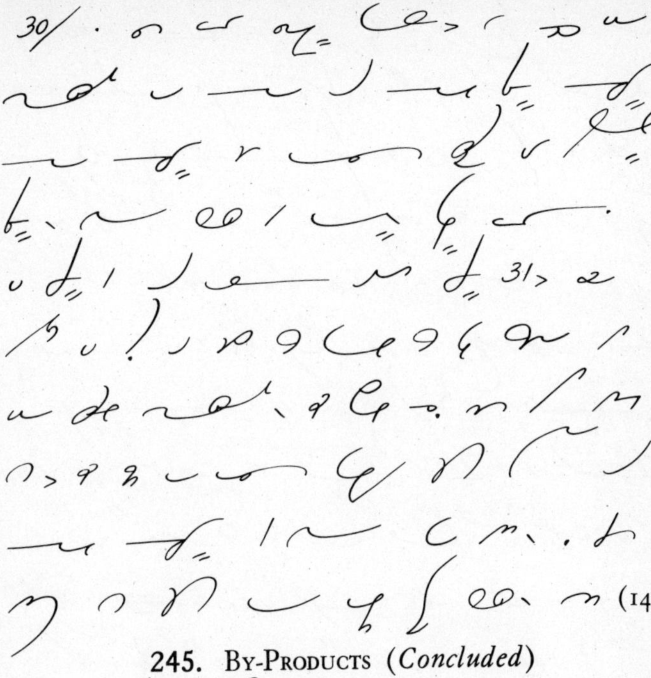

(142)

245. By-Products (*Concluded*)

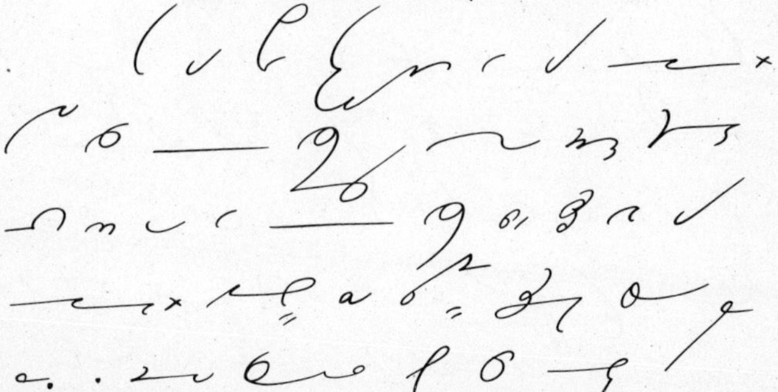

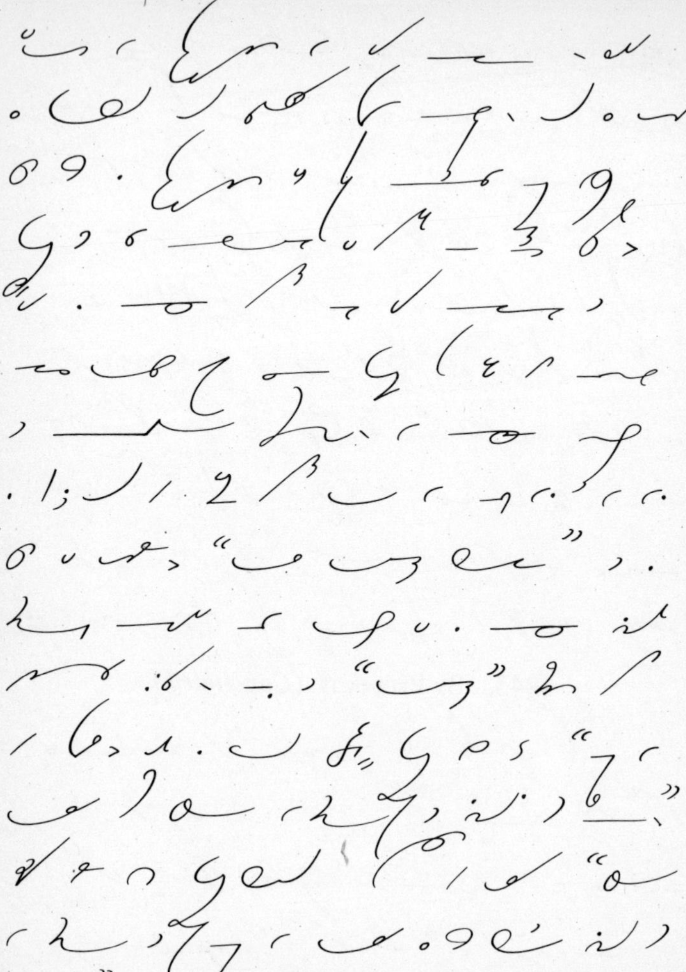

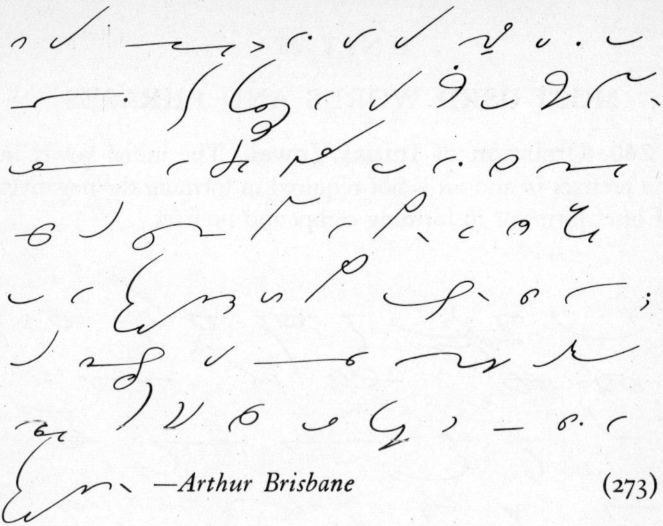

—*Arthur Brisbane* (273)

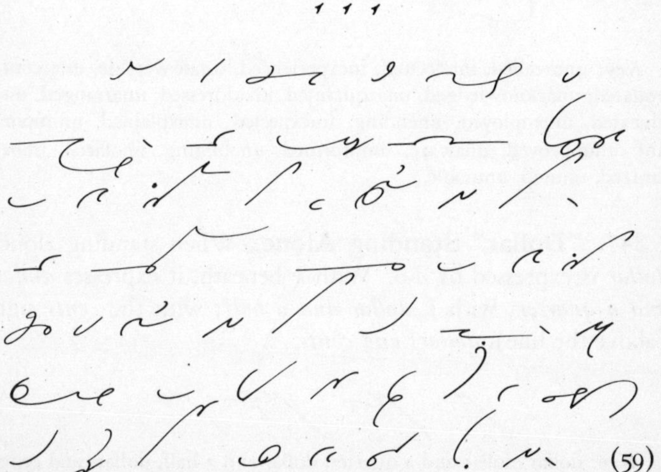

(59)

UNIT 27

MOST-USED WORDS AND PHRASES

246. Omission of Initial Vowel. The initial vowel in the prefixes *in* and *un* is not required in forming the negatives of brief forms or in forming compound prefixes.

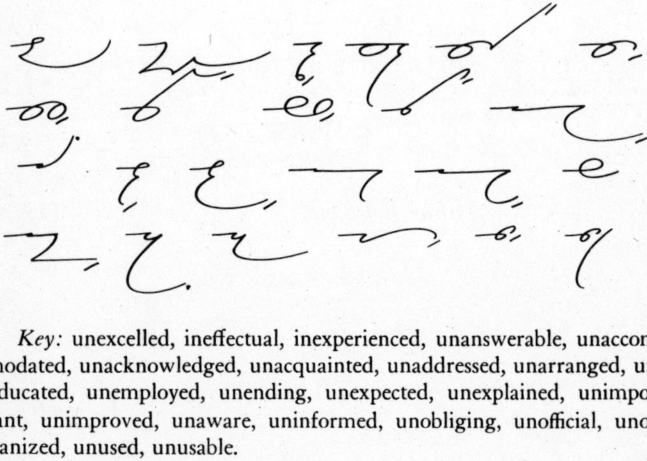

Key: unexcelled, ineffectual, inexperienced, unanswerable, unaccommodated, unacknowledged, unacquainted, unaddressed, unarranged, uneducated, unemployed, unending, unexpected, unexplained, unimportant, unimproved, unaware, uninformed, unobliging, unofficial, unorganized, unused, unusable.

247. "Dollar" Standing Alone. When standing alone, *dollar* is expressed by *d-o*. With *k* beneath, it expresses *dollar and a quarter*; with *f*, *dollar and a half*; with the *cents* sign (above the line), *dollars and cents*.

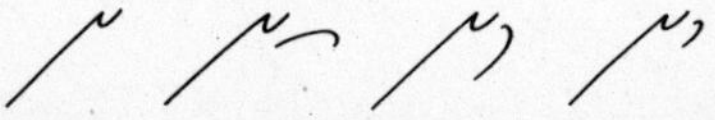

Key: dollar, dollar and a quarter, dollar and a half, dollars and cents.

248. Figures and Measurements

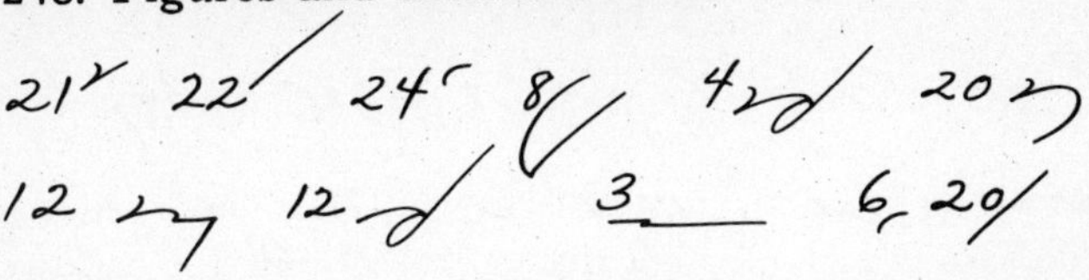

Key: twenty-first, twenty-second, twenty-fourth, $8,000,000,000, 4 square yards, 20 square feet, 12 square inches, 12 cubic yards, 300,000,000, $6,020.

READING AND DICTATION PRACTICE

249.

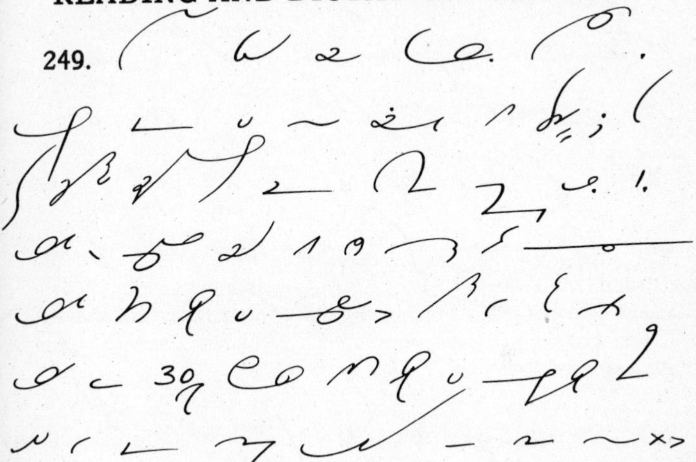

(100)

250.

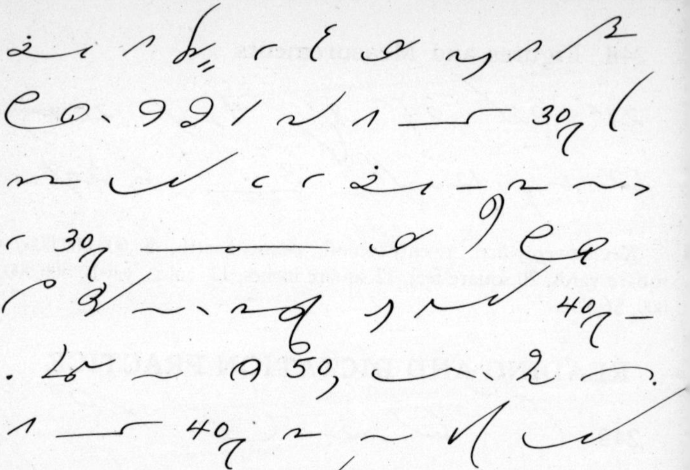

(156)

251.

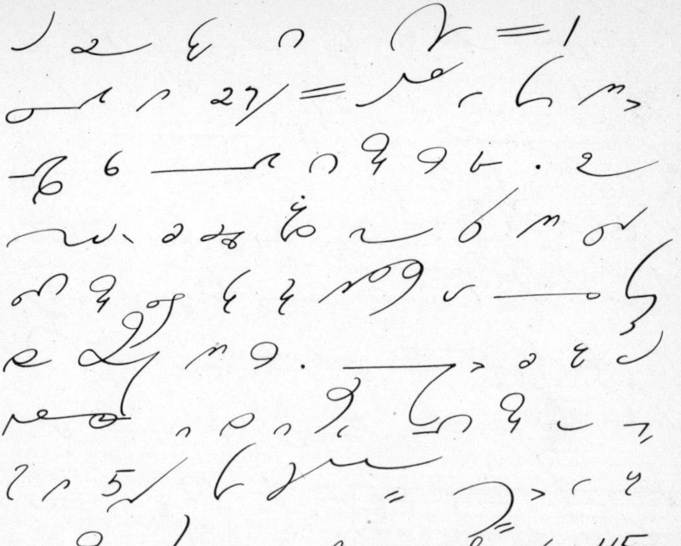

(209)

252.

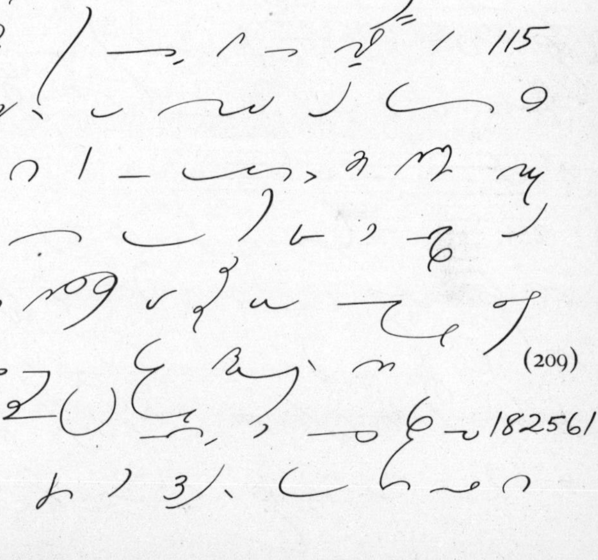

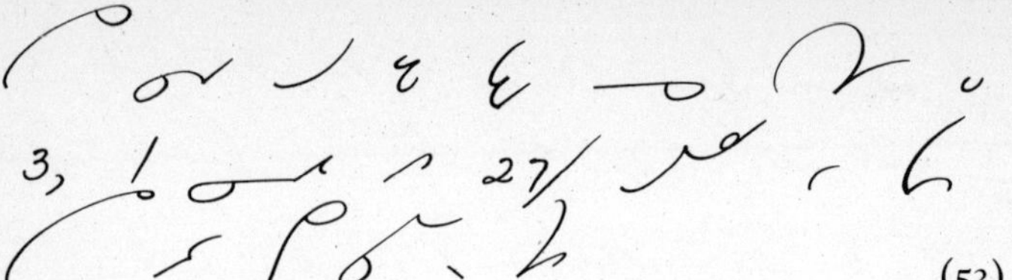

(53)

253.

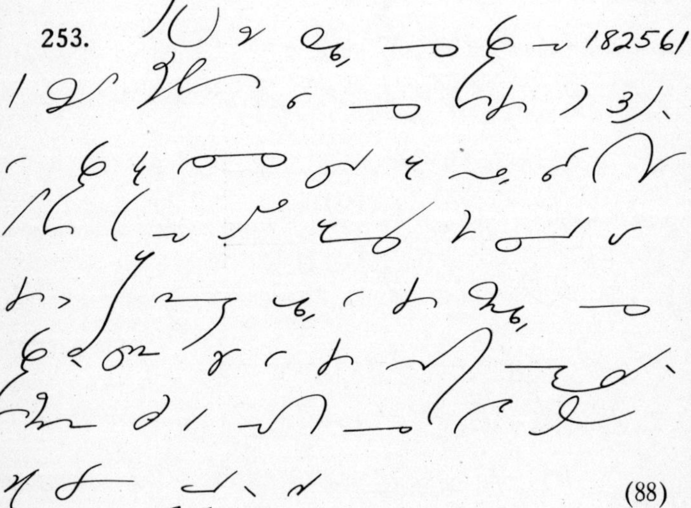

(88)

254.

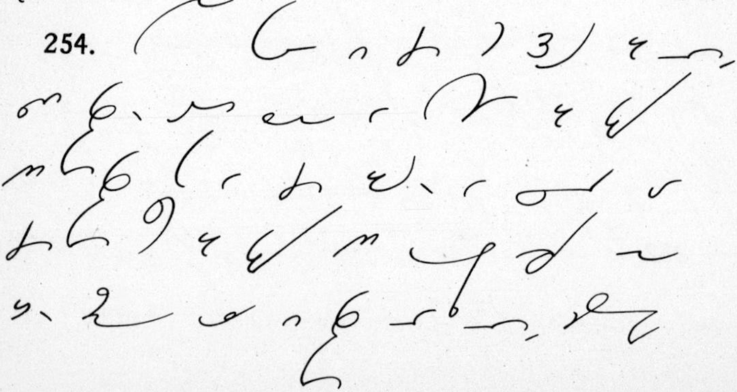

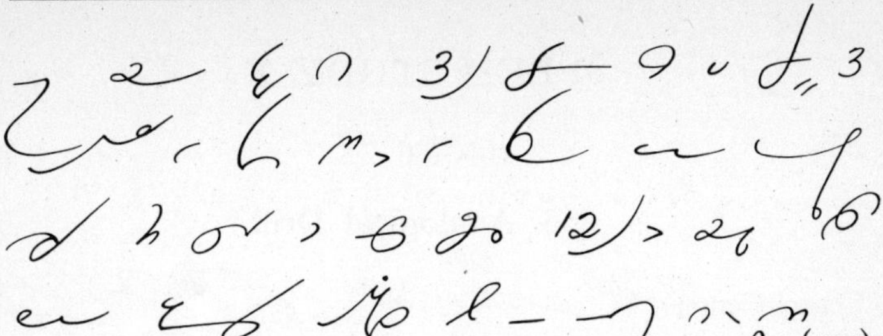

(105)

255.

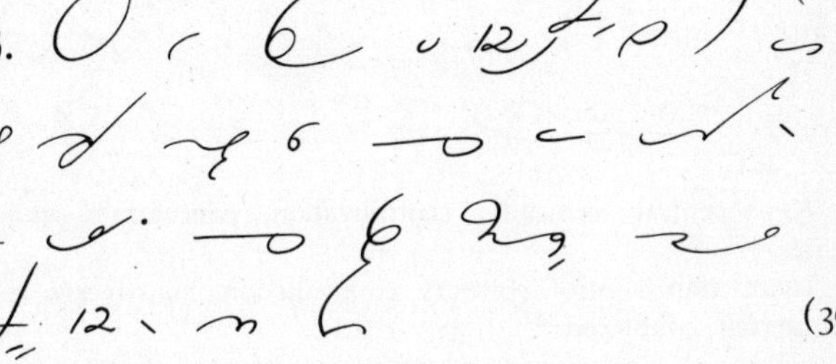

(39)

* * *

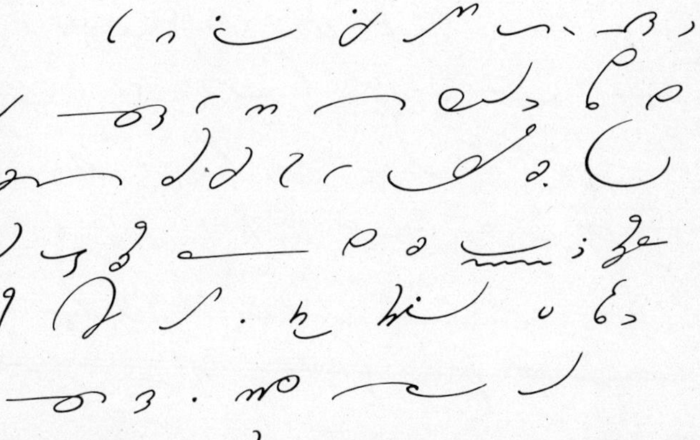

—*Harriet Chalmers Adams* (54)

SPEED STUDY X

UNIT 28

256. Analogical Drill

Centr-, Center

Contr-, Counter

Constr-

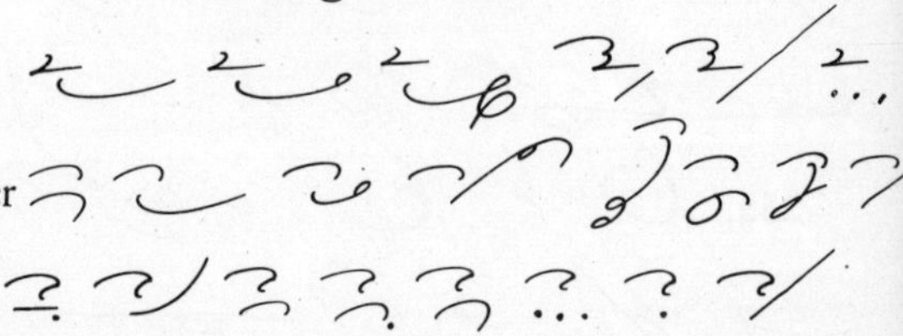

Key: central, centrally, centralization, concentrate, concentrated center.

contraction, control, contrary, contradiction, controversy, counteract, counterfeit, countered.

constrain, constraining, constraint, construct, constructing, construction, construe, construing, construed.

257.

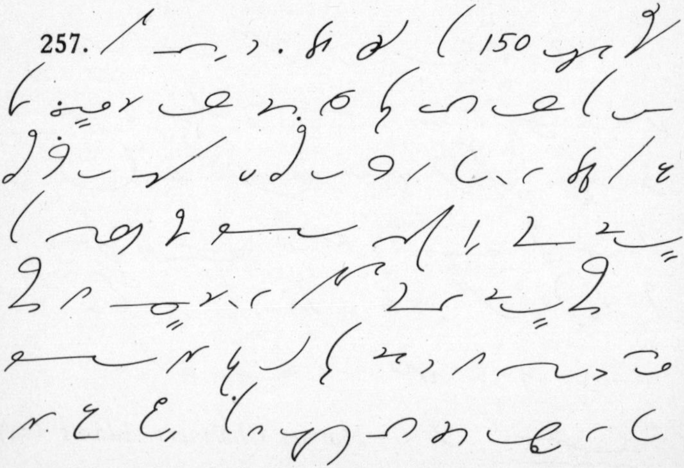

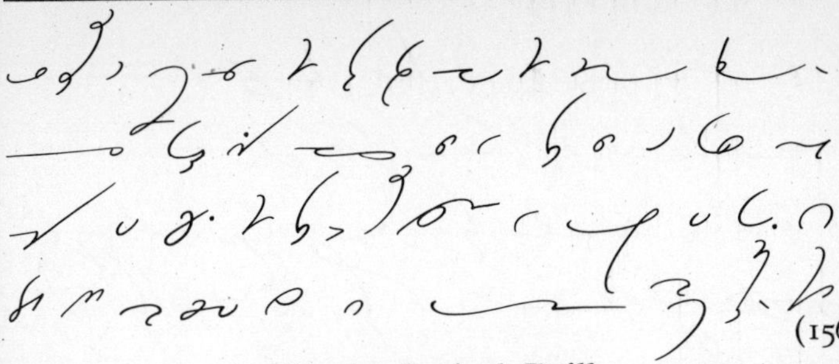

(156)

258. Analogical Drill

Detr-, Deter

Distr-, Destr-

Electr-
(*or* Electric)

Extr-, Exter-
(*or* Excl-)

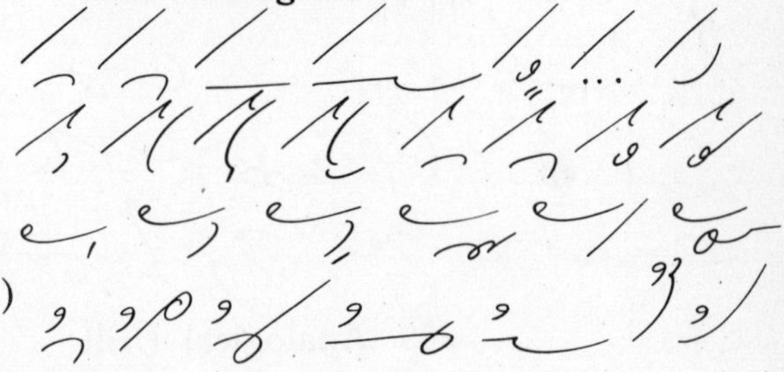

Key: detract, detraction, detriment, detrimental, Detroit, deter, deterrent.

distress, distribute, distribution, distributor, distract, distraction, destroy, destroyed.

electrician, electrify, electrified, electrocute, electrode, electric iron.

extraction, extradite, extricated, exterminate, external, exclusive, exclaimed.

259.

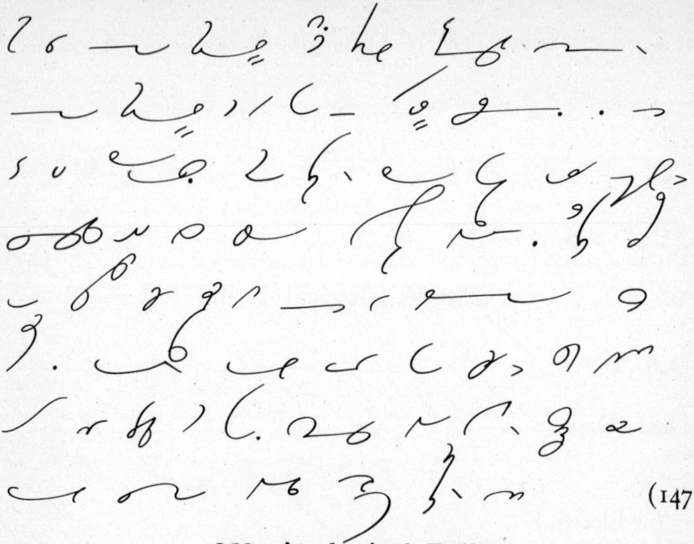

(147)

260. Analogical Drill

Intr-, Inter,
Enter (*or* Intel)
Instr-

Retr-

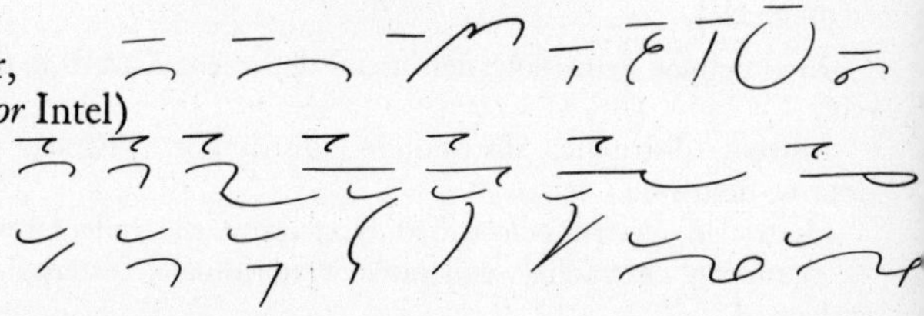

Key: intricate, intrigue, introduction, intrusion, intercept, interchange, intelligent, intellect.

instruct, instruction, instructional, instrument, instruments, instrumental, instrumentally.

retreat, retraction, retrench, retribution, retrieve, retrieved, retrograde, retrogression.

261. 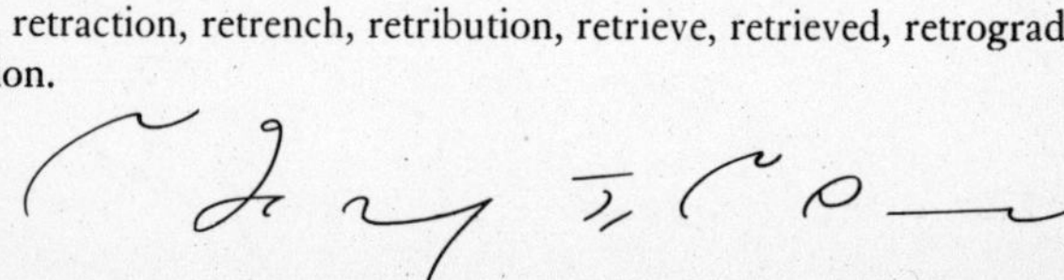

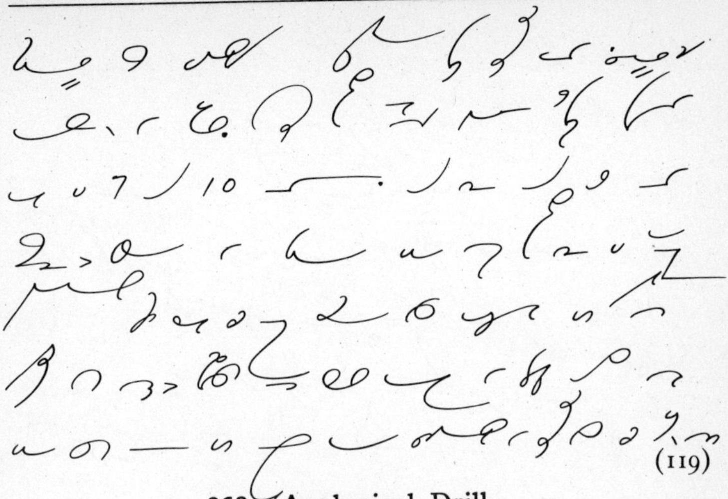

(119)

262. Analogical Drill

Restr- 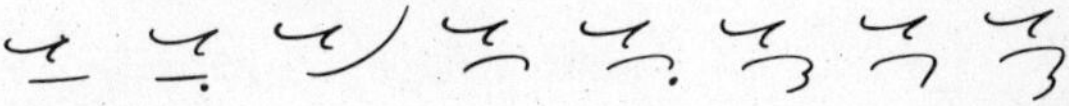

Key: restrain, restraining, restraint, restrict, restricting, restricts, restriction, restrictions.

263. 

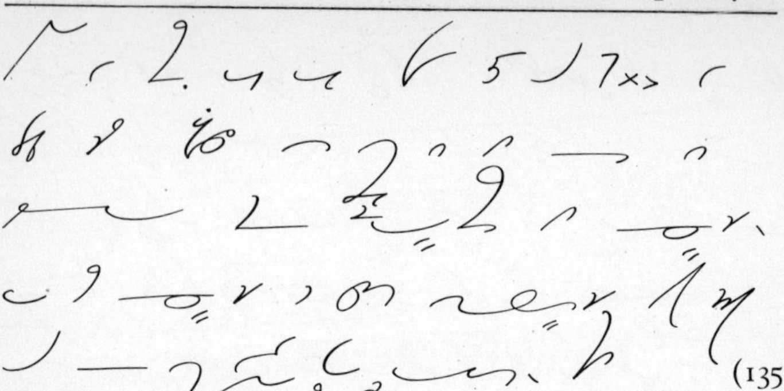

(135)

264.

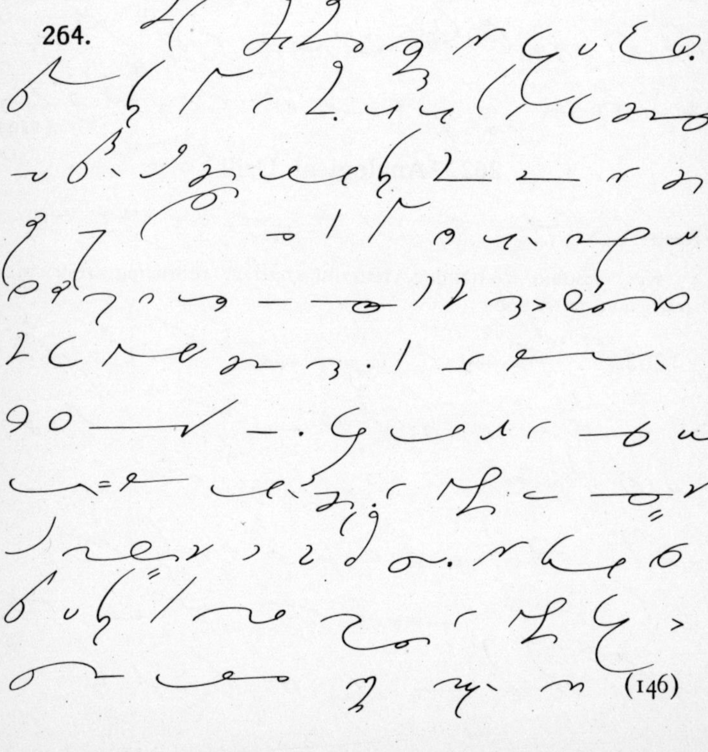

(146)

265. Cold Treatment

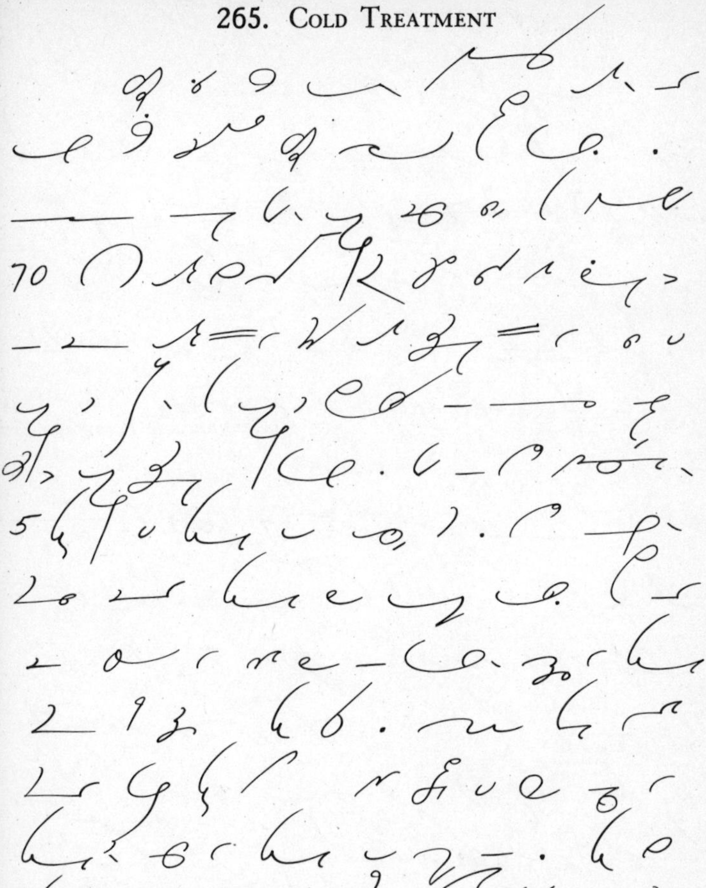

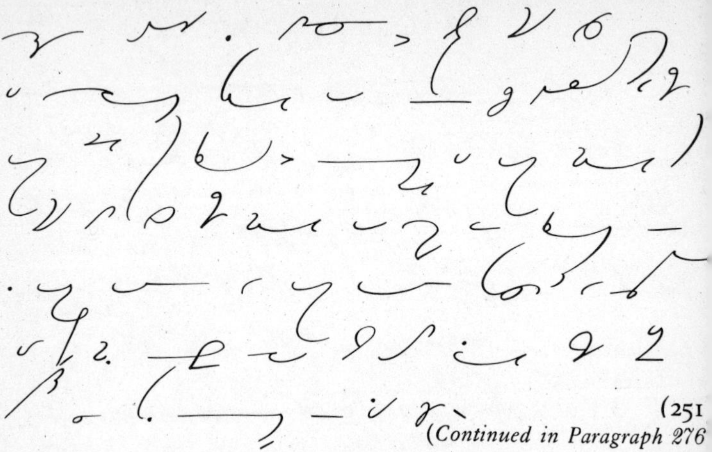

(251

(*Continued in Paragraph 276*

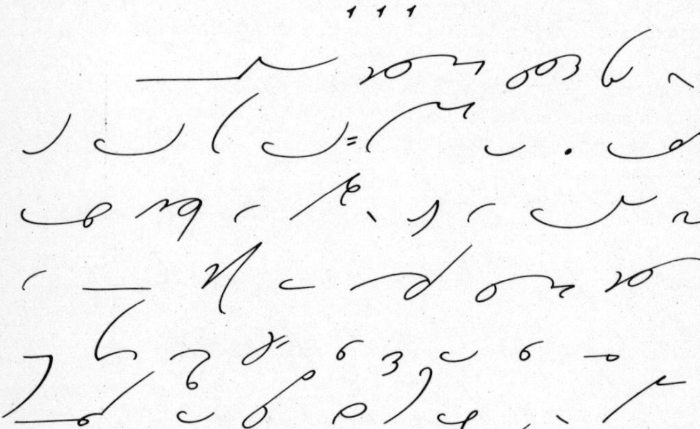

(69)

UNIT 29

266. Analogical Drill

Agr-, Aggr-

Ant-

Decl-

Incl-

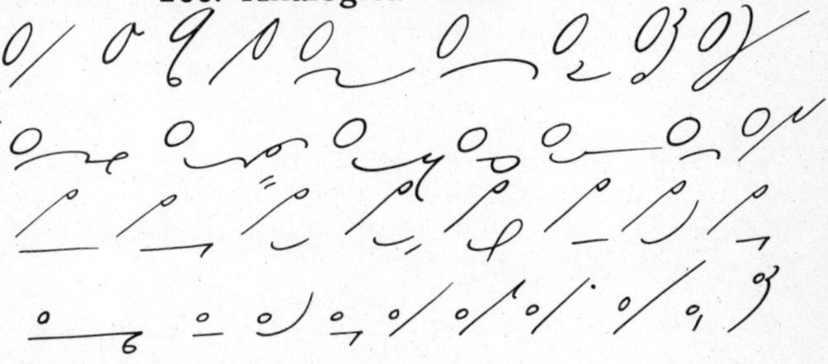

Key: agreed, agrees, agreeably, disagree, agricultural, aggregate, aggressor, aggressively, aggravated.

antagonist, Antarctic, antelope, antenna, anteroom, antique, antidote.

declaim, declamation, declare, declared, declaration, decline, declined, declension.

inclemency, incline, inclined, inclination, include, includes, including, included, inclusion, inclusive.

267.

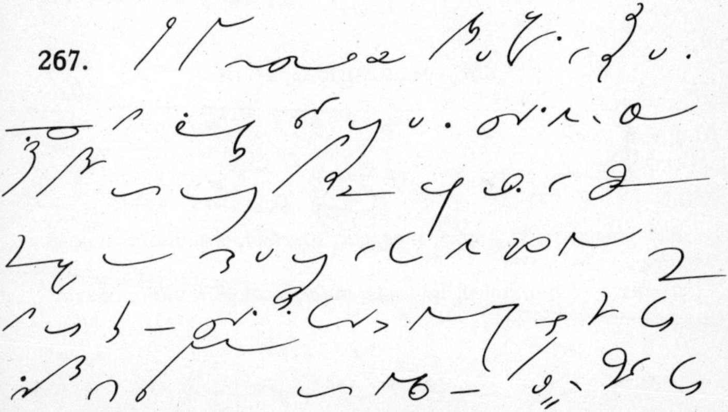

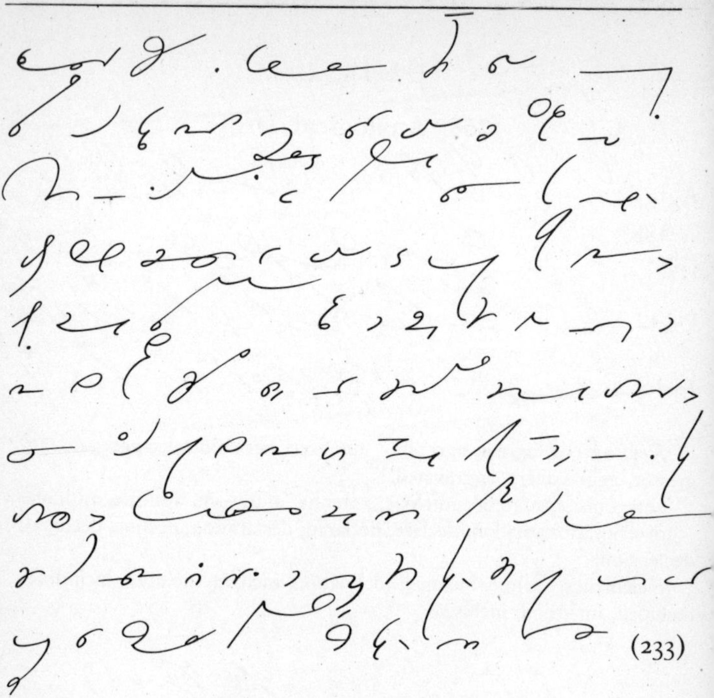

(233)

268. Analogical Drill

Magn-
(*or* Mc)
Multi

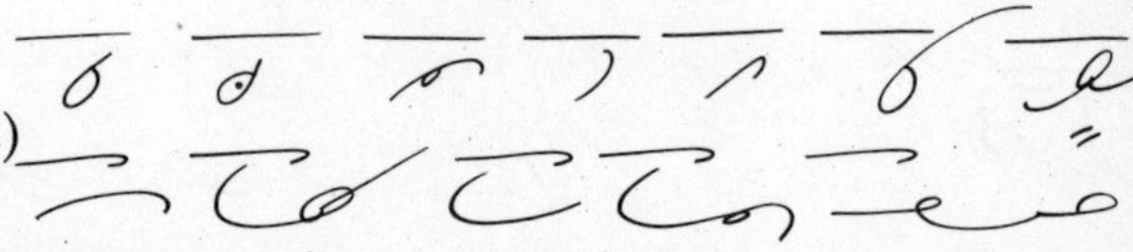

Key: magnate, magnesia, magnetic, magnify, magnitude, macadam, McIntyre.

multigraph, multiplied, multiple, multiplication, multimillionaire.

269.

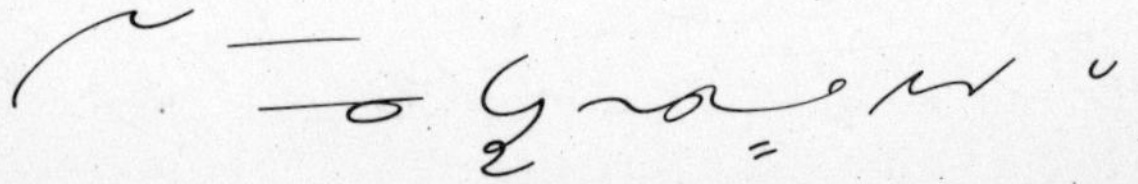

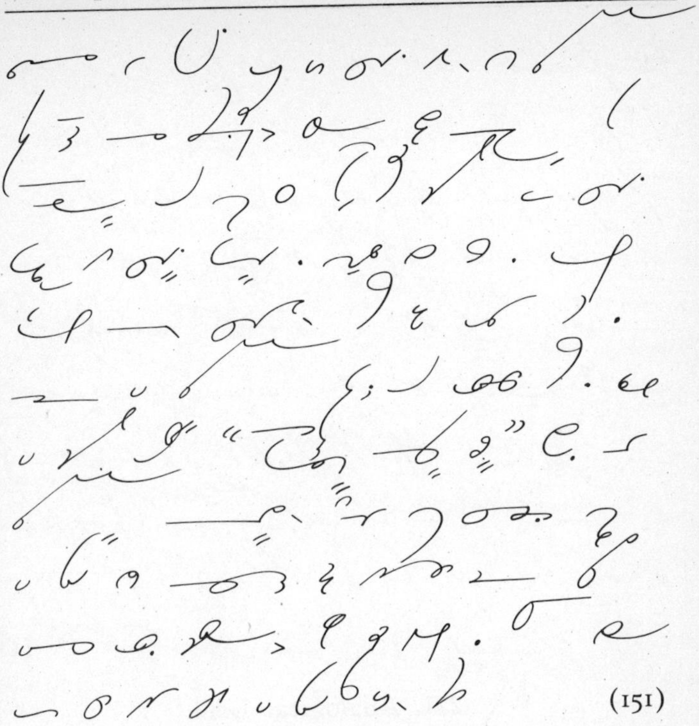

(151)

270.

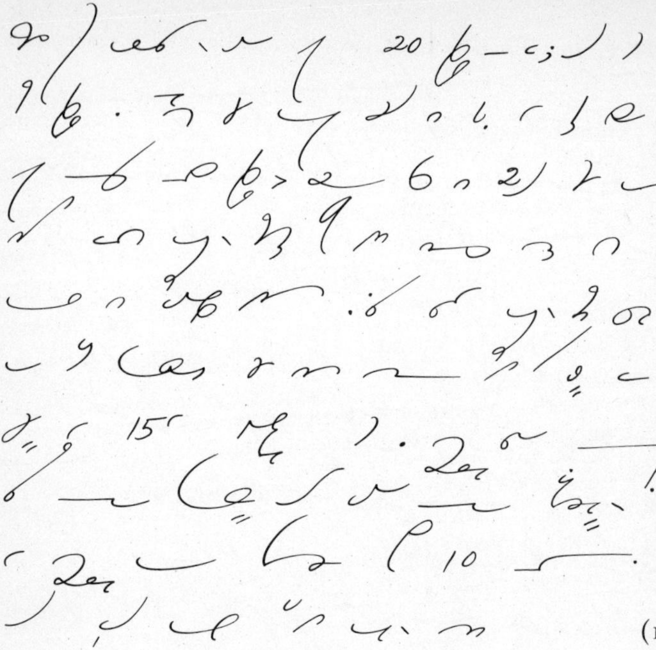

(188)

271. Analogical Drill

Para 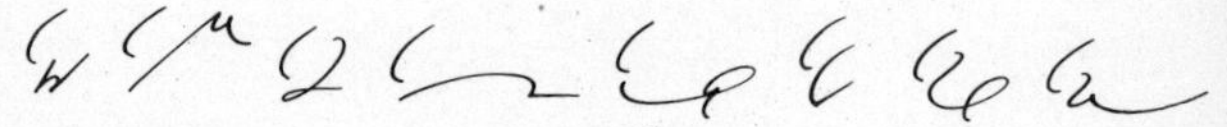

Post 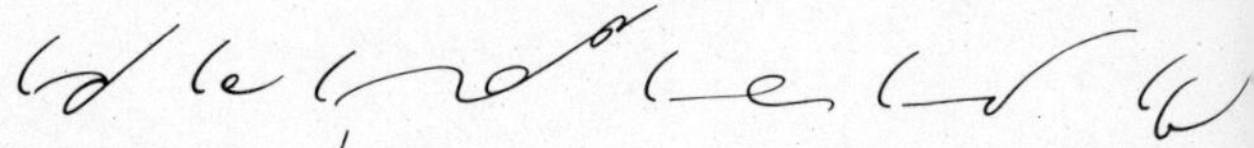

Recl- 

Self, Circu, Circum 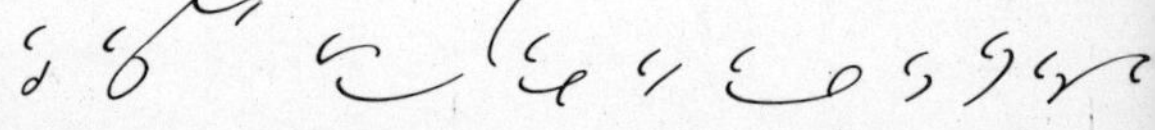

Key: parachute, paradox, paraffin, paragon, paralyze, parapet, paraphrase, parasol.

post card, posterior, postgraduate, postmark, post mortem, postponed.

reclaim, reclaimed, reclamation, reclaimable, recline, reclined, reclination, recluse.

selfishly, self-addressed, self-control, self-respect, circuit, circulate, circus, circumference, circumstance.

272.

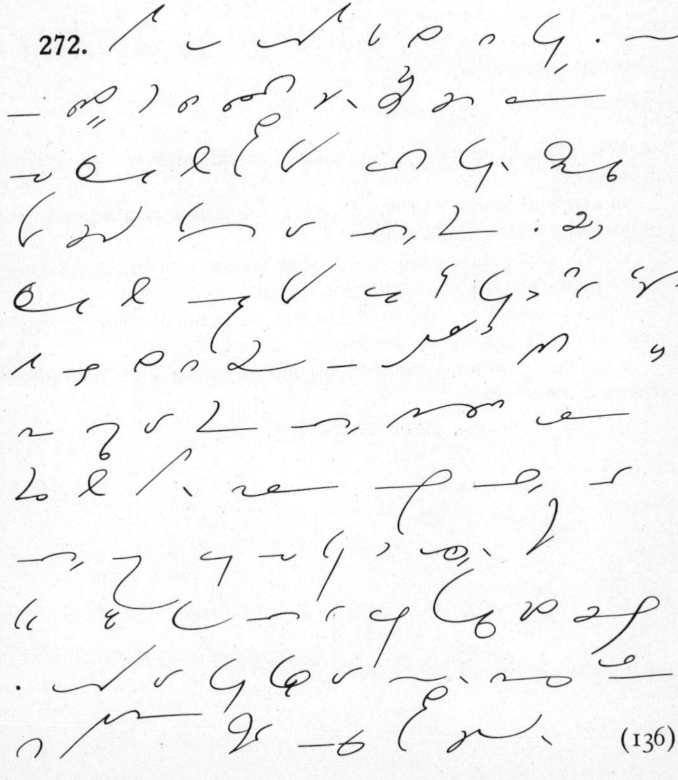

(136)

273. Analogical Drill

Grand
Short, Ship
Super, Supre
Susp-, Suscep
Trans

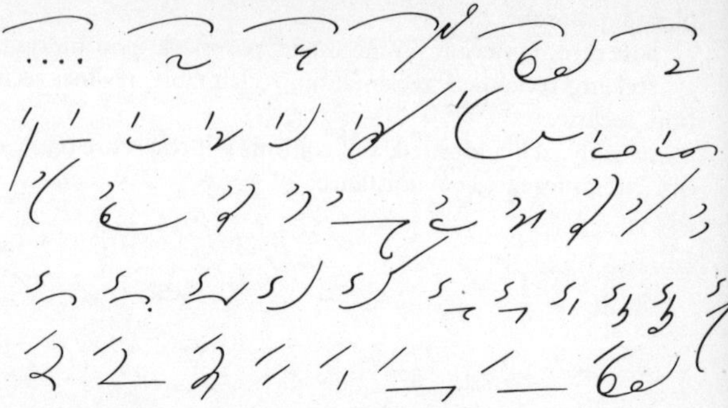

Key: grand, grandeur, grandiose, granddaughter, grandparent, grandson.

shortage, shorten, shorter, shortest, shorthand, shortsighted, shipbuilder, shipowner, shipwreck.

superb, supercilious, superficial, superfluous, superimpose, superior, superstition, supervision, supported, suppress.

suspect, suspecting, suspected, suspend, suspended, suspense, suspension, suspicion, suspicious, suspiciously, susceptible.

transfix, transform, transfusion, transit, transition, transmission, transom, transparent.

274.

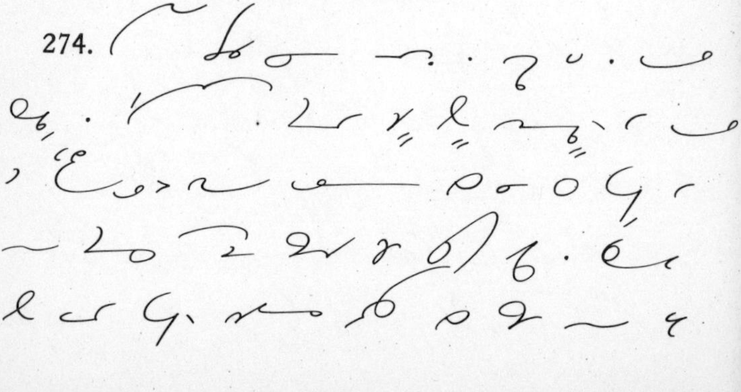

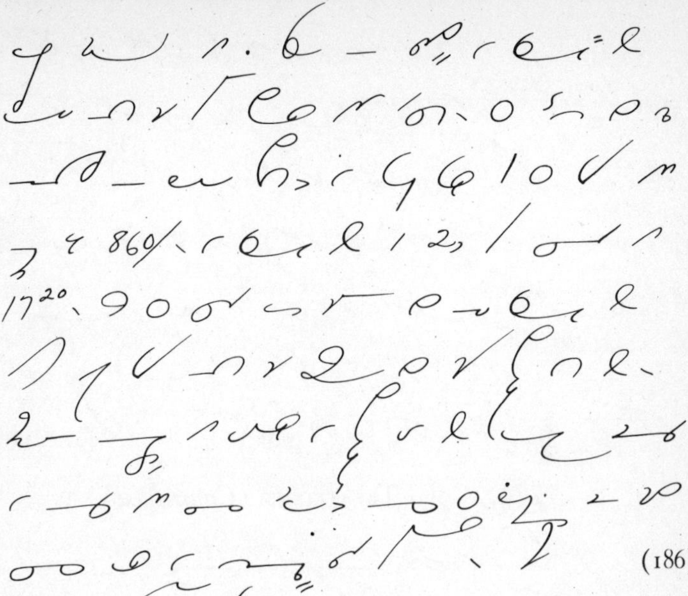

(186)

275.

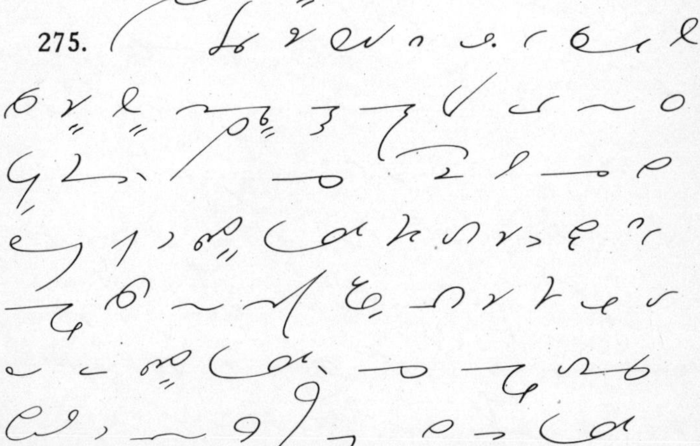

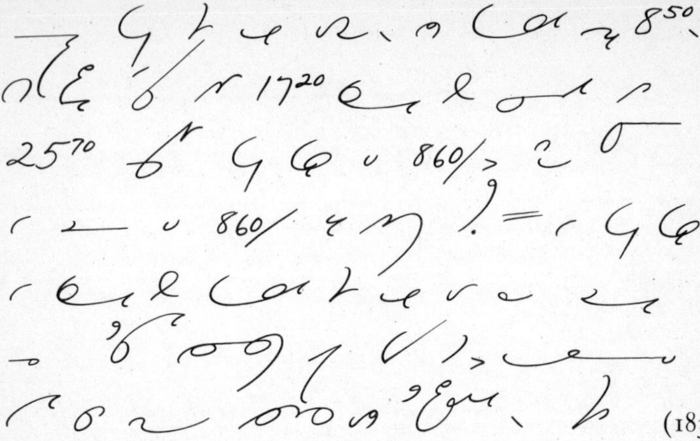

(183)

276. Cold Treatment (*Continued*)

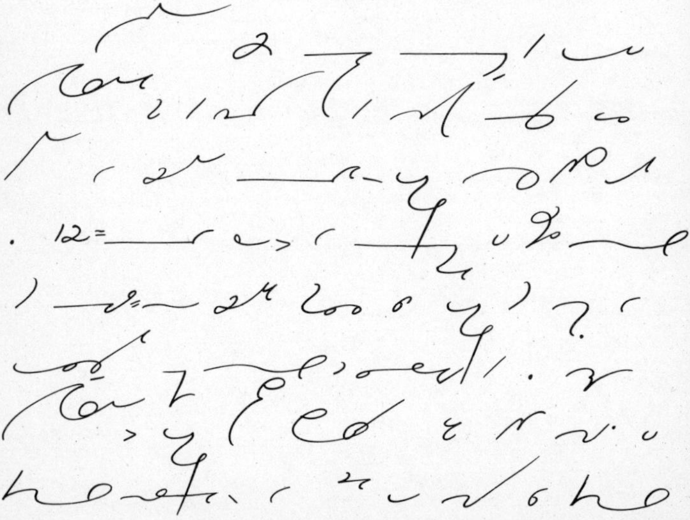

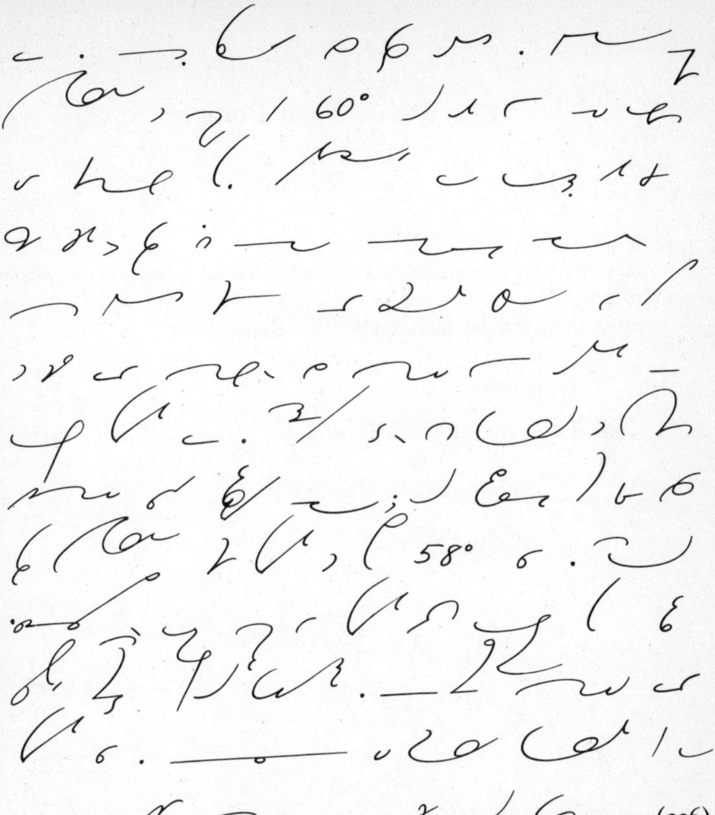

(226)

(*Concluded in Paragraph 288*)

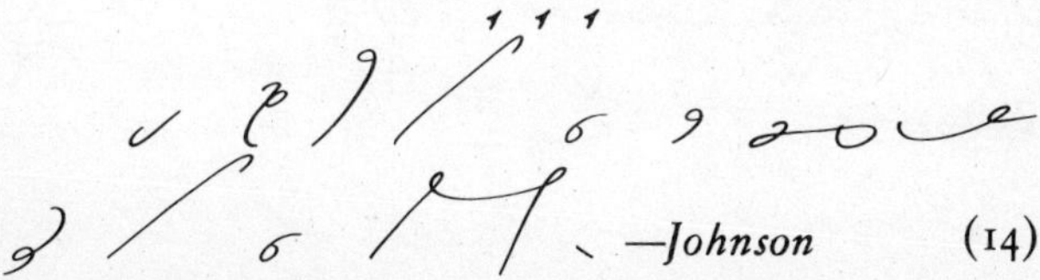

—*Johnson* (14)

UNIT 30

277. Done, Than Phrases

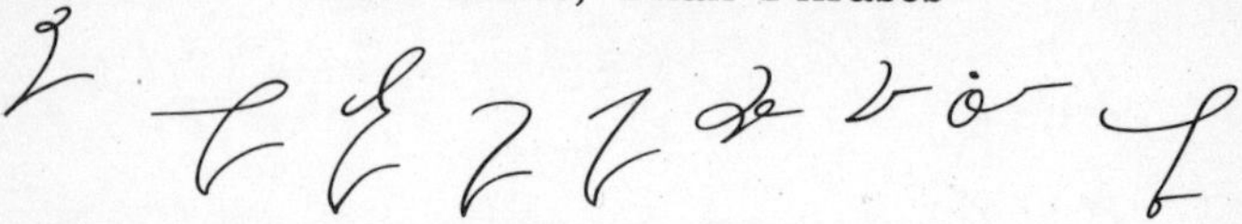

Key: we have done, may be done, what has been done, can be done, to be done.

faster than, further than, higher than, larger than.

278.

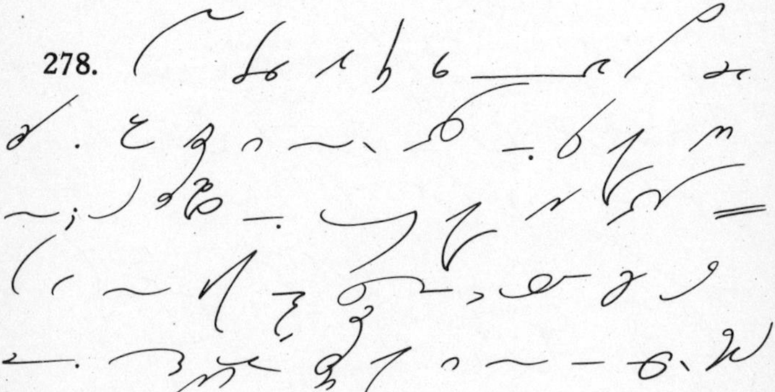

(105)

279.

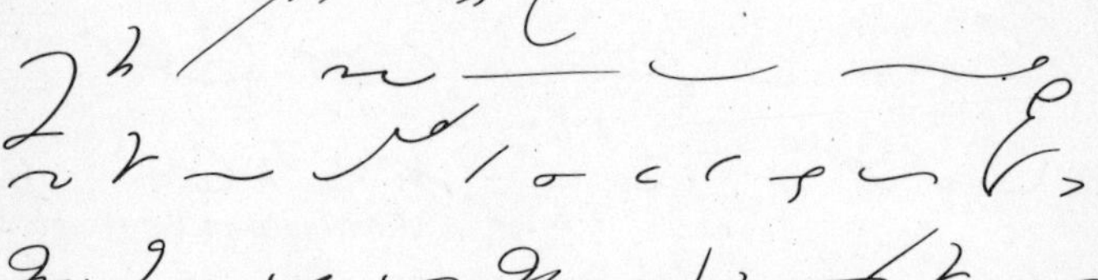

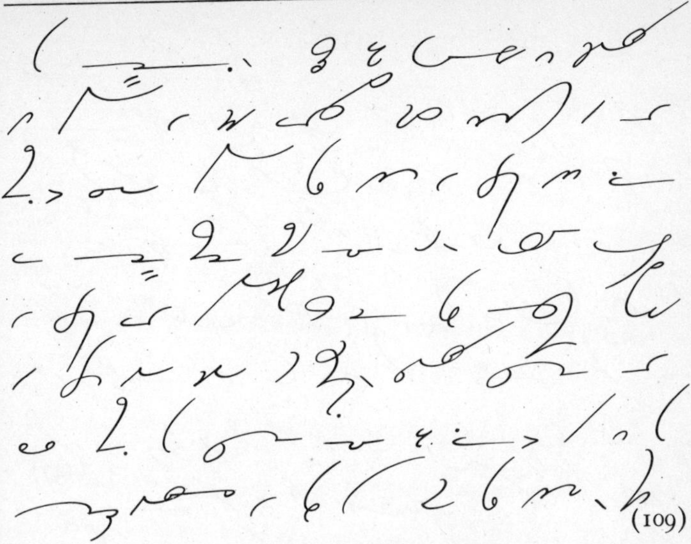

(109)

280. Us, Department Phrases

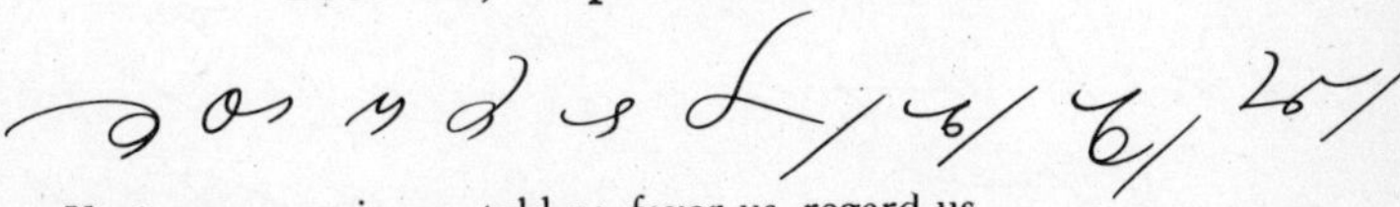

Key: gave us, wire us, told us, favor us, regard us.

banking department, receiving department, repair department, furniture department.

281.

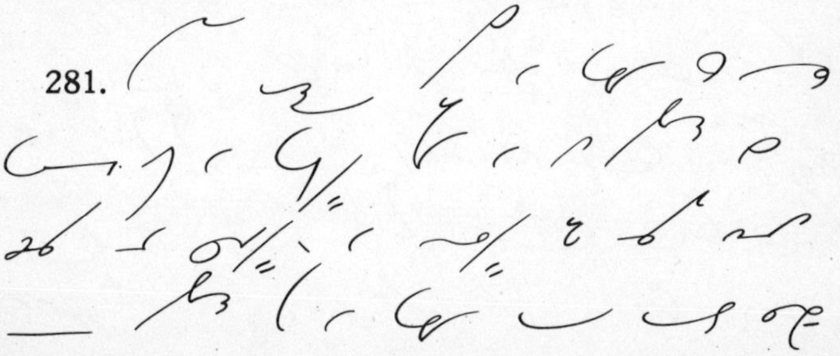

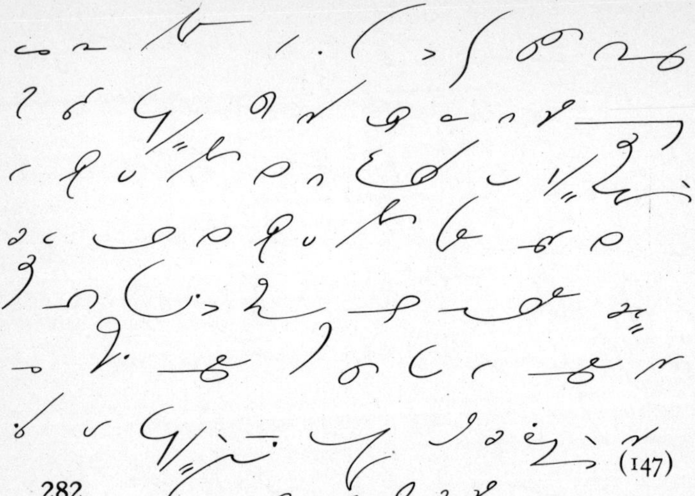

(147)

282.

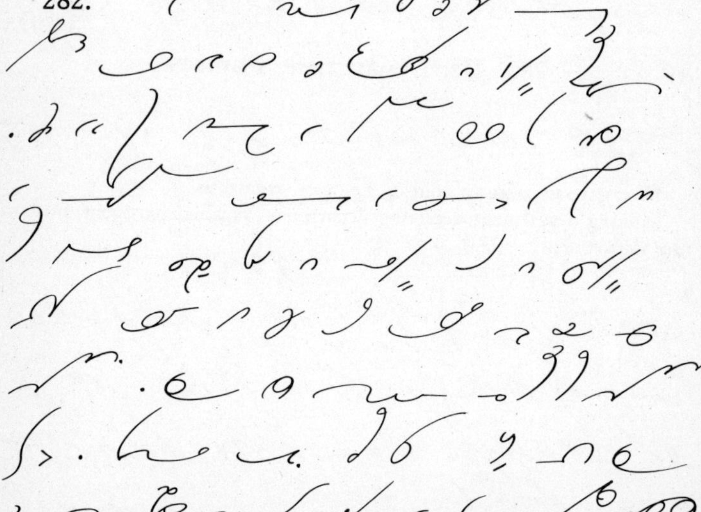

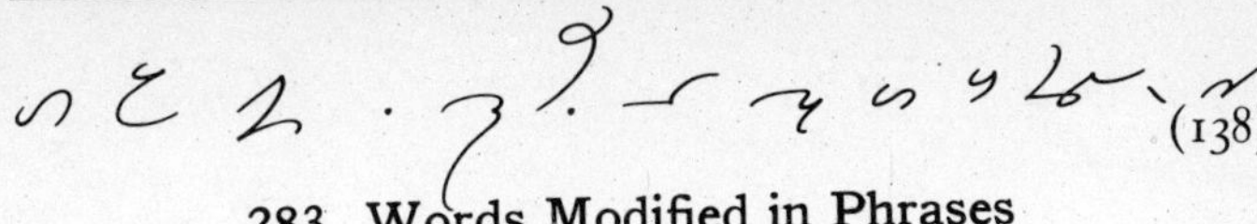

(138)

283. Words Modified in Phrases

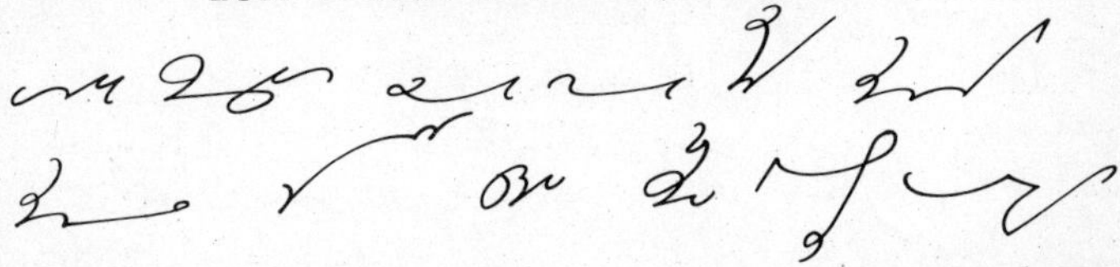

Key: of course it was, as a matter of course, we always, you always, we have your order, first-class condition, first-class manner, sometime or other, out of stock, so far as I know, to a large extent, long past due.

284.

(97)

285.

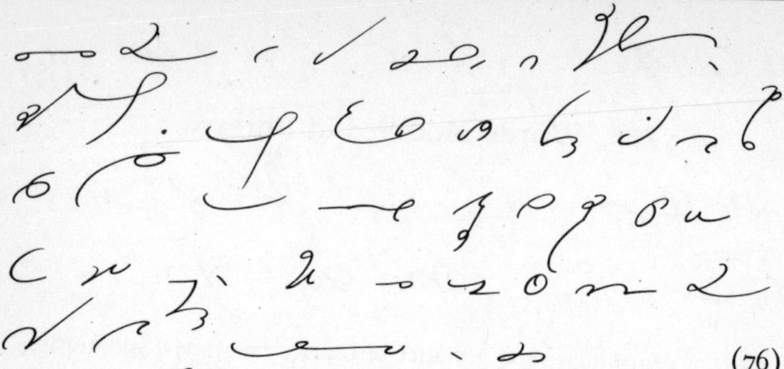

(76)

286.

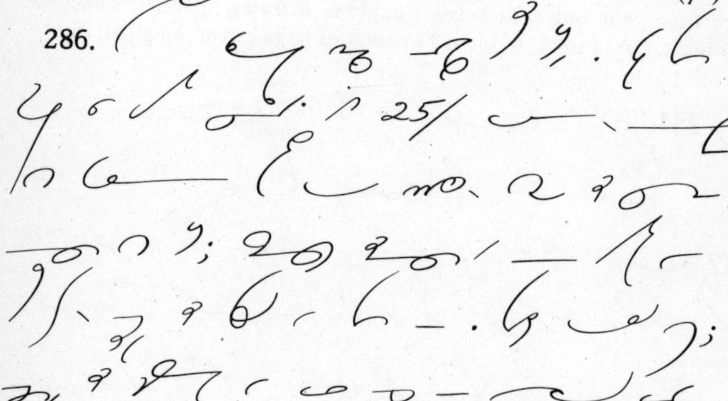

(123)

287.

(169)

288. Cold Treatment (*Concluded*)

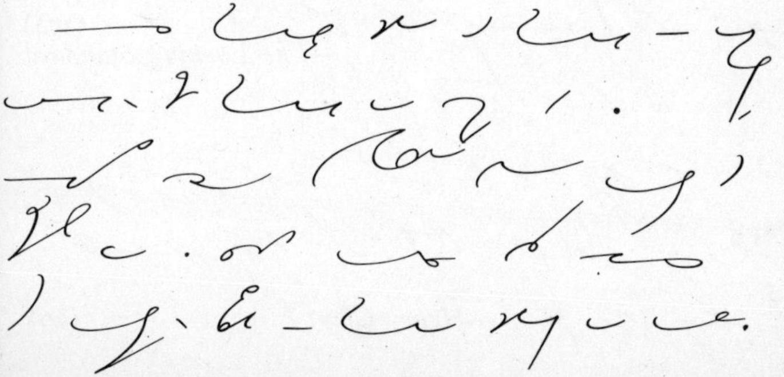

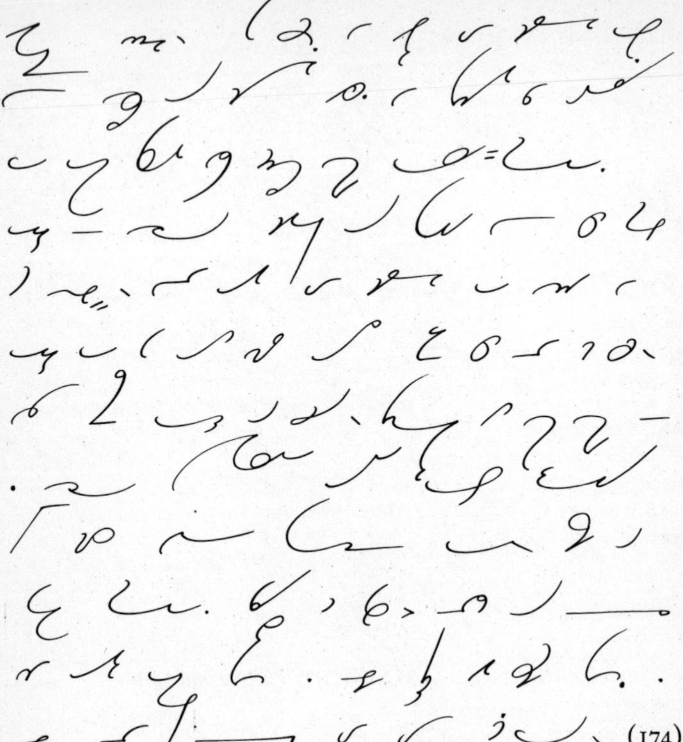

(174)

—The Evening Standard

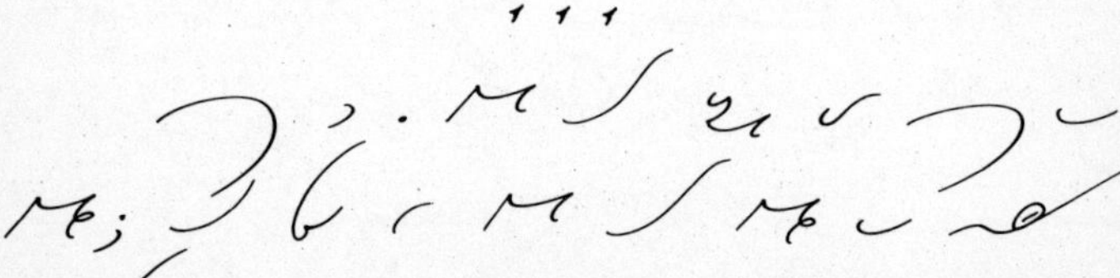

—Henry Clay (29)

SPEED STUDY XI

UNIT 31

289. Analogical Drill

-scribe,
-scription
-cient, -tient,
-ciency
-pose,
-position

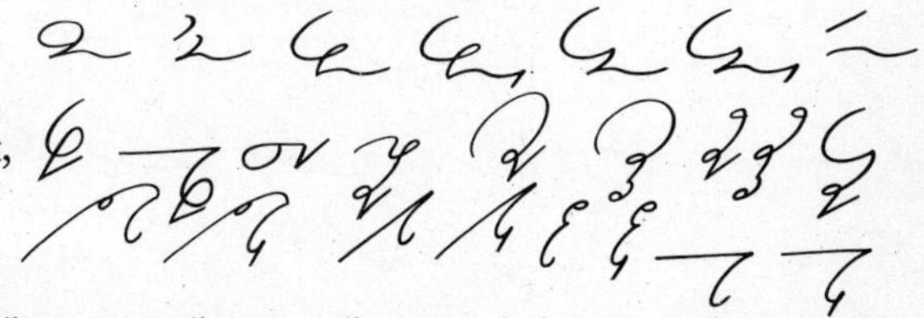

Key: ascribe, superscribe, prescribe, prescription, proscribe, proscription, transcribe.

patient, impatient, ancient, coefficient, deficient, deficiency, efficient, efficiency, proficient.

decompose, decomposition, depose, deposition, expose, exposition, impose, imposition.

290.

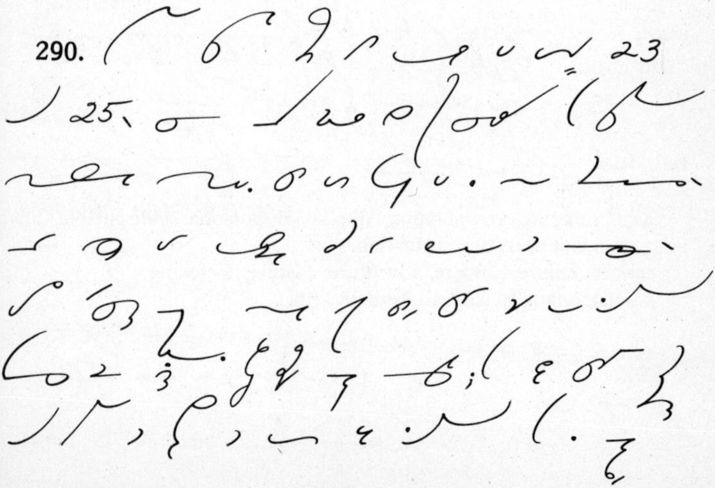

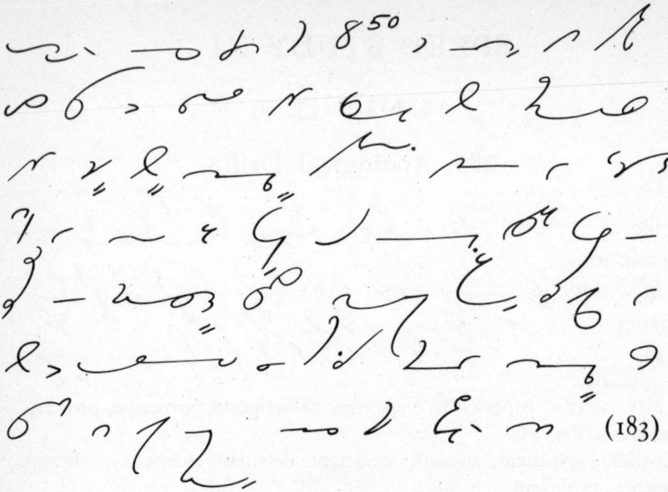

(183)

291. Analogical Drill

-pute,
-putation
-ure, -ture

-ual, -tual

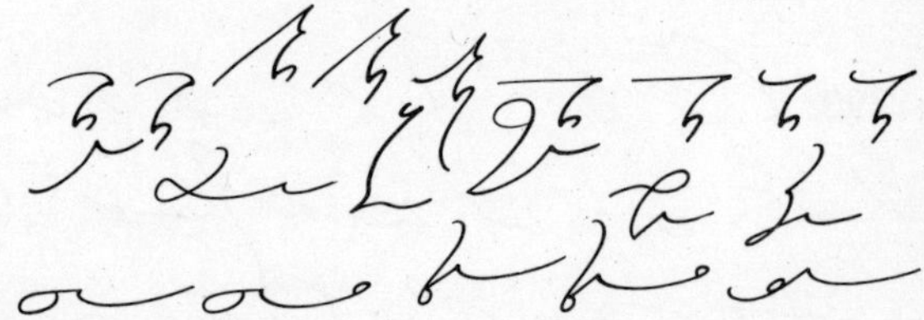

Key: compute, computation, dispute, disputation, indisputable, impute, imputation, repute, reputation.

endure, failure, obscure, adventure, capture, forfeiture.

annual, annually, virtual, virtually, ritual.

292.

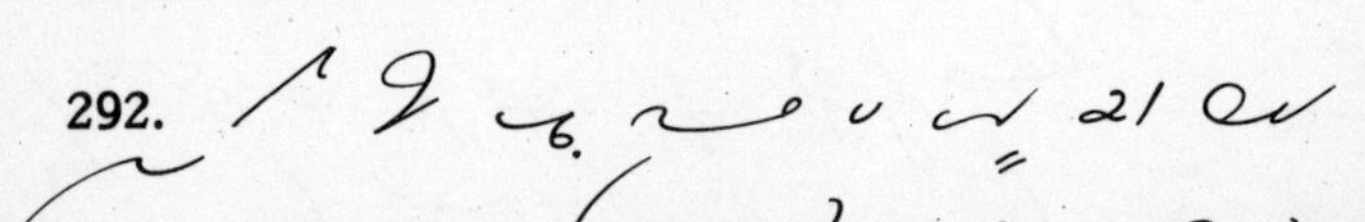

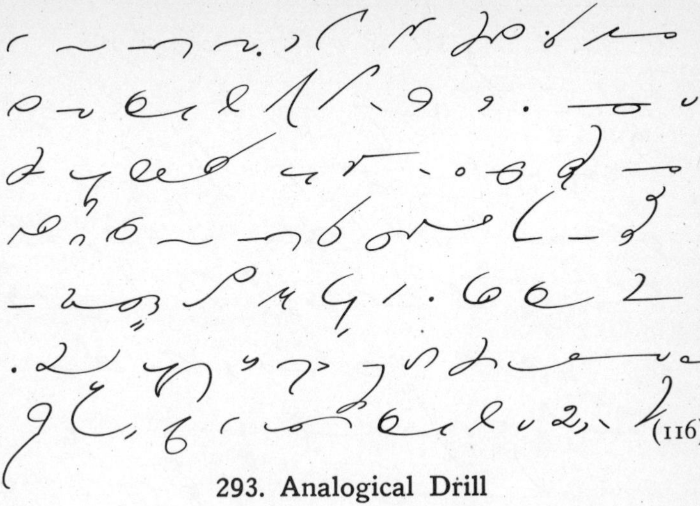

(116)

293. Analogical Drill

-spect, -spection

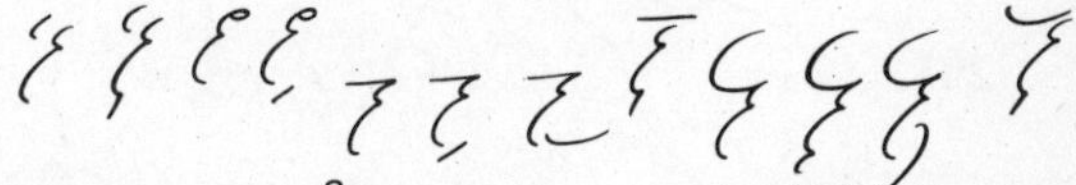

-quire

-pire

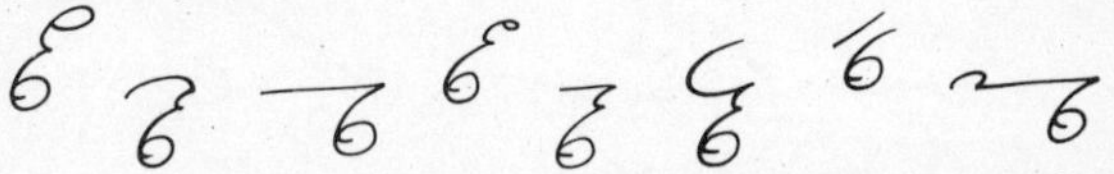

Key: circumspect, circumspection, expect, expected, inspect, inspected, inspector, introspection, prospect, prospects, prospective, retrospection.

acquire, acquires, acquirement, esquire, inquire, inquires, inquirer, requirement.

aspire, conspire, empire, expire, inspire, perspire, transpire, umpire.

294.

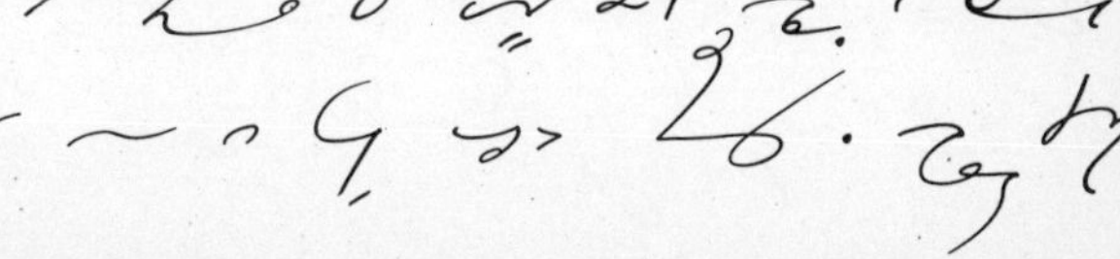

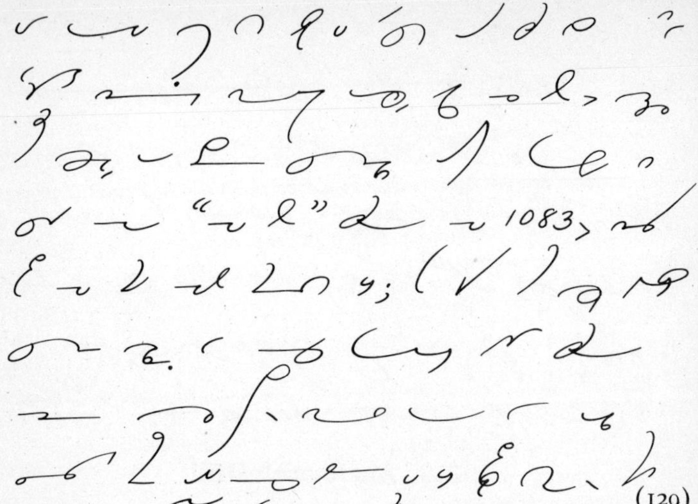

(129)

295.

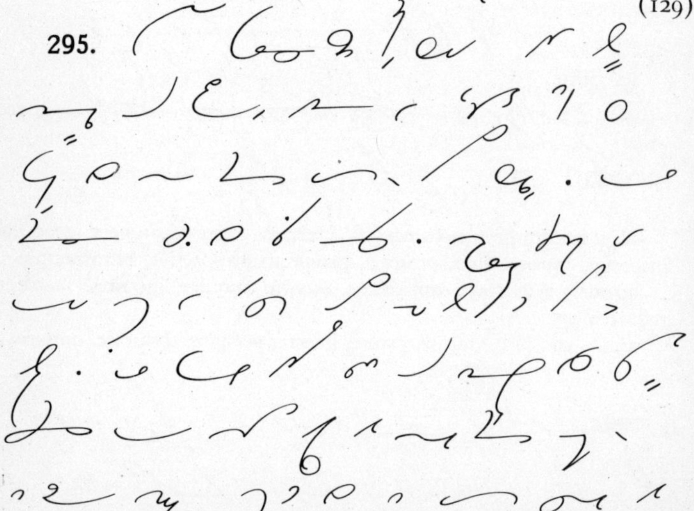

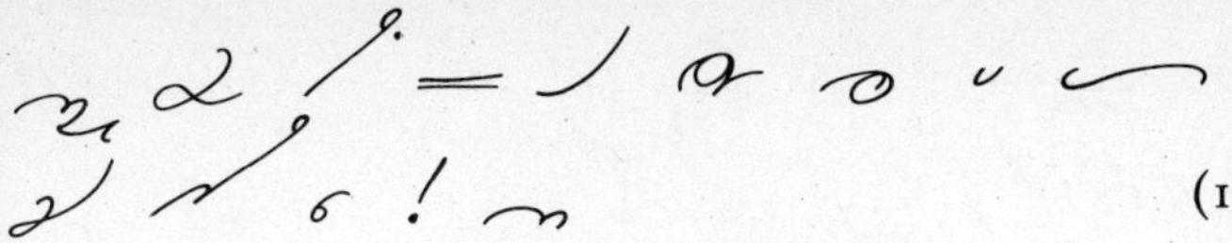

(121)

296. Analogical Drill

-gency

-sure, -jury, -jure

-flect, -flection, -flict, -fliction

-sult

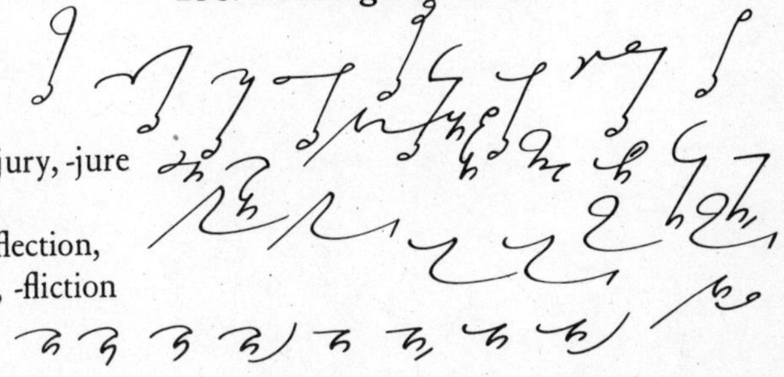

Key: agency, contingency, cogency, emergency, exigency, pungency, regency, stringency, urgency.

censure, composure, disclosure, exposure, assurance, reassure, perjure, injured.

deflect, deflection, reflect, reflection, afflict, affliction.

consult, consultation, consults, consultant, insult, insulted, result, resultant, desultory.

297.

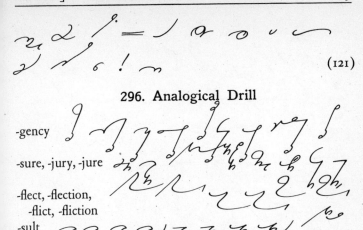

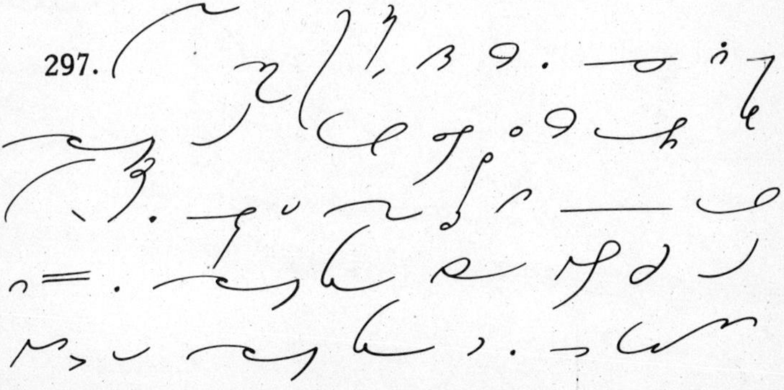

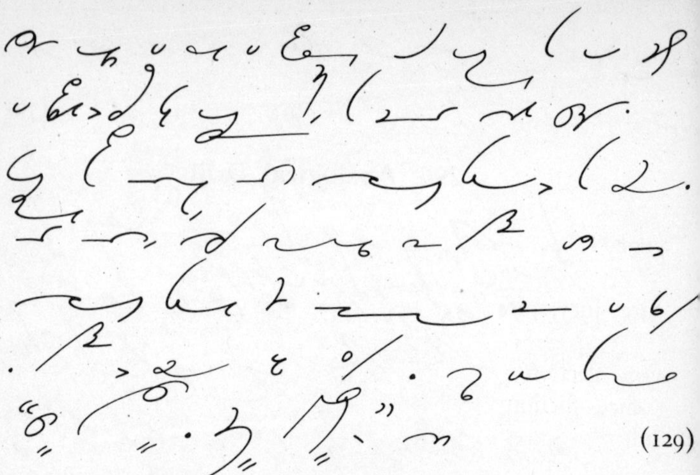

(129)

298. A Typewriter Detective

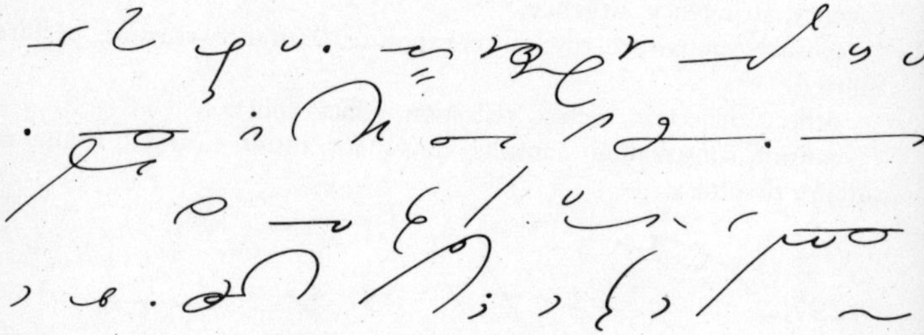

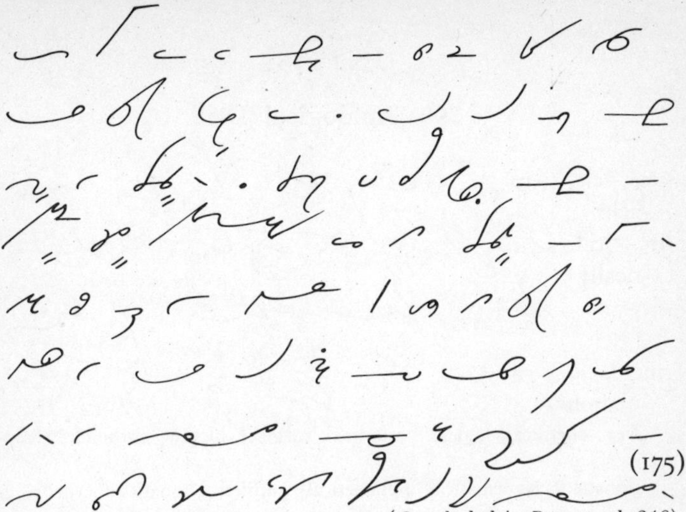

(175)

(*Concluded in Paragraph 310*)

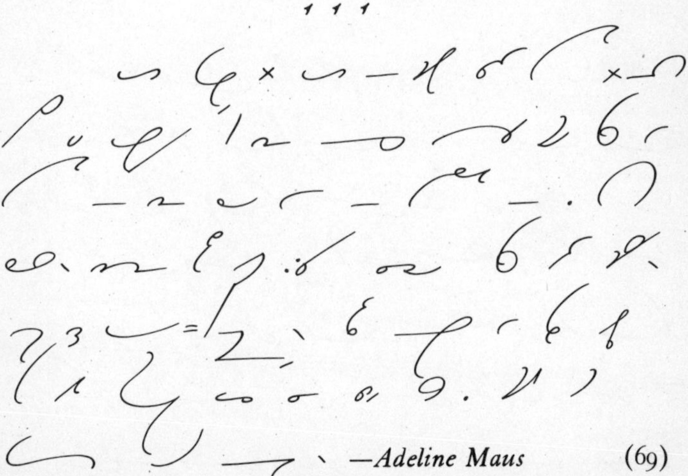

—*Adeline Maus* (69)

UNIT 32

299. Analogical Drill

-ical, -icle, -acle

-tic, -tical, -tically

-lity

-ulate, -ulation

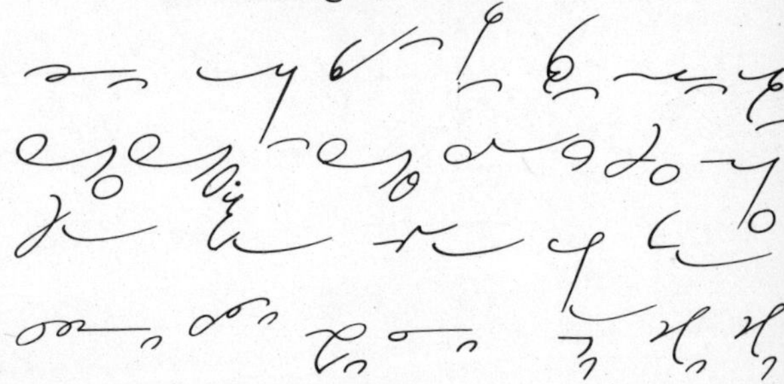

Key: chemical, logical, periodical, surgical, bicycle, chronicle, receptacle.

alphabetic, alphabetical, alphabetically, athletics, fanatic, energetic.

fatality, hospitality, neutrality, originality, penalty.

accumulate, articulate, capitulate, emulate, insulation, stipulate, stipulation.

300.

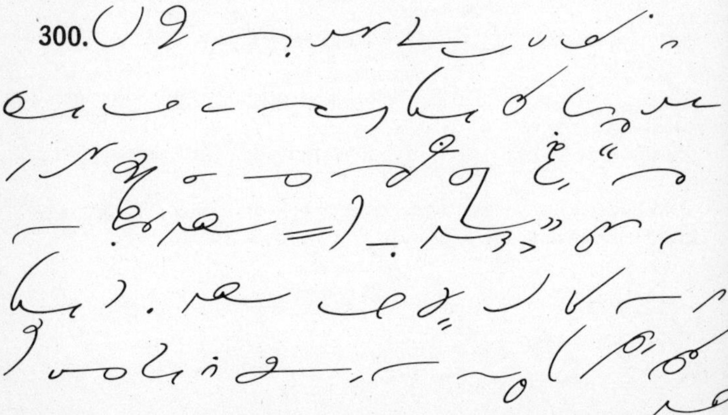

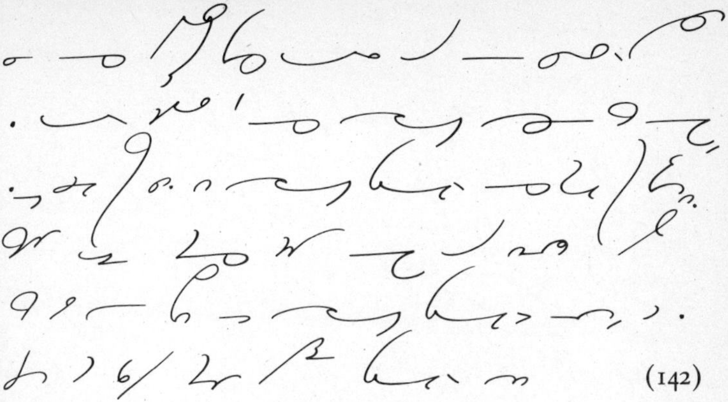

(142)

301. Analogical Drill

-bility

-city

-logy, -logical

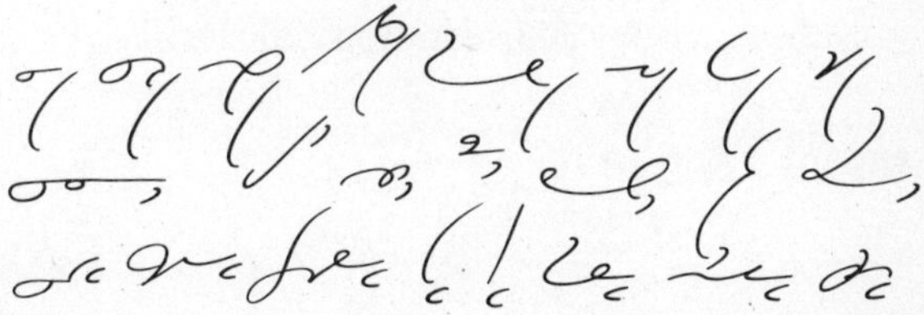

Key: inability, acceptability, capability, disability, flexibility, nobility, probability, stability.

animosity, audacity, curiosity, eccentricity, elasticity, publicity, velocity.

anthology, astrology, bacteriology, biology, geology, phrenology, chronology, psychology.

302.

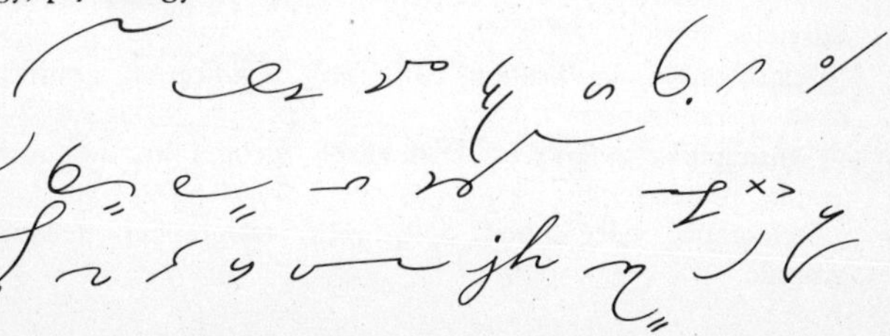

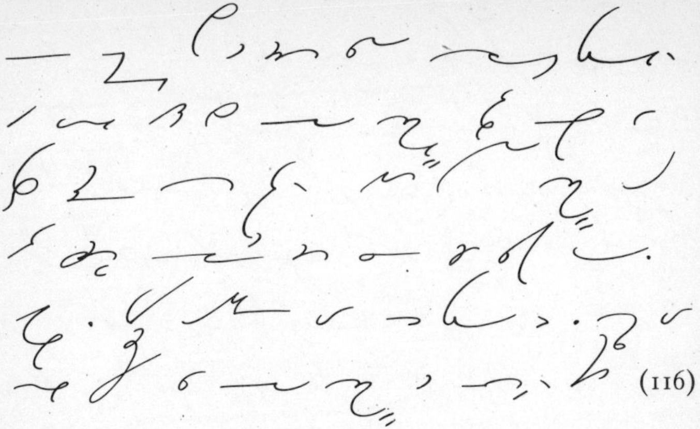

(116)

303. Analogical Drill

-rity

-fication

-ograph-y

-egraph-y

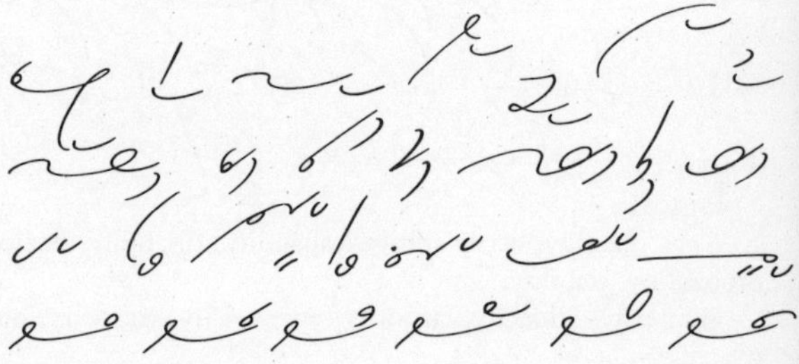

Key: celebrity, charity, clarity, dexterity, inferiority, temerity, superiority.

clarification, certification, edification, fortification, gratification, justification, ratification.

autograph, biography, Dictograph, geography, hectograph, lithograph, Mimeograph.

telegraph, telegraphed, telegraphs, telegrapher, telegraphy, telegraphic.

304.

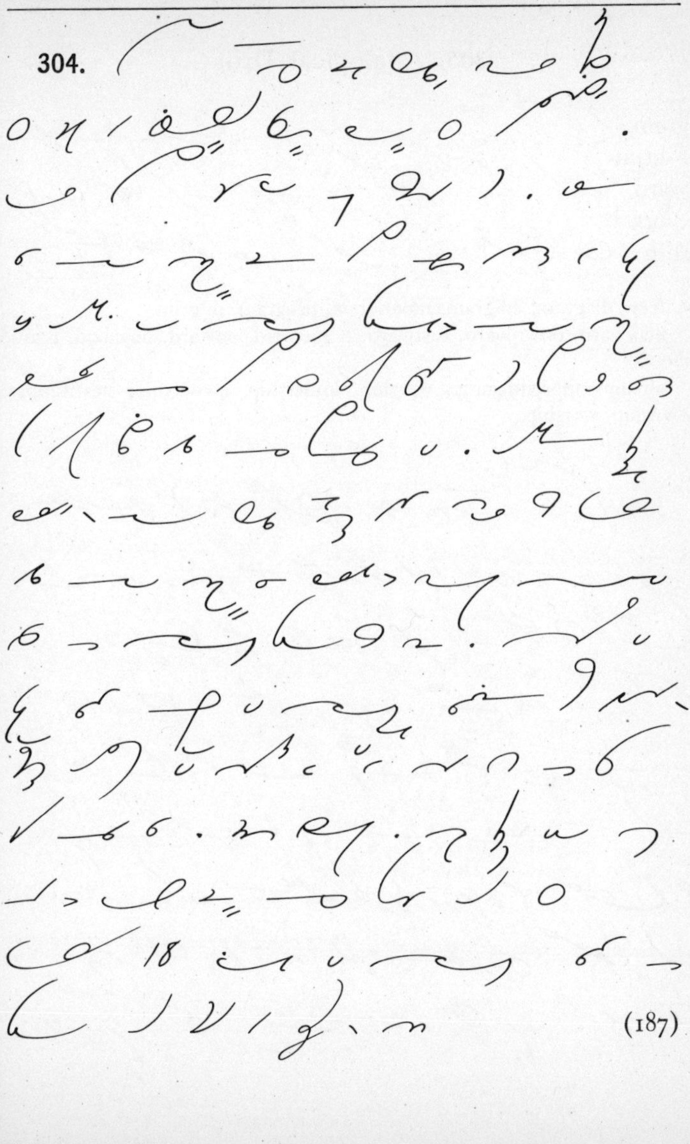

(187)

305. Analogical Drill

-gram,
-grim
-ward,
-hood
-ship

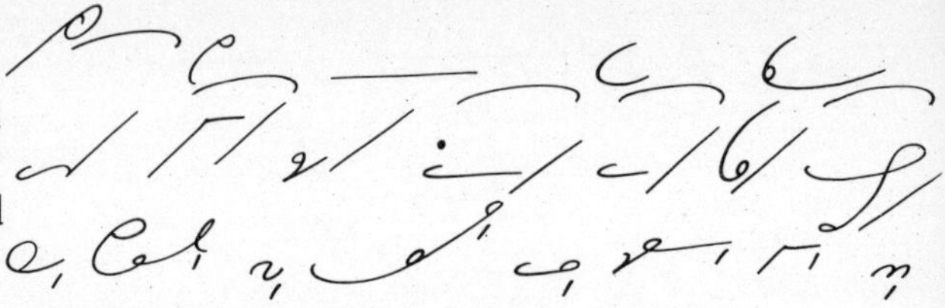

Key: diagram, epigram, monogram, program, pilgrim.

awkward, downward, eastward, homeward, onward, boyhood, livelihood.

airship, apprenticeship, warship, leadership, ownership, steamship, township, worship.

306.

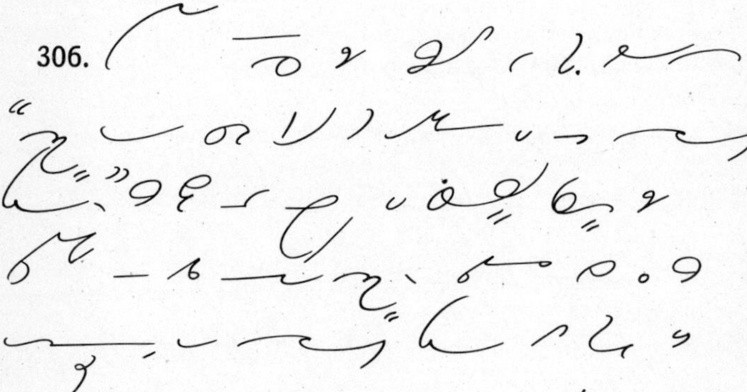

(117)

307. Analogical Drill

-mental

-mity,
-nity

-stic

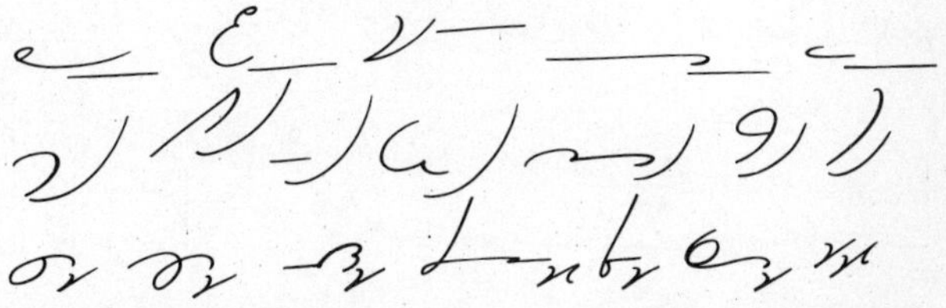

Key: elemental, experimental, fundamental, monumental, ornamental.
conformity, deformity, enmity, proximity, community, affinity, vanity.
acoustic, characteristic, enthusiastic, gymnastics, journalistic, sarcastic, statistics.

308.

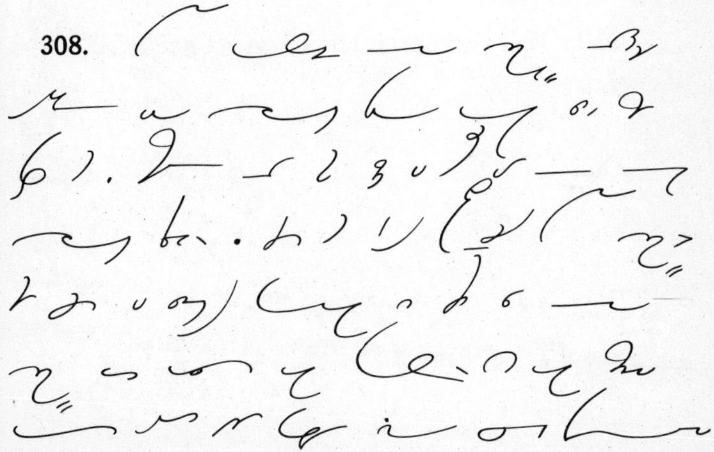

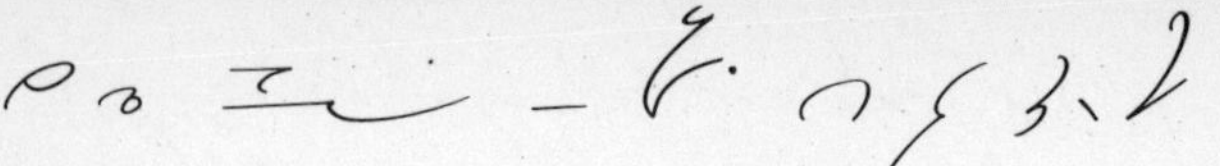 (102)

309.

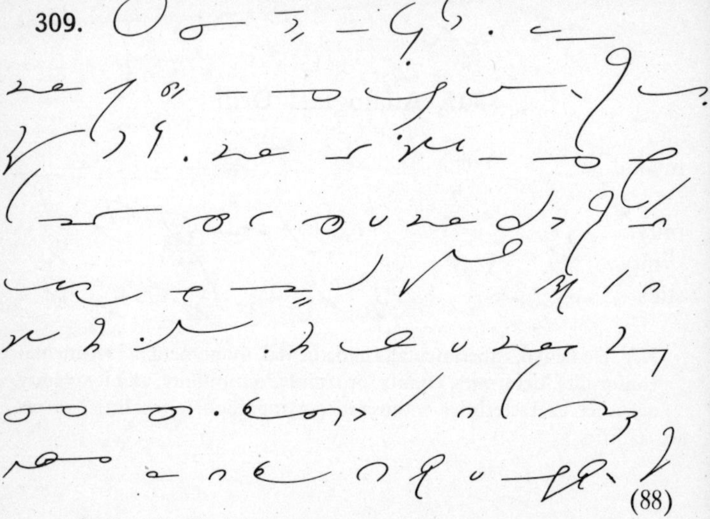

(88)

310. A Typewriter Detective (*Concluded*)

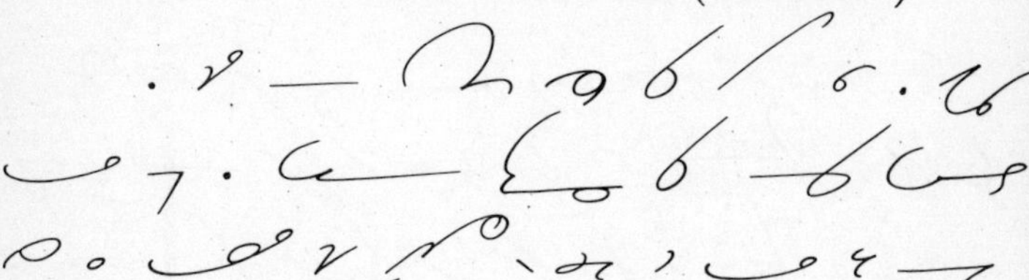

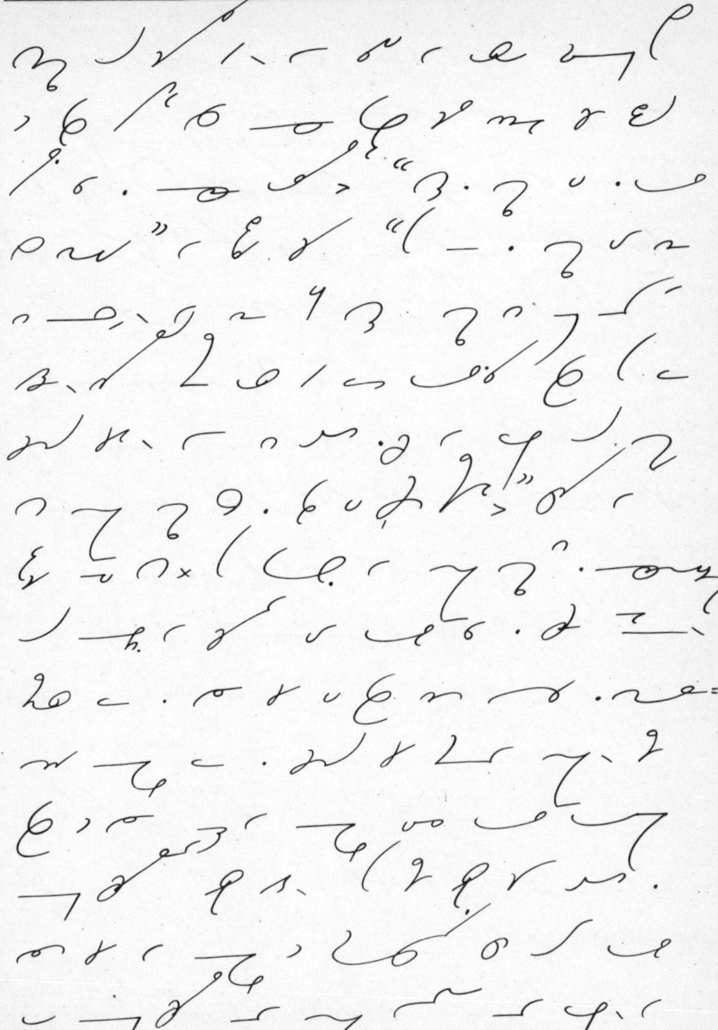

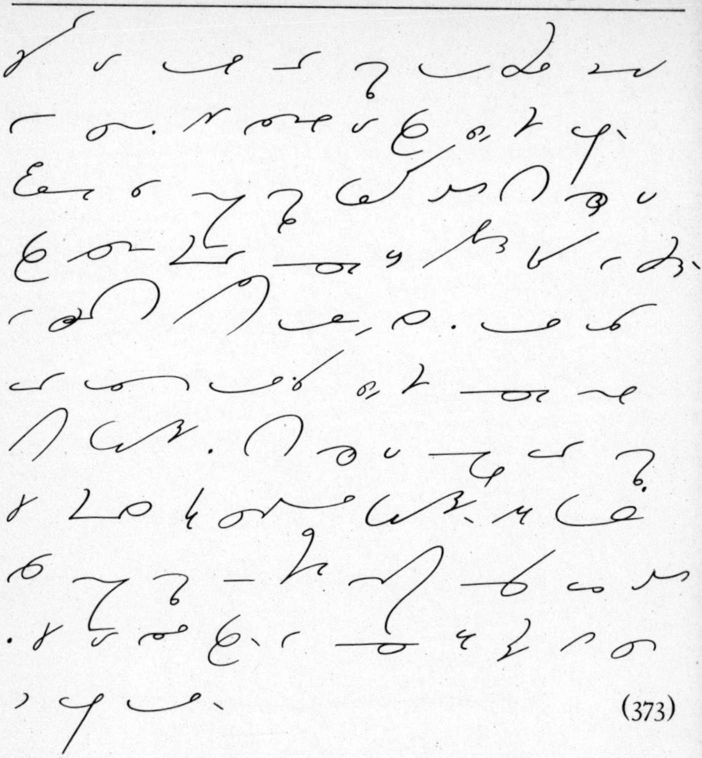

(373)

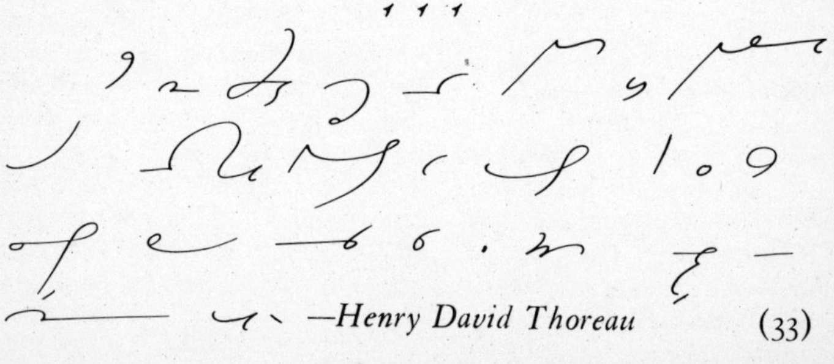

—Henry David Thoreau (33)

UNIT 33

311. Points of the Compass. The following outlines will be found useful in real estate and other types of dictation. Note that the forms for *east* and *west* have been slightly modified.

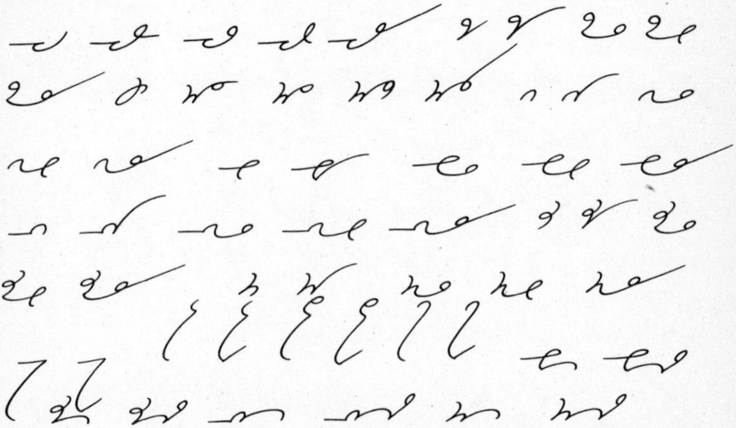

Key: (1) north, northern, northerly, northerly side, northerly direction, east, eastern, easterly, easterly side; (2) easterly direction, south, southern, southerly, southerly side, southerly direction, west, western, westerly; (3) westerly side, westerly direction, northeast, northeastern, northeasterly, northeasterly side, northeasterly direction; (4) northwest, northwestern, northwesterly, northwesterly side, northwesterly direction, southeast, southeastern, southeasterly; (5) southeasterly side, southeasterly direction, southwest, southwestern, southwesterly, southwesterly side, southwesterly direction; (6) northbound, northbound track, southbound, southbound track, eastbound, eastbound track, westbound, westbound track, northeast corner, northeast quarter; (7) southeast corner, southeast quarter, northwest corner, northwest quarter, southwest corner, southwest quarter.

READING AND DICTATION PRACTICE

312.

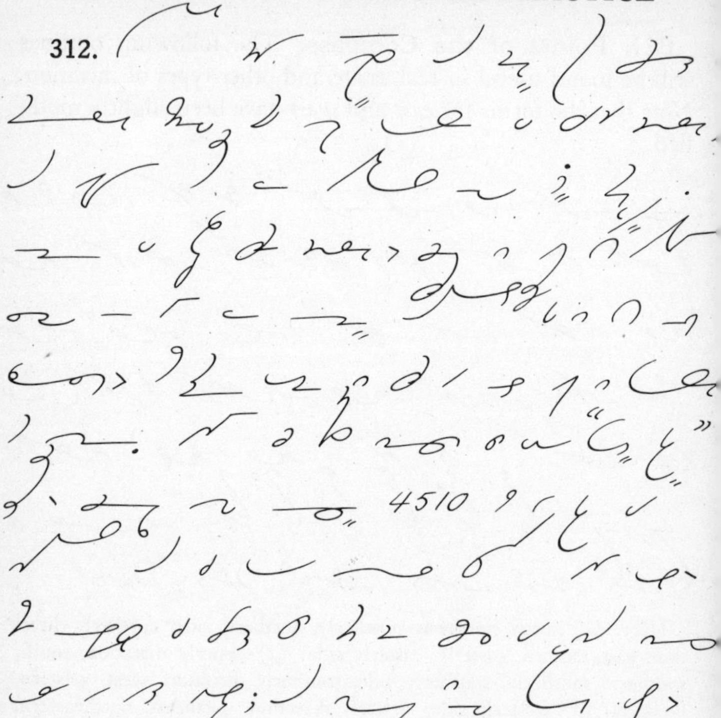

(185)

313.

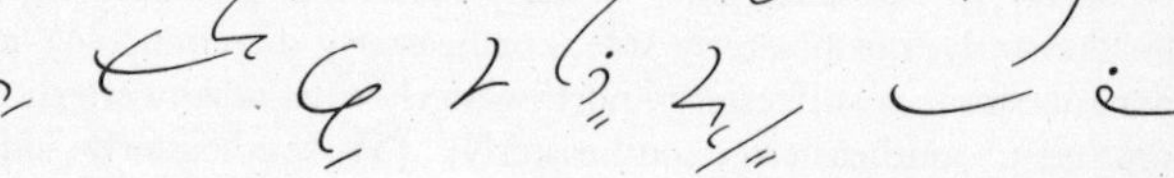

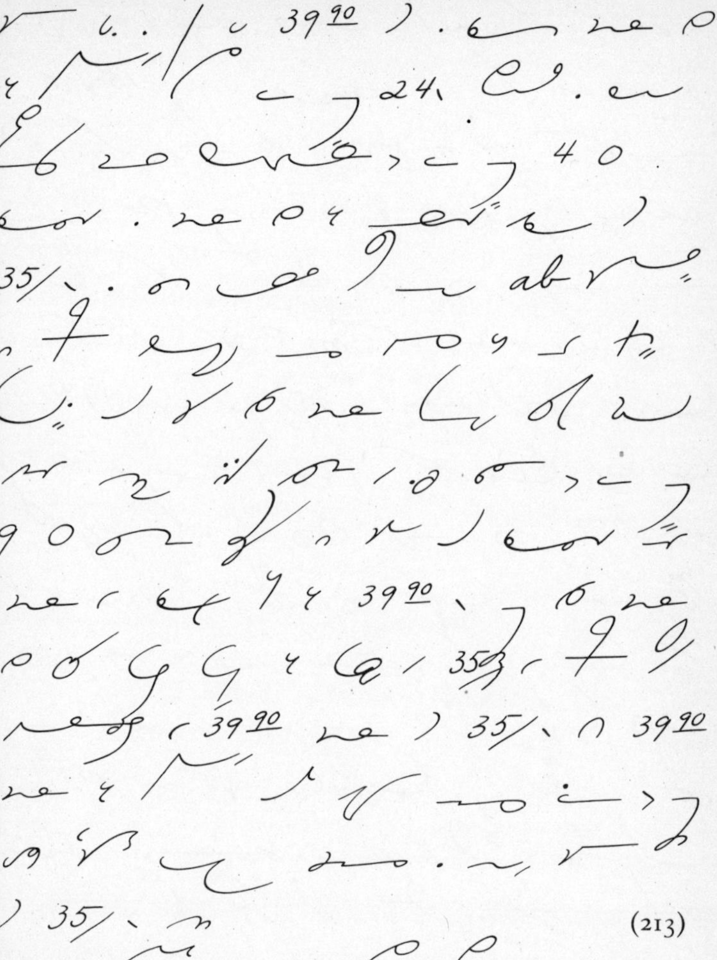

(213)

314. 

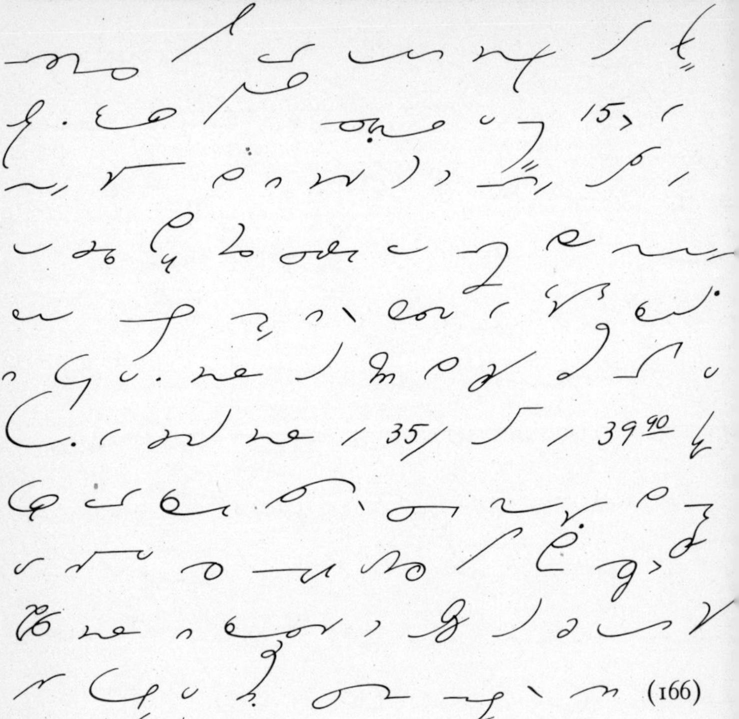

(166)

315. 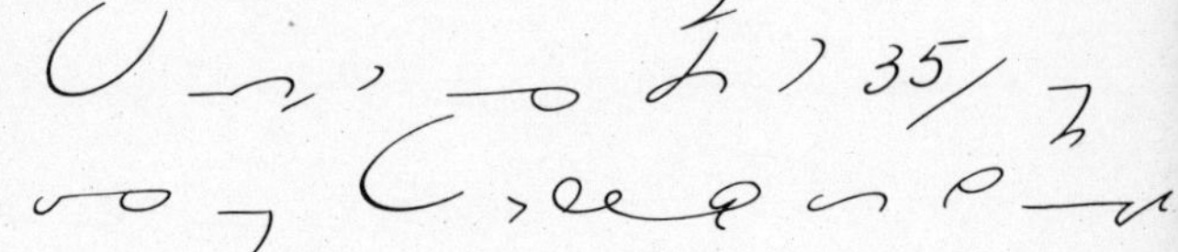

(50)

316. 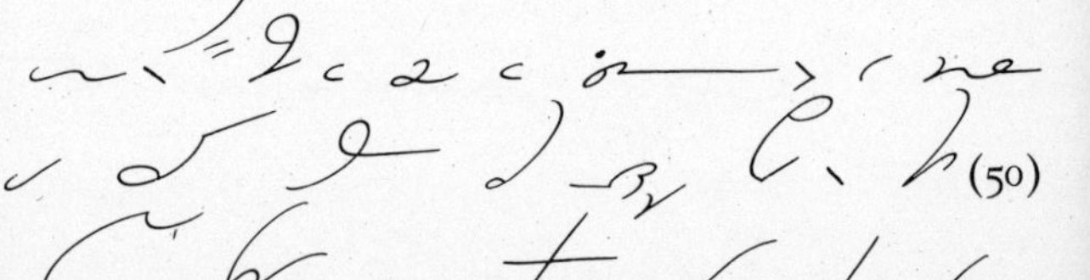

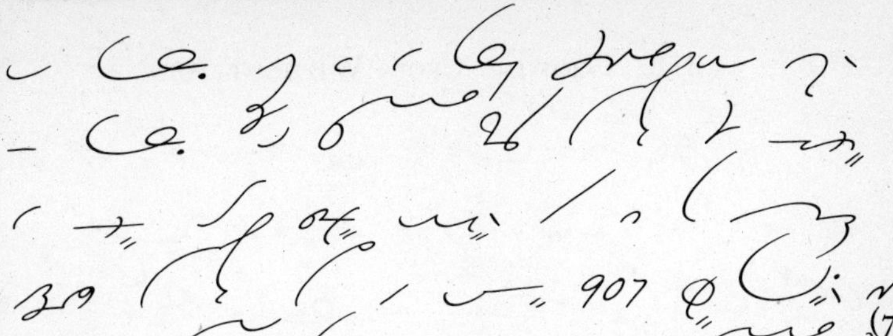

(76)

317.

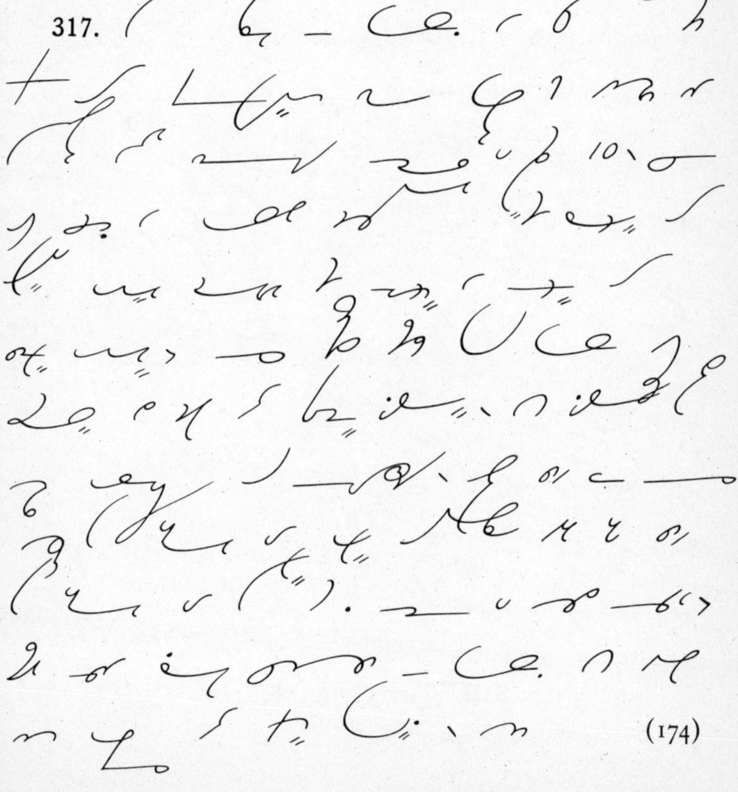

(174)

318. Growing Crops Without Soil

(142)

—*News Chronicle*

319. The Other Fellow

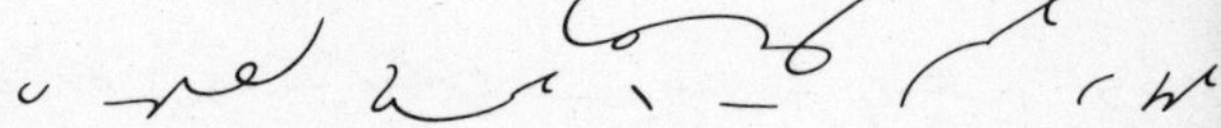

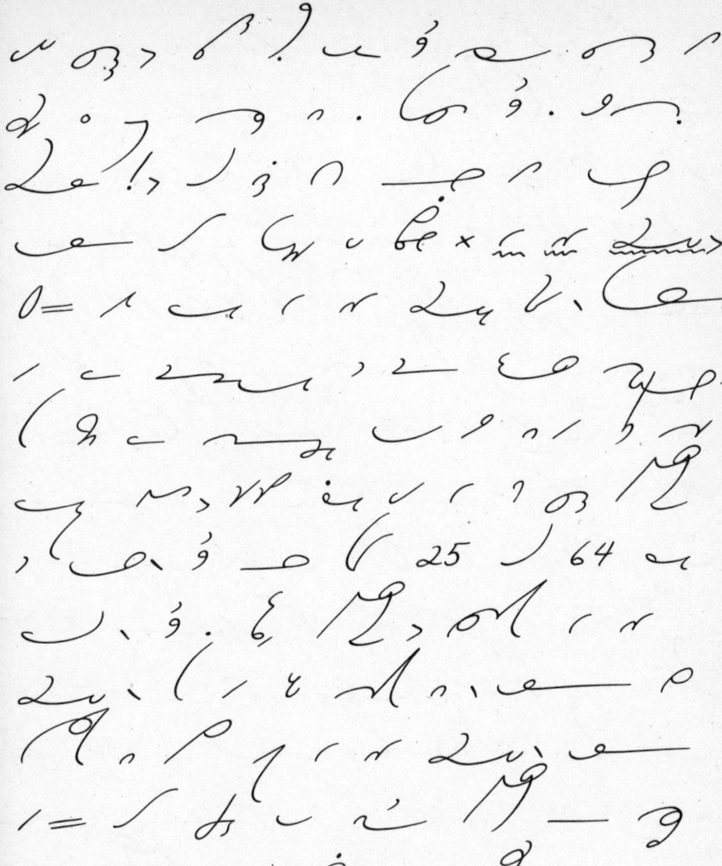
25
64
35
320

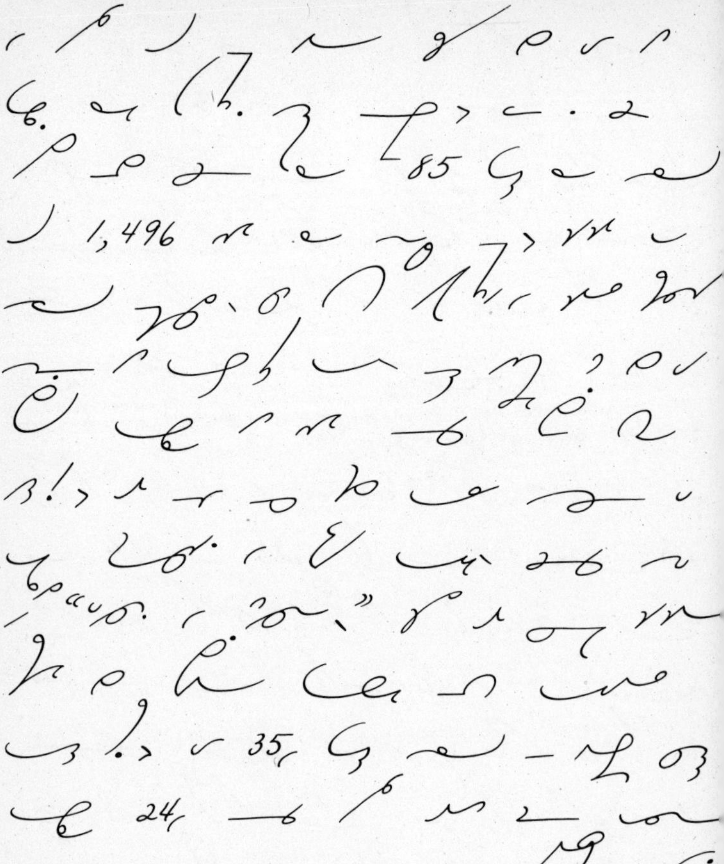
85
1,496
35
24
96

(497)

—*The Travelers Insurance Company*

SPEED STUDY XII

UNIT 34

320. Geographical Names. Shorthand outlines for many foreign countries and cities are given in the following three groups for quick reference. The student should not attempt to memorize all these outlines at one time but should learn them as he finds need for them.

Group *a.*

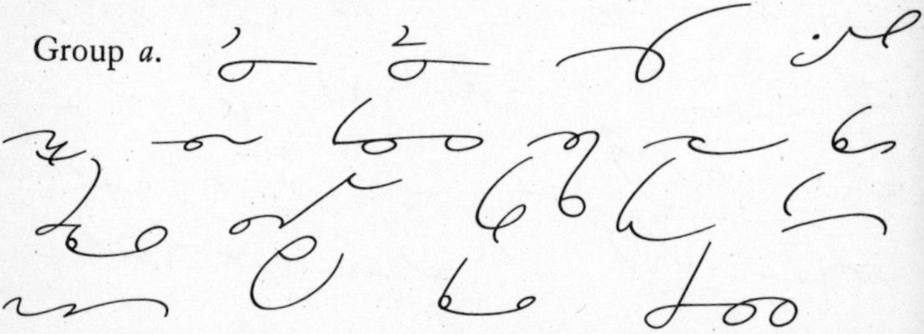

Key: South America, Central America, Guatemala, Honduras, Costa Rica, Nicaragua, Panama, Cuba, Colombia, Peru, Venezuela, Ecuador, Brazil, Bolivia, Paraguay, Uruguay, Argentina, Chile, Jamaica.

Group *b.*

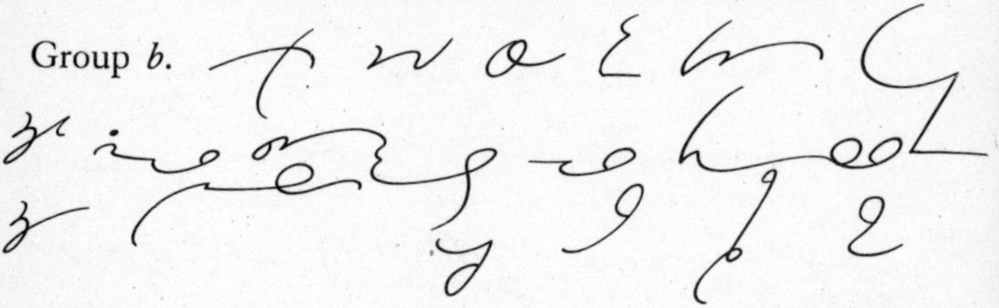

Key: Great Britain, Scotland, Ireland, Spain, Portugal, Belgium, Switzerland, Hungary, Yugoslavia, Norway, Bulgaria, Sweden, Denmark, Russia, India, Egypt, Africa.

Group *c.*

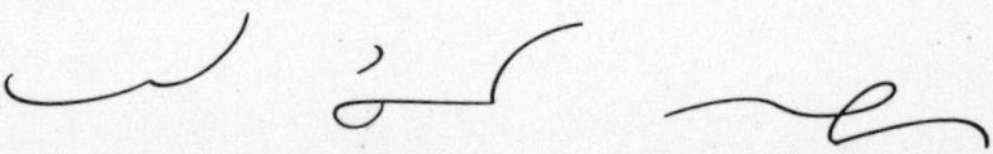

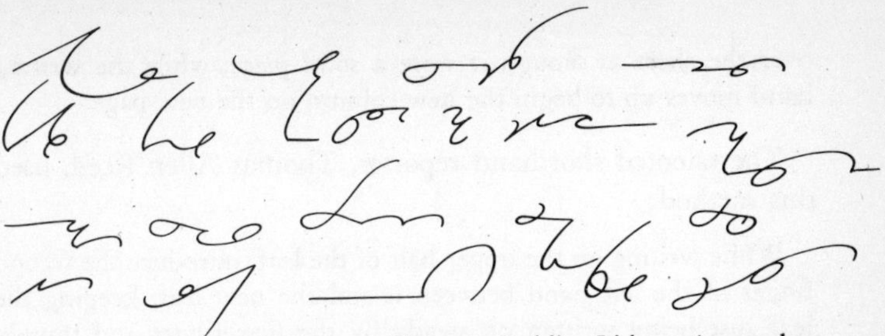

Key: London, Southampton, Glasgow, Dublin, Lisbon, Amsterdam, Munich, Budapest, Bucharest, Athens, Warsaw, Stockholm, Copenhagen, Moscow, Angora, Bangkok, Singapore, Shanghai, Tokyo, Rio de Janeiro, Montevideo, Buenos Aires, Santiago.

SPEED POINTER

Turning the Page. There are a number of satisfactory methods of turning the page, two of which are given here. Martin J. Dupraw, World's Champion Shorthand Writer, uses this method:

Consider the whole notebook as a solid block until you are ready to turn the page, and then consider the *page* as a solid block.

Push up the entire notebook as a block, as you write down the first column of the notebook. When you are ready to start on the second column, the left hand pulls the notebook down, while the right hand comes up until it is on the top line of the second column.

As the writing hand goes down the second column, the other hand pushes the entire notebook up. When the writing hand is within a few lines of the end of the second column, the other hand prepares for turning the page by turning up the corner of the page. As the writing hand starts on the last line of the second column, the other hand grasps the little corner that has been turned up. When the last outline on the page is written, the one hand turns over the sheet as though it were a solid piece, while the writing hand moves up to begin the new column on the new page.

The talented shorthand reporter, Thomas Allen Reed, used this method:

While writing on the upper half of the leaf, introduce the second finger of the left hand between it and the next leaf, keeping the leaf just being written on steady by the first finger and thumb. While writing on the last part of the page, shift the leaf by degrees until it is about halfway up the book; when it is convenient, lift the first finger and thumb, and the leaf will turn by itself.

Mr. Reed apparently used a one-column notebook. The writer who prefers a two-column notebook may also use this method by applying Mr. Reed's suggestions as he is coming down the second column.

READING AND DICTATION PRACTICE

321. State Names

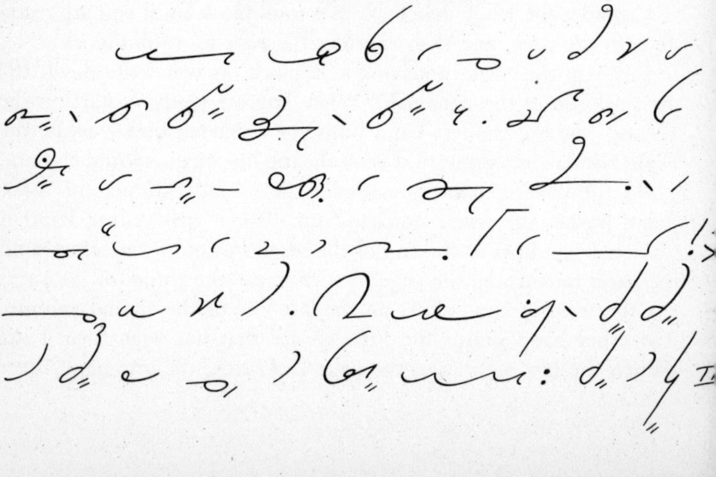

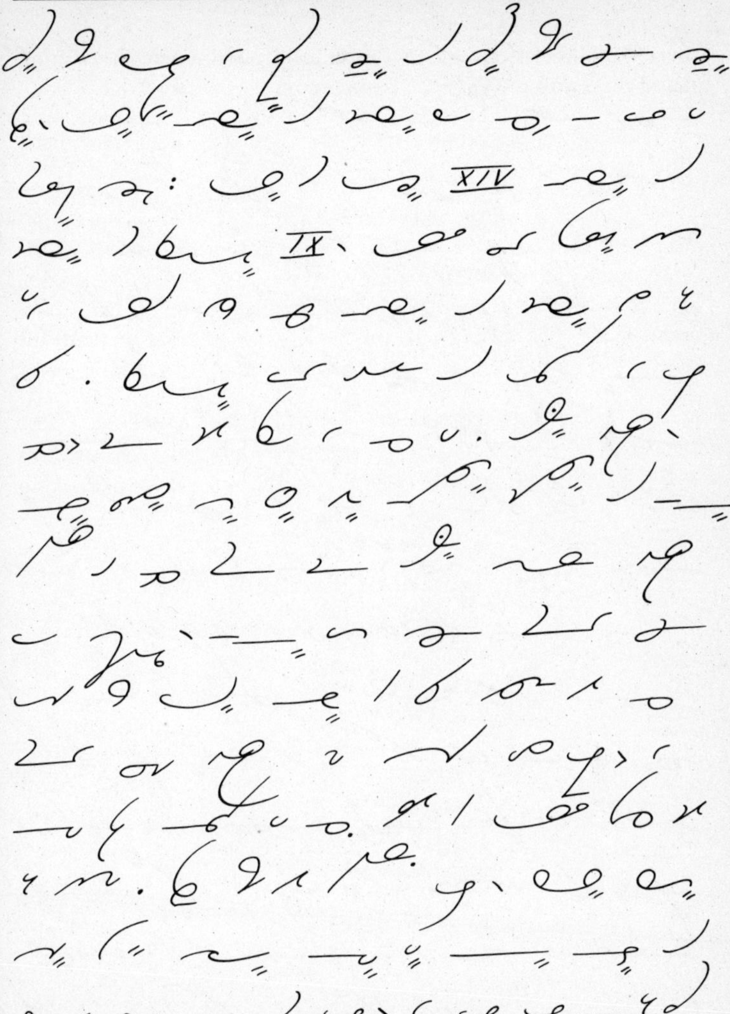
XIV
IX

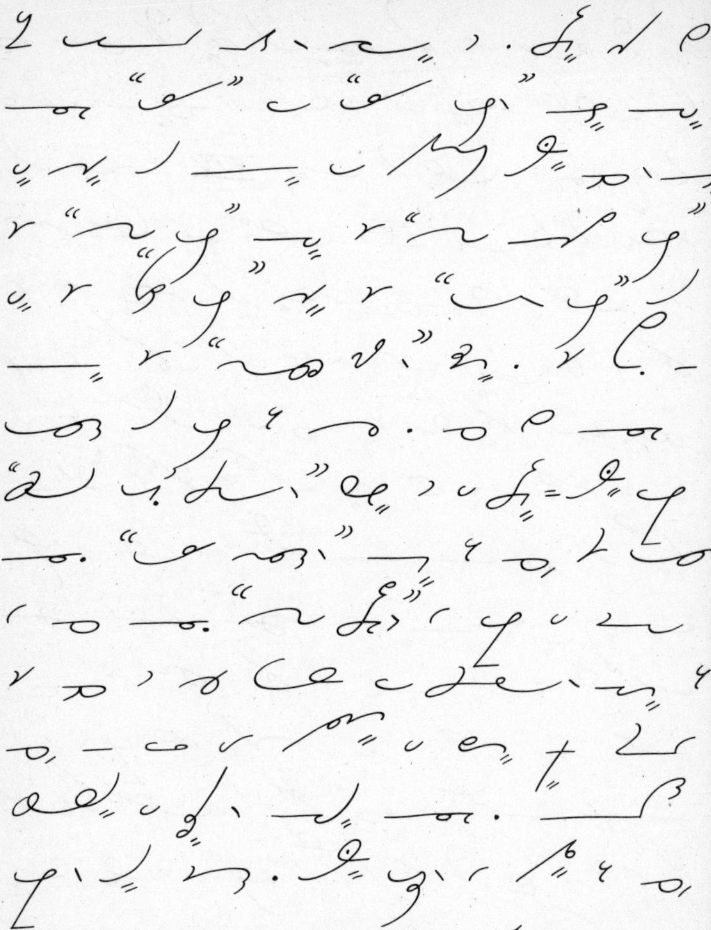

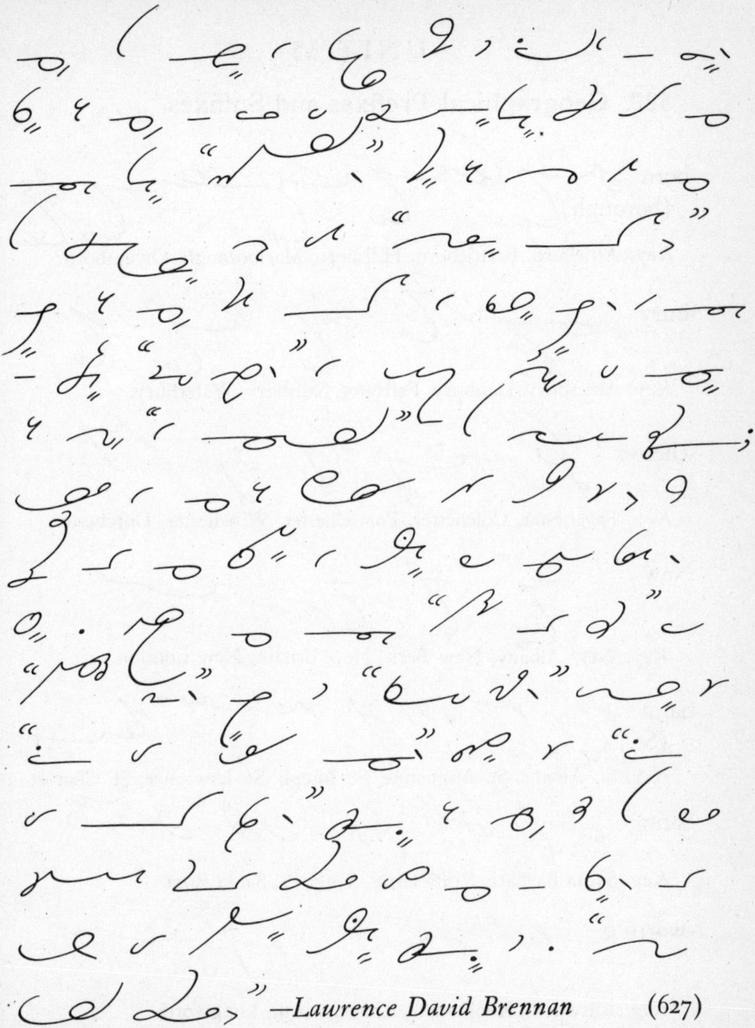

—*Lawrence David Brennan* (627)

UNIT 35

322. Geographical Prefixes and Suffixes

-boro
(borough)

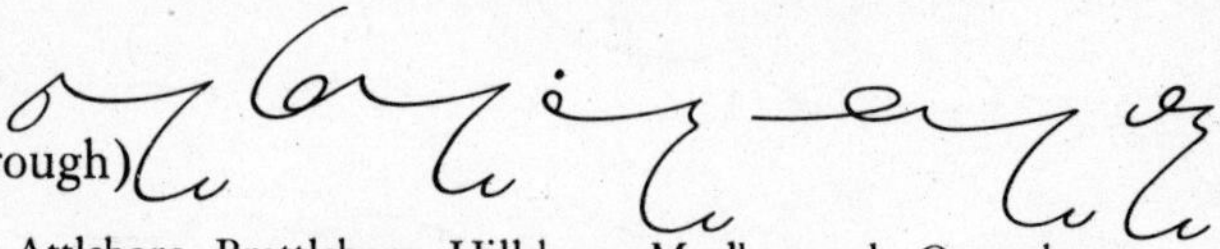

Key: Attleboro, Brattleboro, Hillsboro, Marlborough, Owensboro.

-bury

Key: Amesbury, Danbury, Fairbury, Salisbury, Waterbury.

-chester

Key: Baychester, Colchester, Port Chester, Winchester, Dorchester.

New

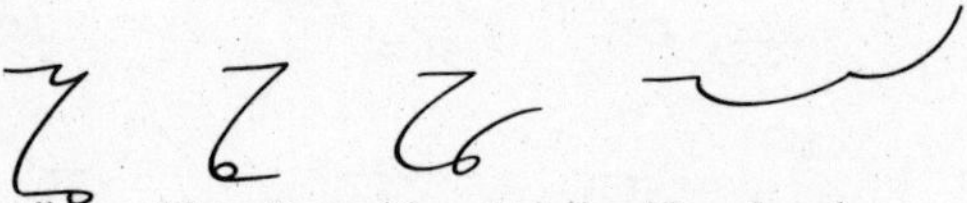

Key: New Albany, New Bern, New Britain, New London.

Saint
(St.)

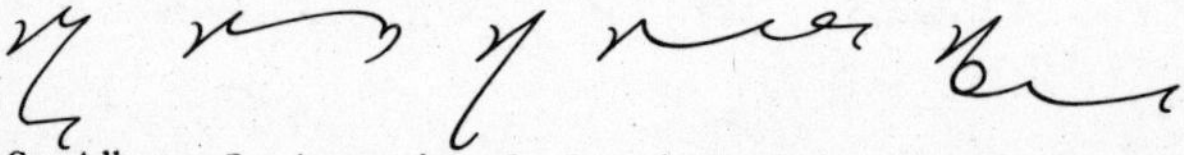

Key: St. Albans, St. Augustine, St. Joseph, St. Lawrence, St. Charles.

Santa

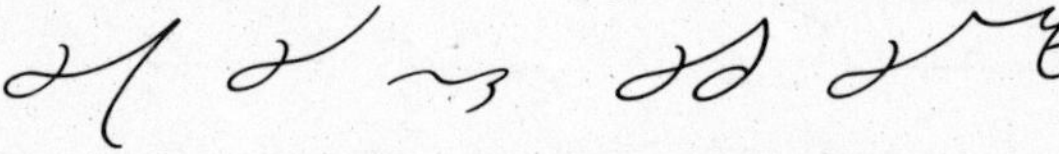

Key: Santa Barbara, Santa Cruz, Santa Fe, Santa Rosa.

-worth

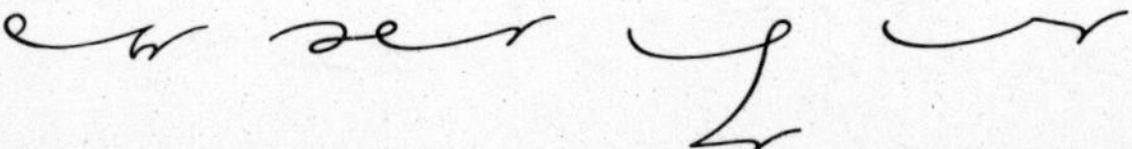

Key: Ellsworth, Kenilworth, Leavenworth, Longworth.

READING AND DICTATION PRACTICE

323.

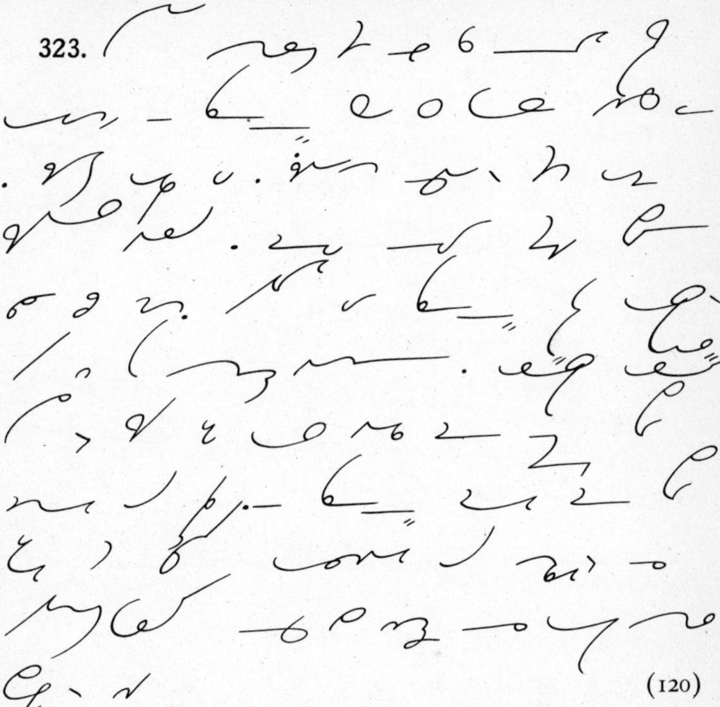

(120)

324.

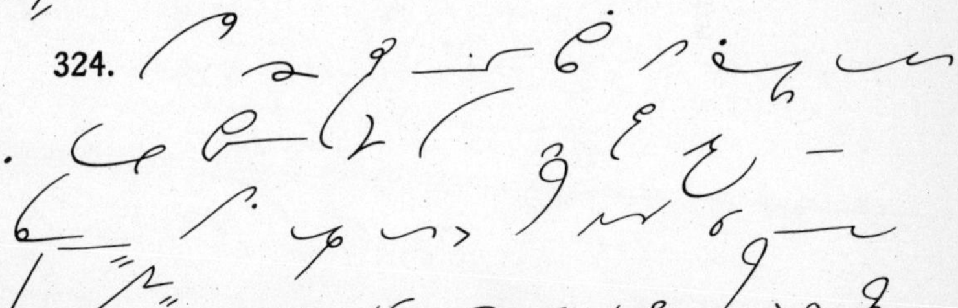

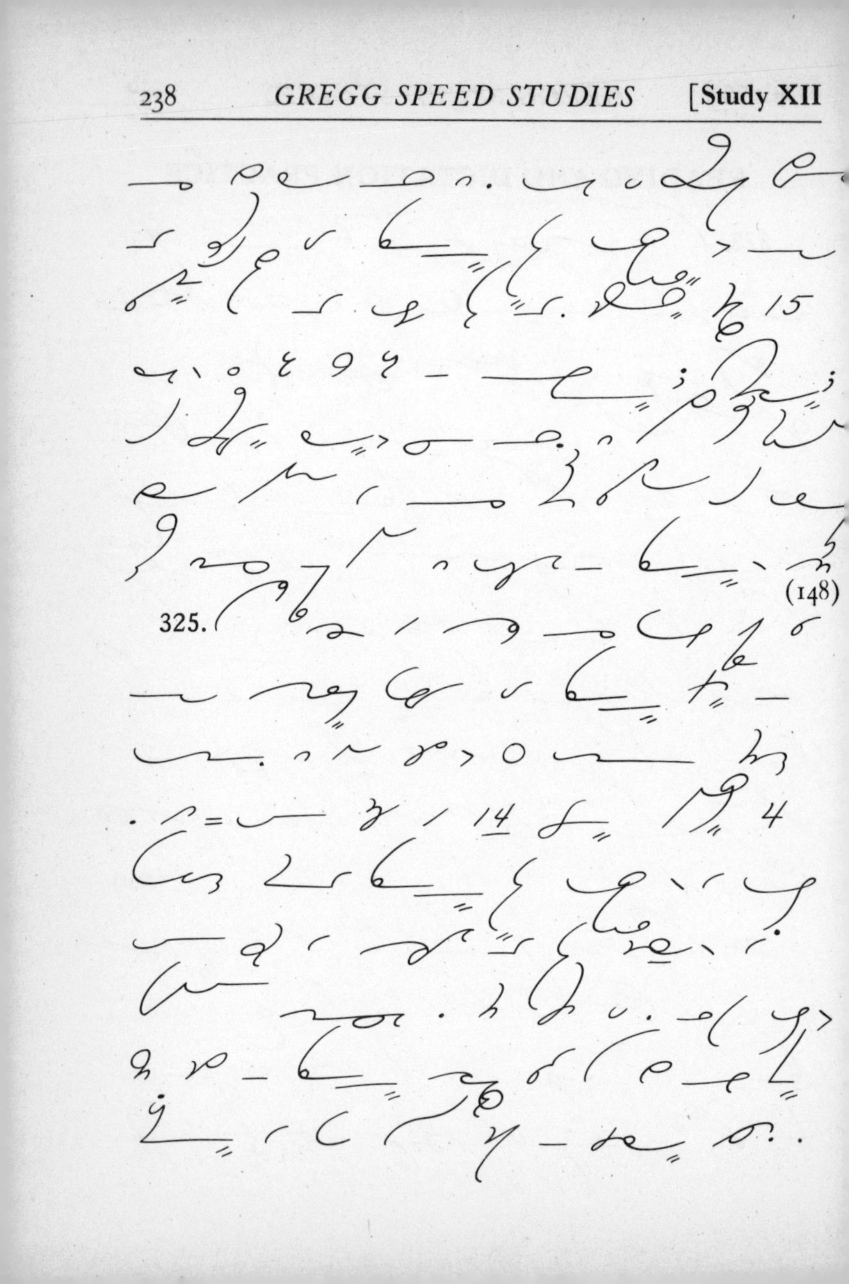

15

(148)

325.

14 4

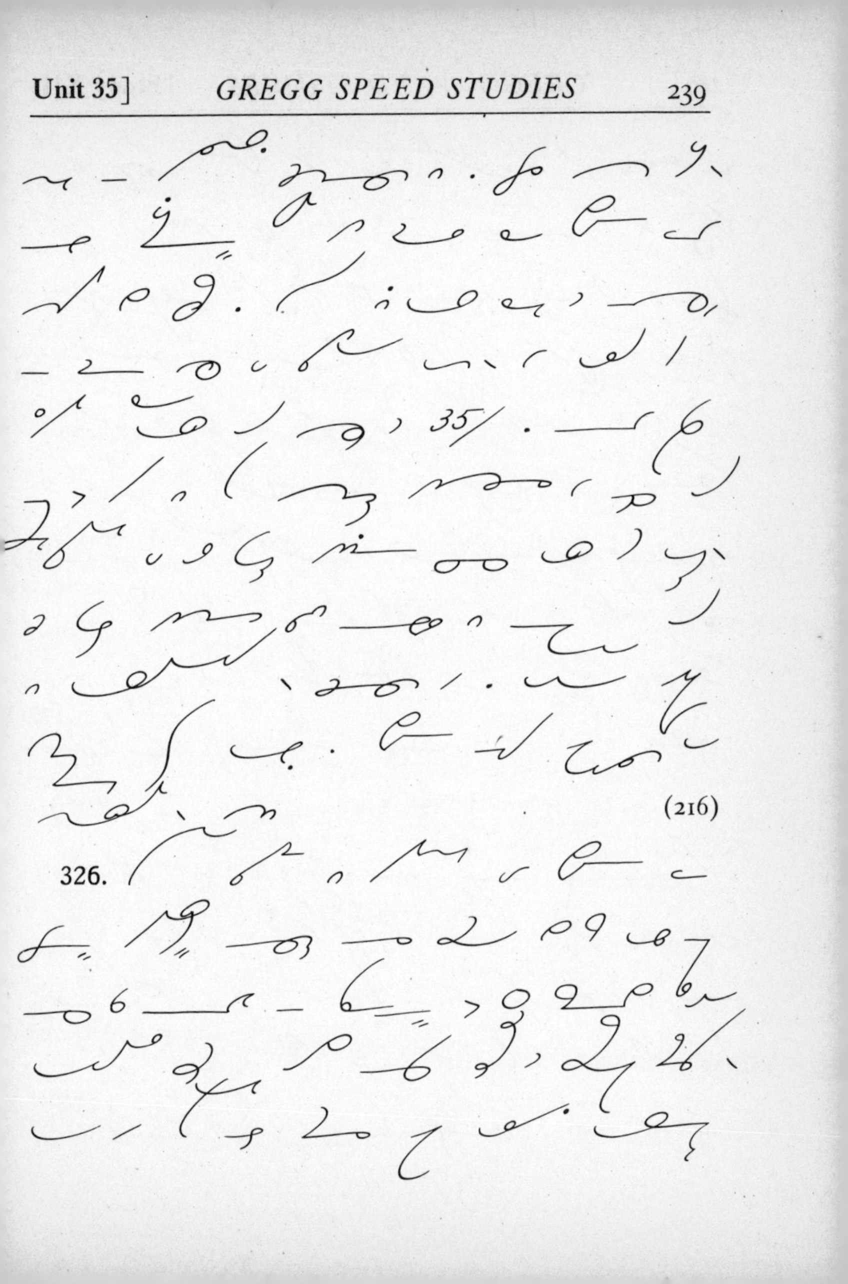

(216)

326.

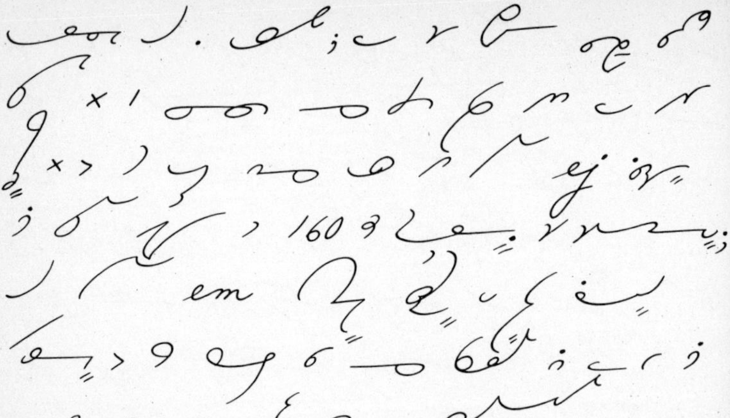

(171)

327.

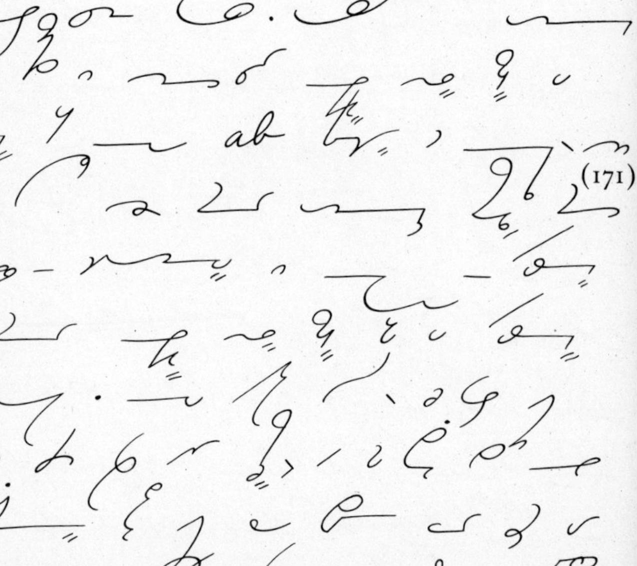

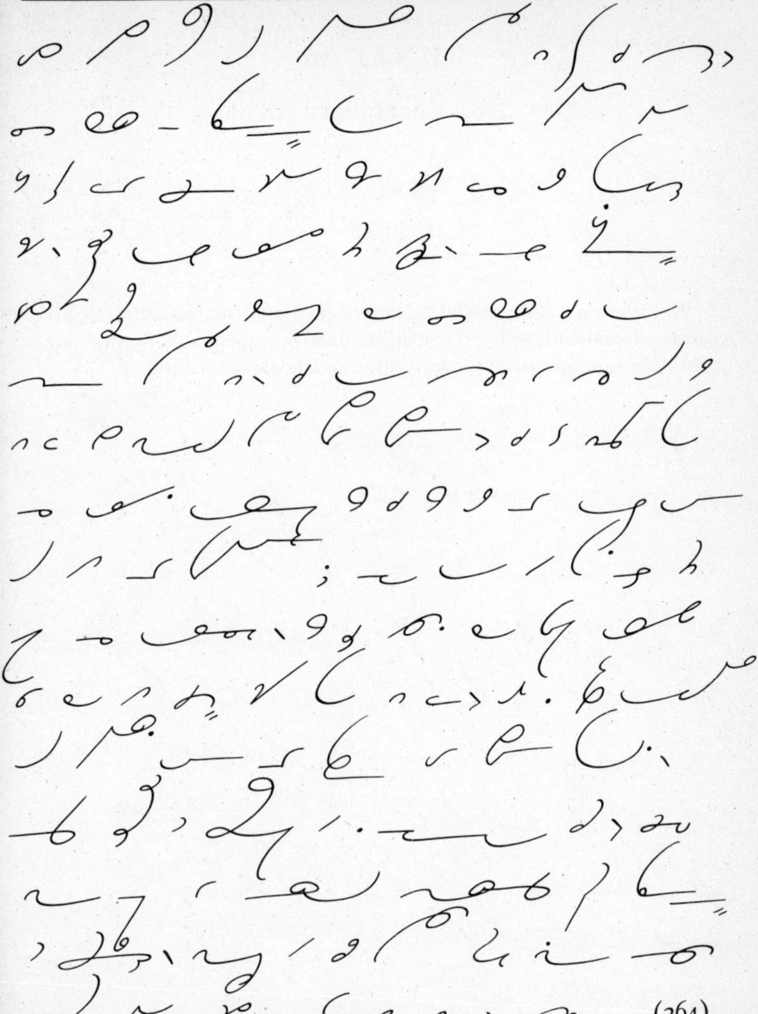

(264)

UNIT 36

328. Vocabulary Drill

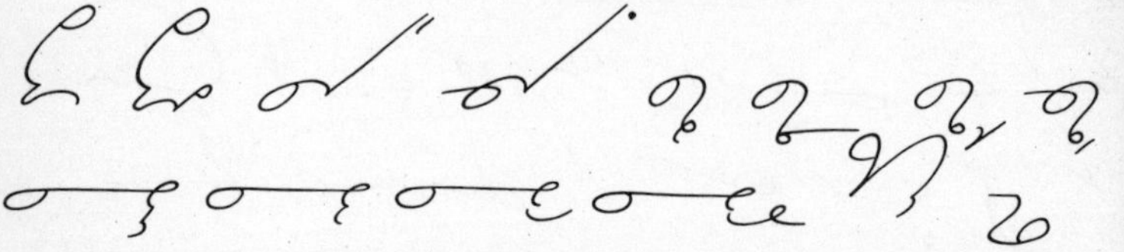

Key: abstract, abstractedly, accommodated, unaccommodating, accompanies, accompaniment, accompanist, unaccompanied, administrations, administers, administrator, administratrix, affidavits, unafraid.

329.

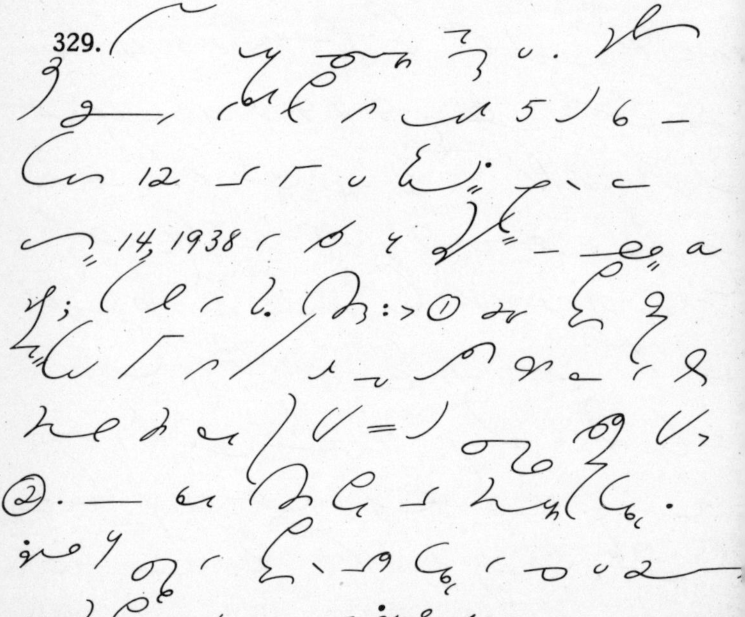

(306)

330. Vocabulary Drill

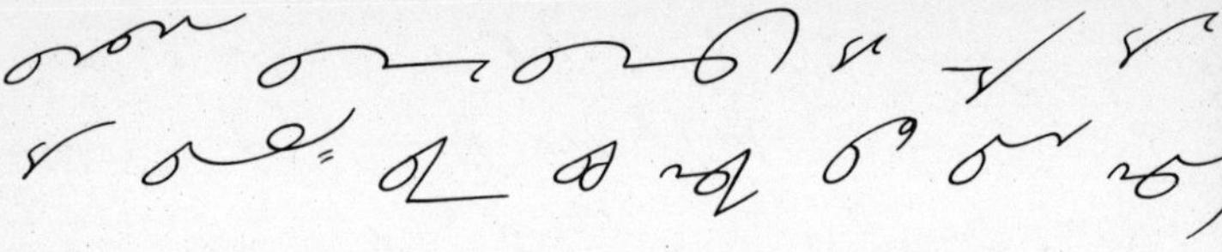

Key: Americans, un-American, application, applications, disapproval, architects, architecture, arguments, argumentative, assists, unassisted, assistance, assistant, Atlantic, attachment, attaché, unattached, attorneys, attracted, unattractive.

331.

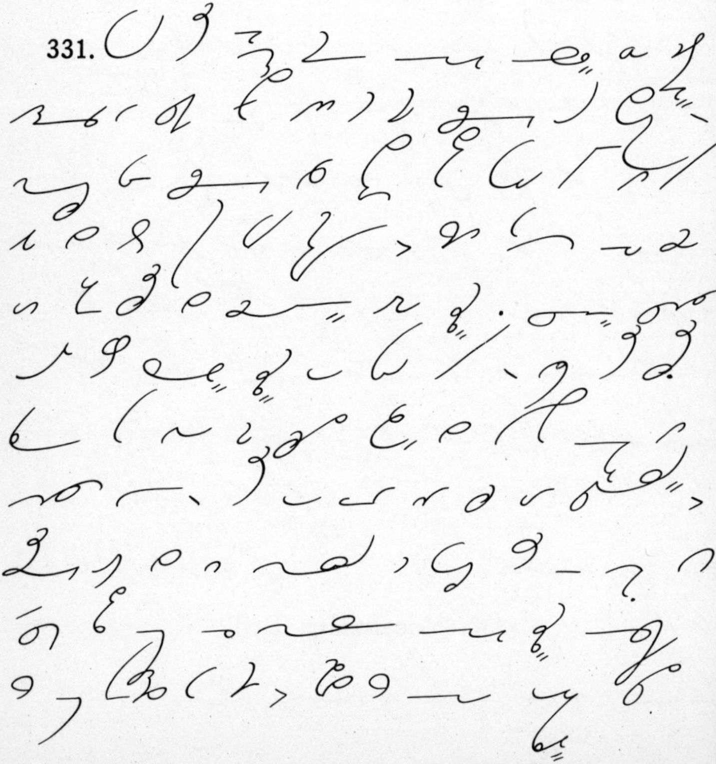

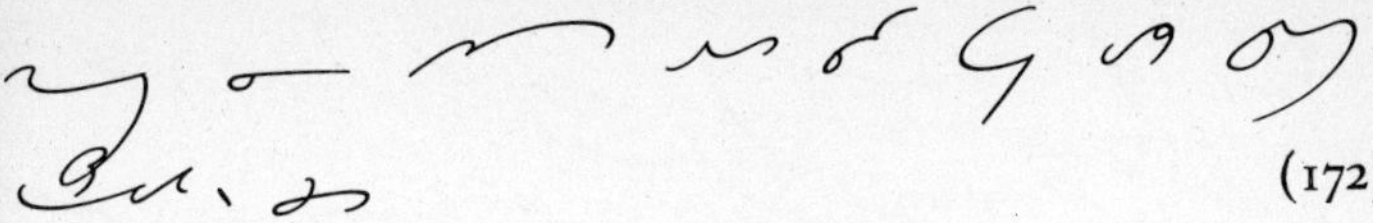

(172)

332. Vocabulary Drill

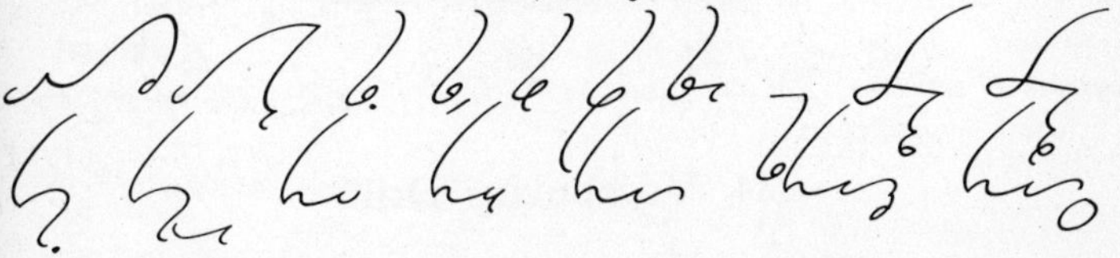

Key: authoritatively, automobiles, avoiding, avoided, avoids, avoidable, avoidance, unavoidable, bankruptcy, bankruptcies, bookkeeping, bookkeepers, bureau, bureaus, bureaucrat, bureaucracy, bureaucratic.

333. 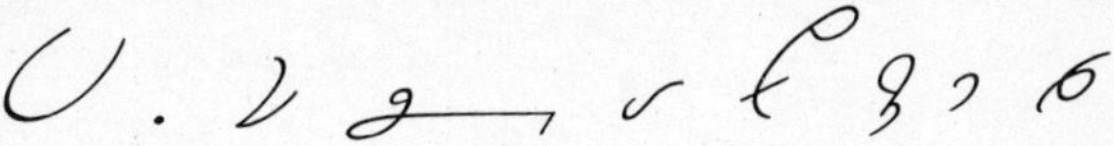

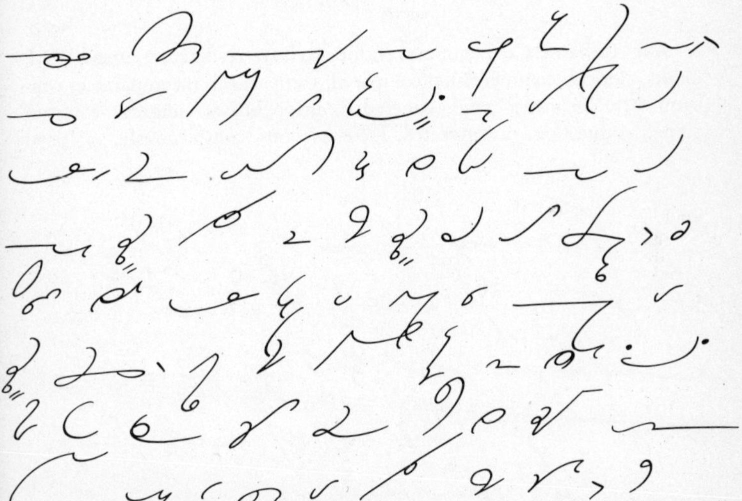

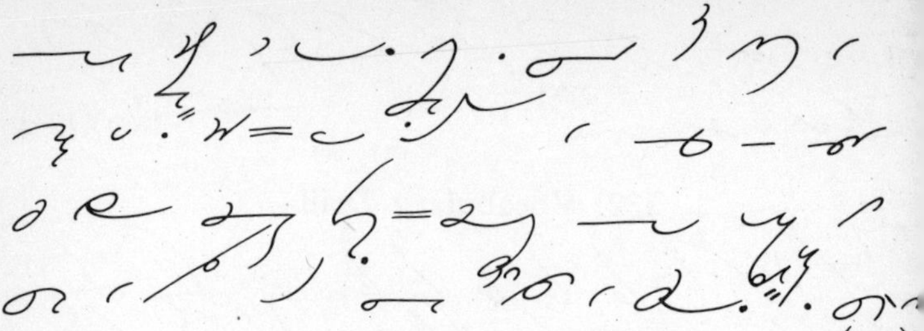

(171)

334. Vocabulary Drill

Key: Christmas, citizens, citizenship, civilian, civilization, uncivilized, clerks, clerical, commercially, compared, comparison, incomparable, consequently, inconsequential, concluded, inconclusive, congress, congressional, connection, disconnected, inconspicuous, conspicuously.

335.

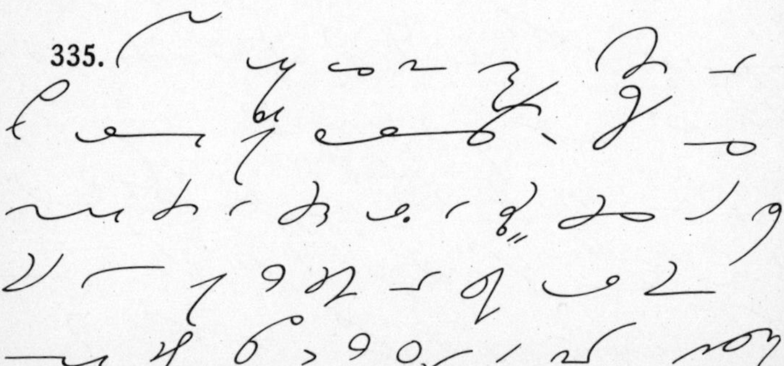

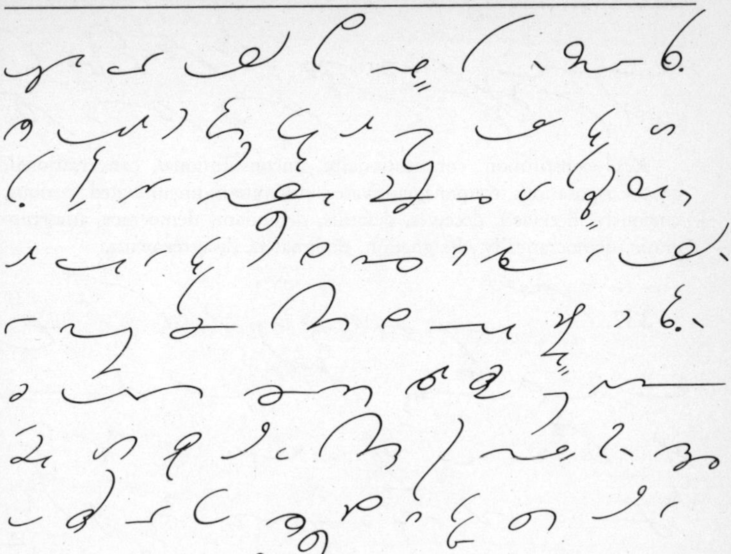

(249)

336. Vocabulary Drill

Key: constitution, constitutionally, unconstitutional, conversational, crops-corporations, coupons, cultivates, cultivation, uncultivated, curious, curiously, deceived, deceives, defaults, defendant, democracy, undemocratic, democratically, designation, designated, disagreements.

337.

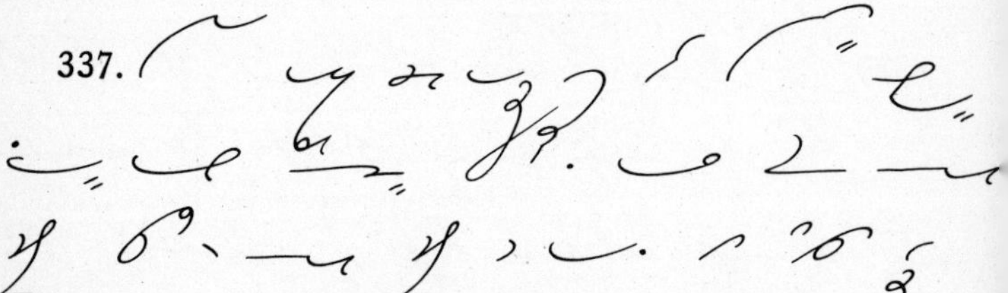

(116)

338. Vocabulary Drill

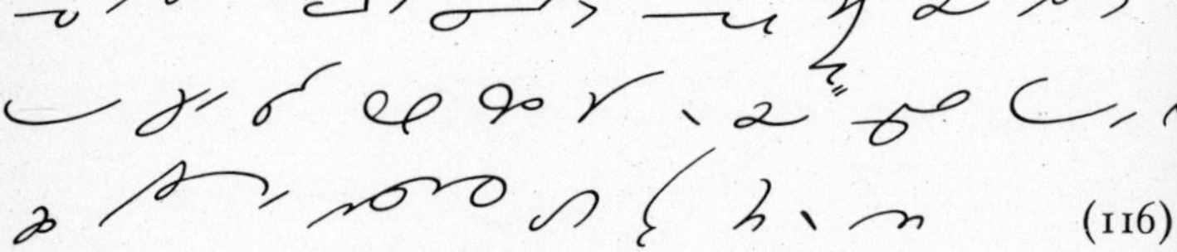

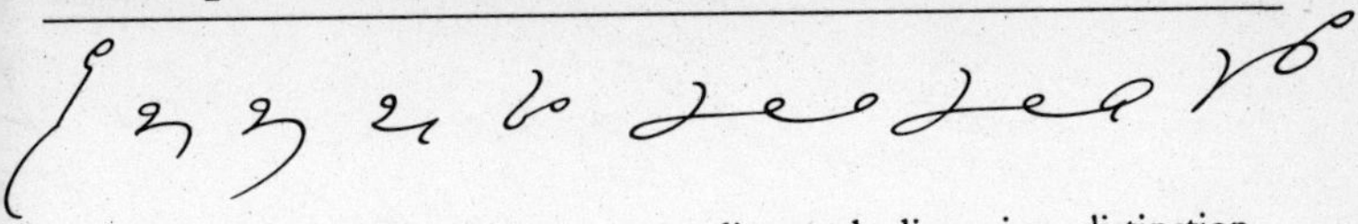

Key: disappointed, disappointment, discussed, discussion, distinction, distinguishable, indistinct, disturbance, doctrines, emphasized, energies, energize, Englishman, entitled, estates, exchanged, exchangeable, execution, executive, exercises, faulty, familiarly, familiarize, fortunately.

339.

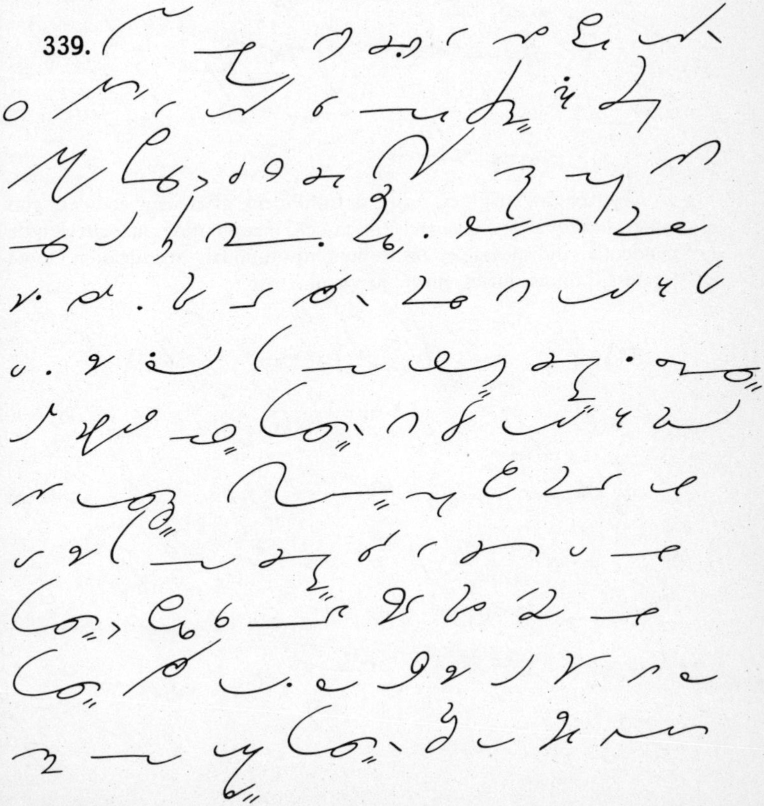

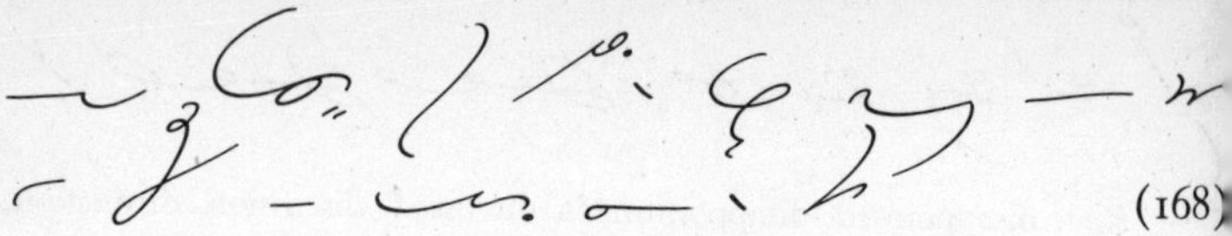

(168)

340. Vocabulary Drill

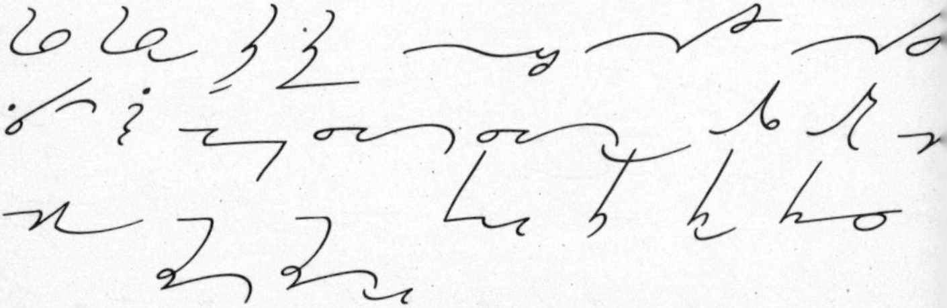

Key: freight, freighter, fulfilled, fulfillment, gloriously, godsend, godfather, headquarters, husbands, inasmuch, inauguration, inaugural, independently, indispensable, institution, institutional, investigation, investigators, juniors, juries, juror, juryman.

341.

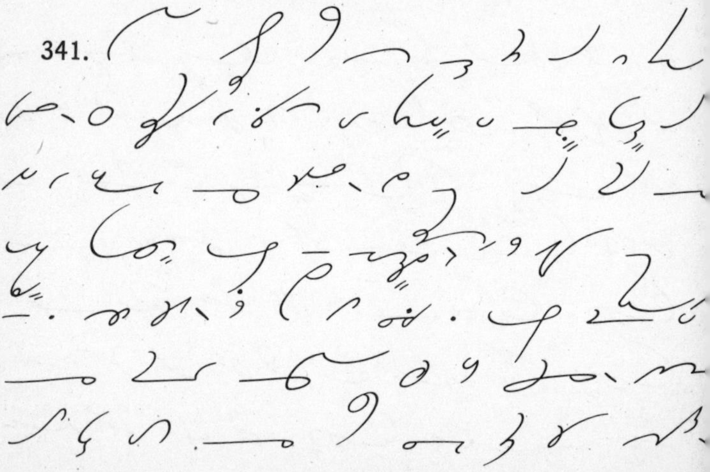

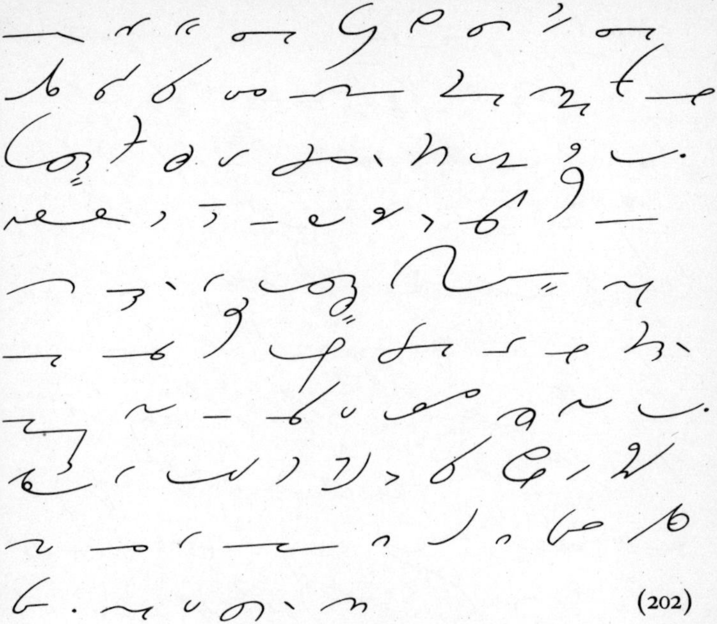

(202)

342. Vocabulary Drill

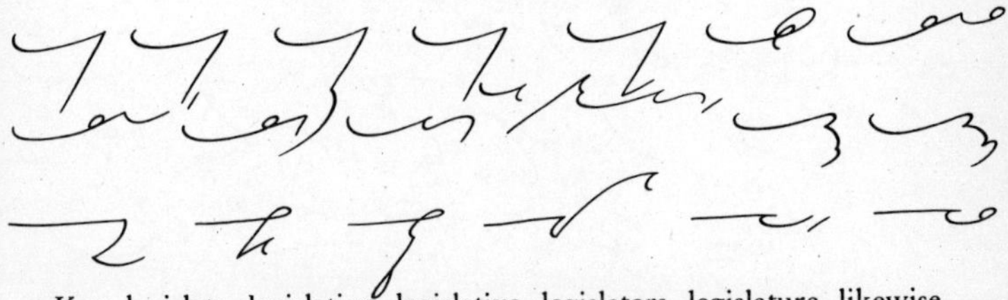

Key: legislate, legislation, legislative, legislators, legislature, likewise, literary, literature, litigation, location, dislocated, luxuries, luxurious, manufacturer, merchants, messengers, misdemeanors, mortgaged, mortgagee.

343.

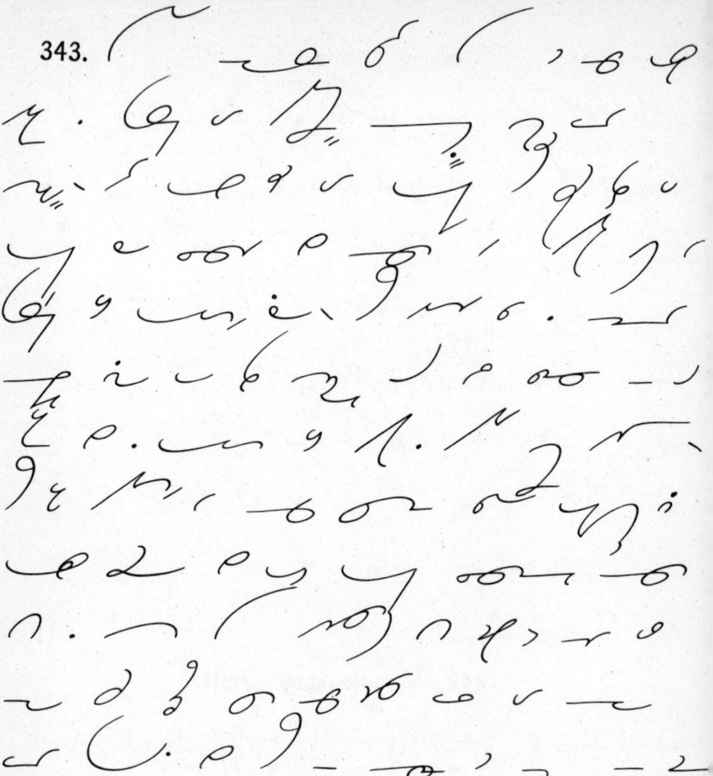

(187)

344. Vocabulary Drill

Key: neglected, negligence, negligent, negotiated, negotiable, novelty, novelties, observer, observance, observation, obstruction, obstructing, unobstructed, obviously, occupancy, occupant, unoccupied, preoccupied, Pacific, parcels, partiality, impartial.

345.

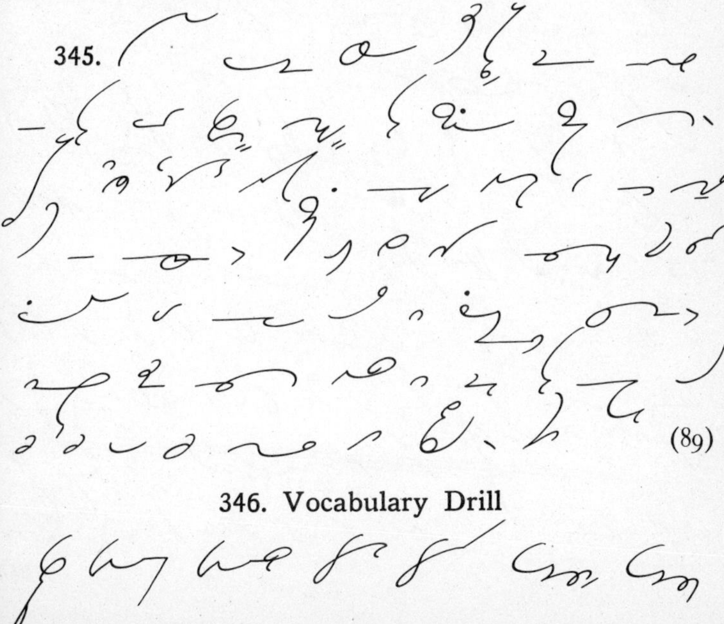

(89)

346. Vocabulary Drill

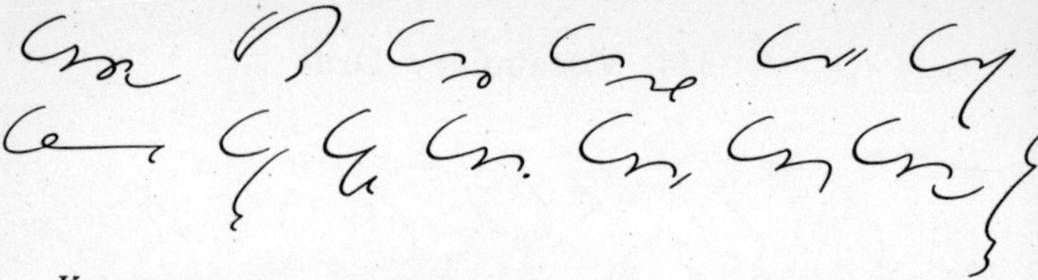

Key: passengers, patronage, patronize, patterns, patterned, persecuted, persecution, persecutor, plaintiffs, practically, practicalness, practiced, practicable, premiums, probabilities, properties, prosecuting, prosecuted, prosecution, prosecutor, publications.

347.

(139)

348. Vocabulary Drill

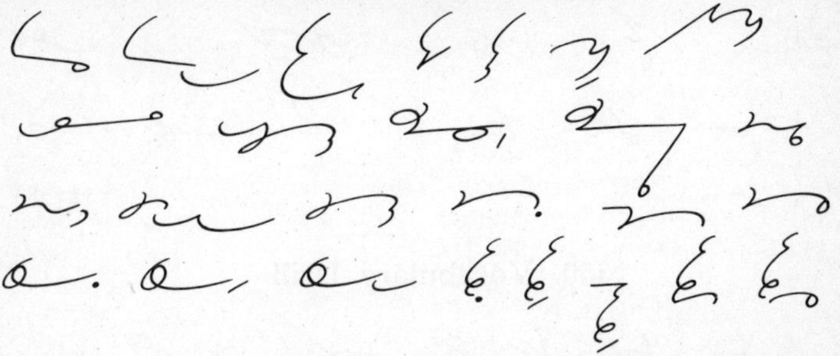

Key: punctually, punctuality, pupils, pushed, pushes, qualified, disqualify, remainder, resignations, salesmanship, sales manager, scarcely, scarcity, secretarial, signatures, signifying, insignificant, significantly, silencing, silenced, silencer, specifying, specified, unspecified, specific, specifically.

349.

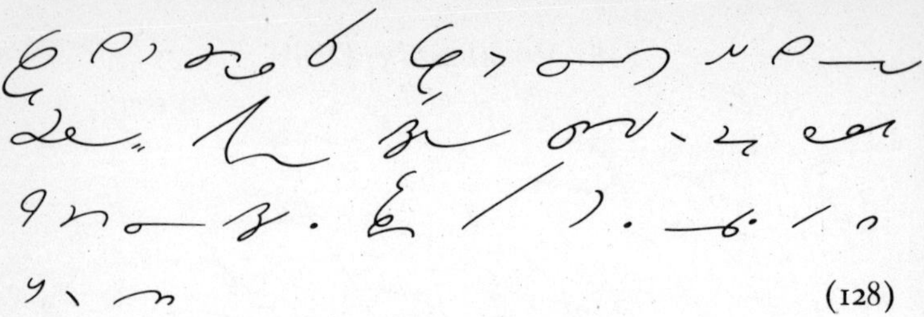

(128)

350. Vocabulary Drill

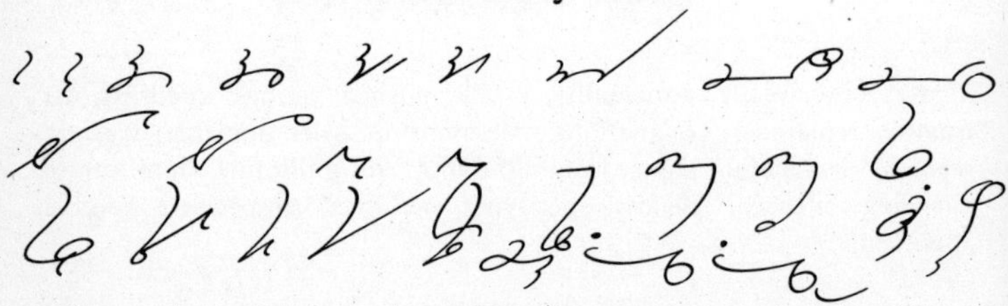

Key: society, societies, subsequent, subsequently, substituted, substitution, succeeded, sympathize, sympathetic, testimonials, testimony, texts, textbook, unavoidably, universal, universally, variety, varieties, verdicts, votes, voted, voter, warehouses, wholesale, wholesaler, housewife, wives.

351.

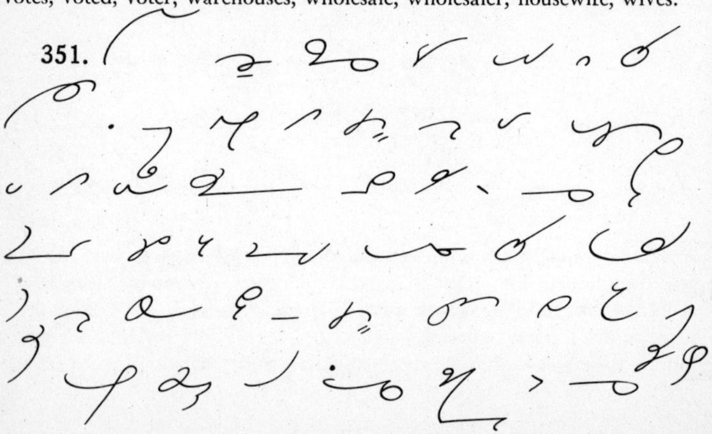

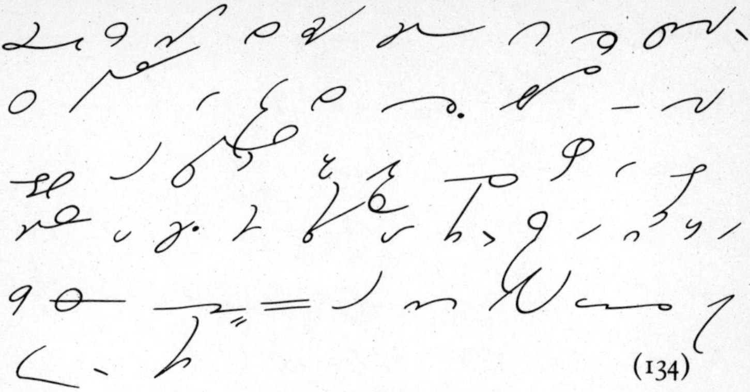

(134)

352. Vocabulary Drill

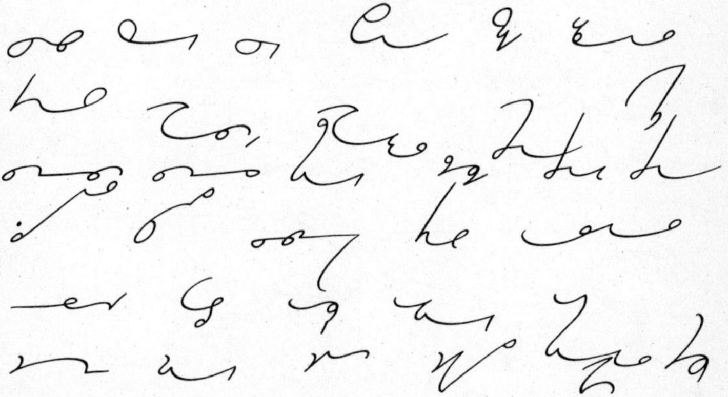

Key: accurately, allusion, anguish, apparel, associate, auxiliary, chocolate, complicated, compulsory, congenial, dangerous, economic, economy, evolution, exquisite, generous, genial, hereditary, identity, innumerable, jurisdiction, literally, mercantile, precisely, requisition, resolution, revolutionary, signal, solution, struck, stupidity, topic, vocation.

353.

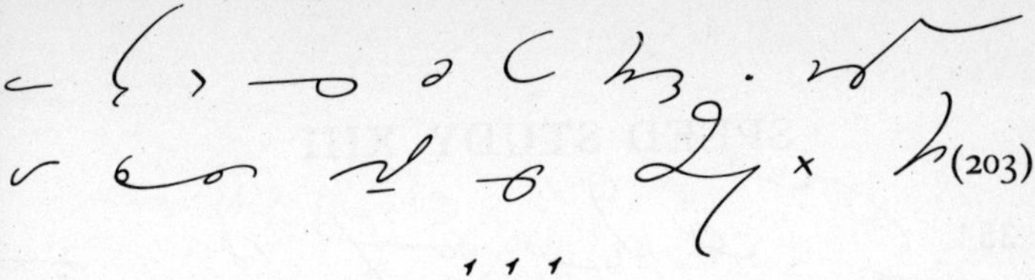

(203)

(93)

SPEED STUDY XIII

354.

(78)

355.

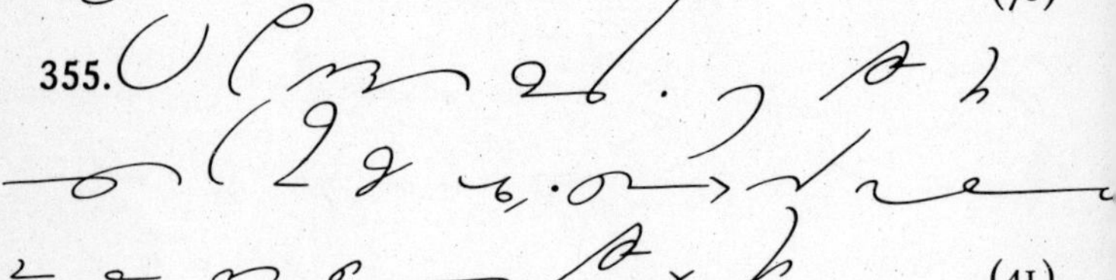

(41)

356.

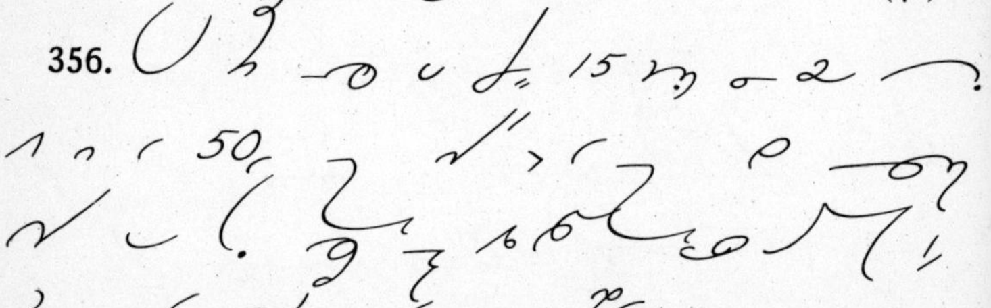

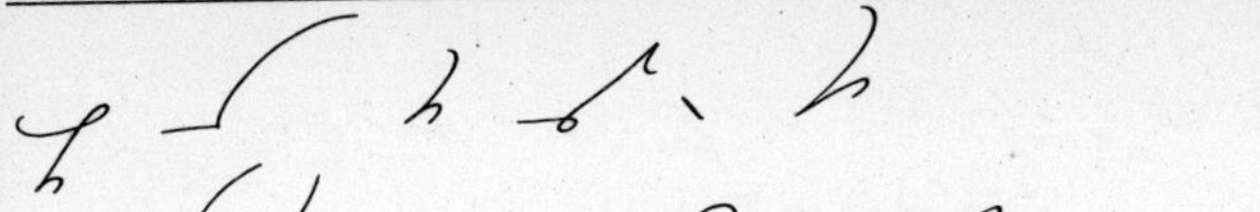

(67)

357.

(170)

358.

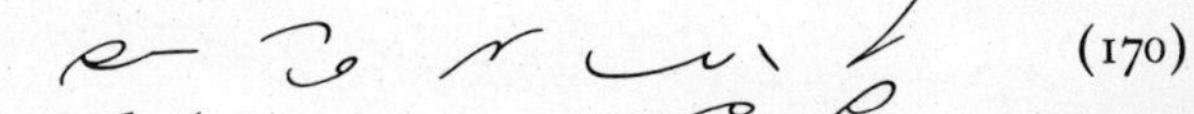

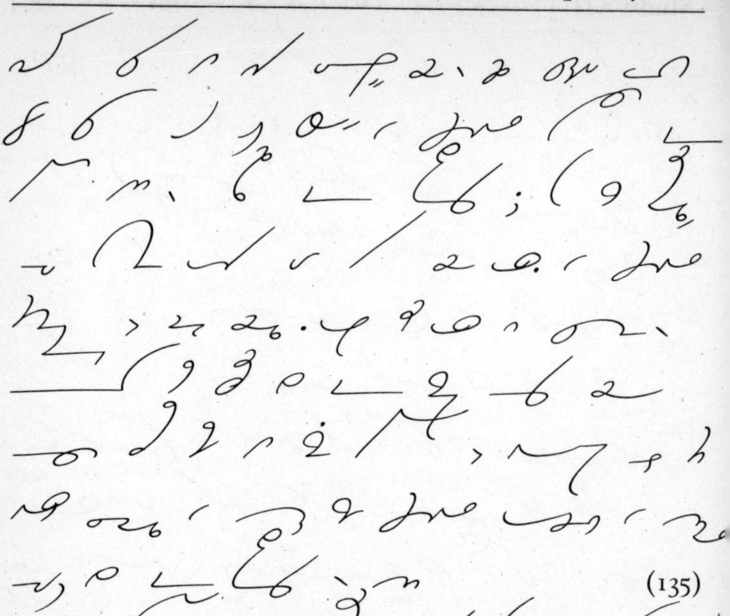

(135)

359.

(176)

360.

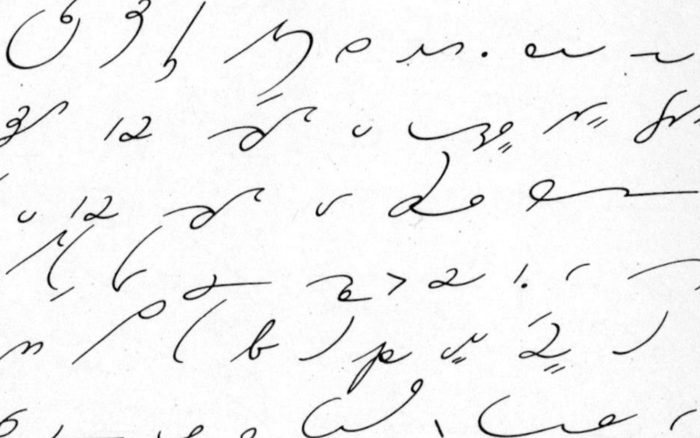

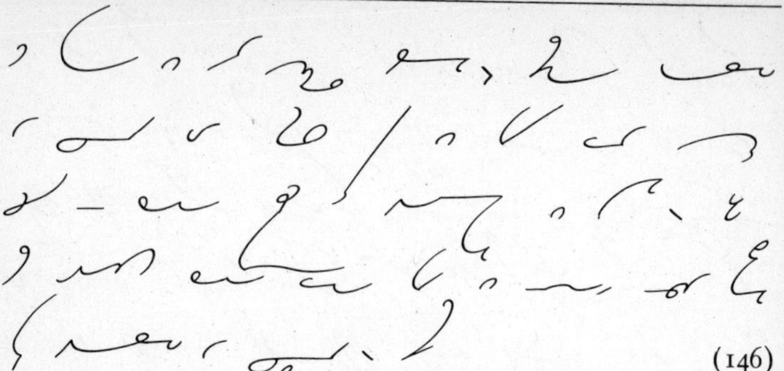

(146)

361.

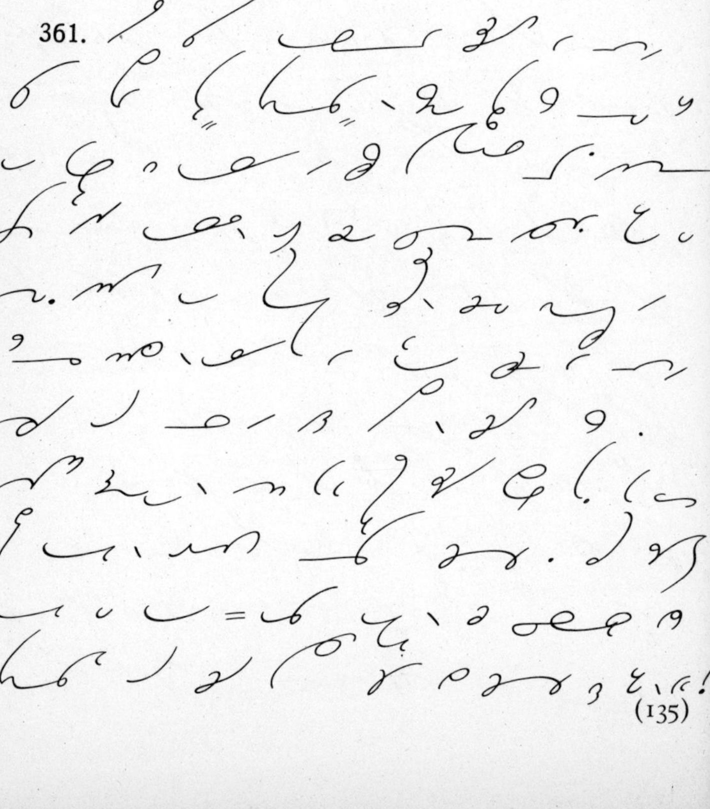

(135)

362. [shorthand outlines]

[shorthand outlines] 450/;

[shorthand outlines] 275⁸⁶

[shorthand outlines] 15.

[shorthand outlines]

60 [shorthand outlines]

[shorthand outlines] 60=

[shorthand outlines]

[shorthand outlines]

[shorthand outlines]

[shorthand outlines]

(207)

363. [shorthand outlines]

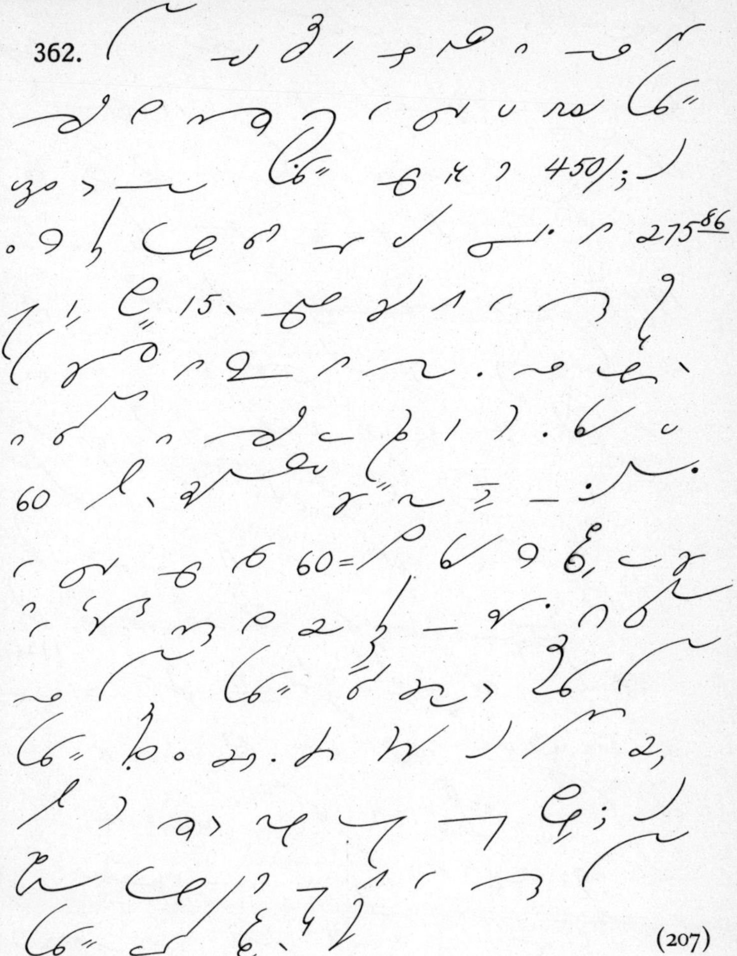

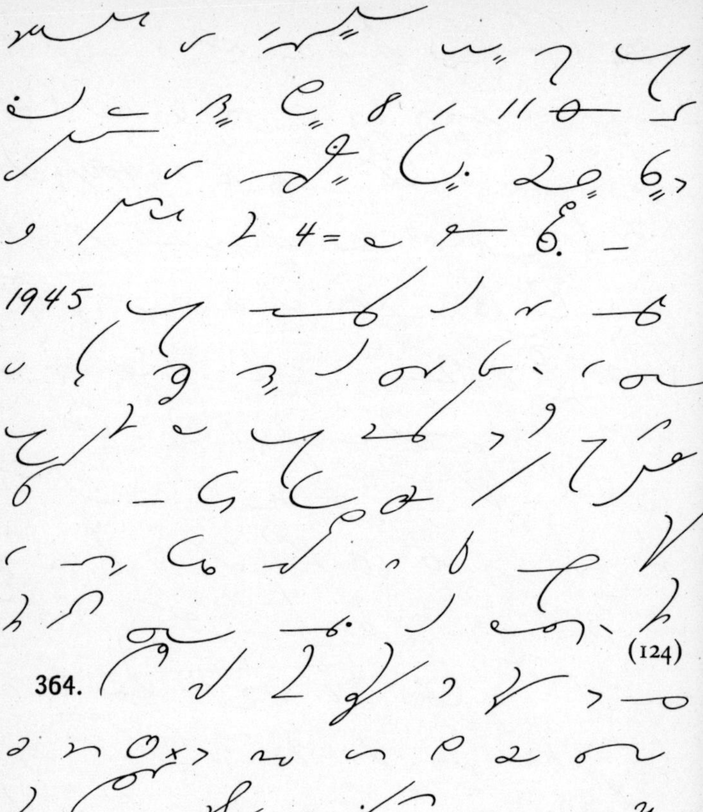

(124)

364.

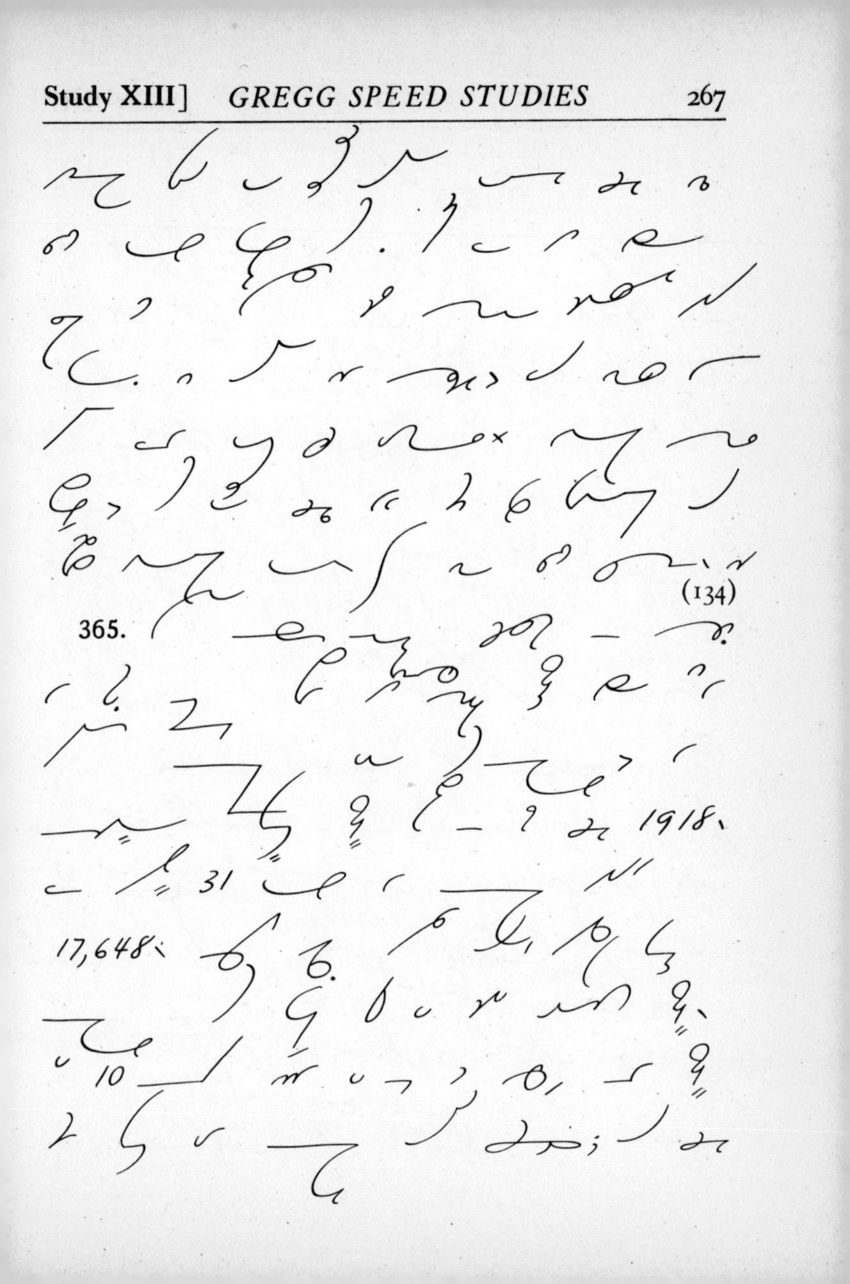

(134)

365.

1918.

31

17,648.

10

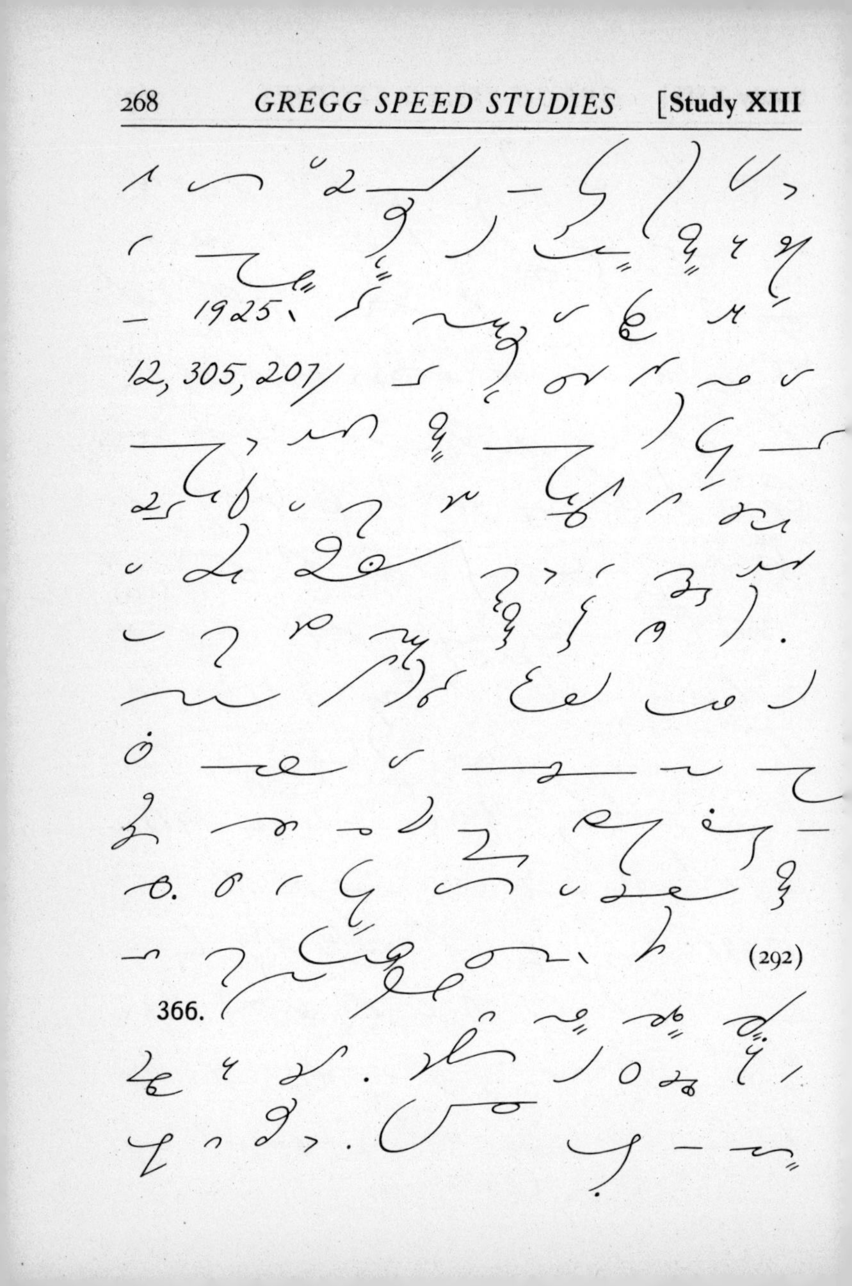

1925

12,305,207

(292)

366.

(164)

367.

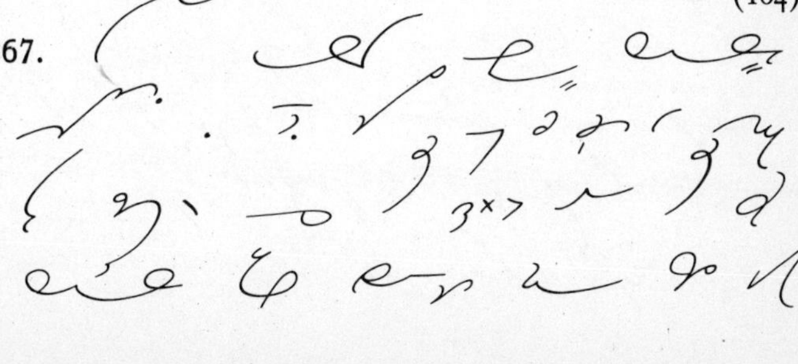

(225)

368.  (159)

369. 

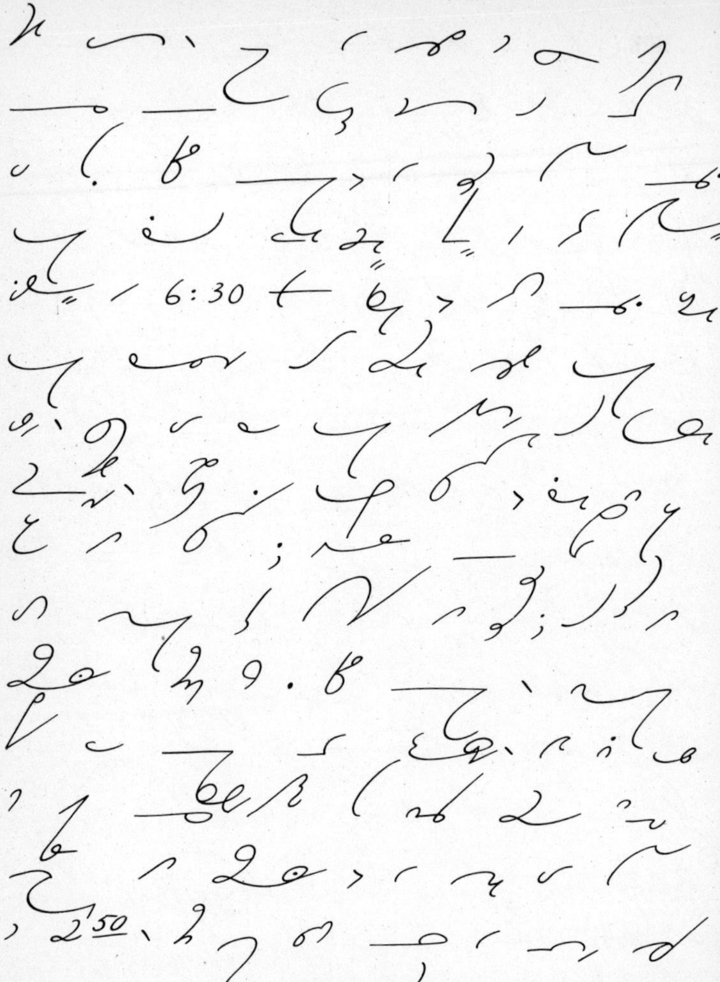

(191)

370.

(97)

371.

(276)

372.

(119)

373.

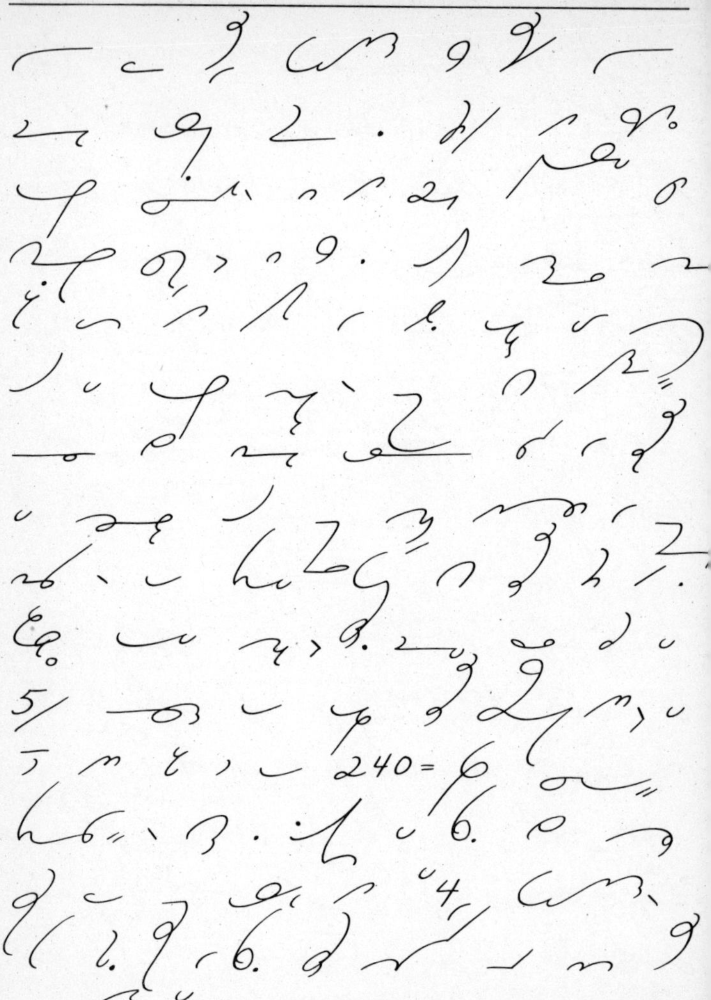

(313)

374.

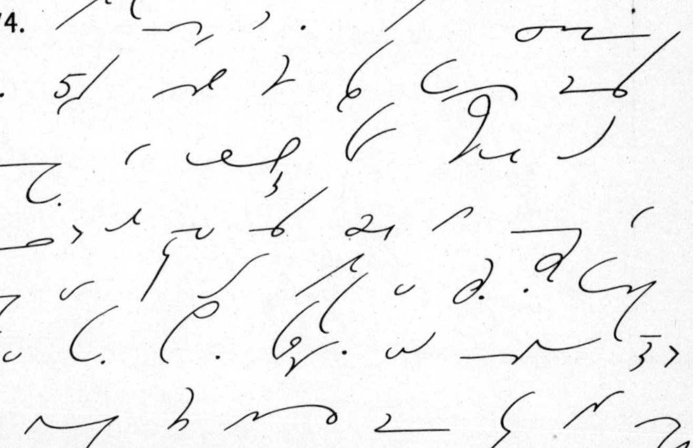

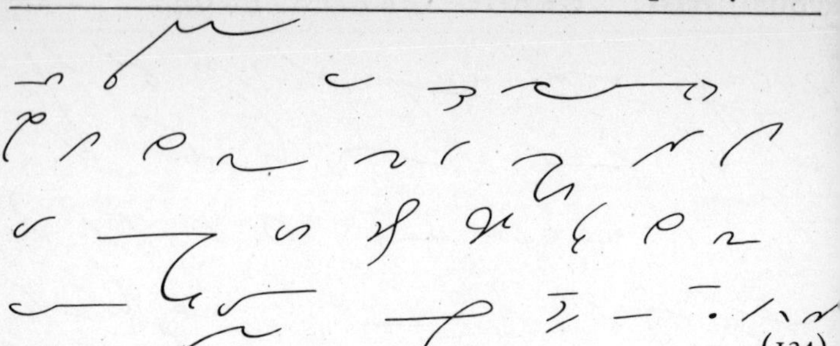

(134)

375.

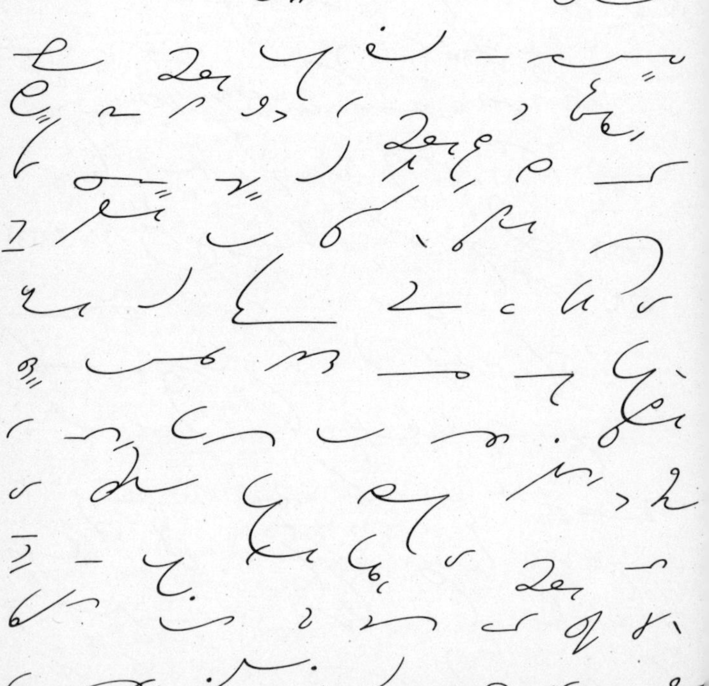

(188)

376.

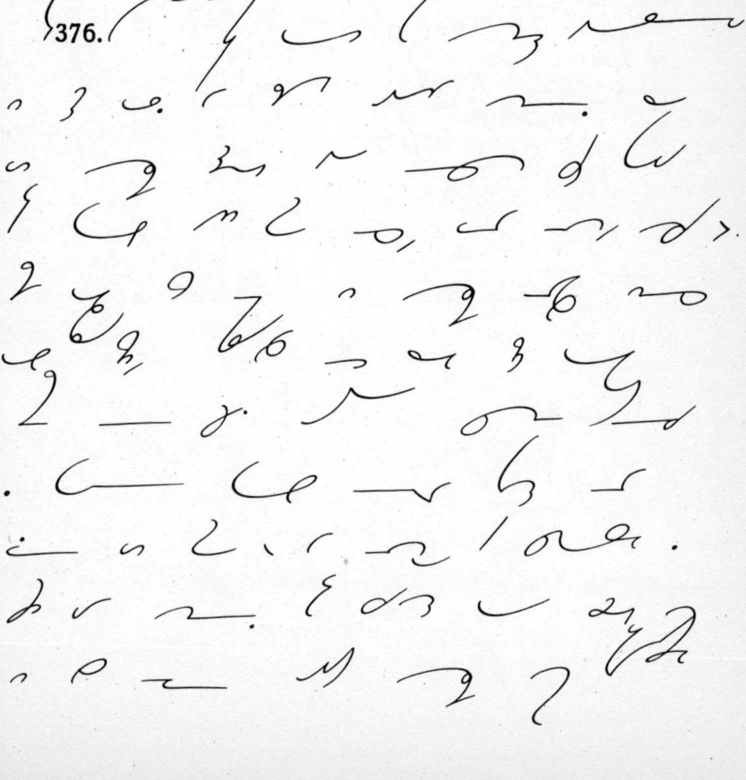

(236)

377.

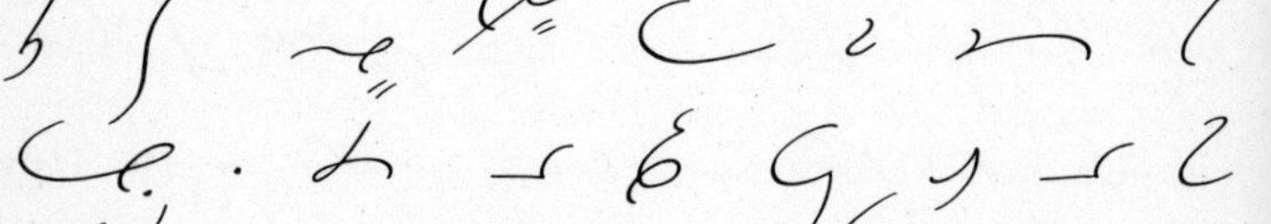

(123)

378.

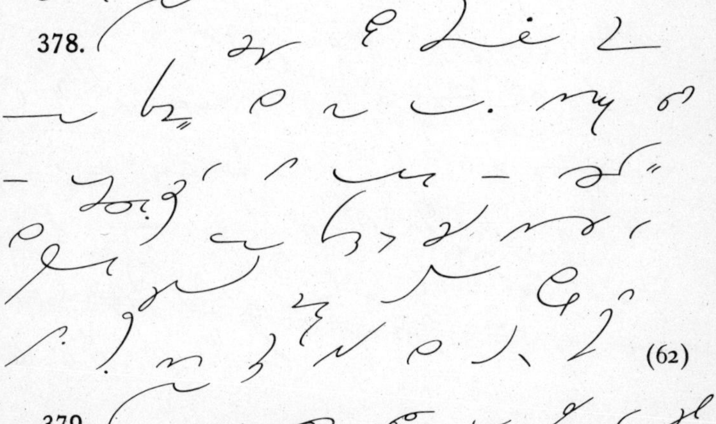

(62)

379.

(99)

380.

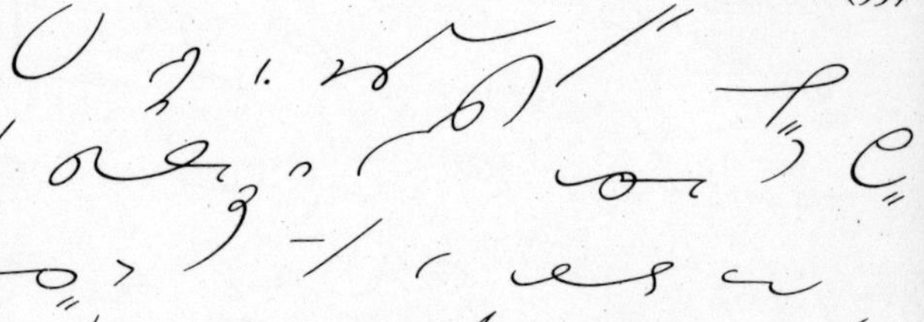

(66)

381. Use Simple Words

 —*The Light-Liner* (336)

382. Why Sleep?

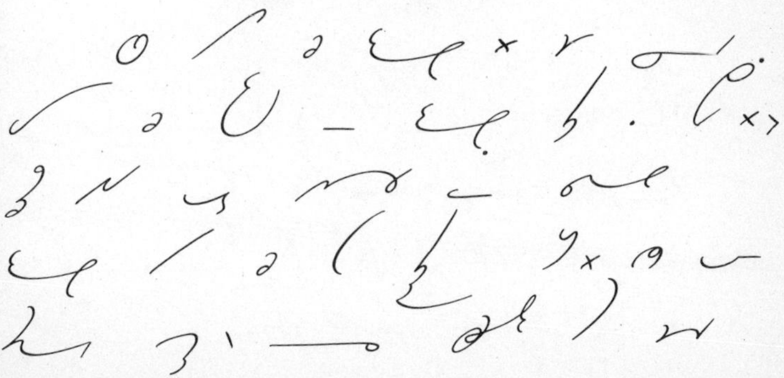

—Adapted from Metropolitan Life Ins. Co. Health Bulletins (424)

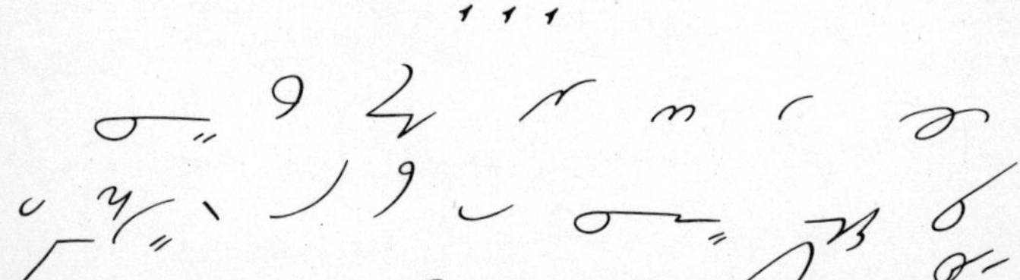

—Daniel Webster (36)

383. There's No Way Like the American Way

BECAUSE:

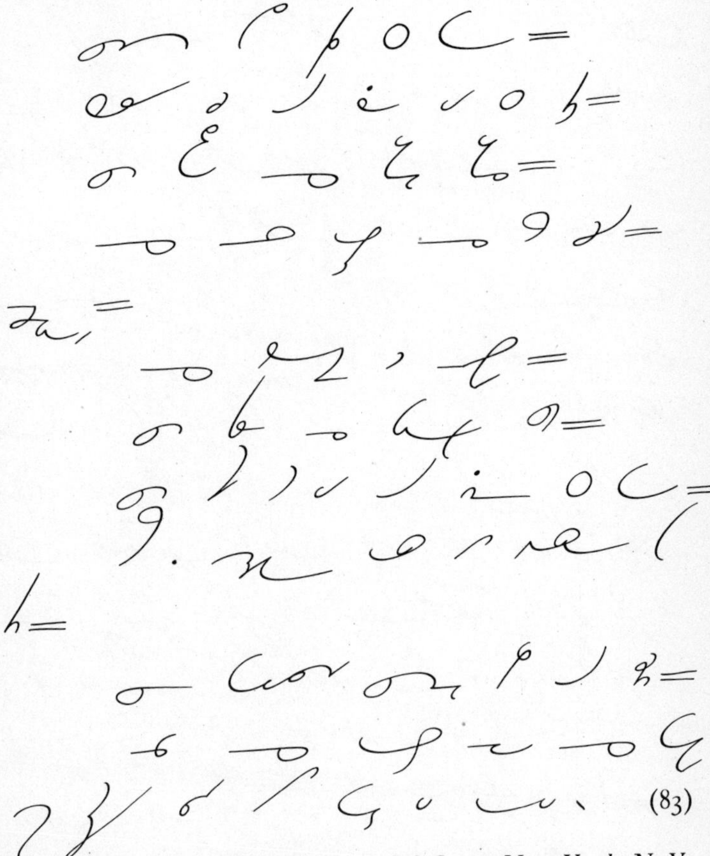

—*Ever Ready Label Corp., New York, N. Y.*

SPEED STUDY XIV

384.

(96)

385.

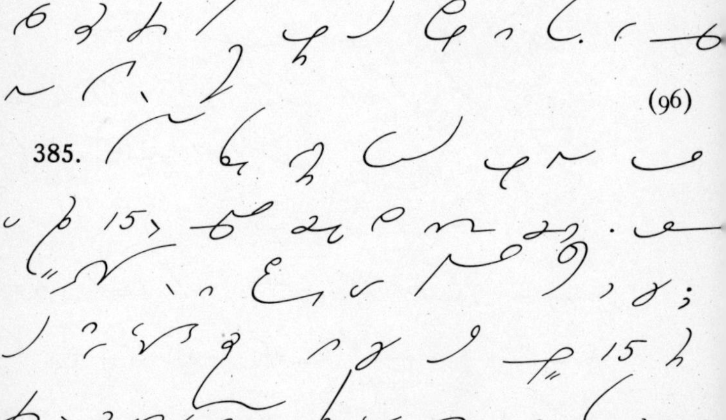

(86)

386.

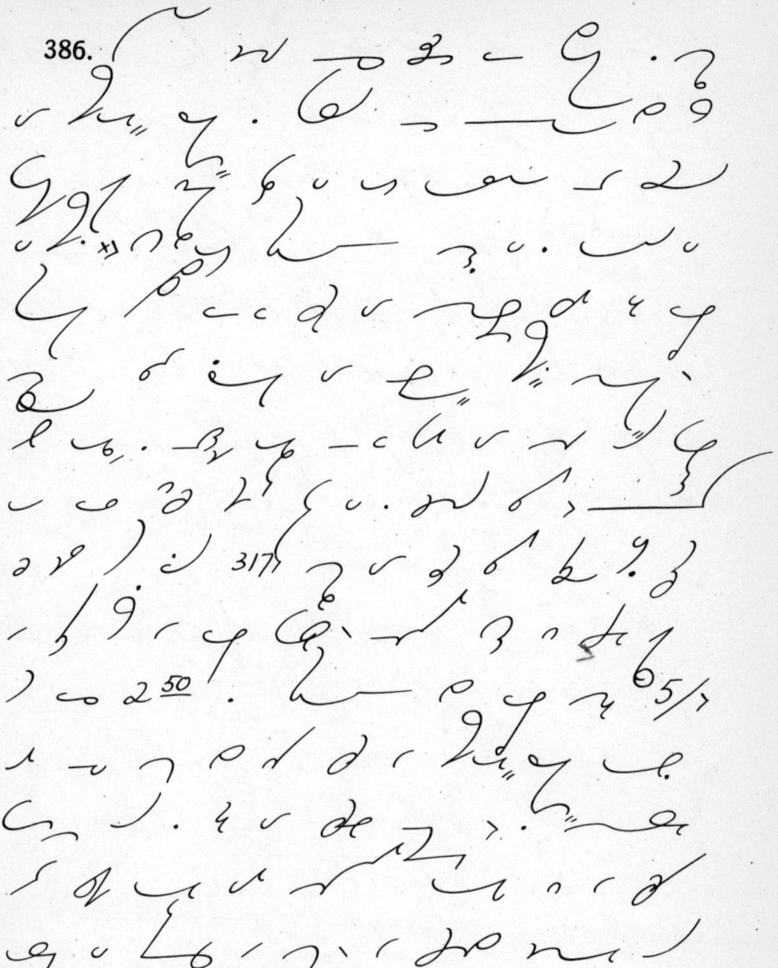

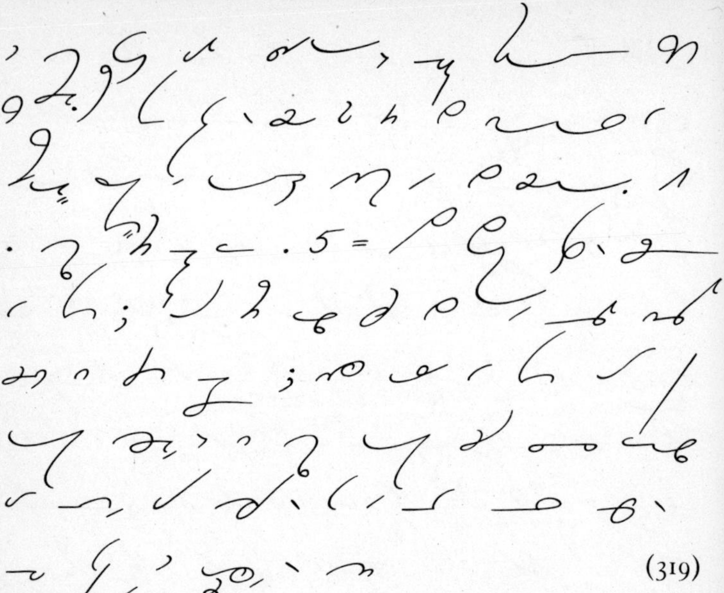

(319)

387.

(68)

388.

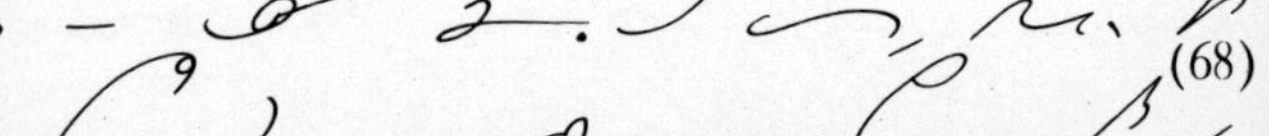

(315)

389.

(81)

390.

(98)

391.

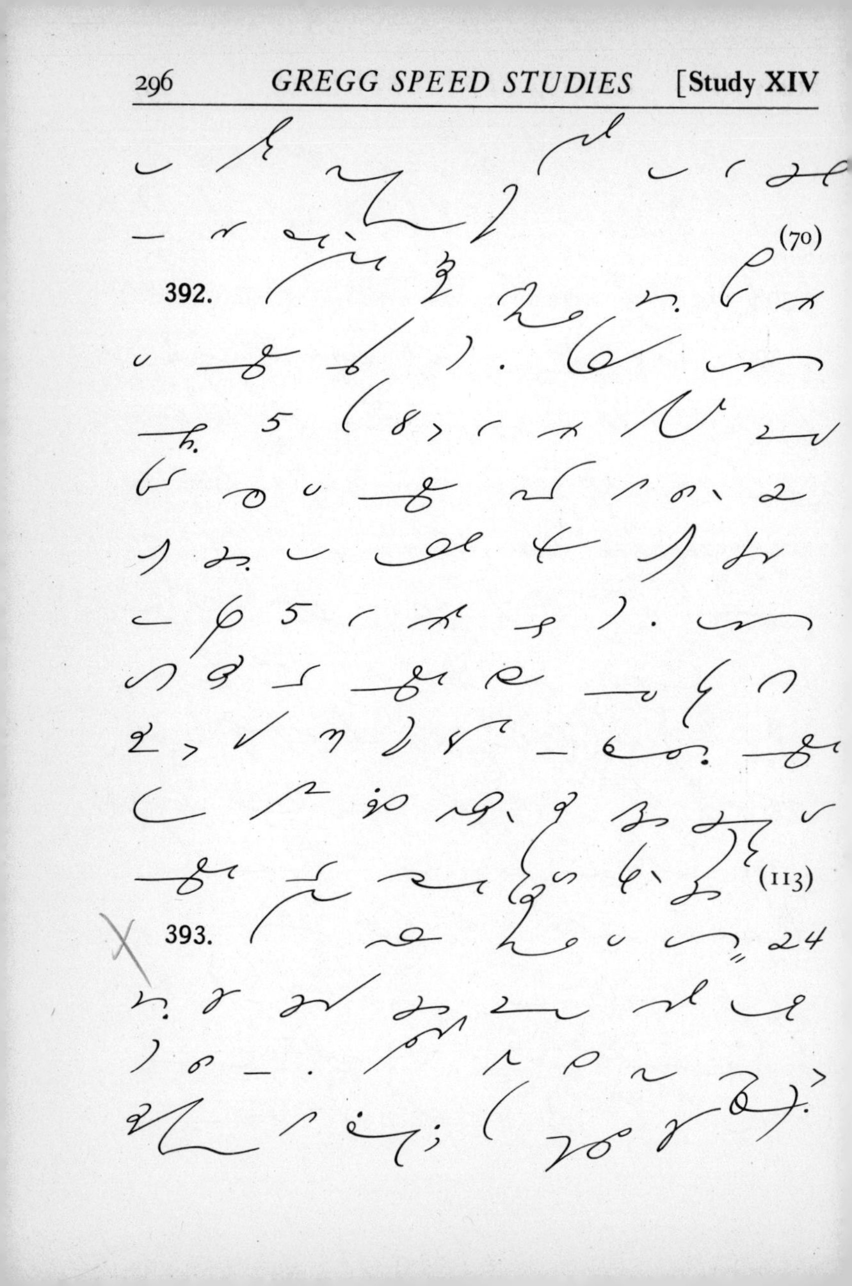

(70)

392.

(113)

393.

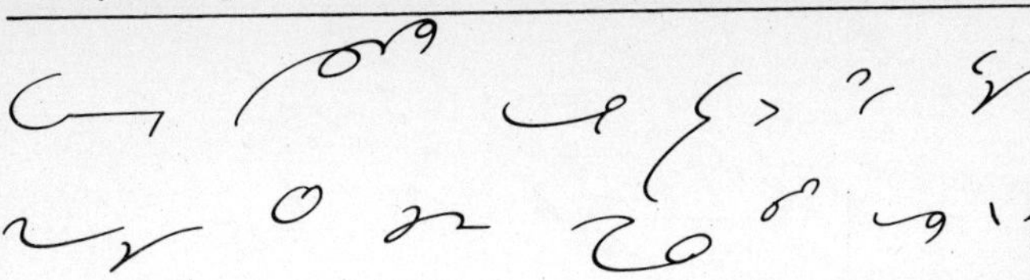

(69)

394. A Letter from Lincoln to His Stepbrother

—*A. Lincoln* (506)

395.

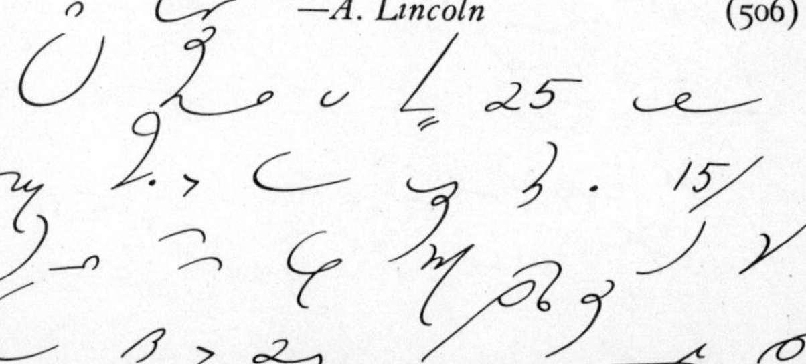

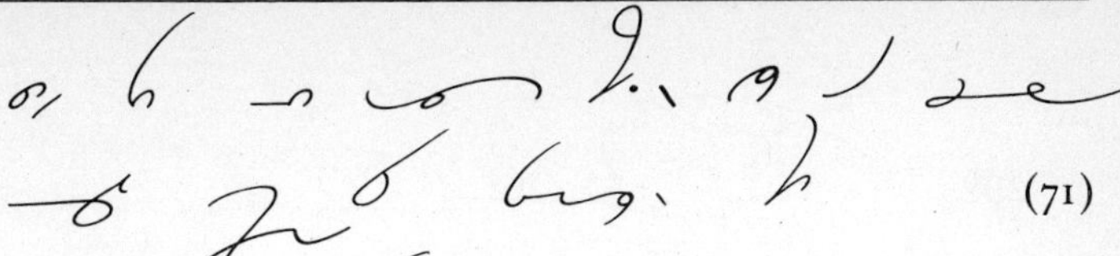

(71)

396.

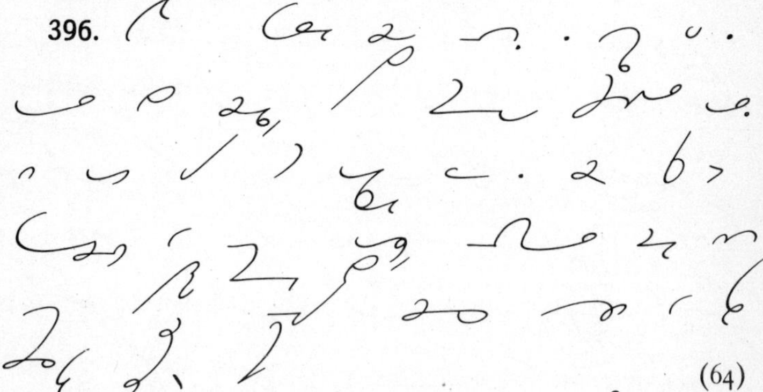

(64)

397.

(80)

398.

(14

399.

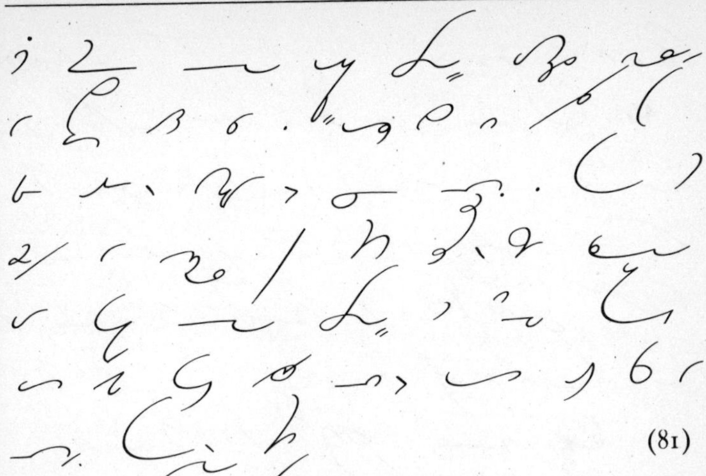

(81)

400.

(104)

401.

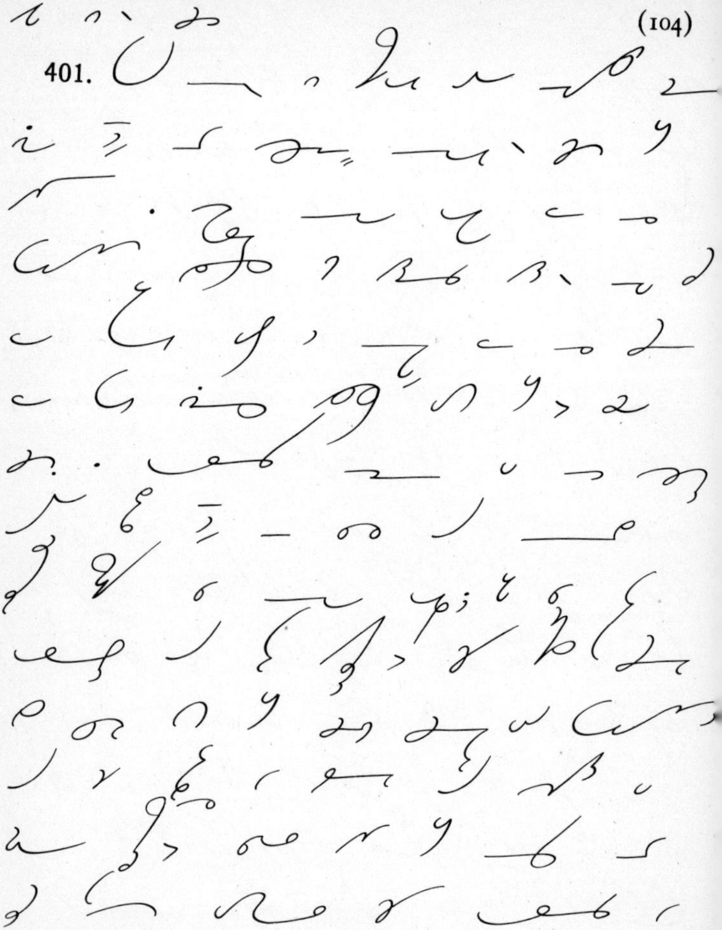

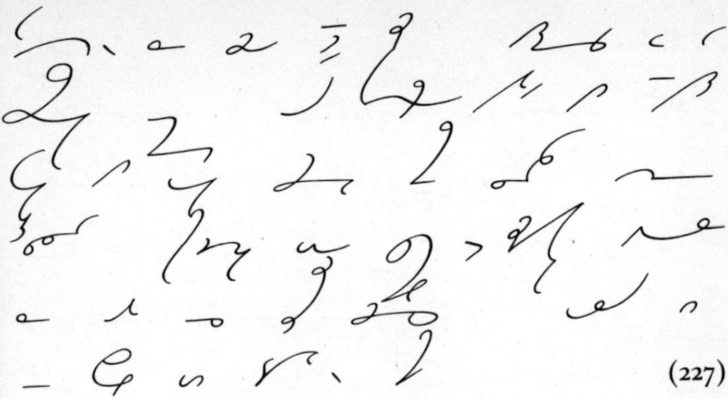

(227)

402.

(102)

403.

(132)

404.

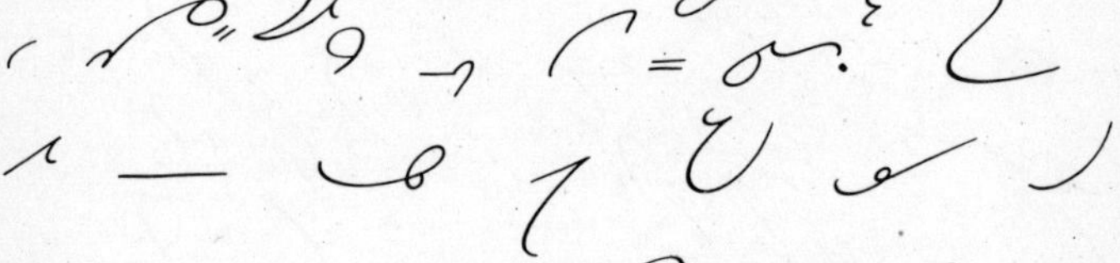

(116)

405.

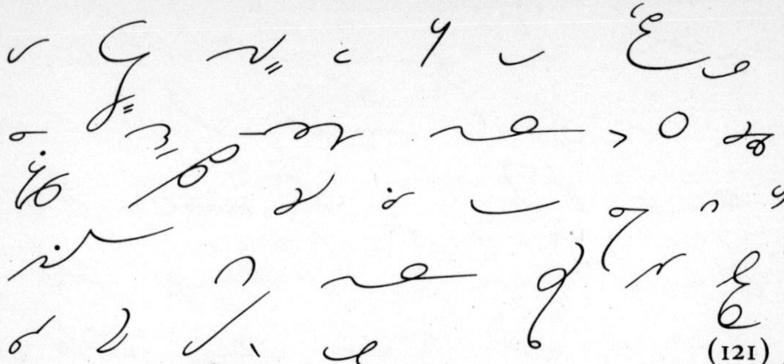

(121)

406.

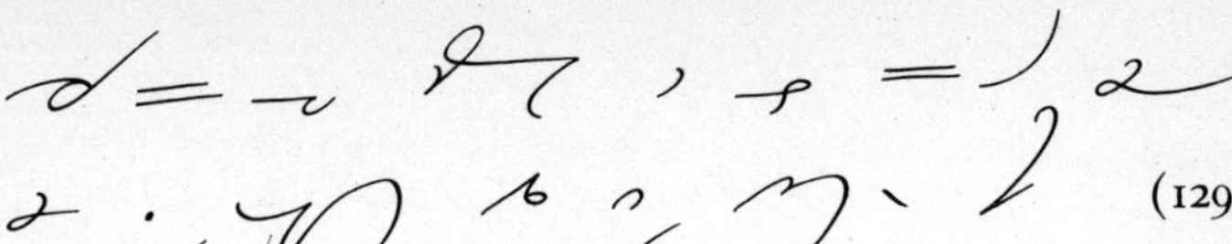

(129)

407.

(115)

408.

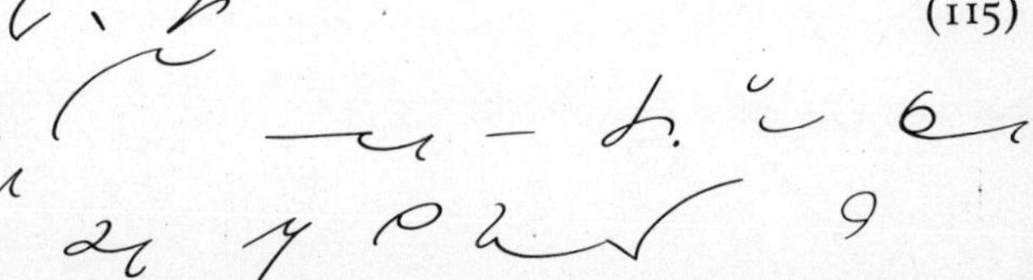

(154)

409.

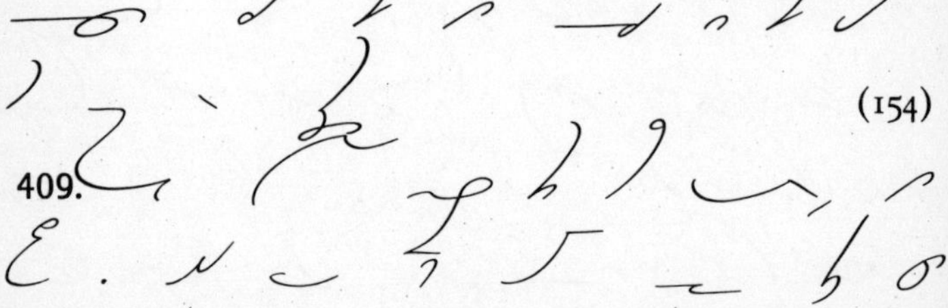

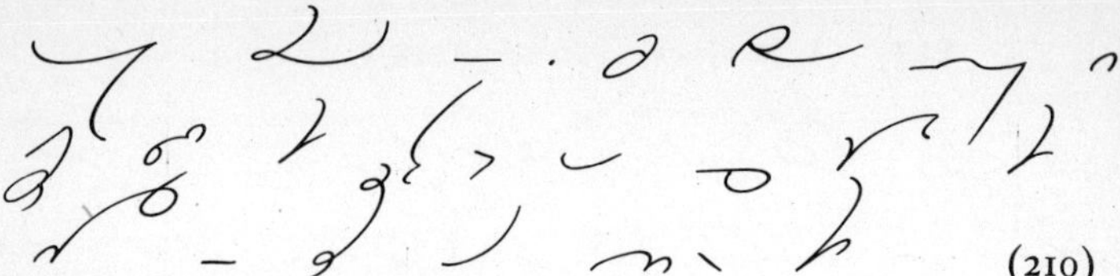

(210)

410.

(135)

411. One Good Thing About People

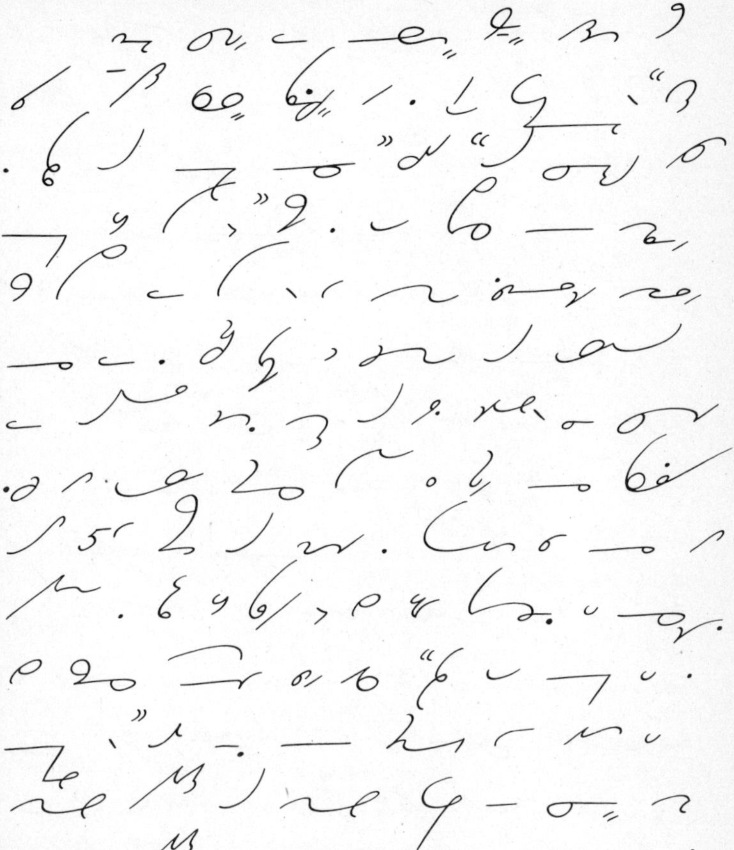

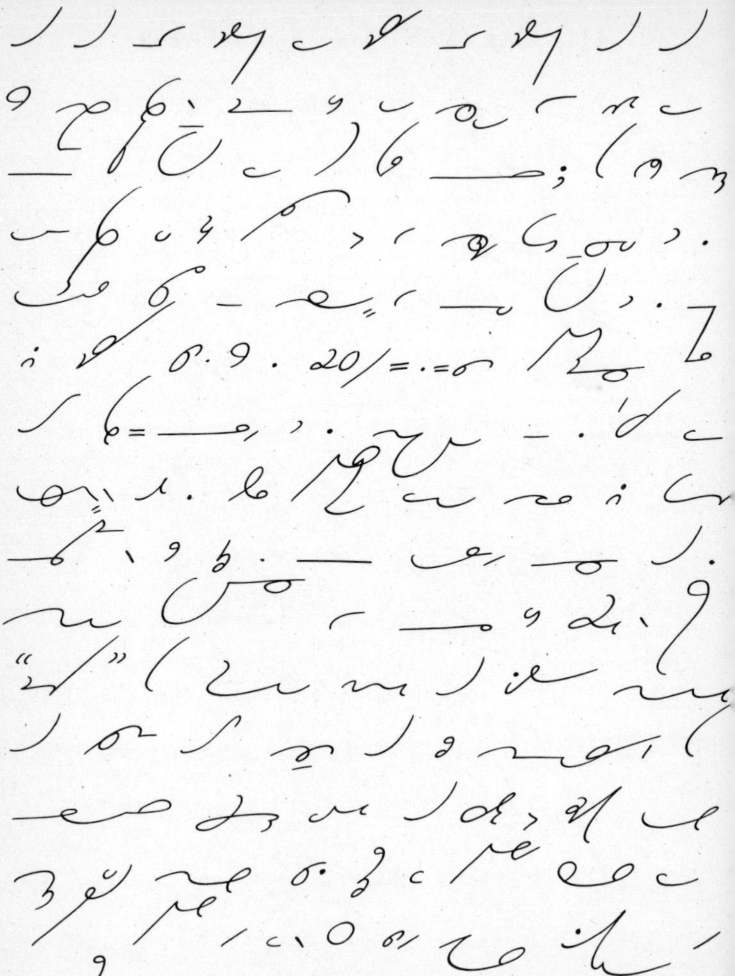
ymca

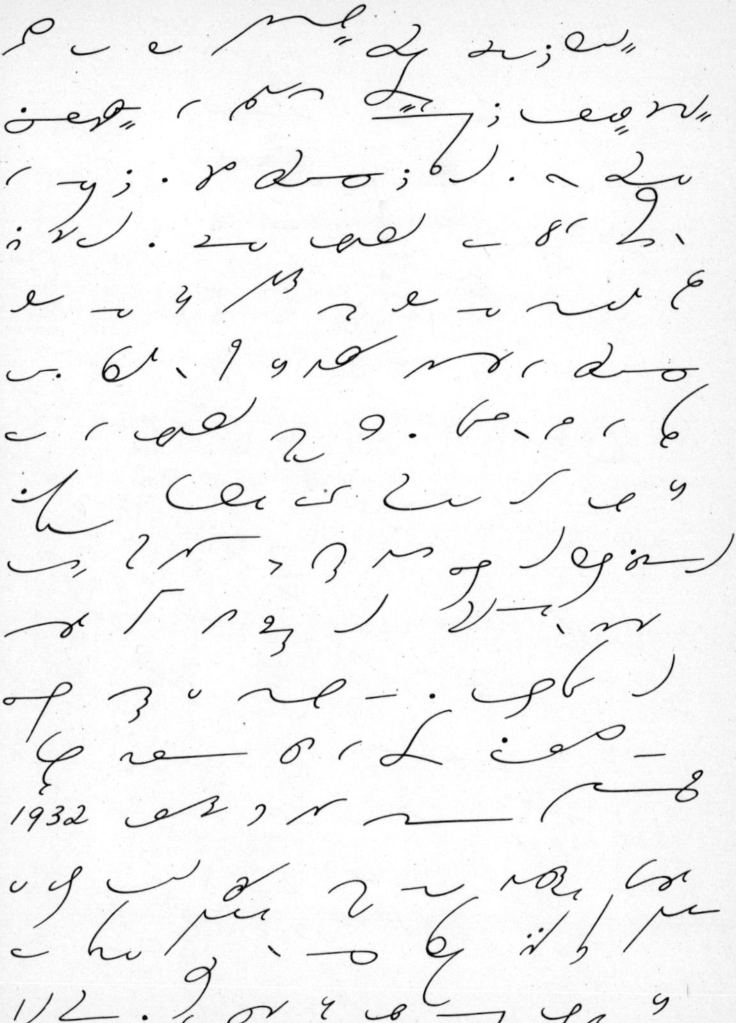
1932

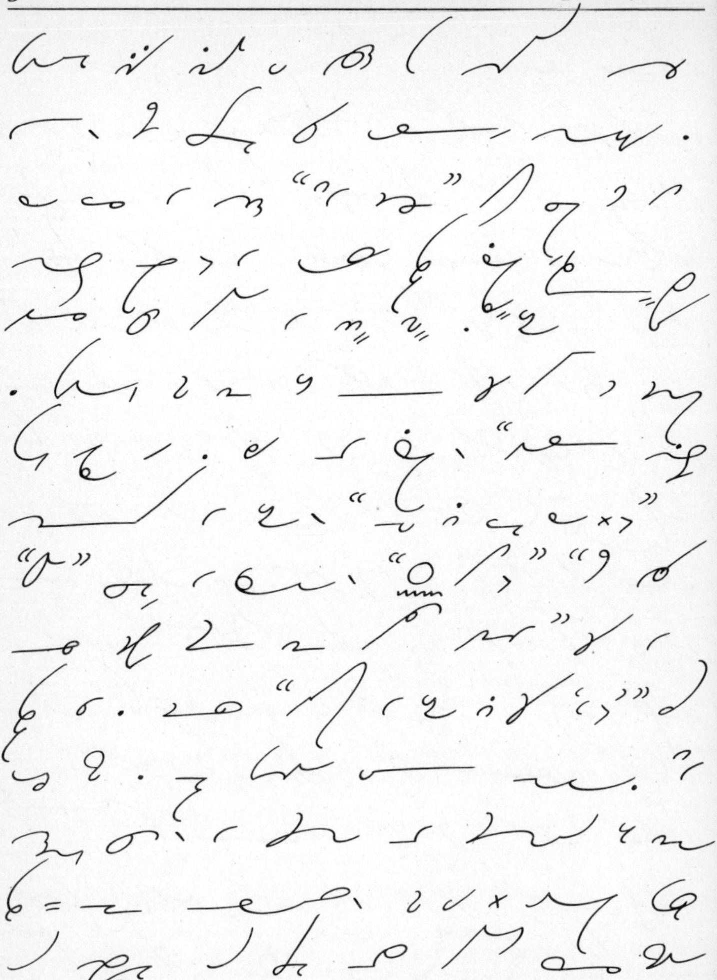

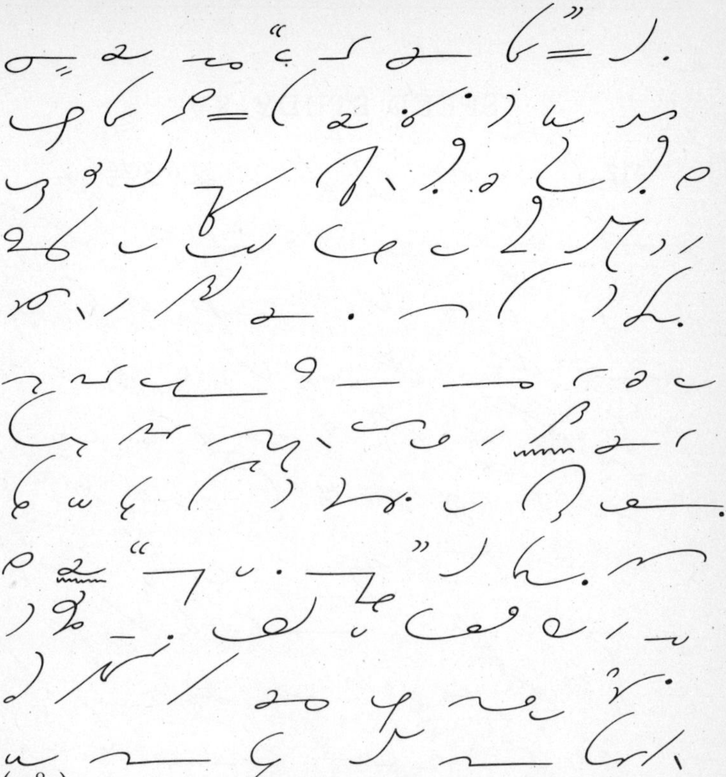

(1083) Channing Pollack, *This Week Magazine* *

* * *

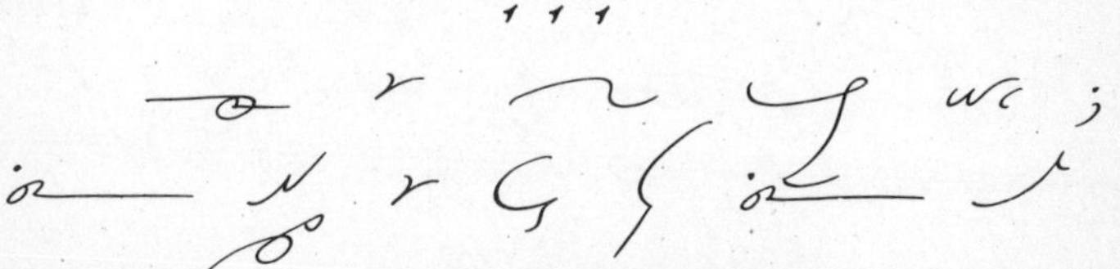

—*Daniel Webster* (20)

SPEED STUDY XV

412. *(shorthand outline)* 243 $\frac{80}{}$

(shorthand outlines) 10

(shorthand outlines)

(shorthand outlines)

(shorthand outlines)

(shorthand outlines) 10

(shorthand outlines) 30

(shorthand outlines)

(shorthand outlines)

(133)

413. *(shorthand outlines)*

(shorthand outlines)

(shorthand outlines) 10 $\frac{75}{}$

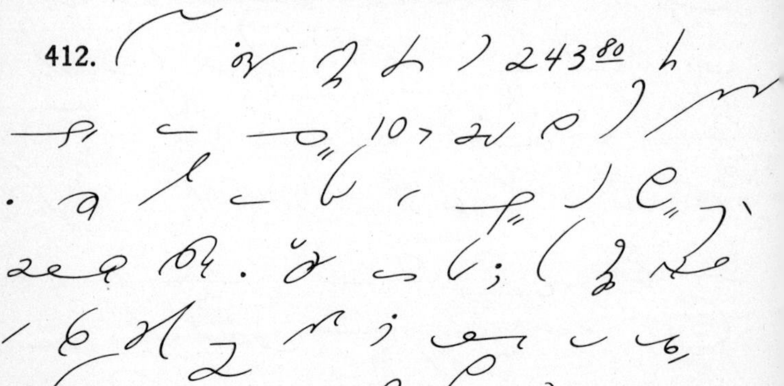

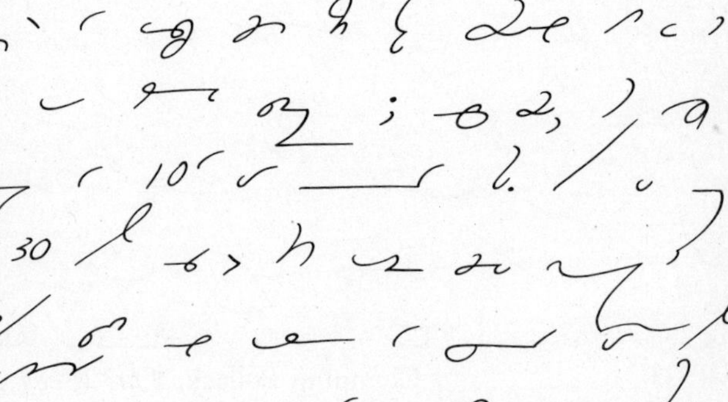

(84)

414.

(126)

415.

1941 [shorthand outlines]

[shorthand outlines] 50 [shorthand] 60,

[shorthand outlines]

[shorthand outlines]

[shorthand] *52* / *53* [shorthand outlines]

[shorthand outlines]

[shorthand outlines]

[shorthand outlines]

[shorthand outlines]   (124)

416. [shorthand outlines]

[shorthand outlines]

[shorthand outlines]

[shorthand outlines] *20* [shorthand outlines]

[shorthand outlines]

[shorthand outlines] 50/ [shorthand] 75/,

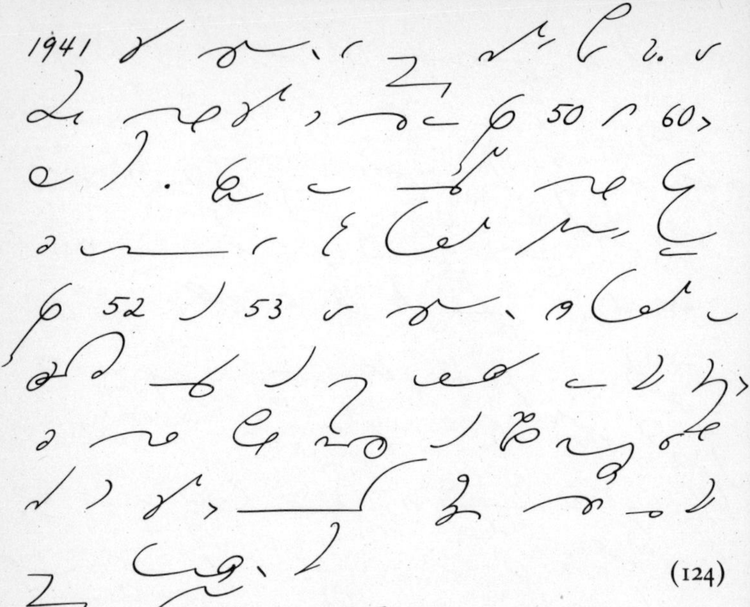

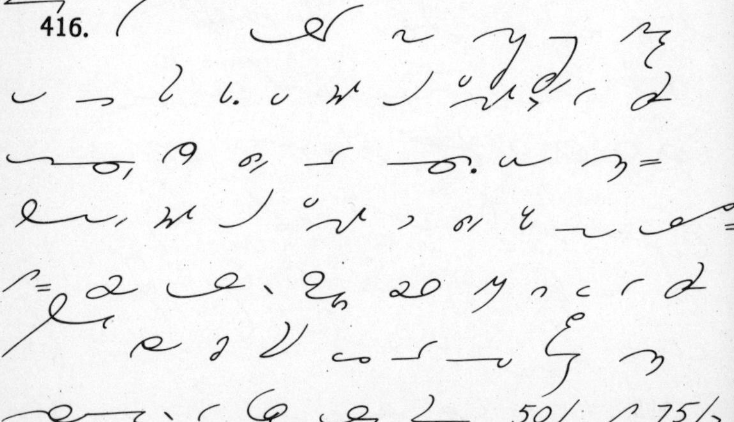

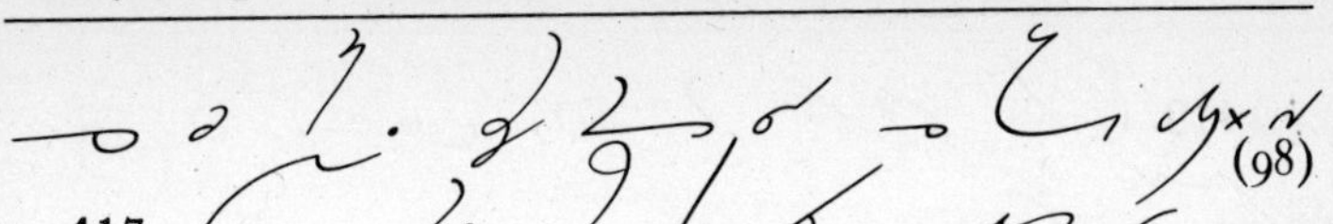

(98)

417.

(91)

418.

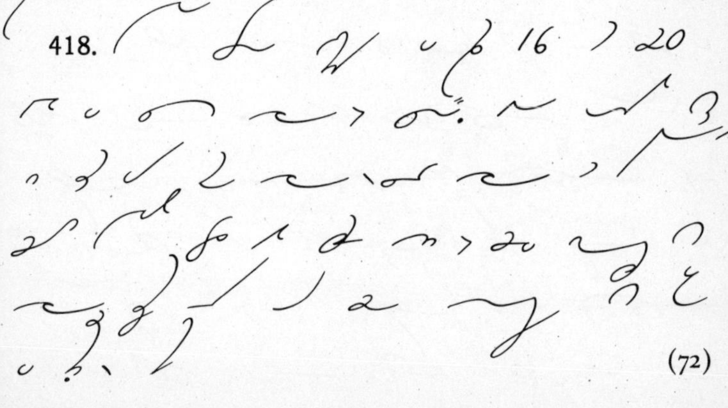

(72)

419. *[shorthand outlines]* 50 *[shorthand outlines]*

[shorthand outlines]

[shorthand outlines]

[shorthand outlines] 26 *[shorthand outlines]*

[shorthand outlines]

[shorthand outlines]

[shorthand outlines]

[shorthand outlines]

[shorthand outlines] (92)

420. *[shorthand outlines]*

[shorthand outlines]

[shorthand outlines] 8 *[shorthand outlines]*

[shorthand outlines]

[shorthand outlines]

[shorthand outlines]

[shorthand outlines]

[shorthand outlines]

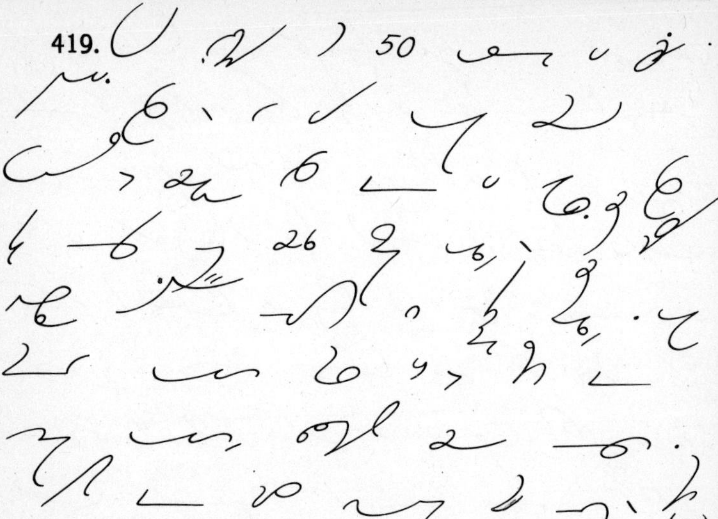

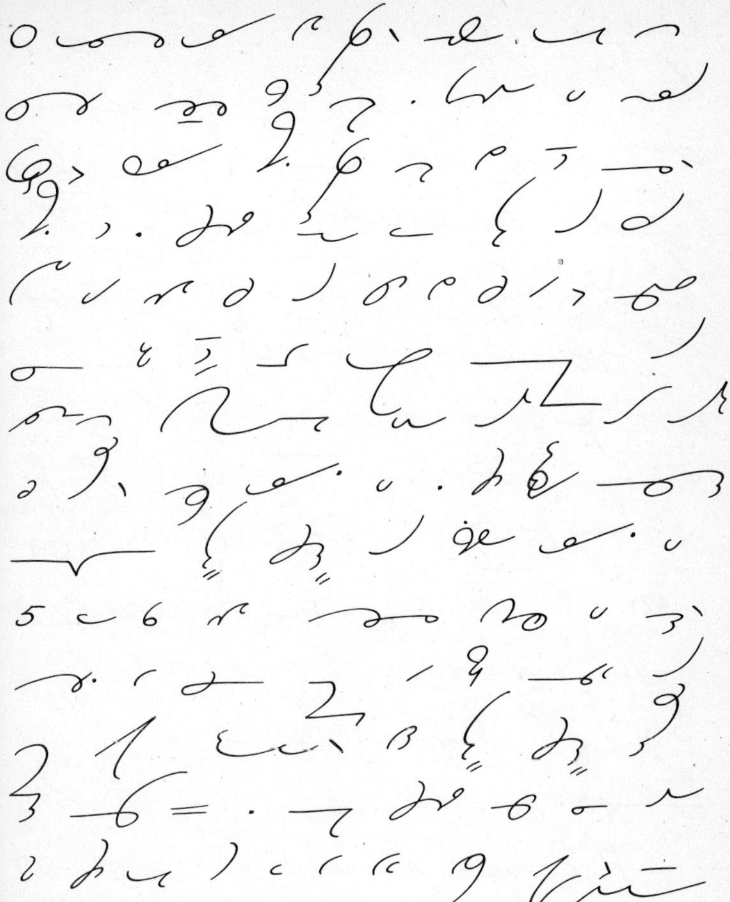

(336)

421.

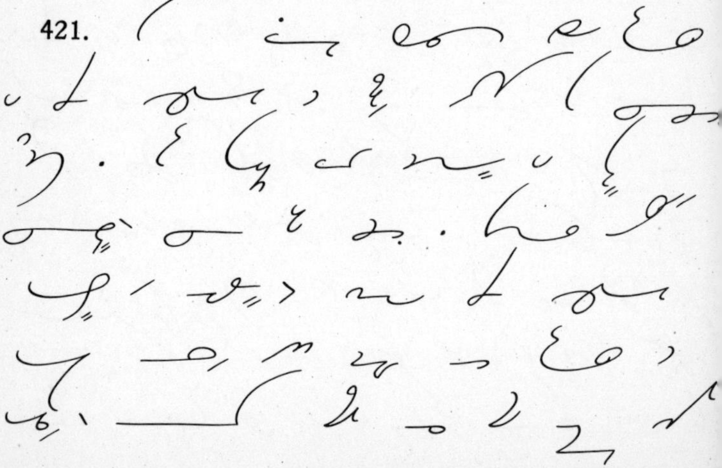

(87)

422.

(87)

423. A Letter from William James on Receiving a Gift of an Azalea from Some of His Students

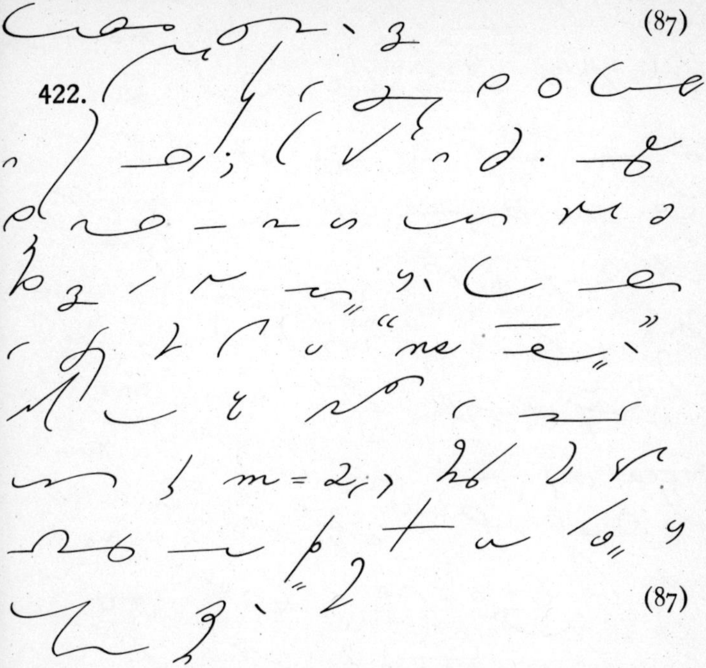

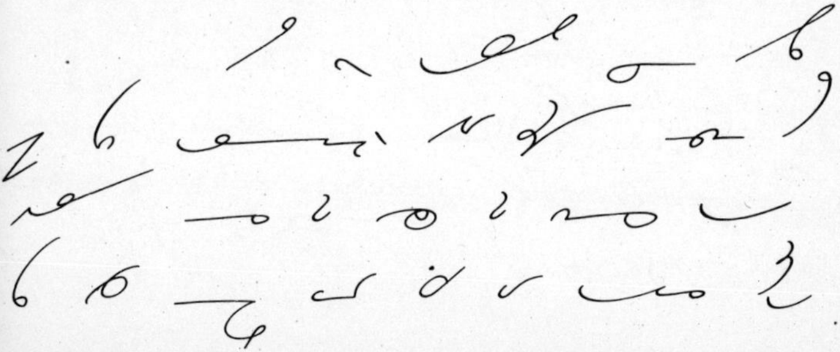

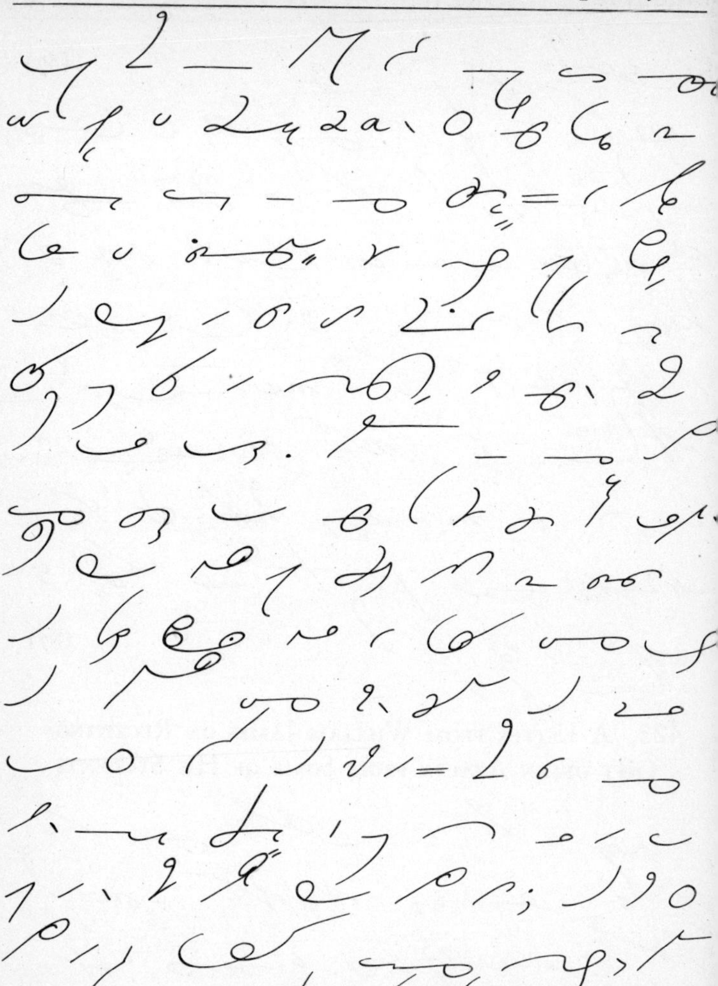

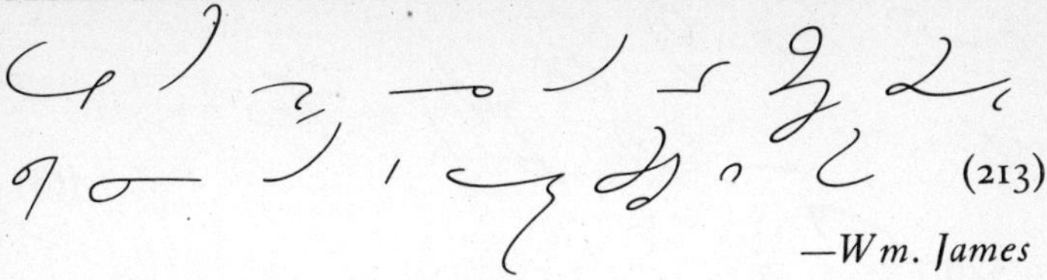

(213)

—*Wm. James*

424.

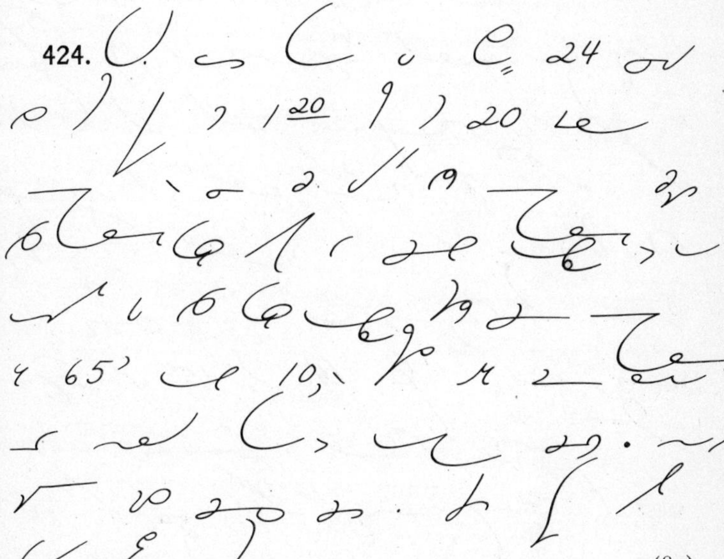

(89)

425.

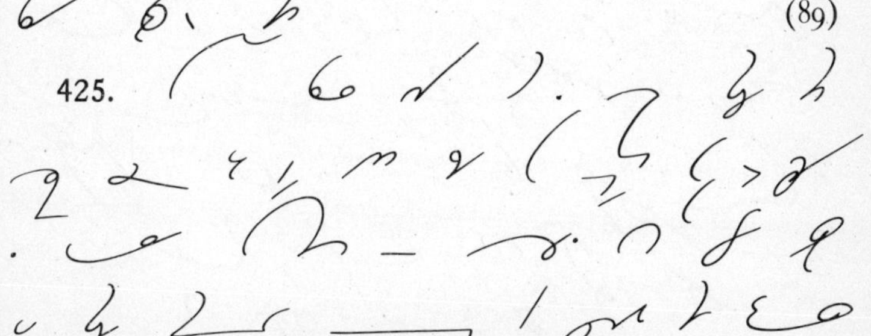

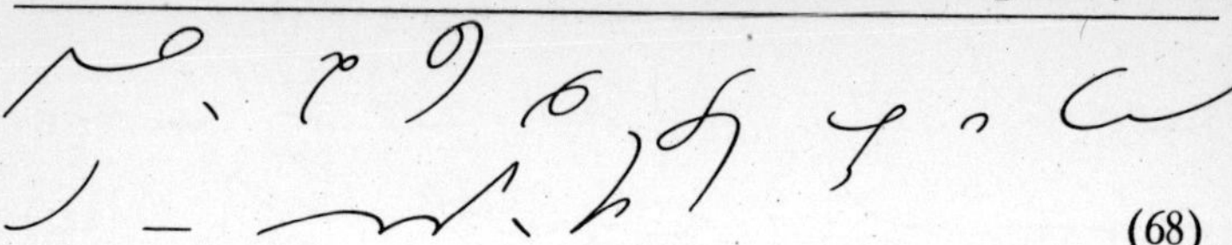

(68)

426.

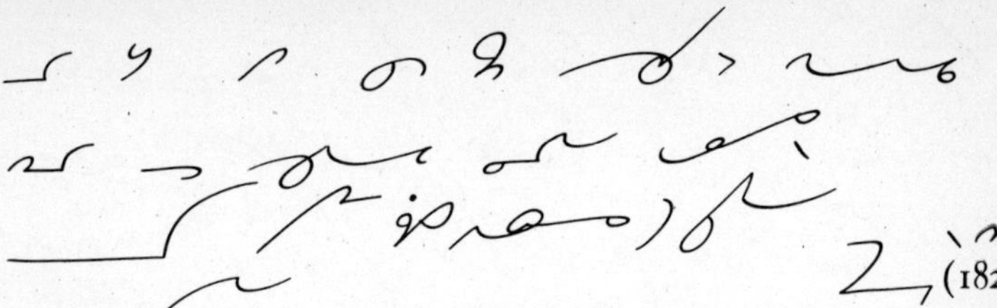

(182)

427.

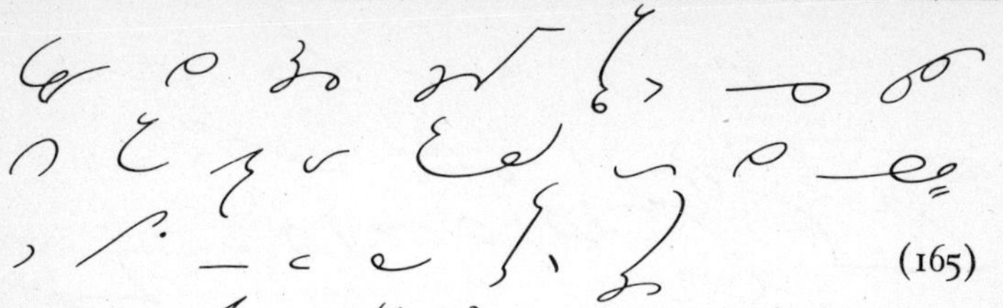

(165)

428.

(127)

429.

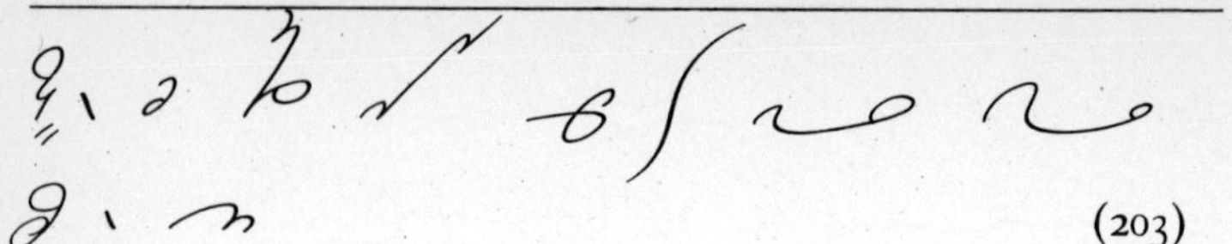

(203)

430.

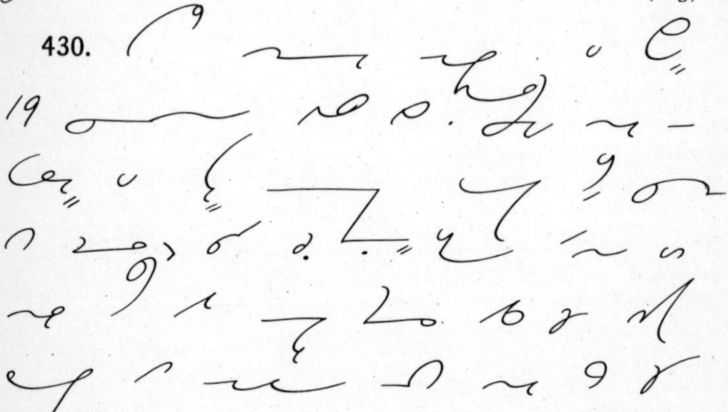

(128)

431.

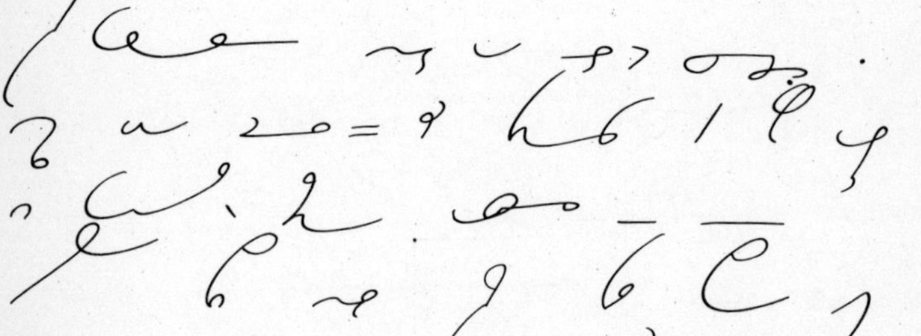

(162)

432. 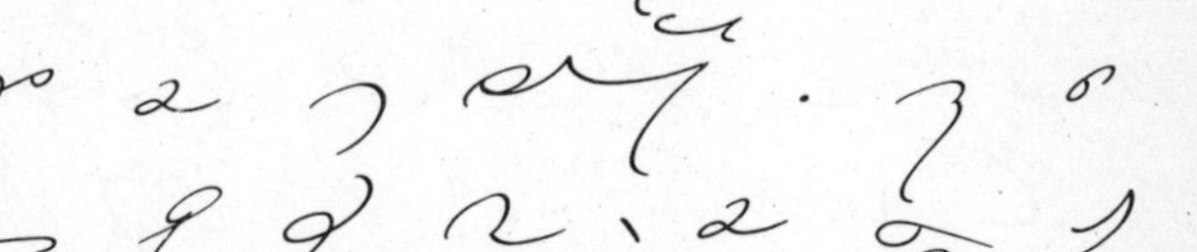

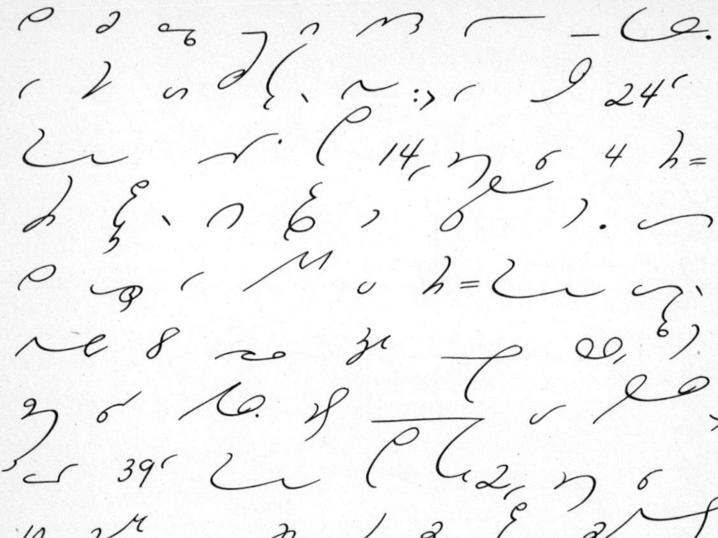

(174)

433.

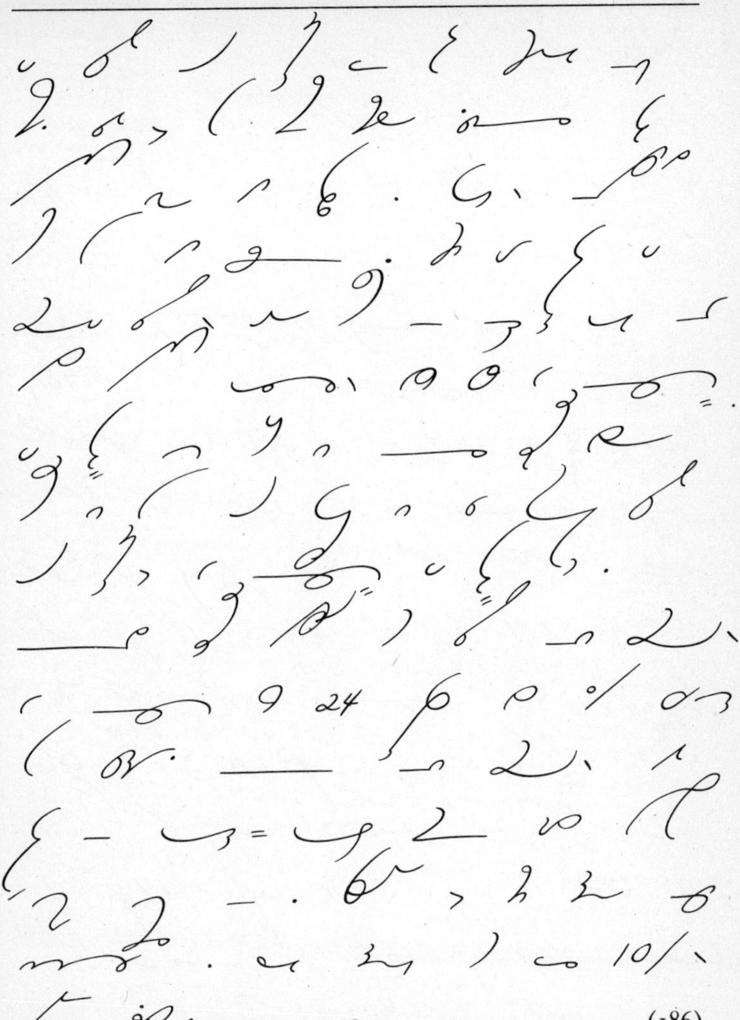

(186)

434.

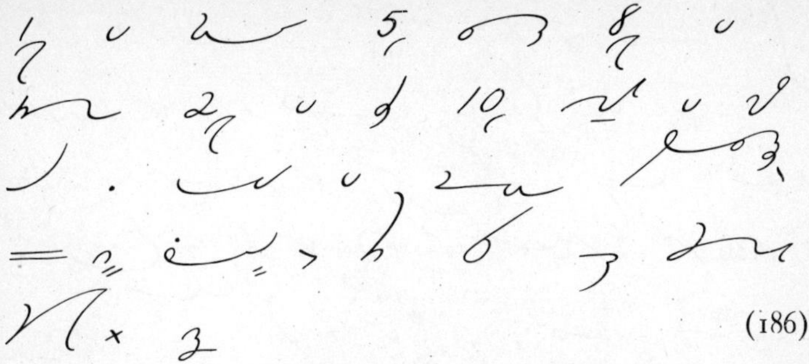

(186)

435.

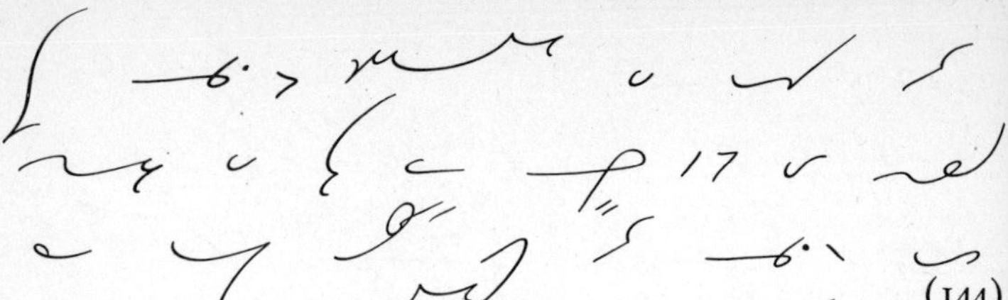

(144)

436.

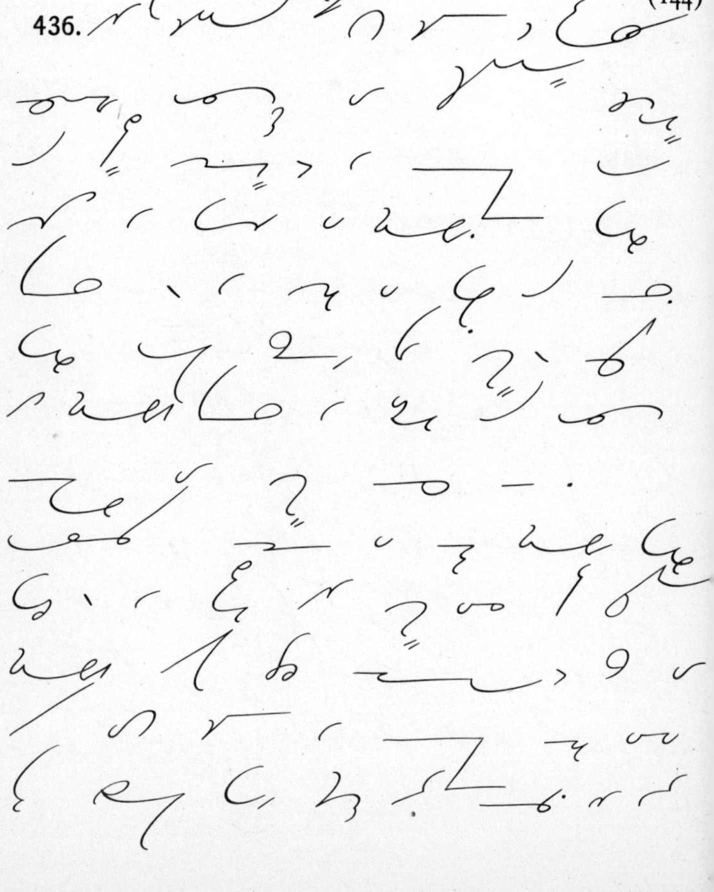

20
(160)
437.
(65)
438.

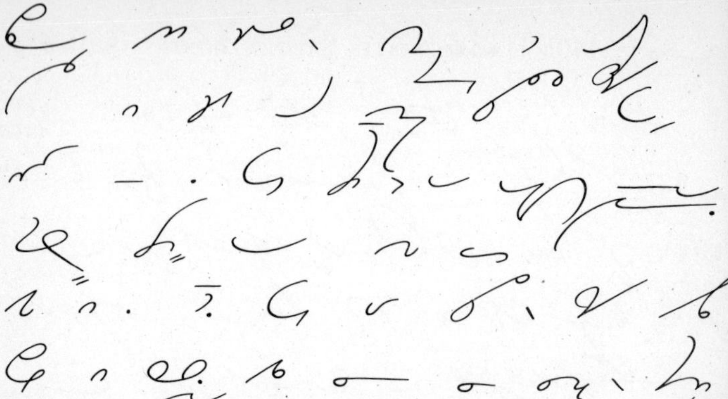

(144

439.

(111)

440. United States Savings Bonds

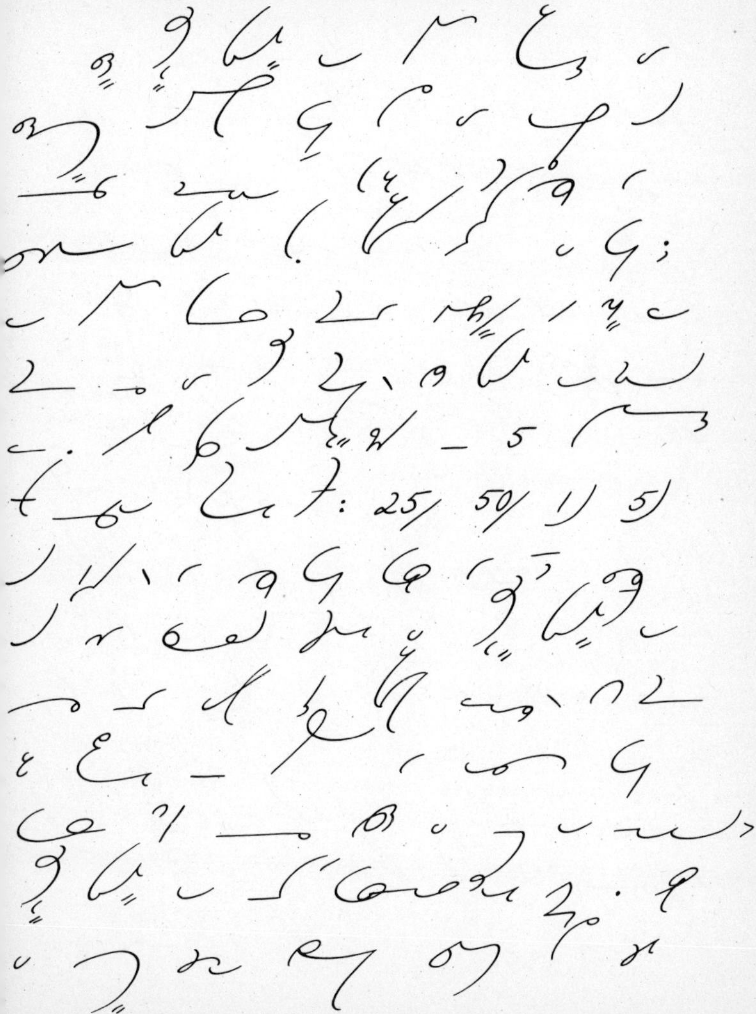

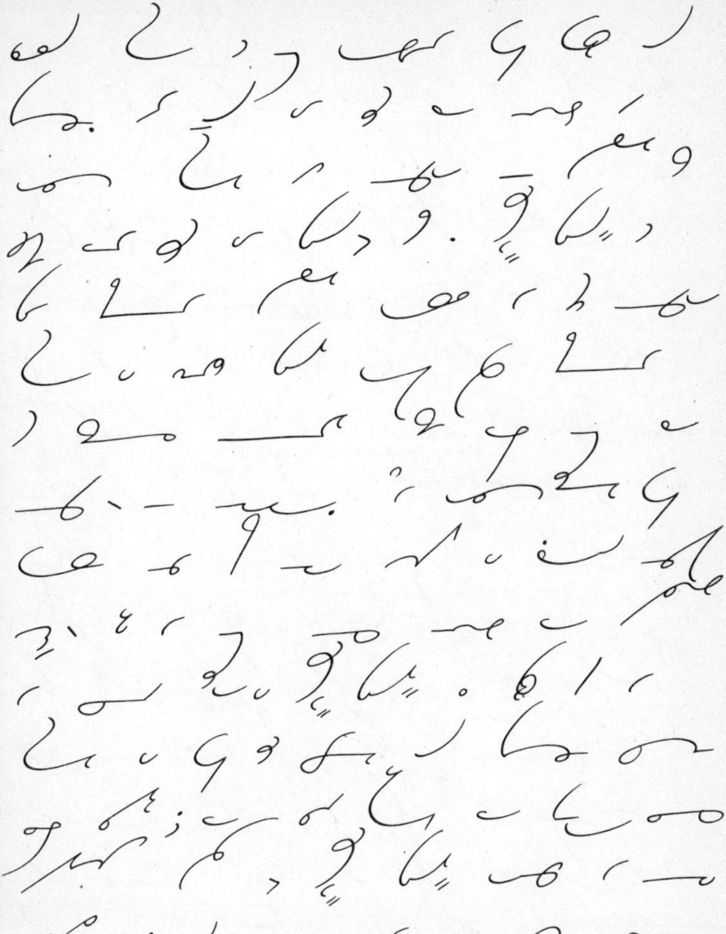

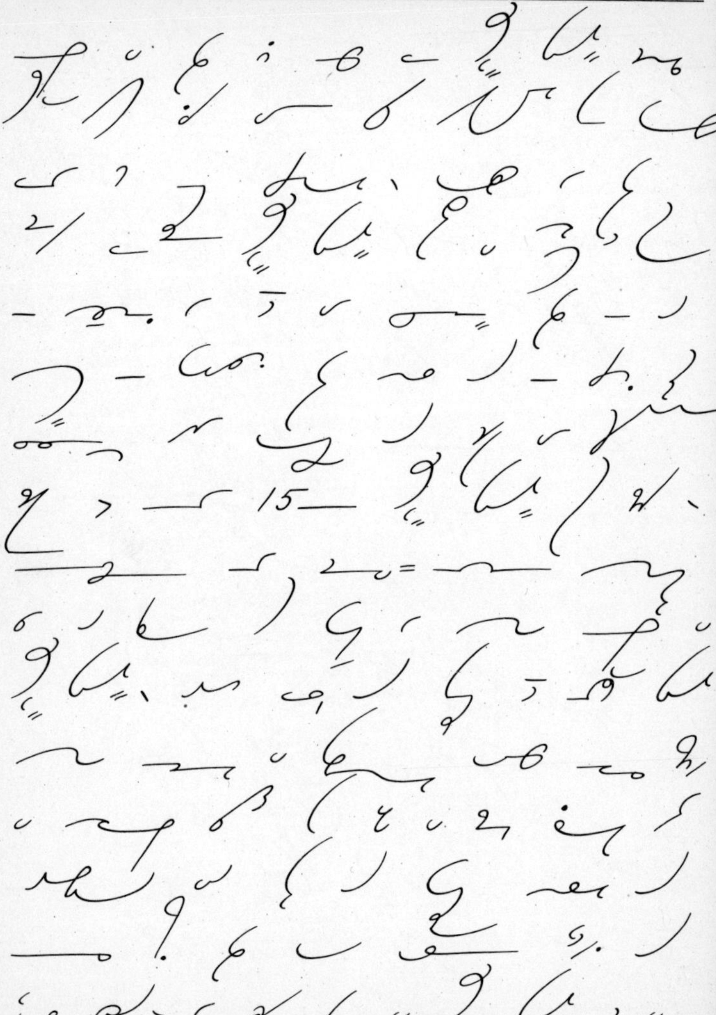

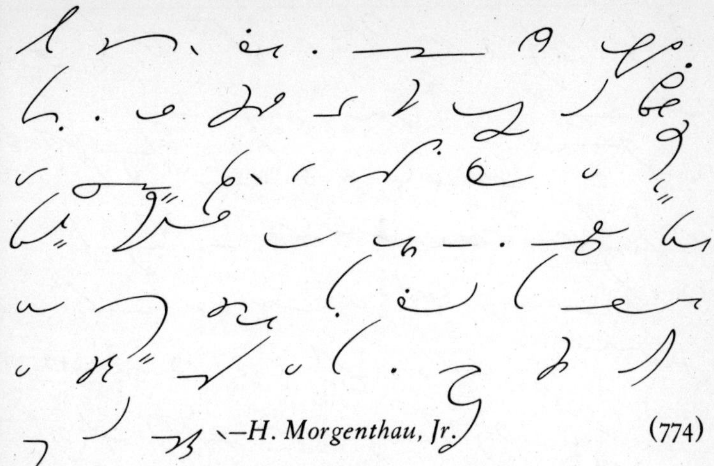

—*H. Morgenthau, Jr.* (774)

441. A New Philosophy of Trusteeship

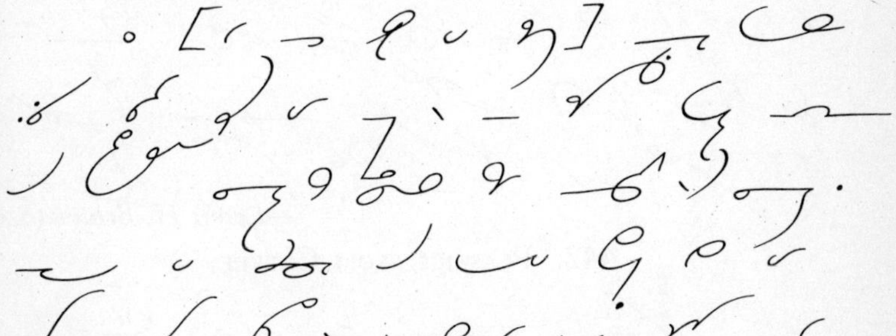

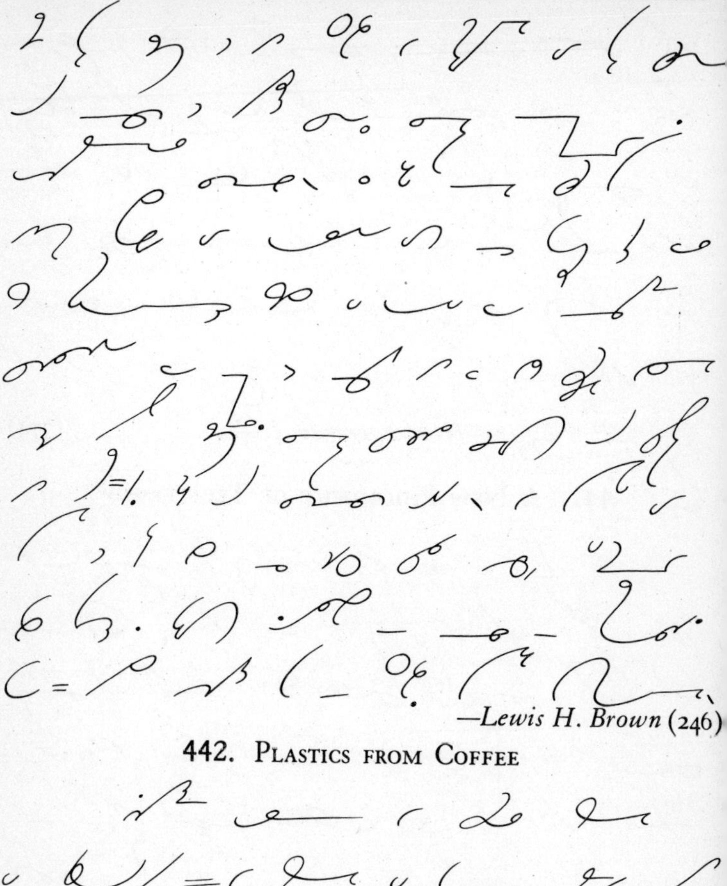

—*Lewis H. Brown* (246)

442. Plastics from Coffee

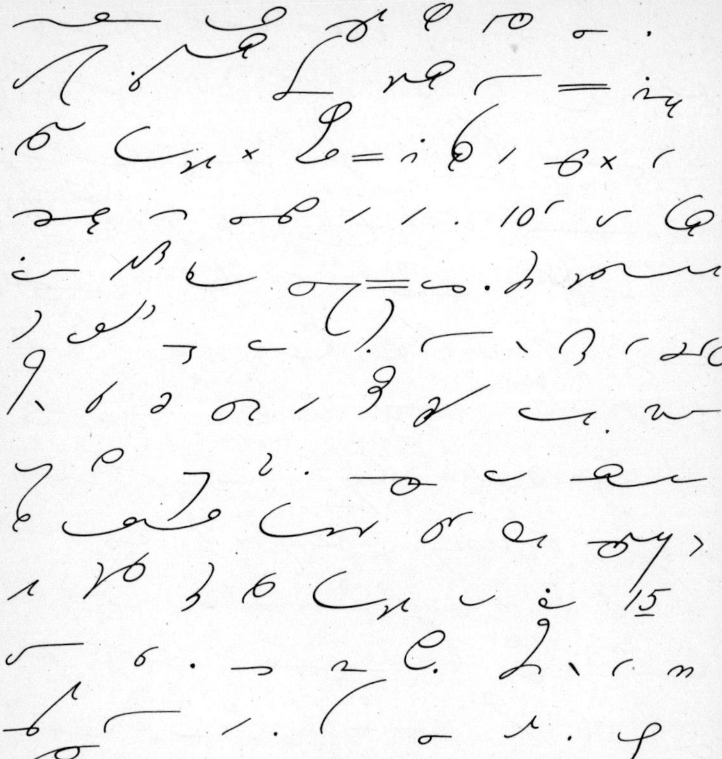

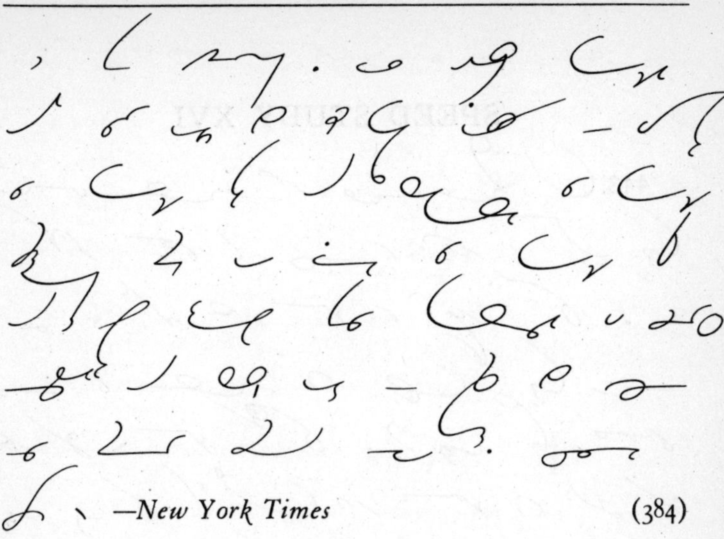

—*New York Times* (384)

(56)

SPEED STUDY XVI

443.

(86)

444.

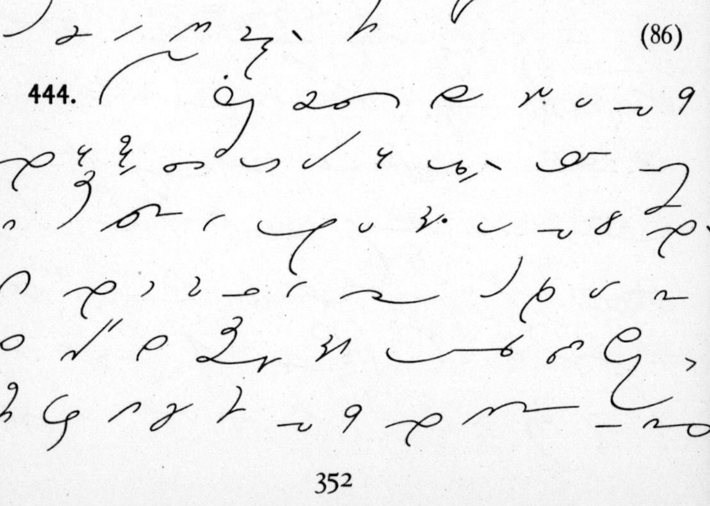

(87)

445.

(67)

446.

(74)

447.

(66)

448.

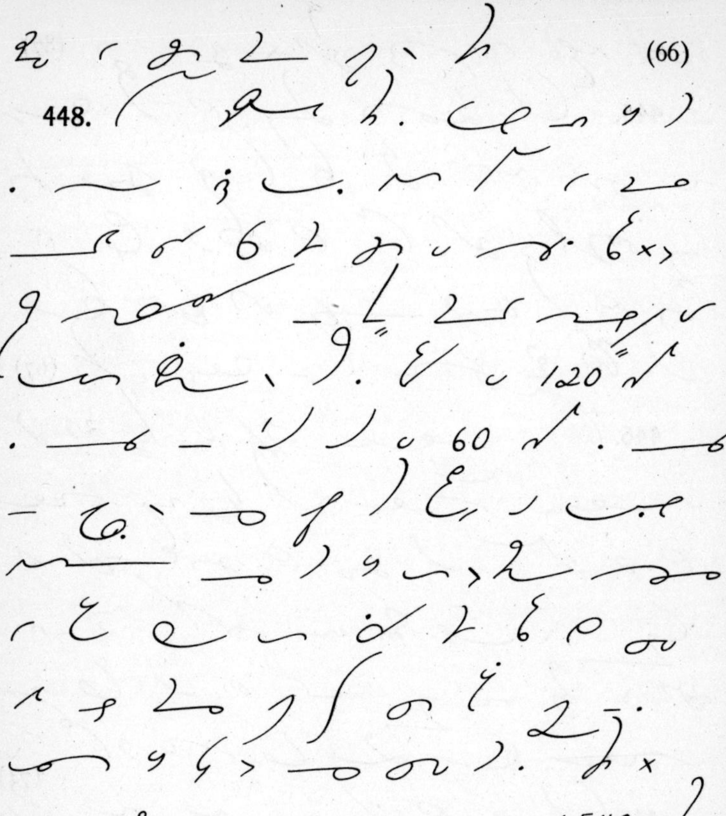

(132)

449.

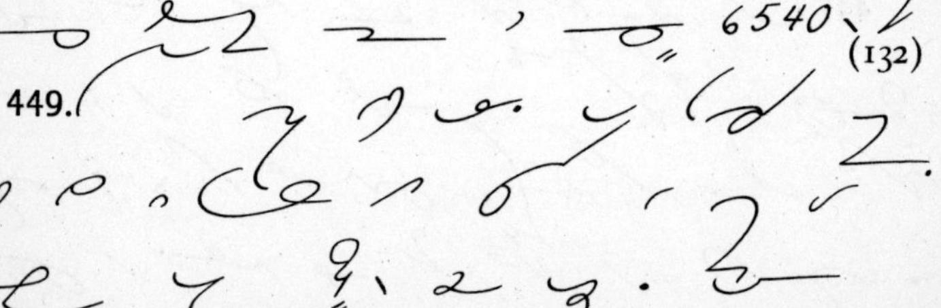

(75)

450.

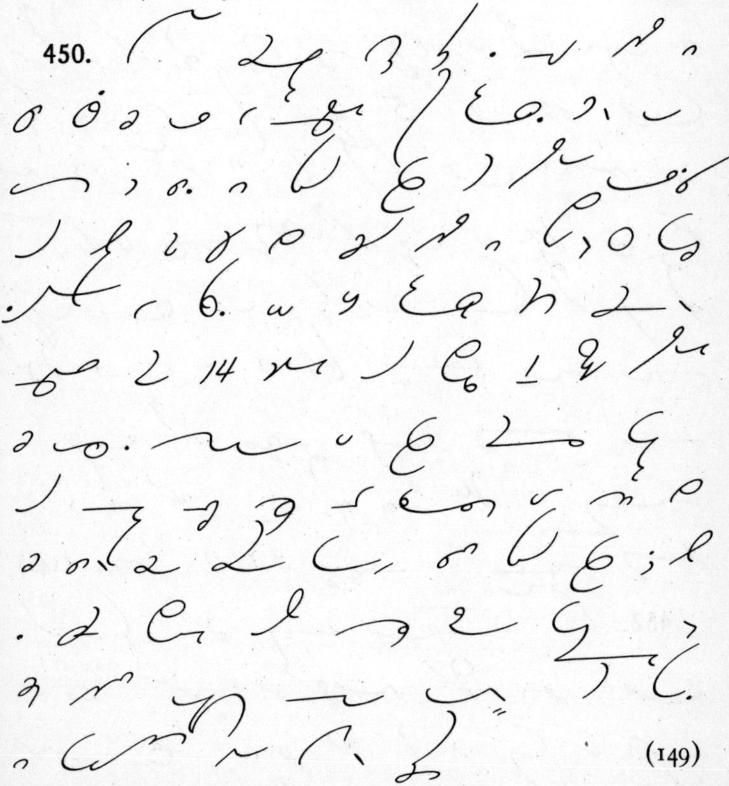

(149)

451.

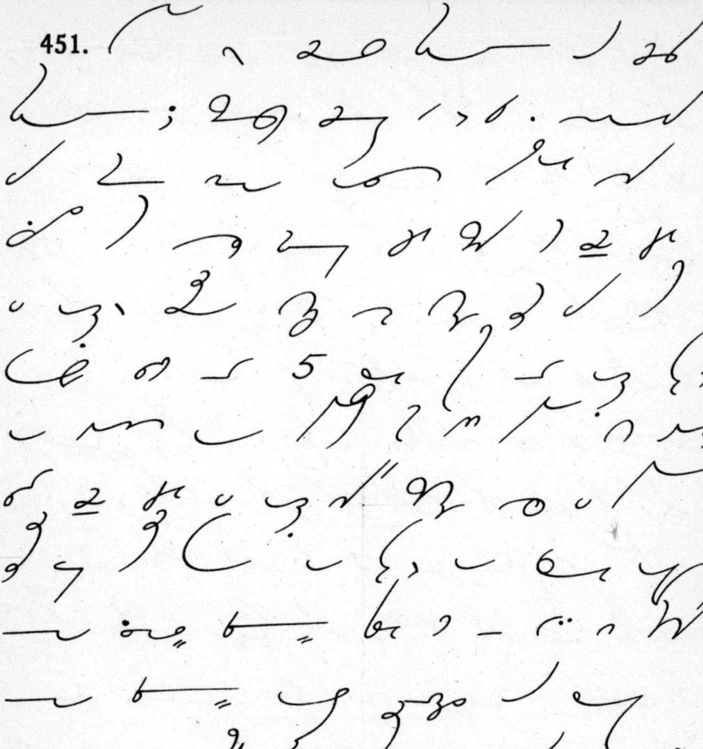

(146)

452.

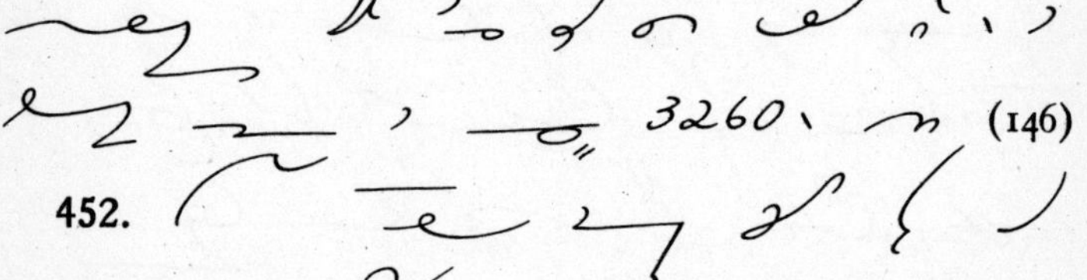

(155)

453.

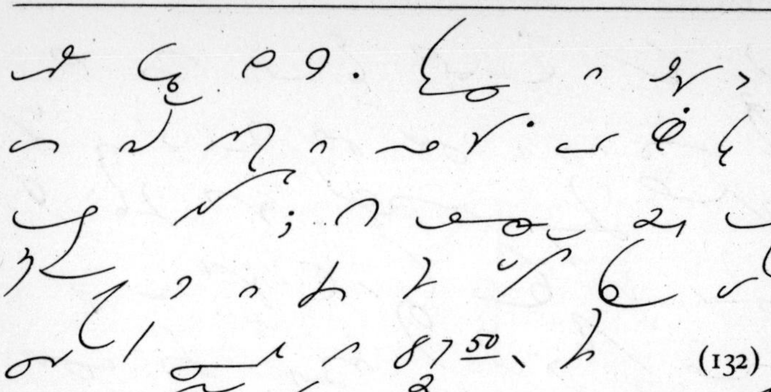

(132)

454.

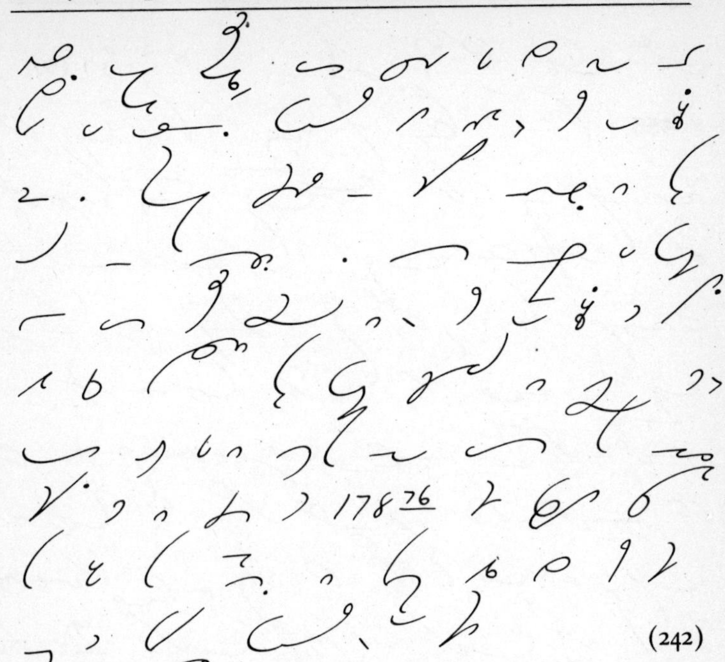

(242)

455.

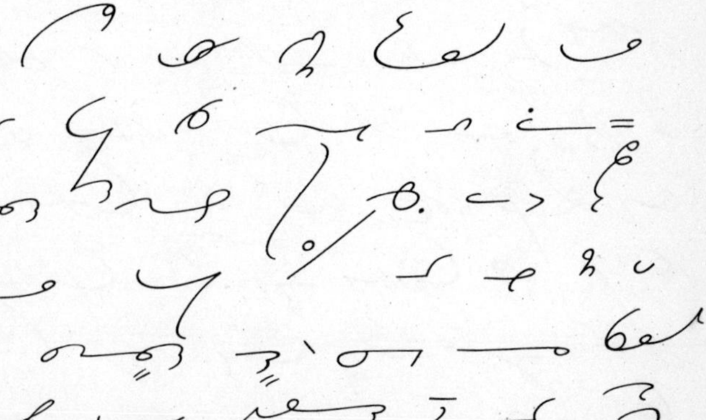

(66)

456.

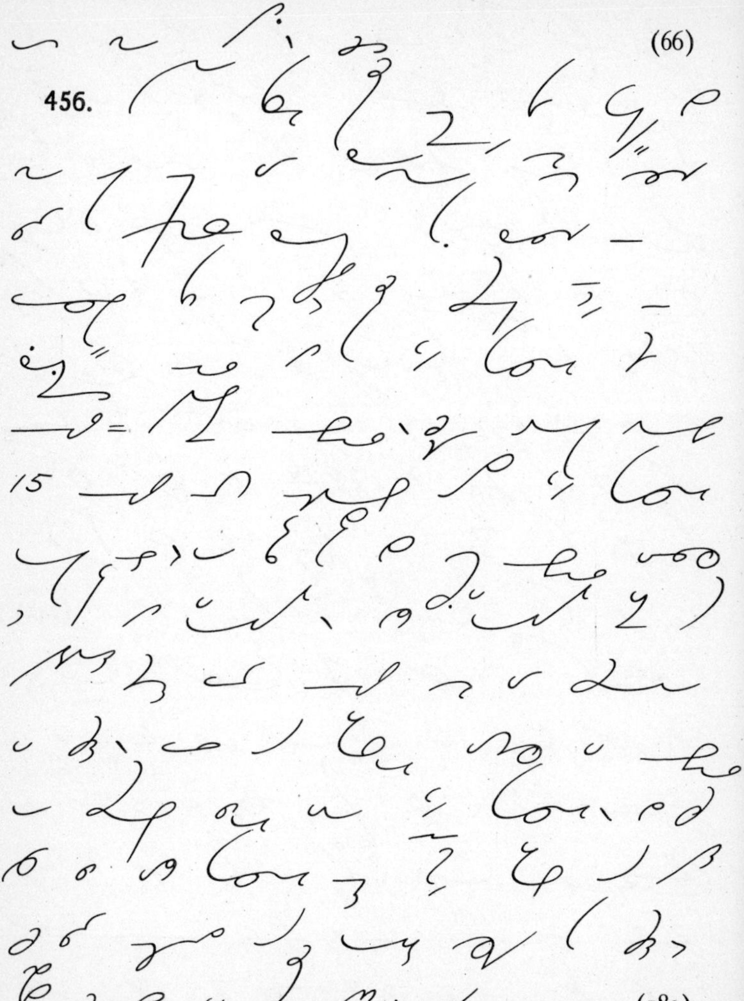

(182)

457.

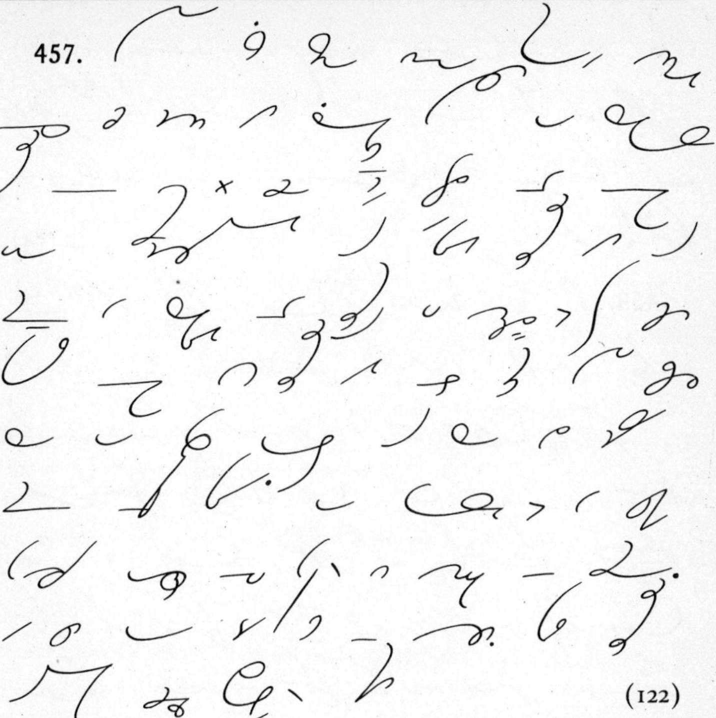

(122)

458.

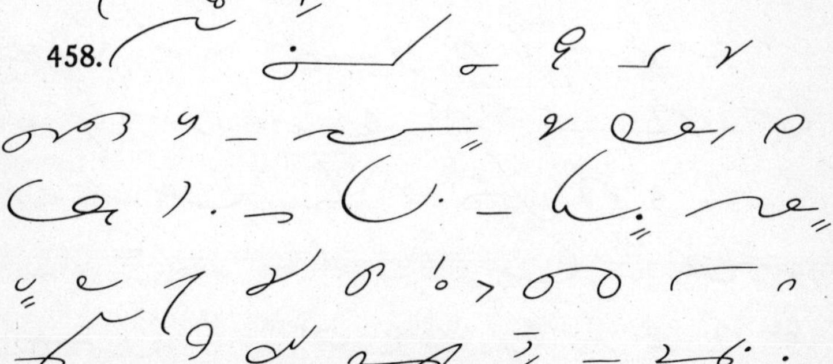

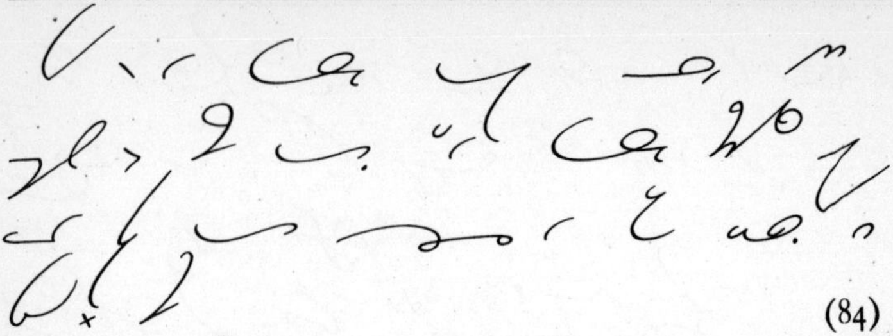

(84)

459.

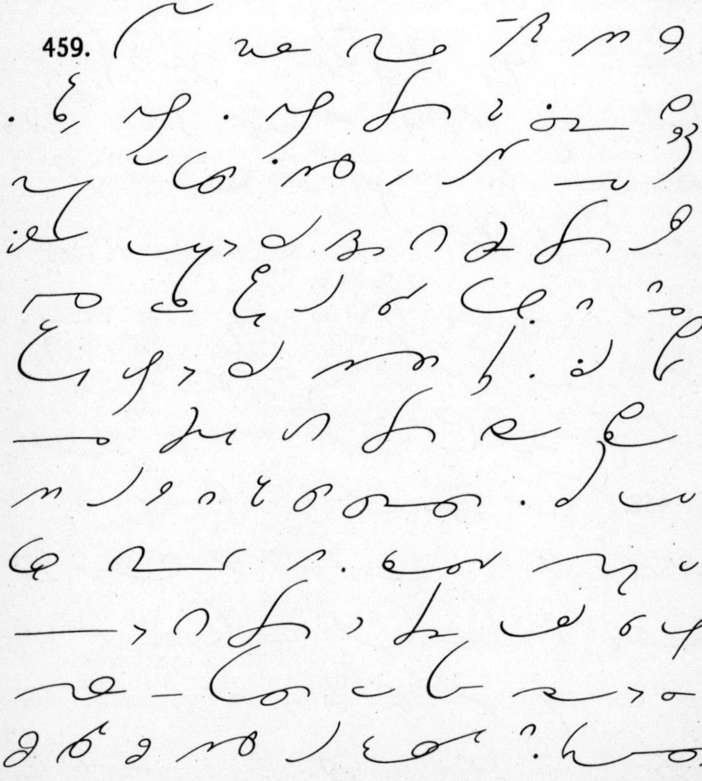

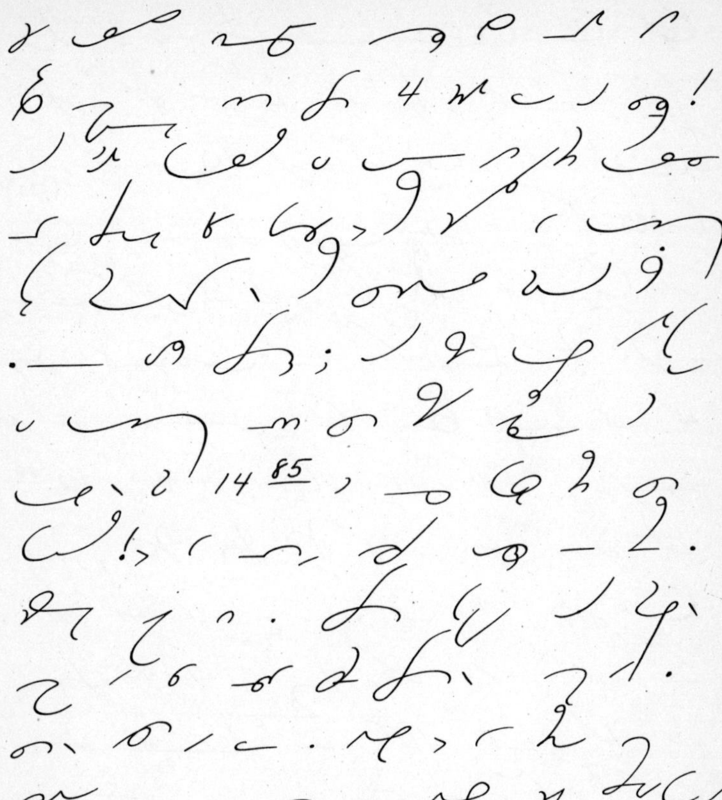

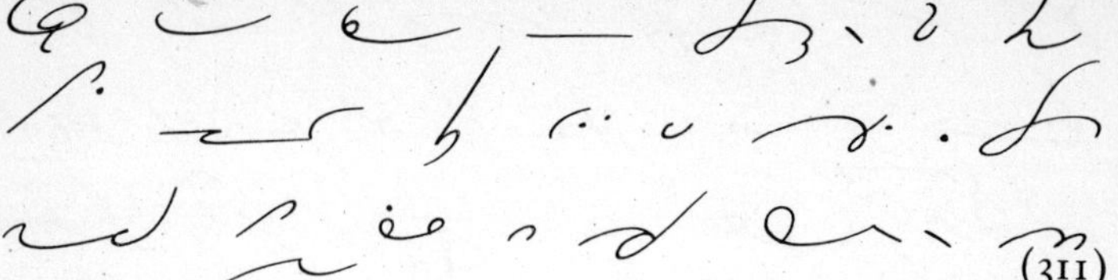

(311)

460.

(120)

461.

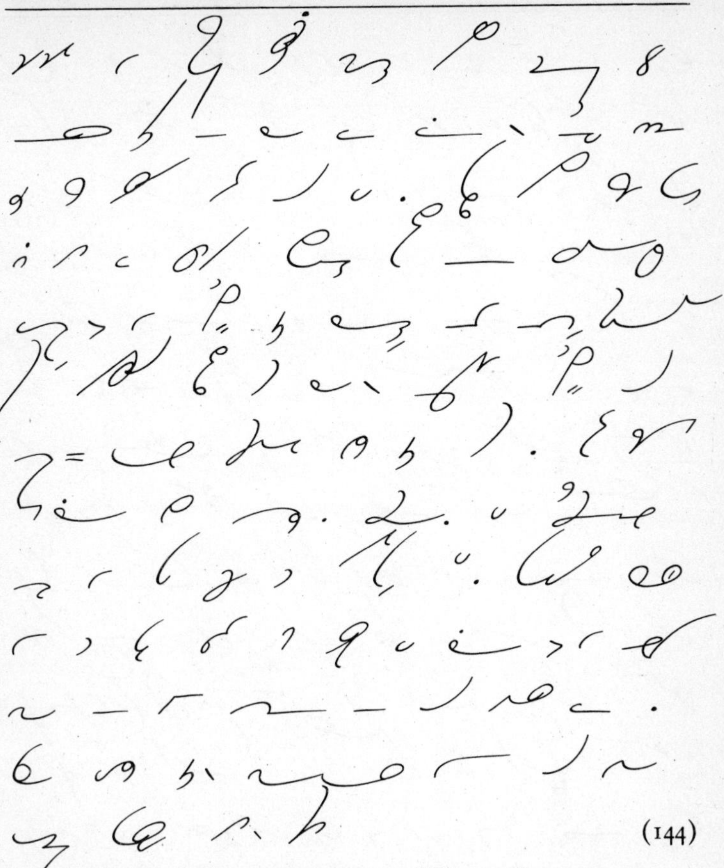

(144)

462. A Letter from Ralph Waldo Emerson to Walt Whitman

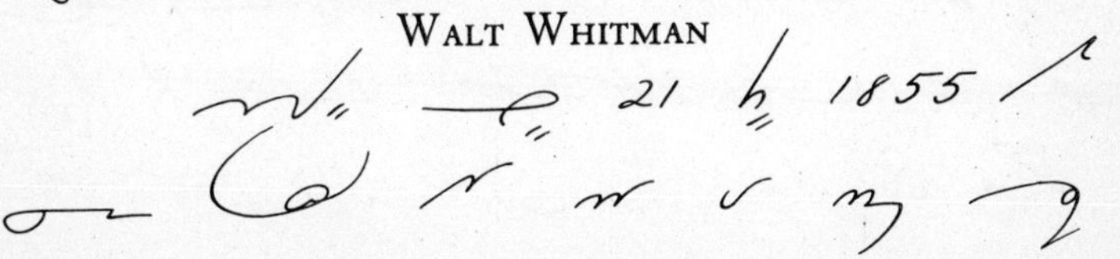

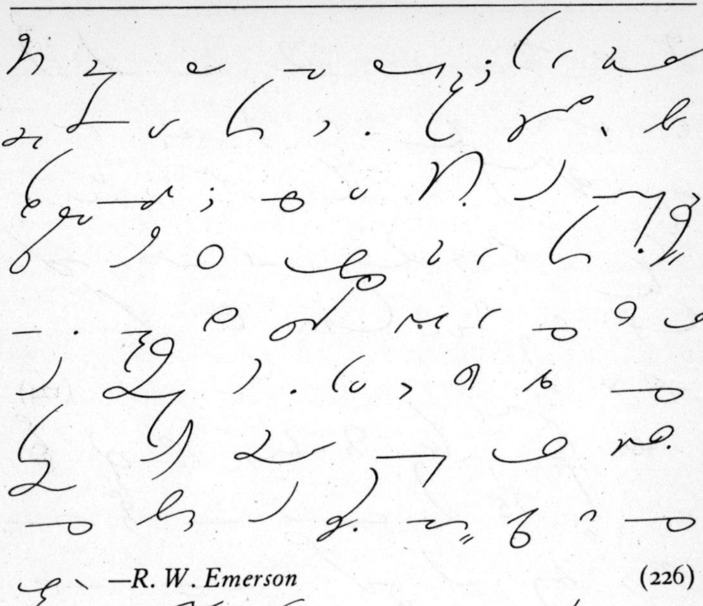

—*R. W. Emerson* (226)

463.

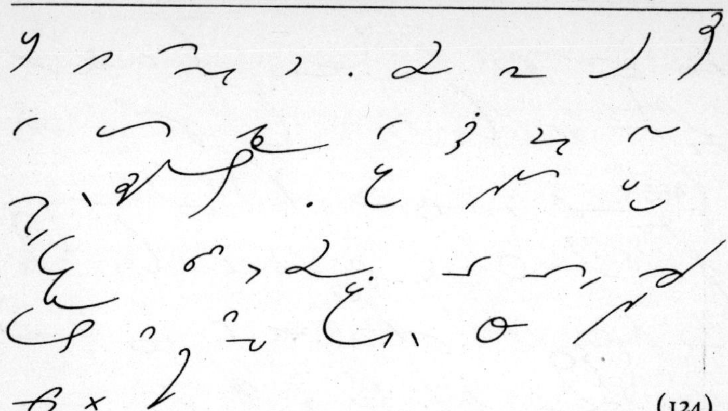

(124)

464.

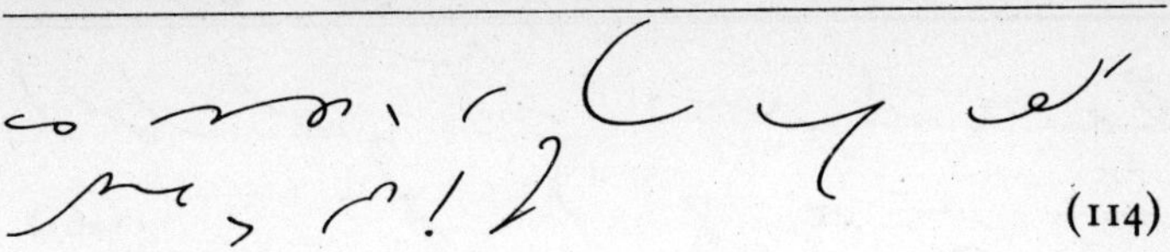

(114)

465.

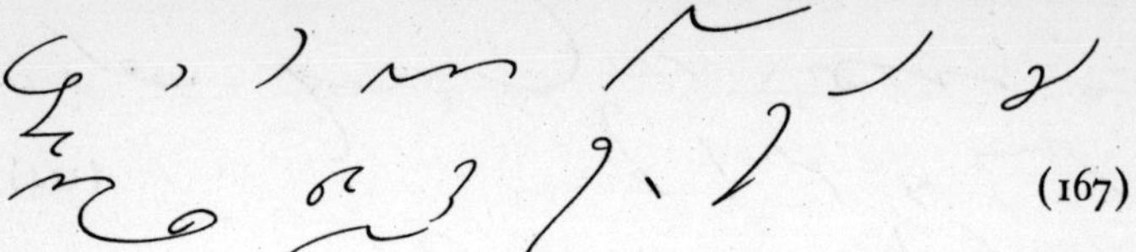

(167)

466.

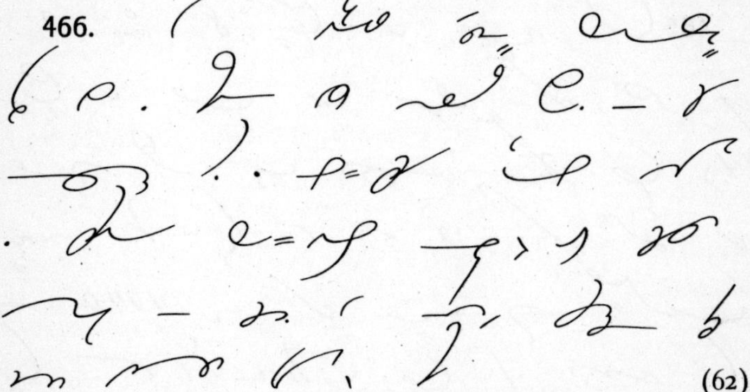

(62)

467.

(190)

468.

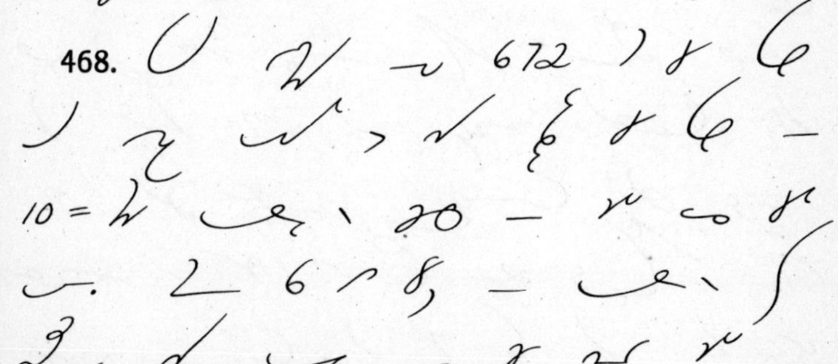

(71)

469.

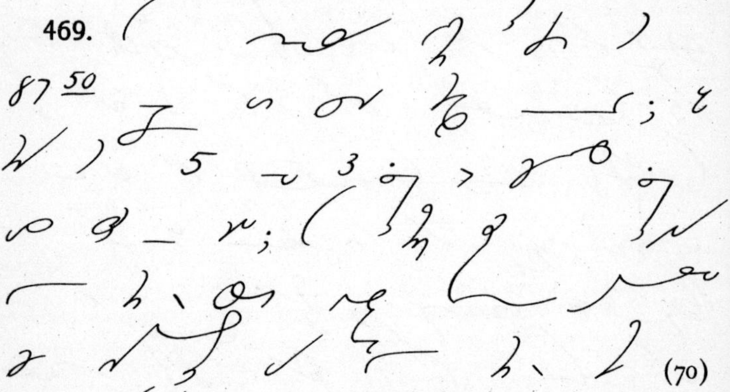

(70)

470.

(90)

471.

(131)

472.

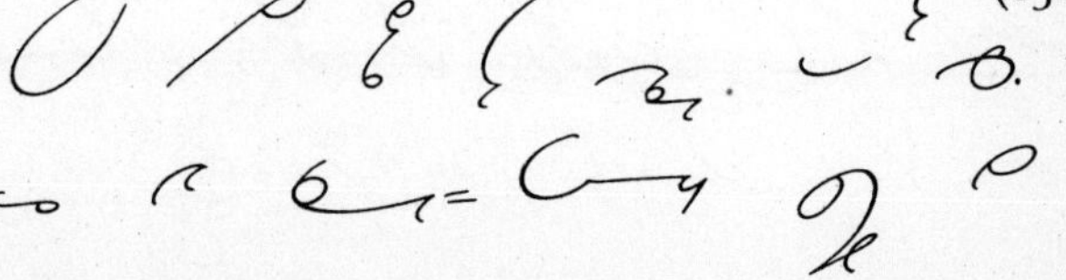

(116)

473.

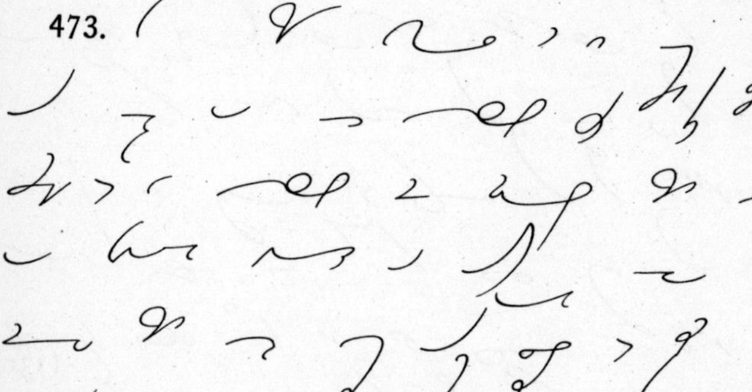

(59)

474. Taking the "Irk" Out of Work

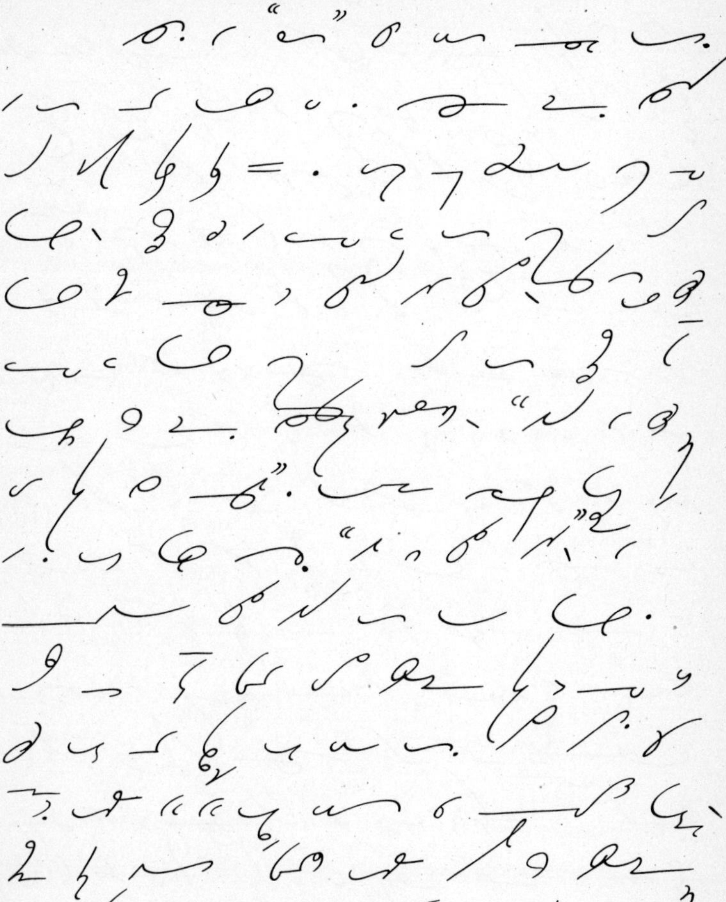

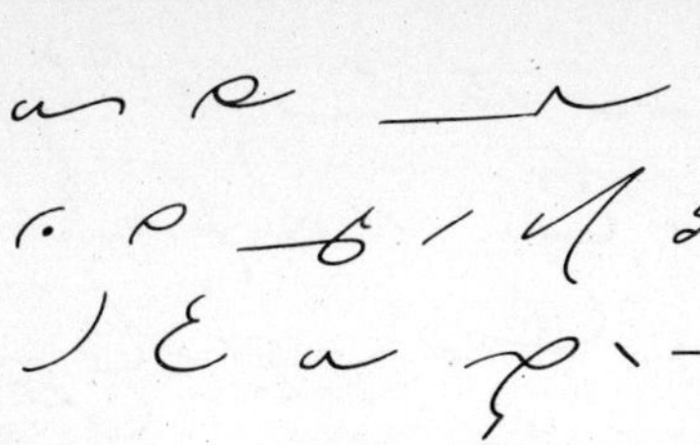

—*Callisthenes* (379)

475. How About Ourselves?

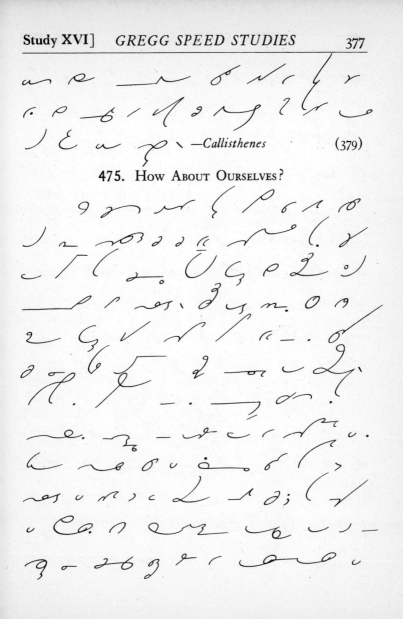

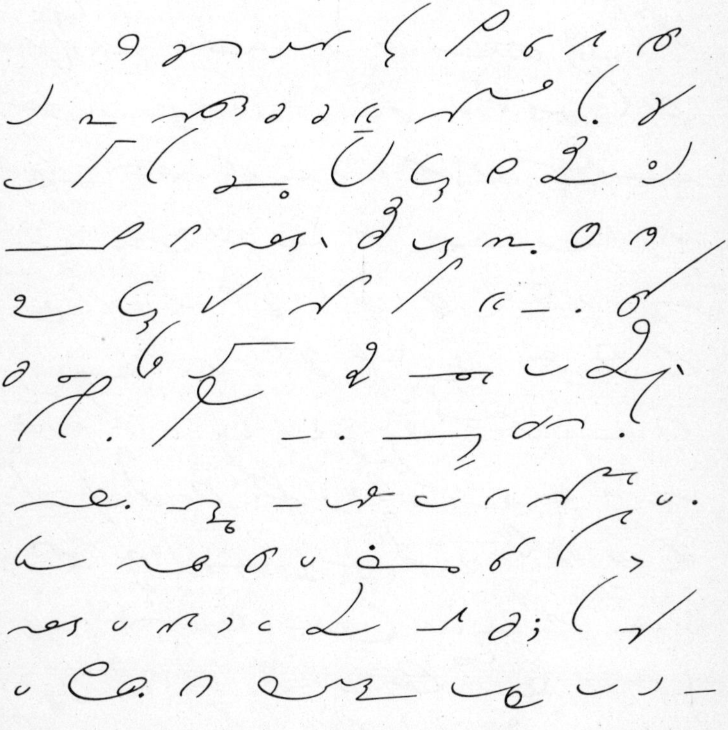

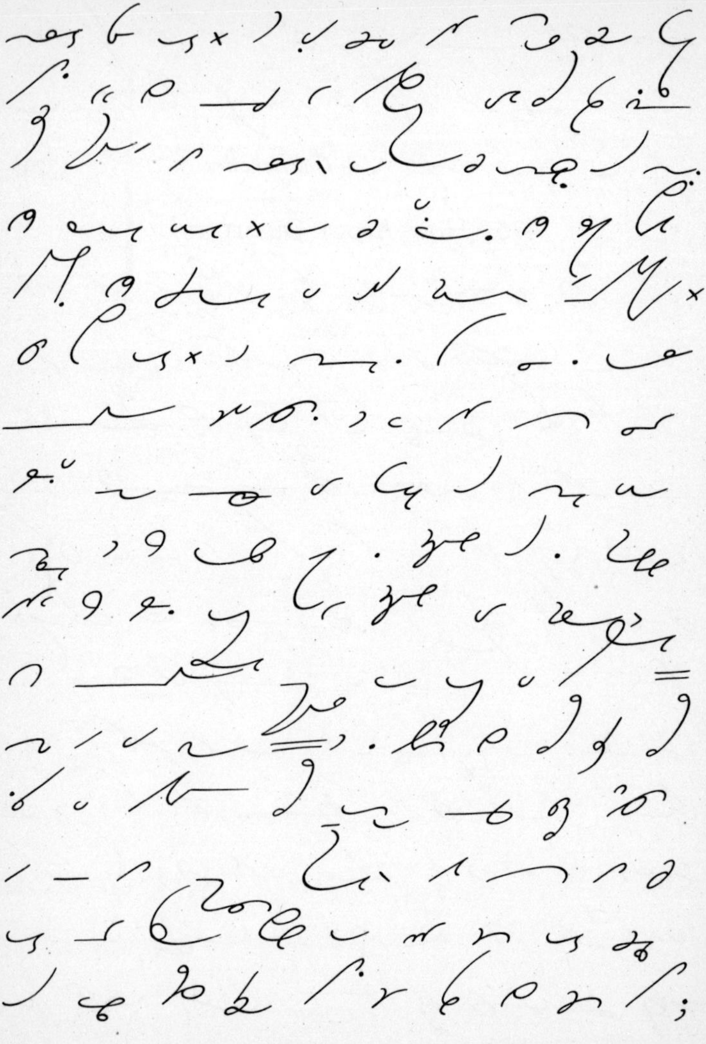

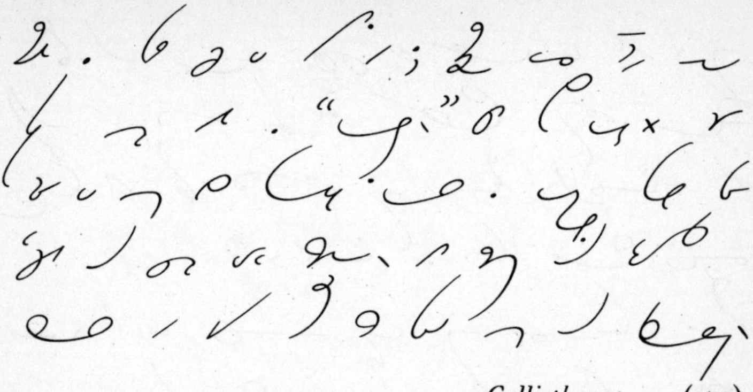

—*Callisthenes* (373)

476. An Asset to One's Personality

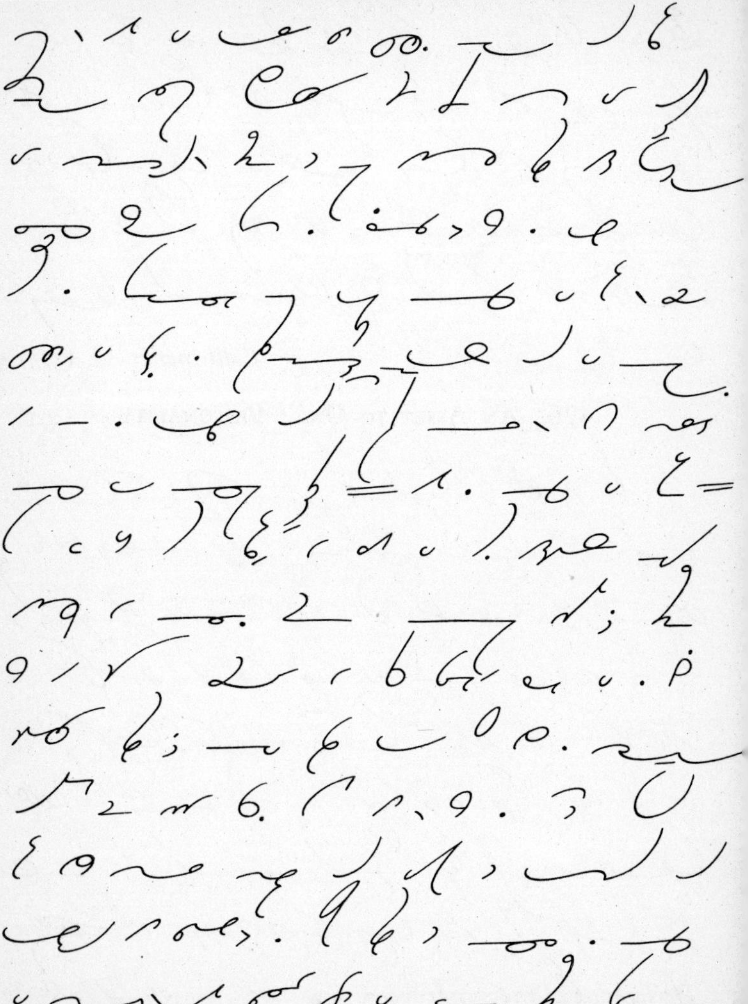

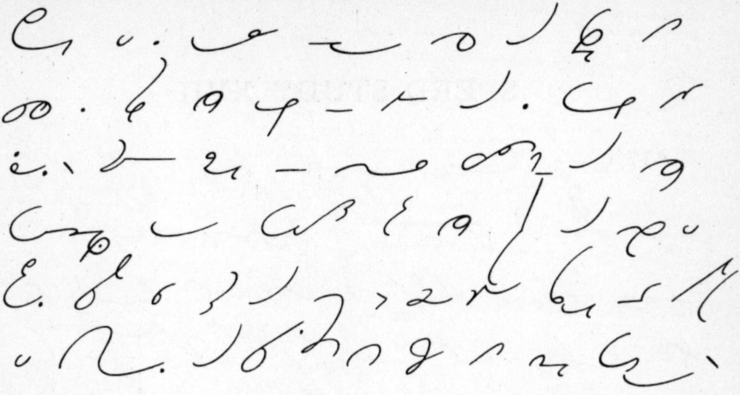

—*Callisthenes* (394)

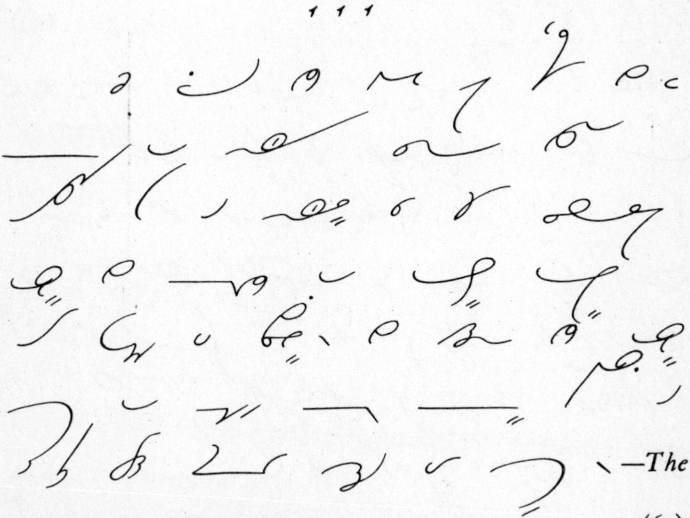

—*The Declaration of Independence* (63)

SPEED STUDY XVII

477.

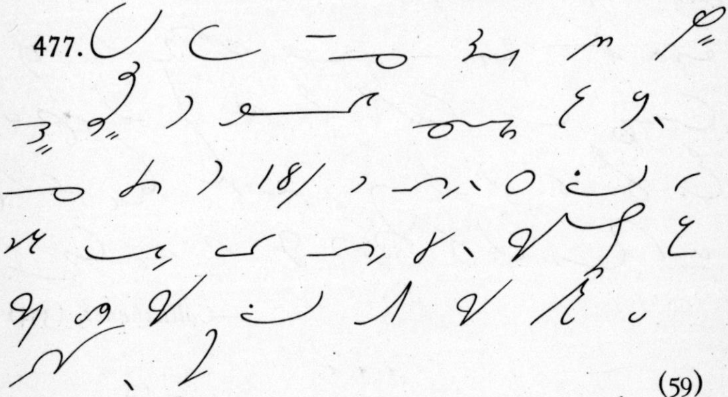

(59)

478.

(58)

479.

(66)

480.

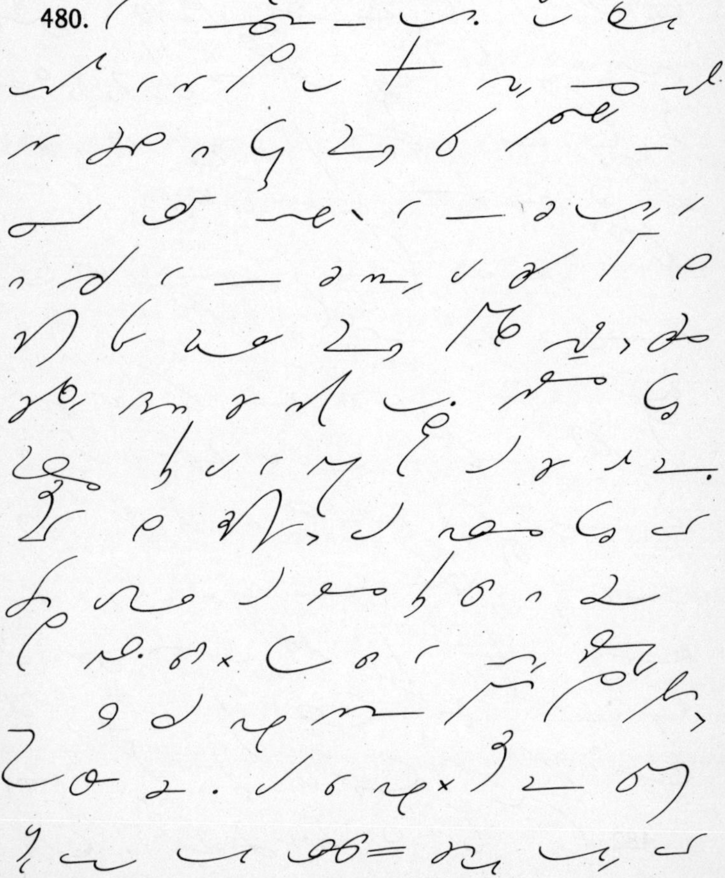

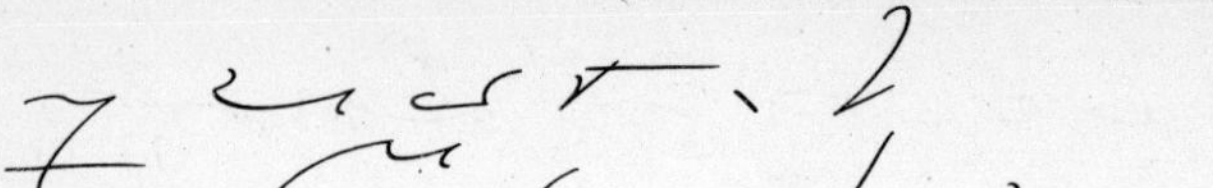

(164)

481. 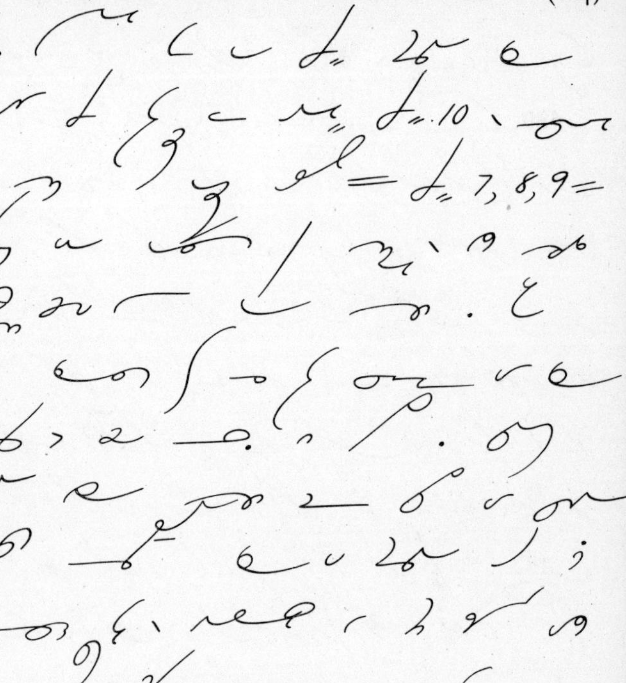

(157)

482. 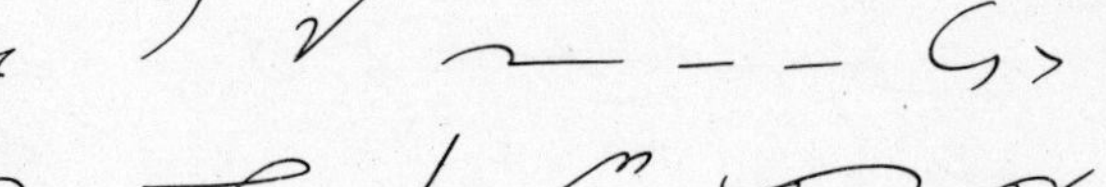

(128)

483.

(156)

484.

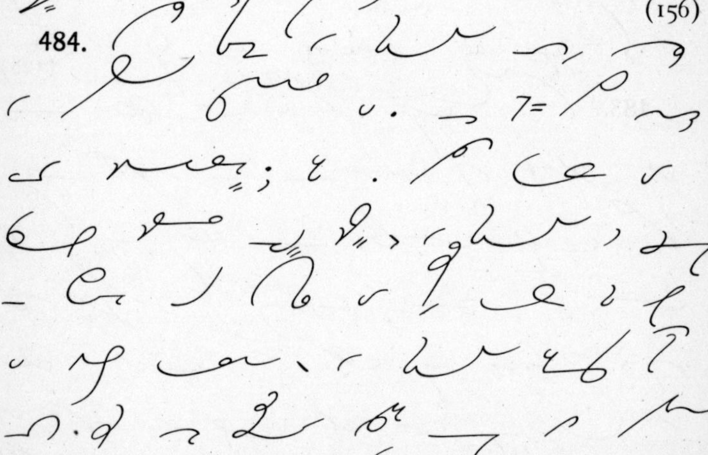

(200)

485.

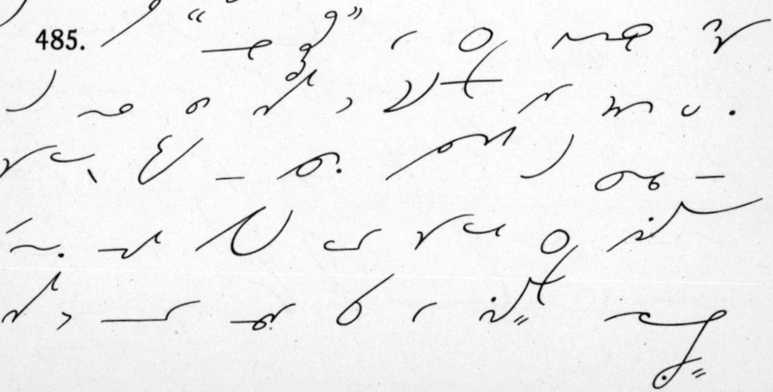

(164)

486.

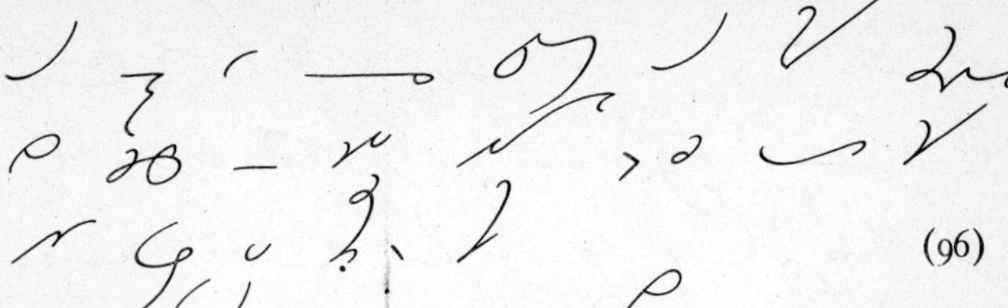

(96)

487.

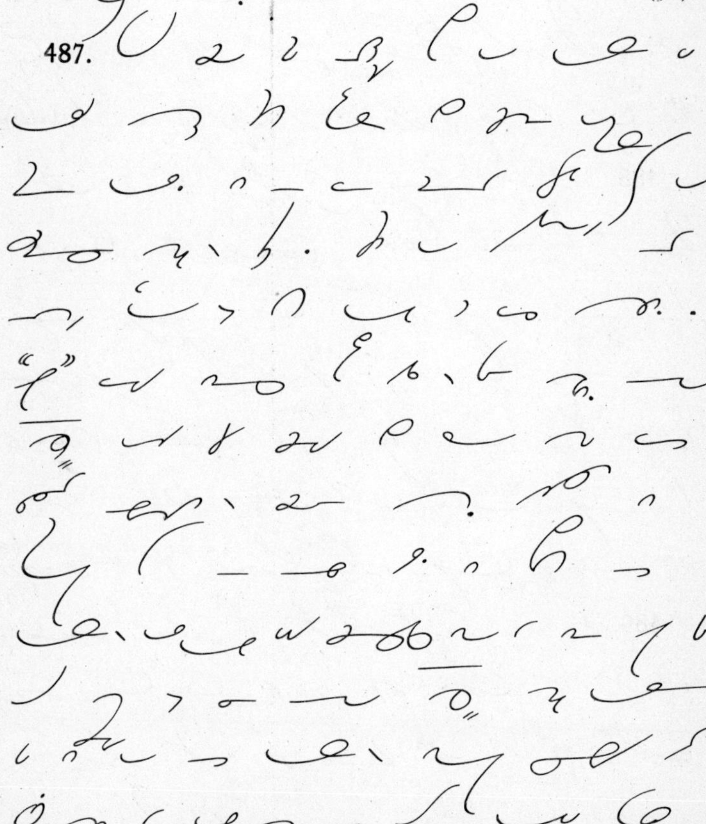

(196)

488. 20 320 4 (75)

489.

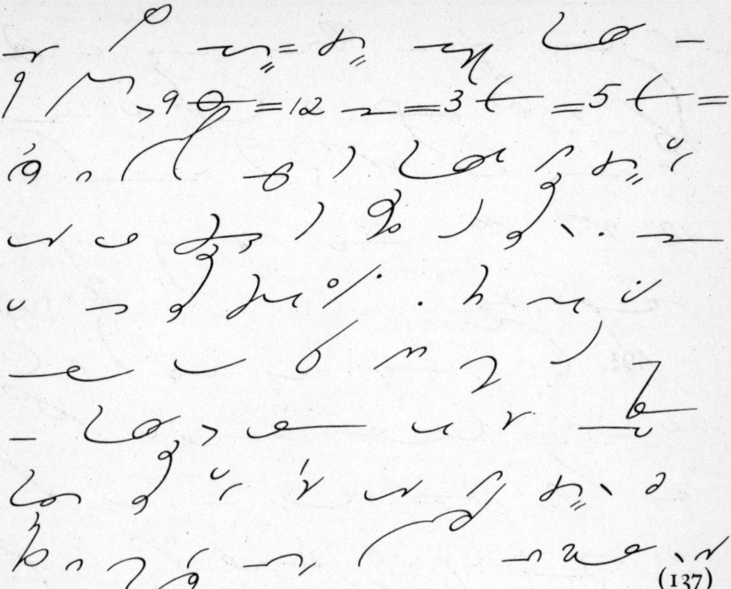

(137)

490.

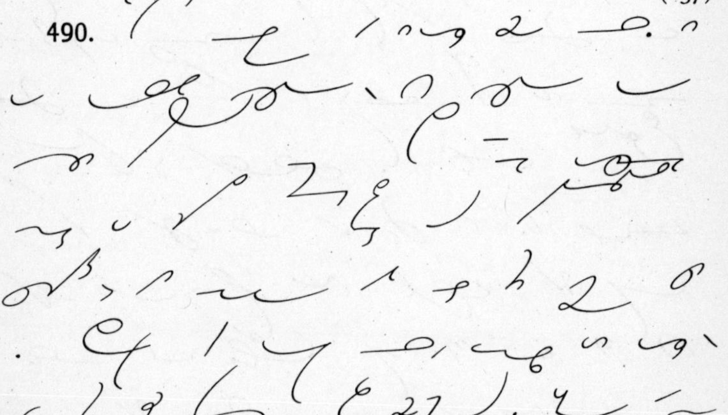

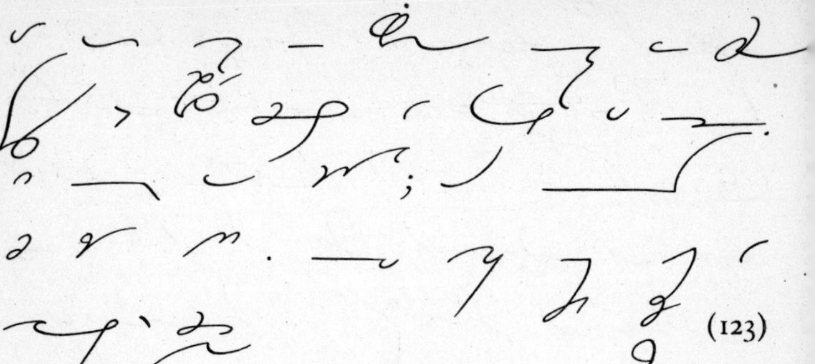

(123)

491.

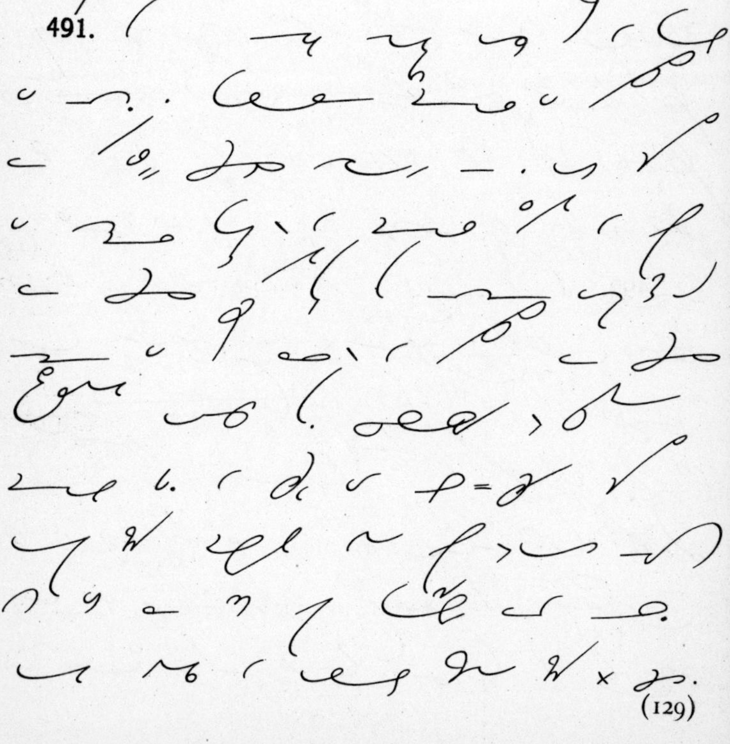

(129)

492.

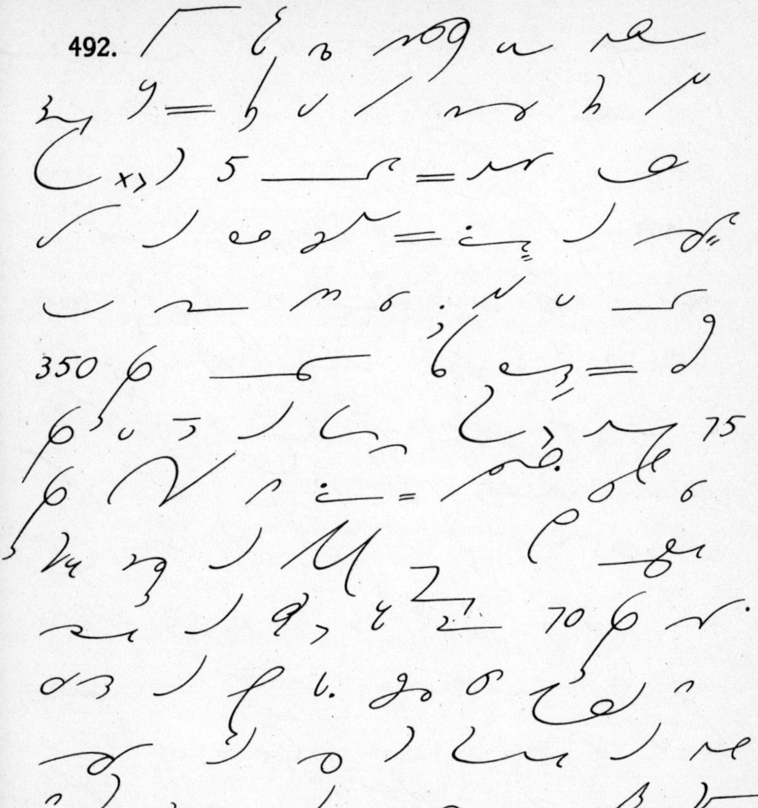

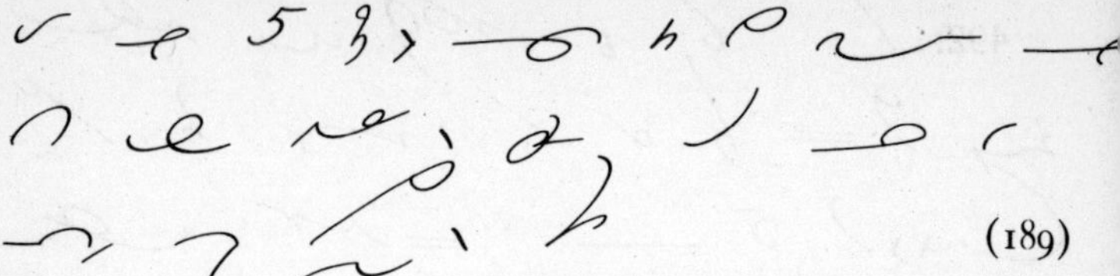

(189)

493.

(131)

494.

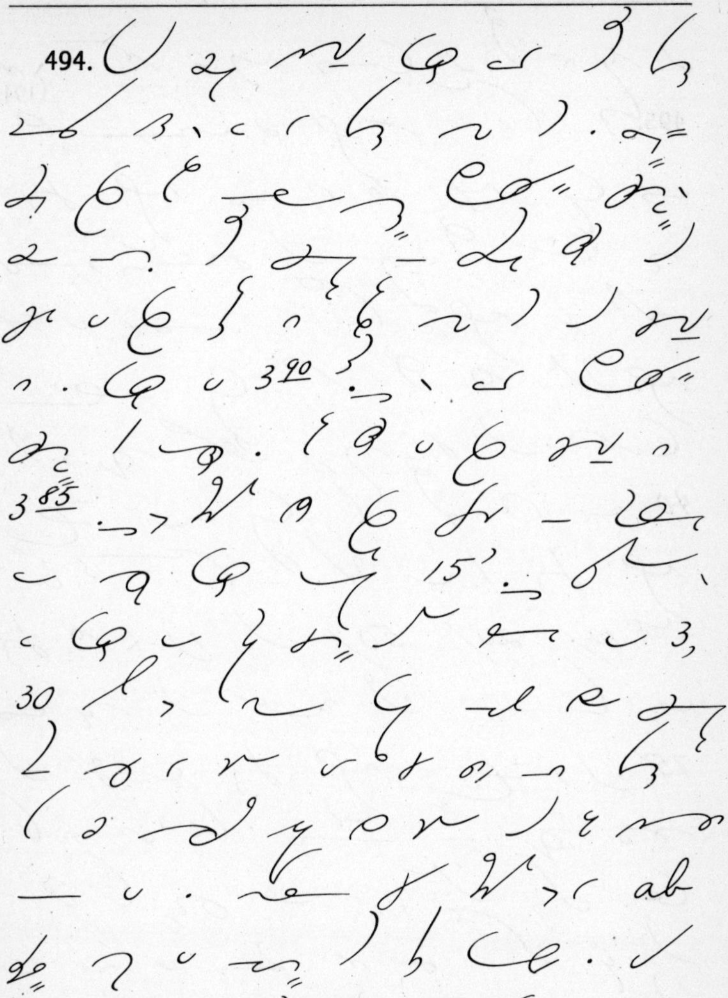

(194)

495.

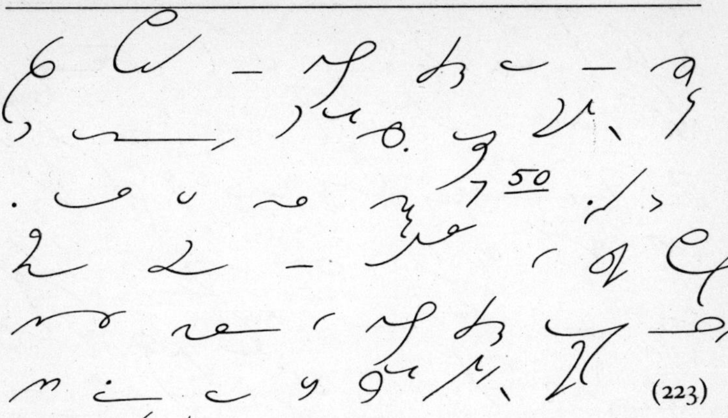

(223)

496.

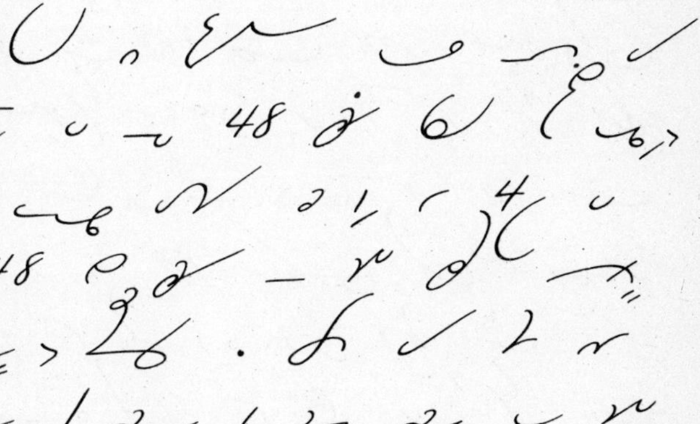

(96)

497.

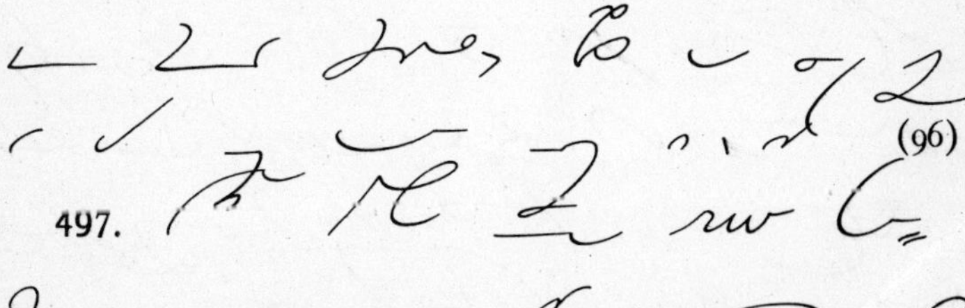

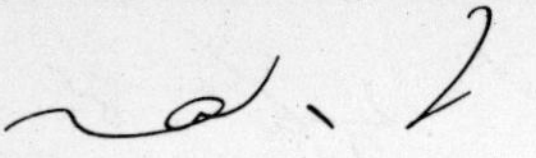

(206)

498.

50

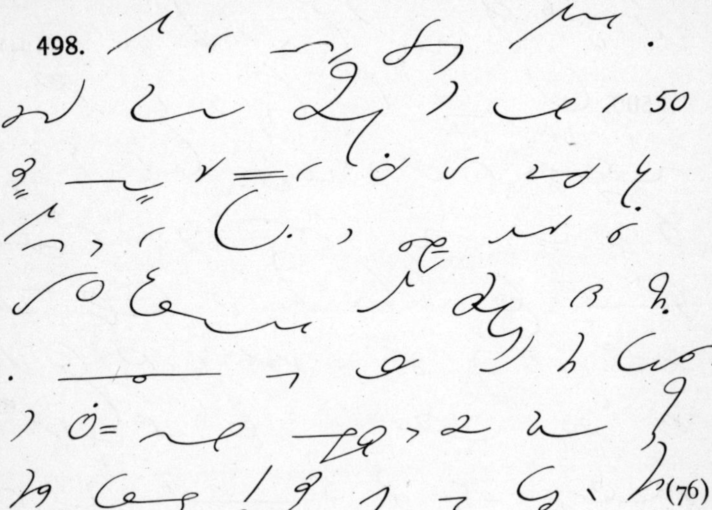

(76)

499.

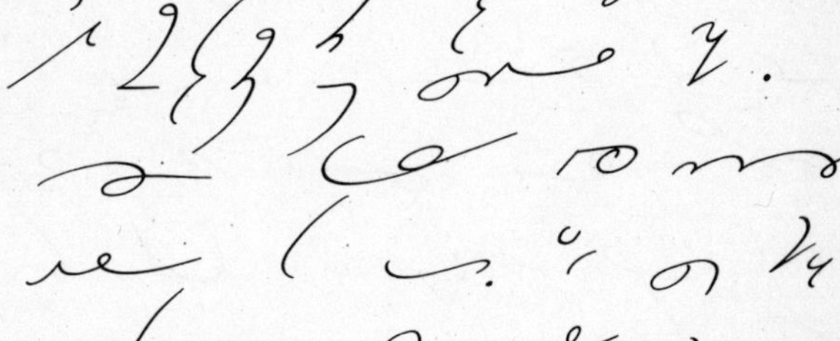

(94)

500.

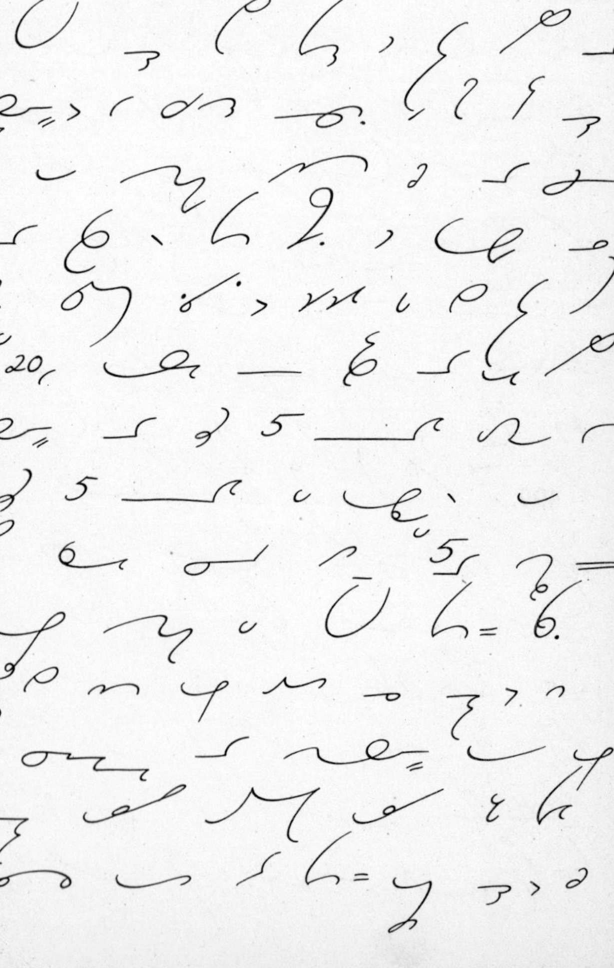

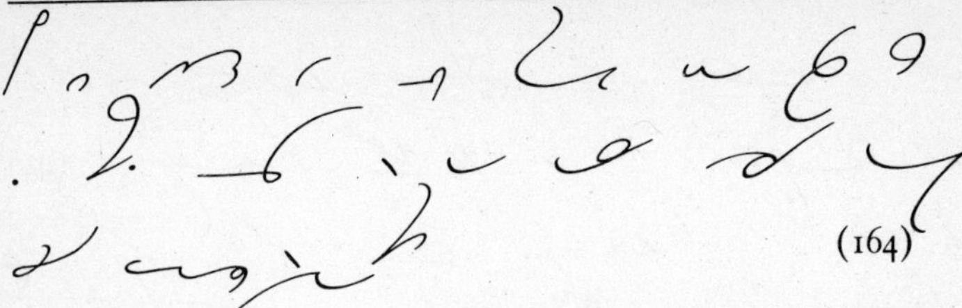

(164)

501.

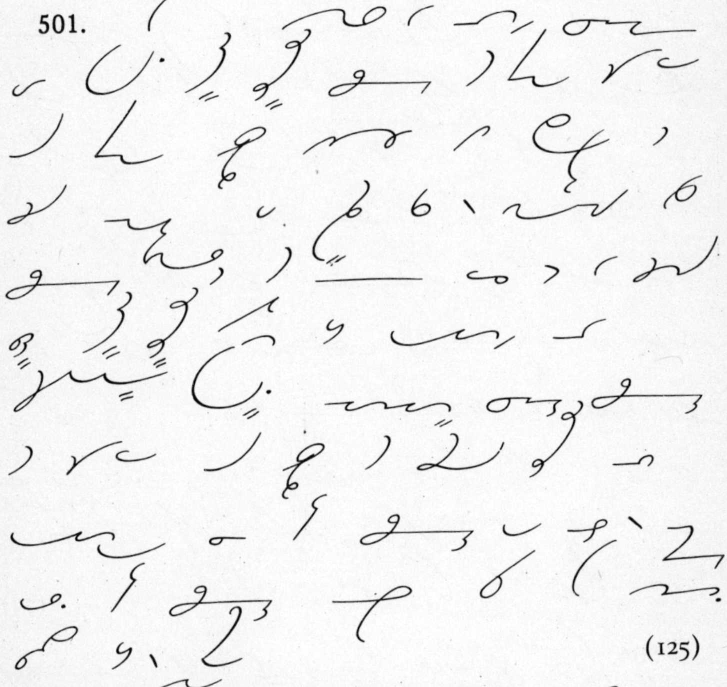

(125)

502.

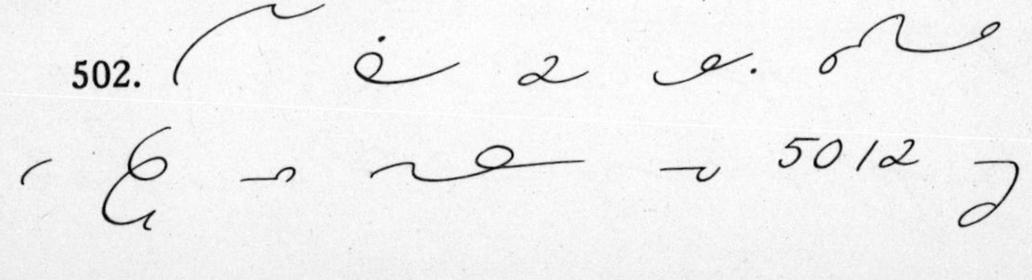

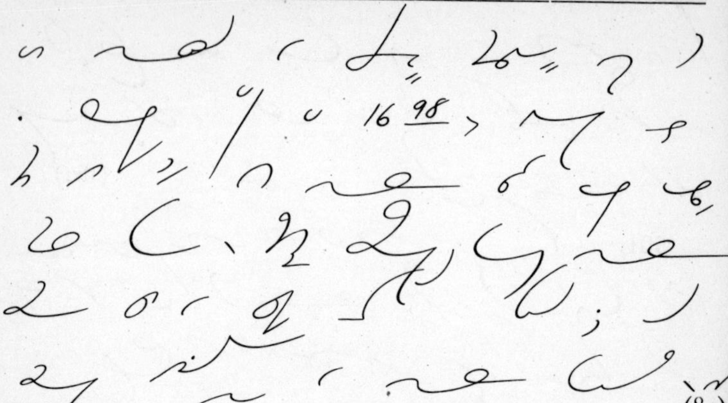

(84)

503.

(70)

504.

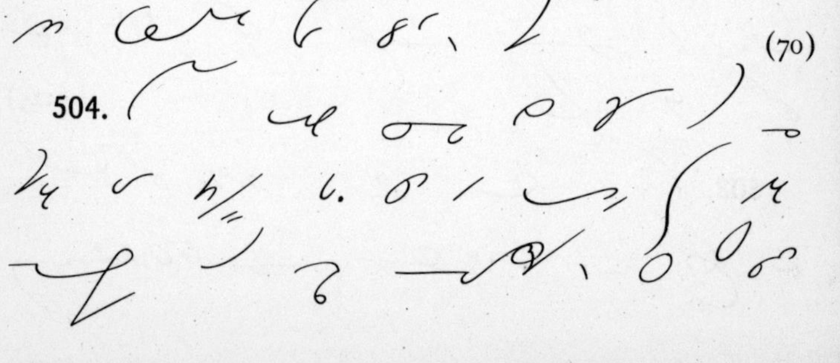

(144)

505.

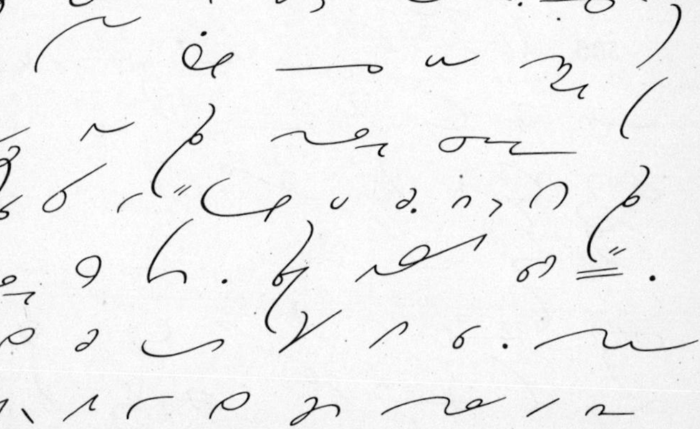

(181)

506.

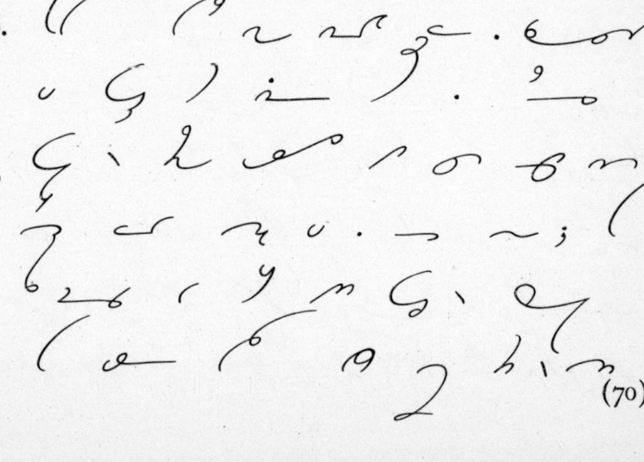

(70)

507. How Can We Keep Water Pure?

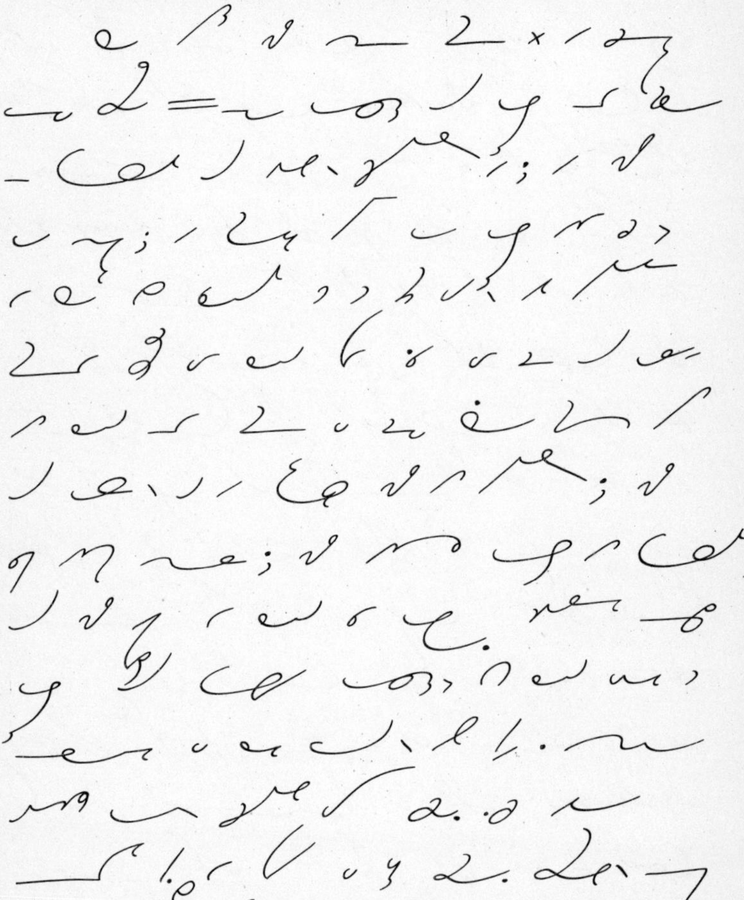

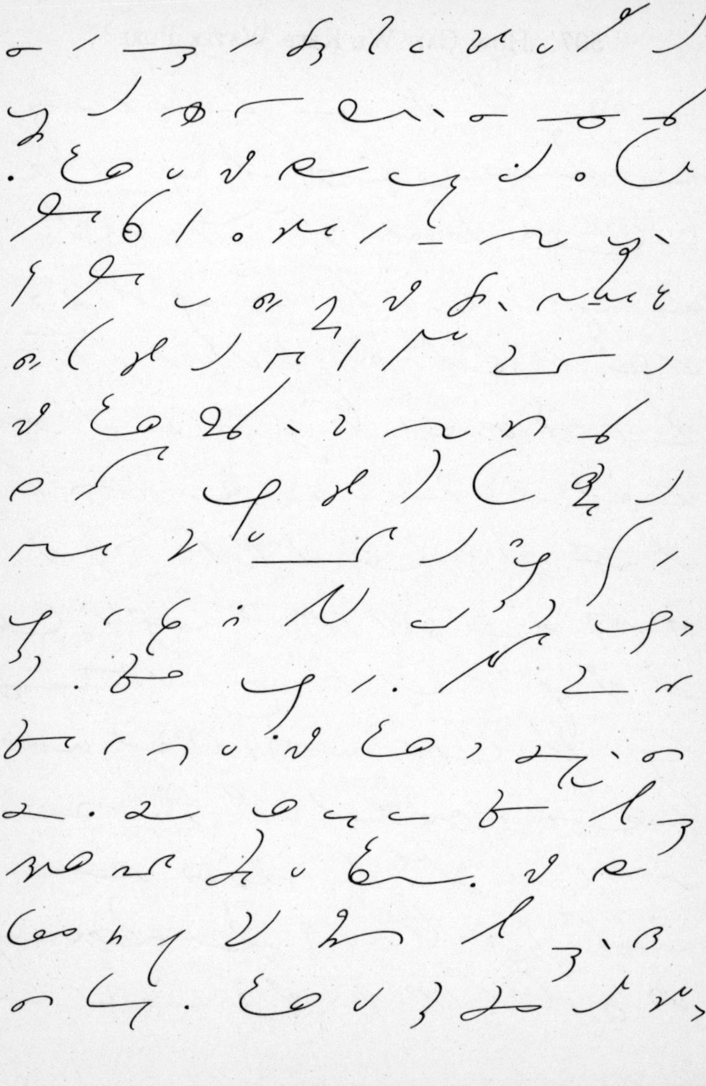

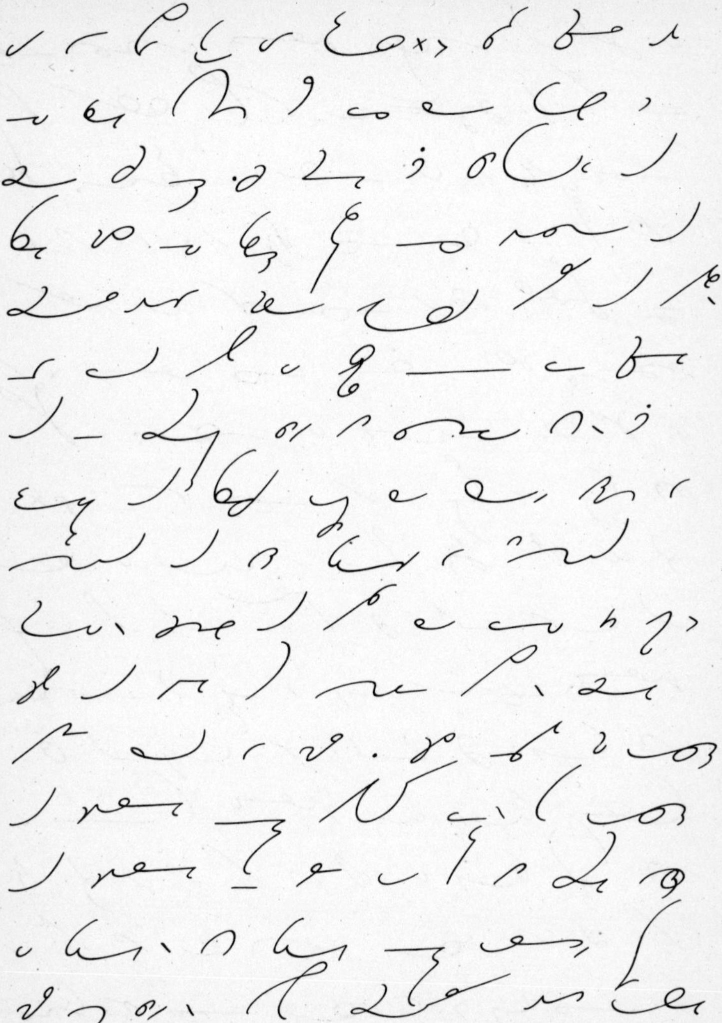

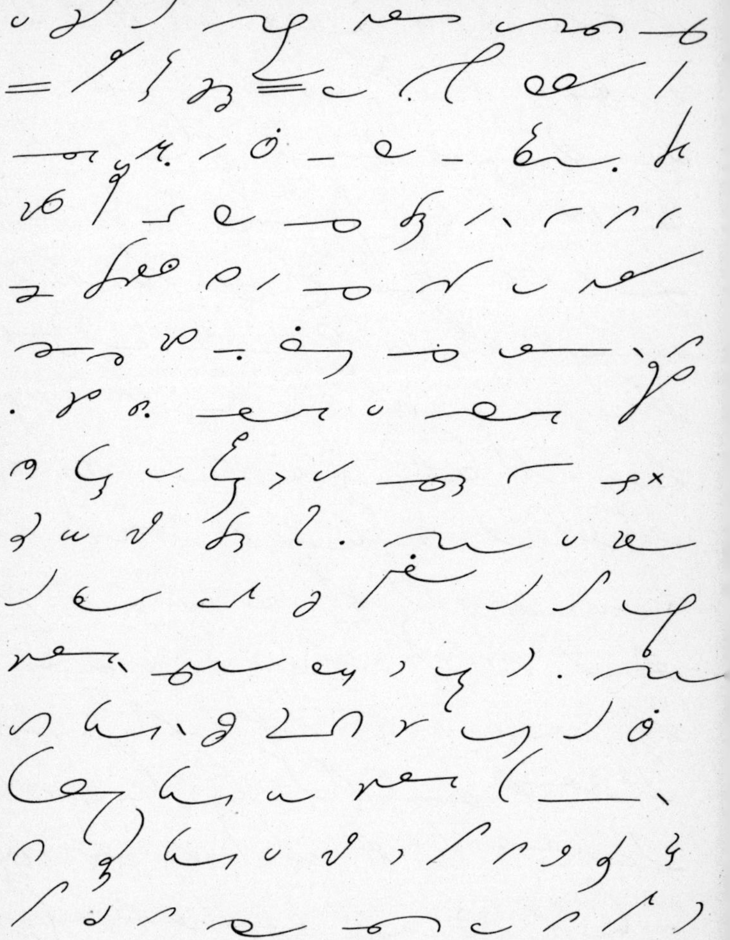

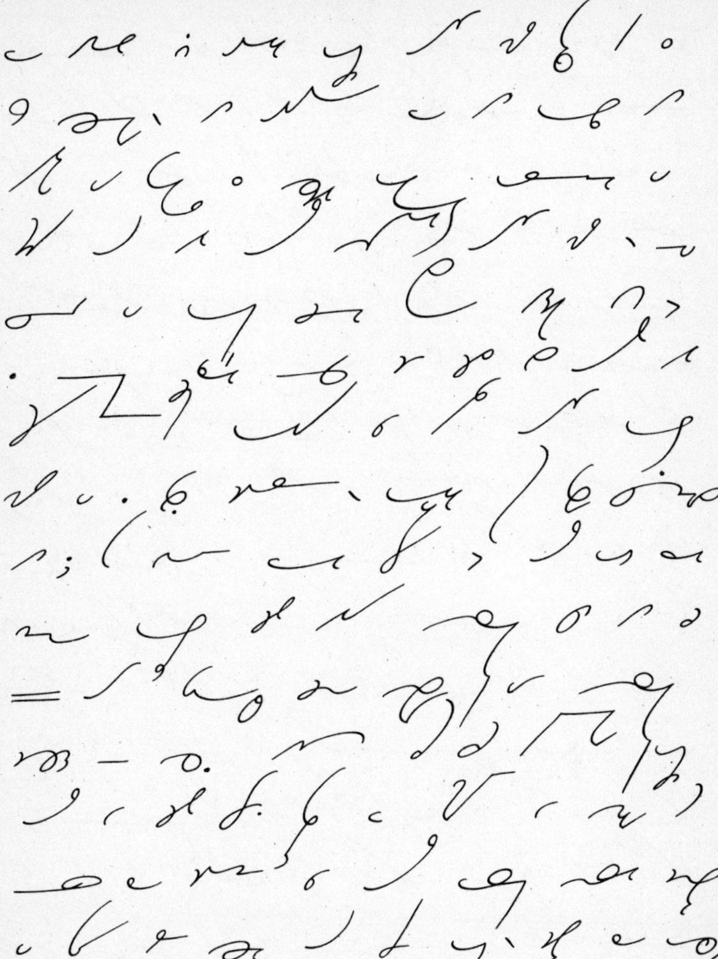

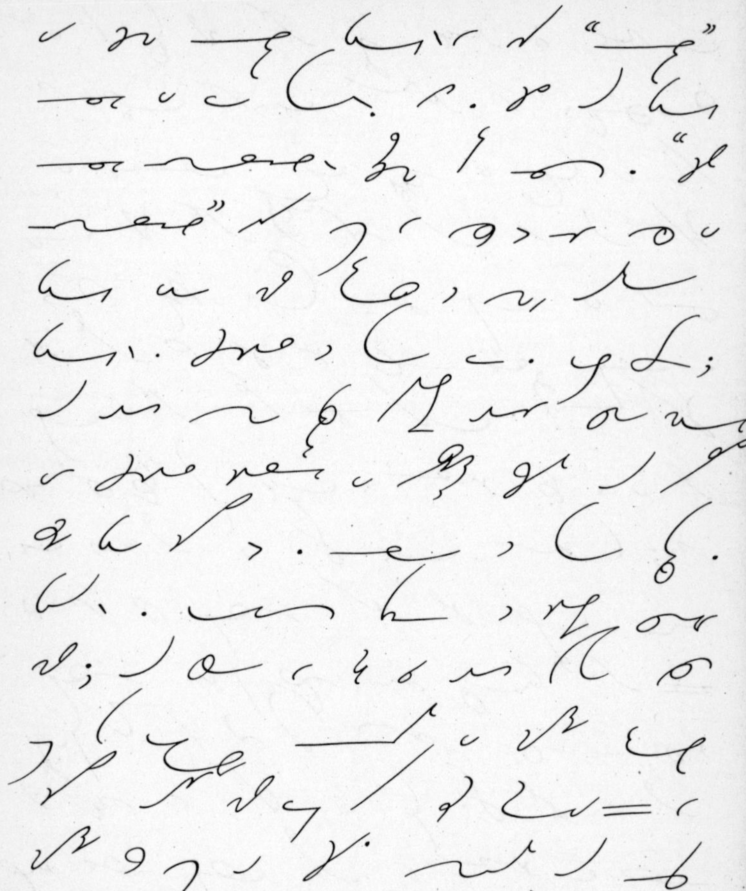

—*National Wildlife Federation*

(959)

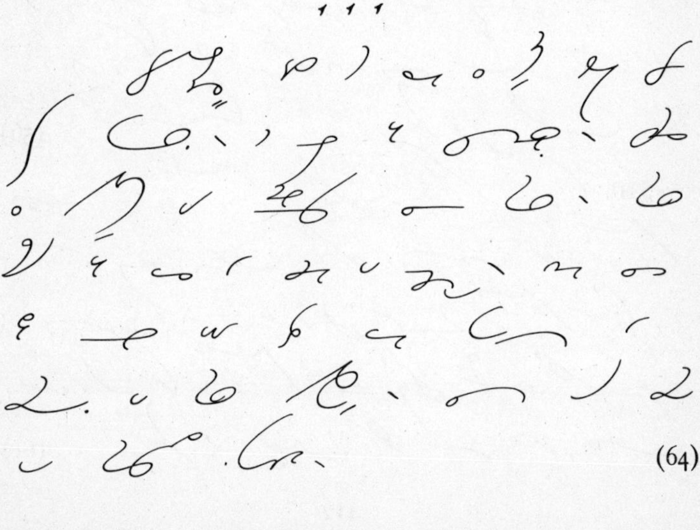

(64)

SPEED STUDY XVIII

508.

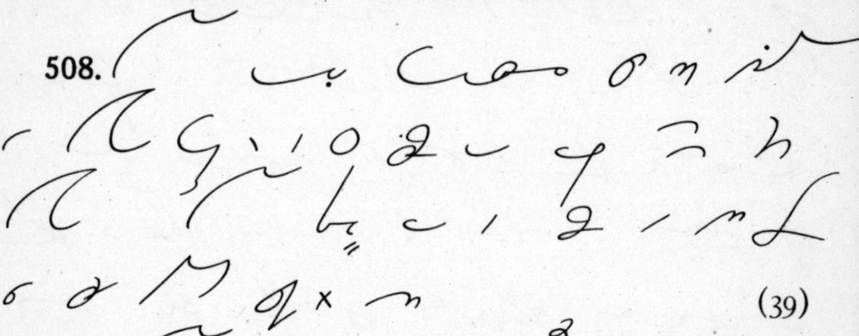

(39)

509.

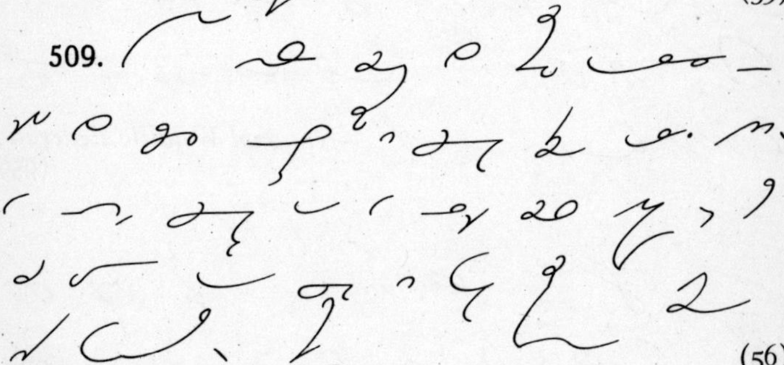

(56)

510.

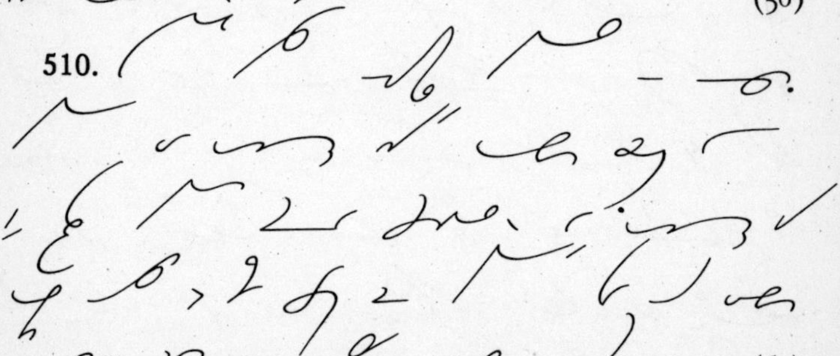

(61)

511.

(144)

512.

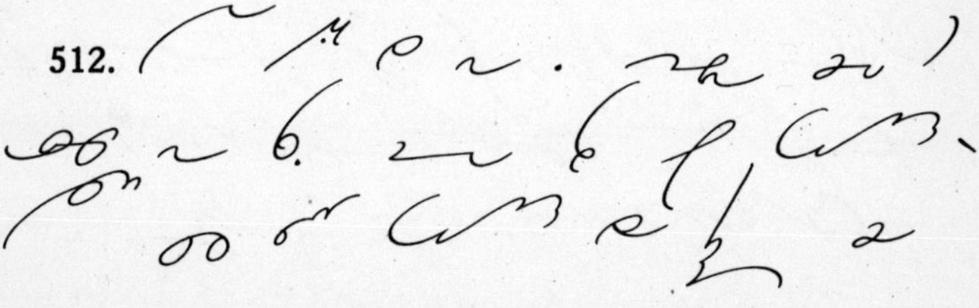

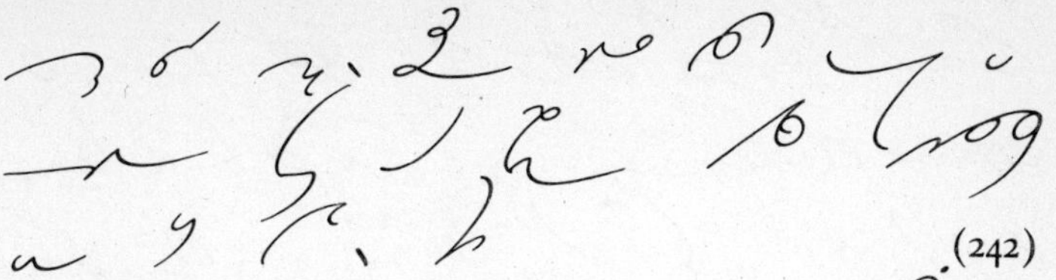

(242)

513.

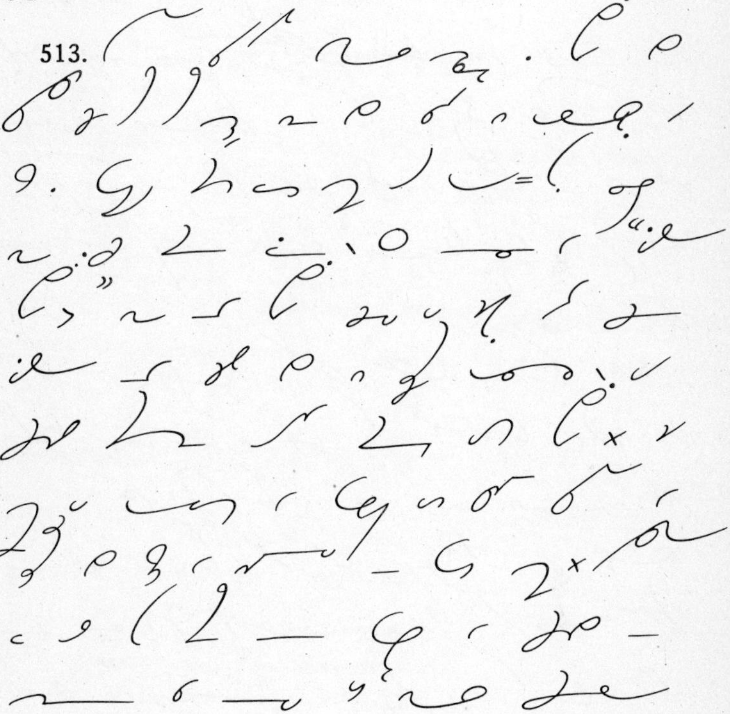

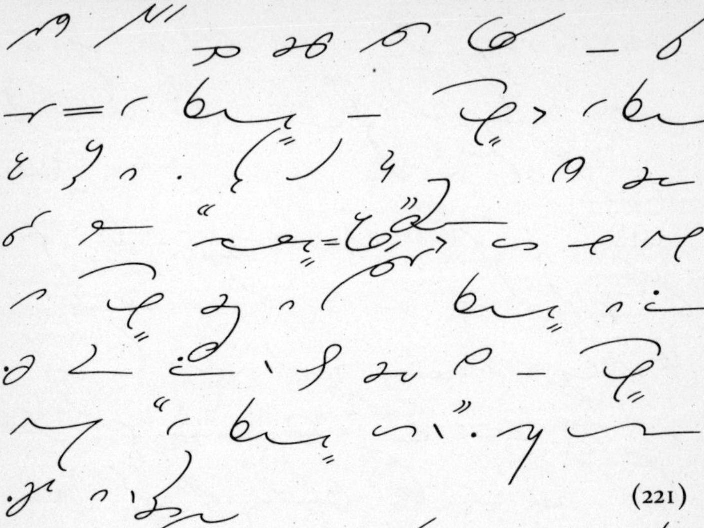

(221)

514.

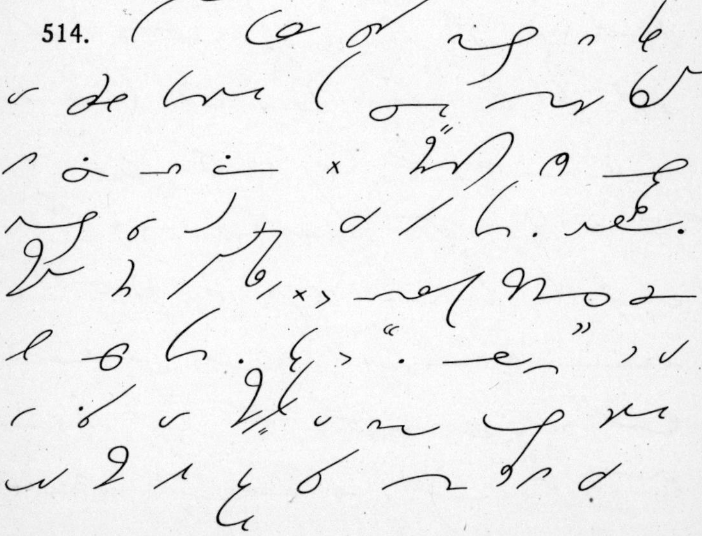

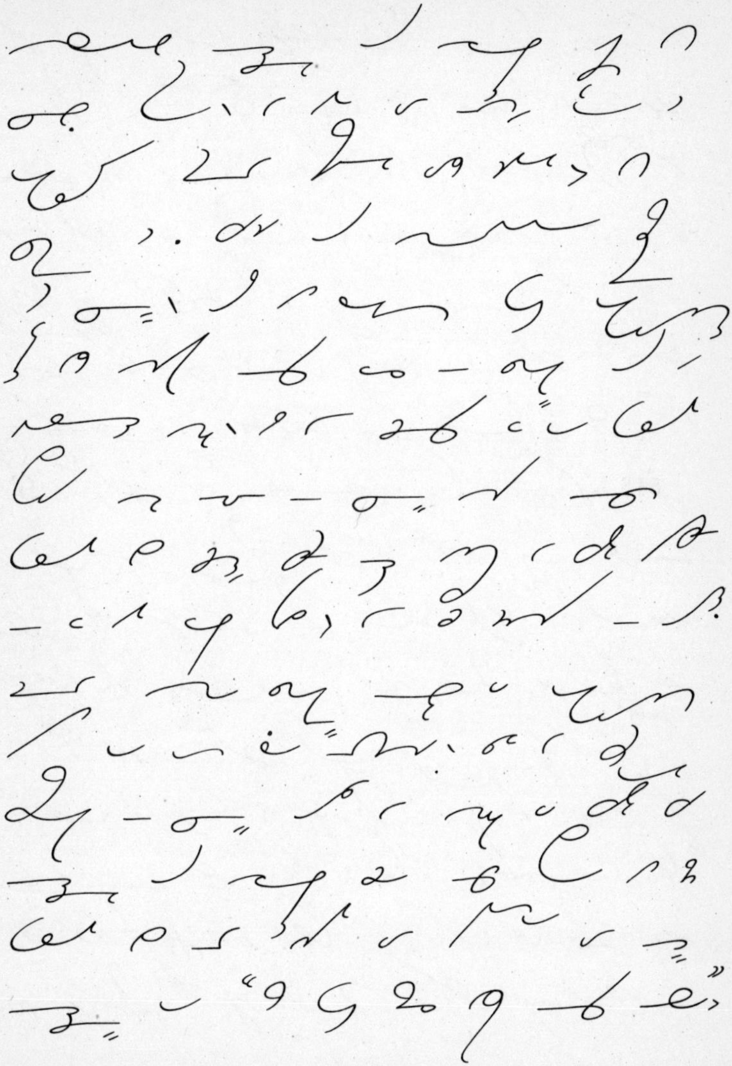

(328)

515.

(224)

516.

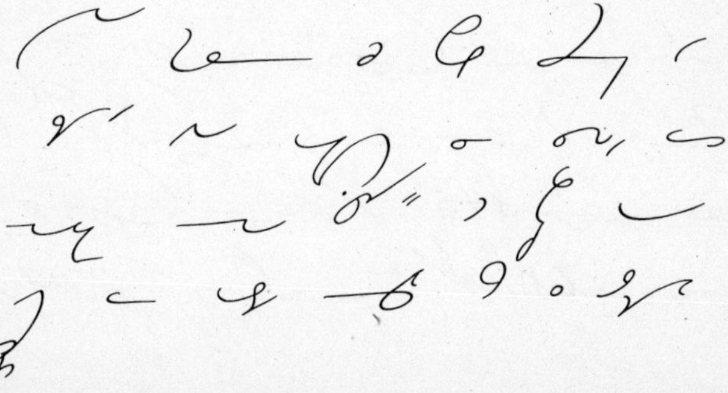

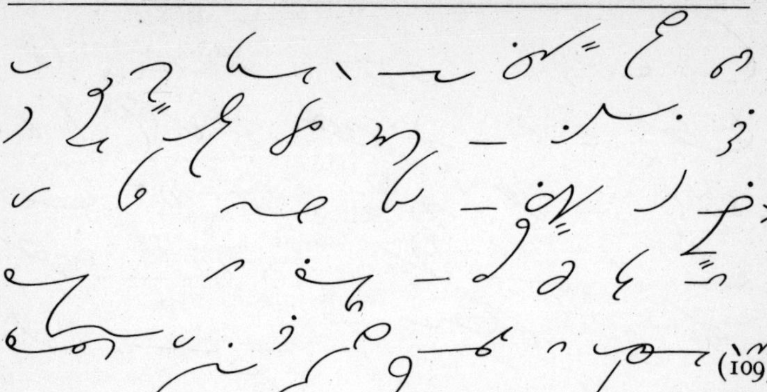

(109)

517.

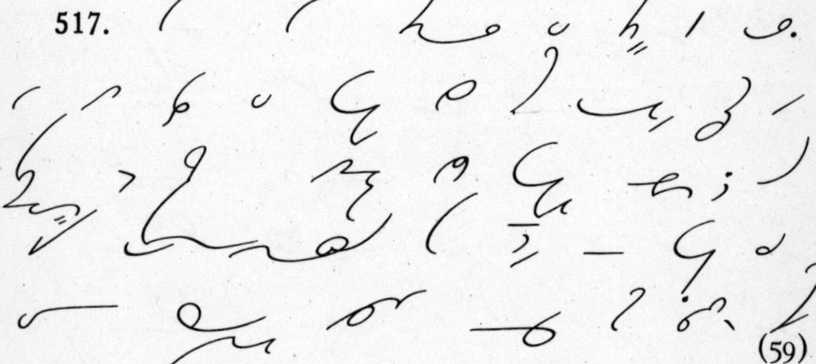

(59)

518.

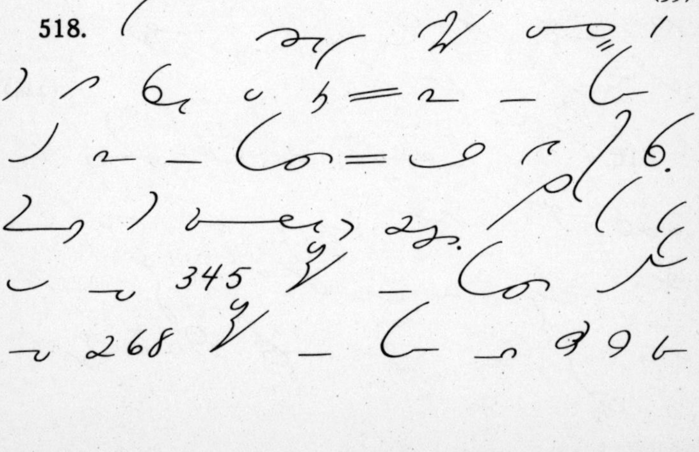

[Gregg shorthand outlines]

(106)

519. *[Gregg shorthand outlines]* 26

[Gregg shorthand outlines] 26

[Gregg shorthand outlines] 26

[Gregg shorthand outlines] 20 . *[outline]*

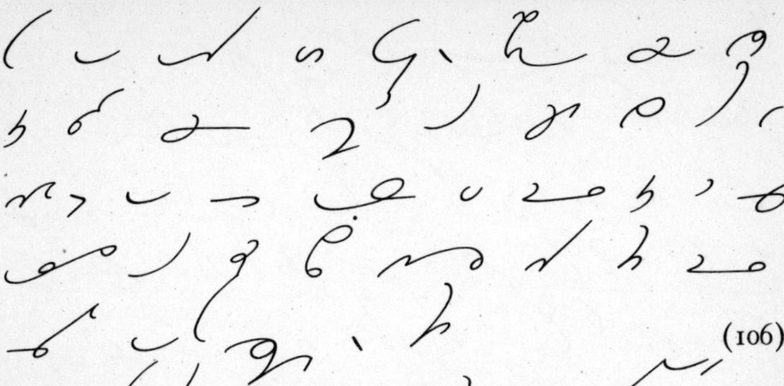

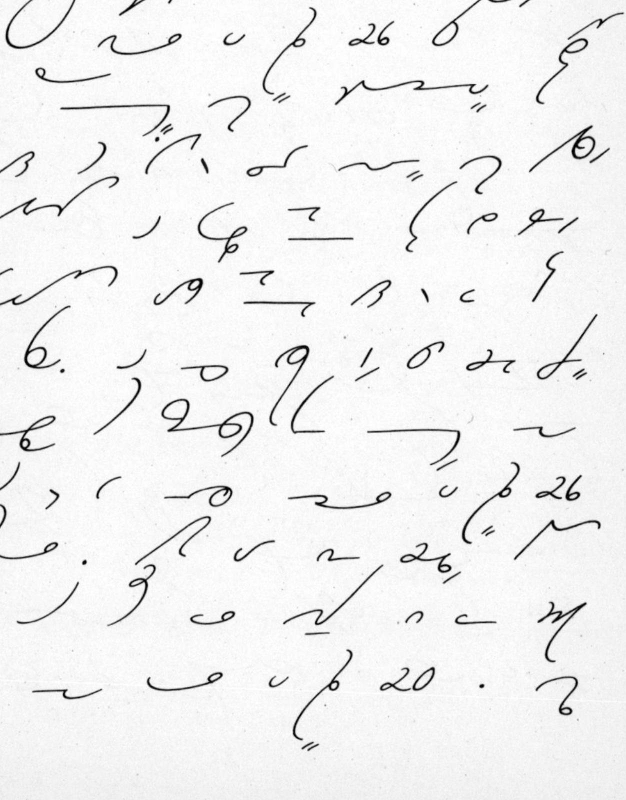

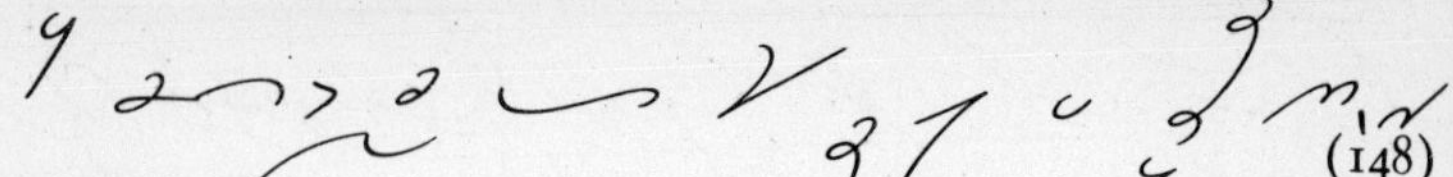

(148)

520.

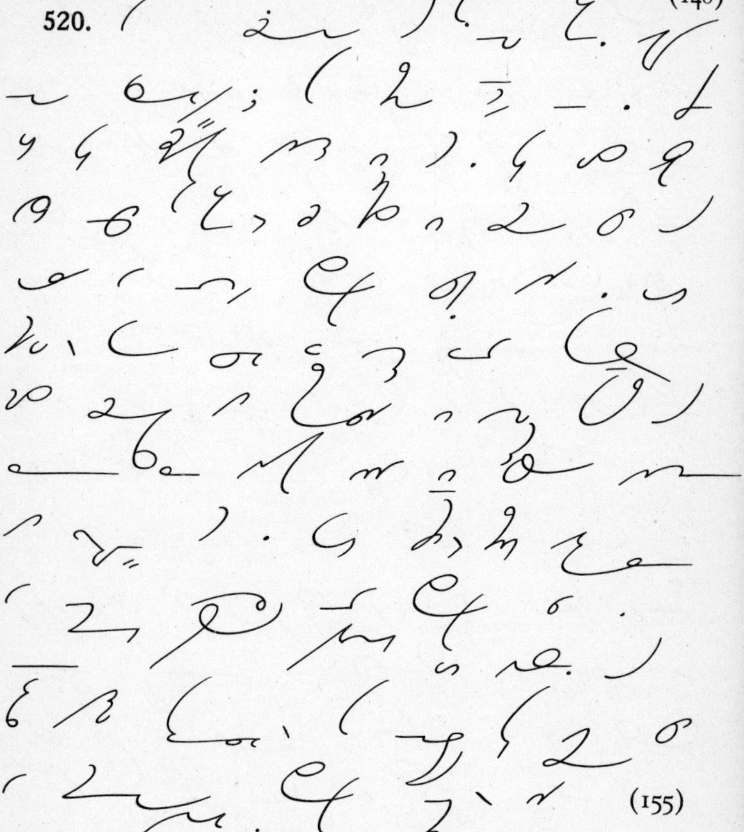

(155)

521.

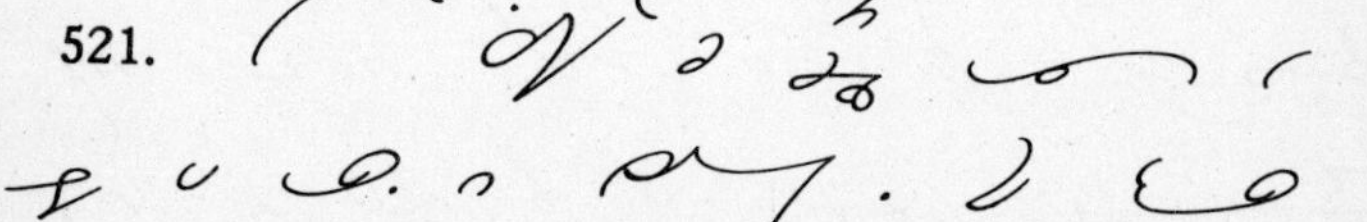

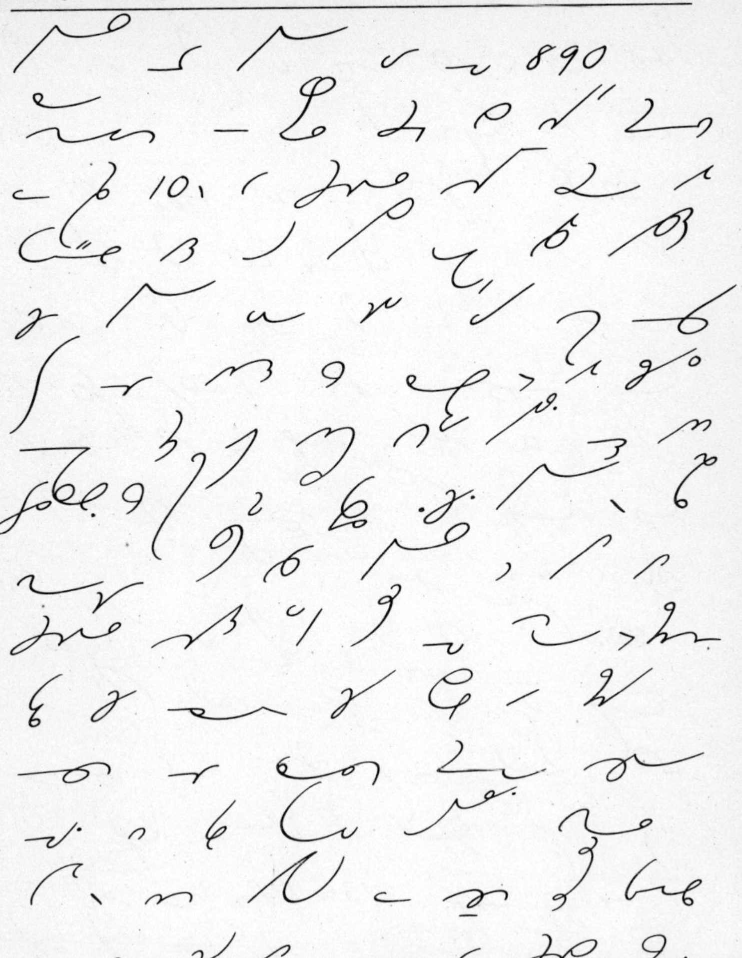
890
10

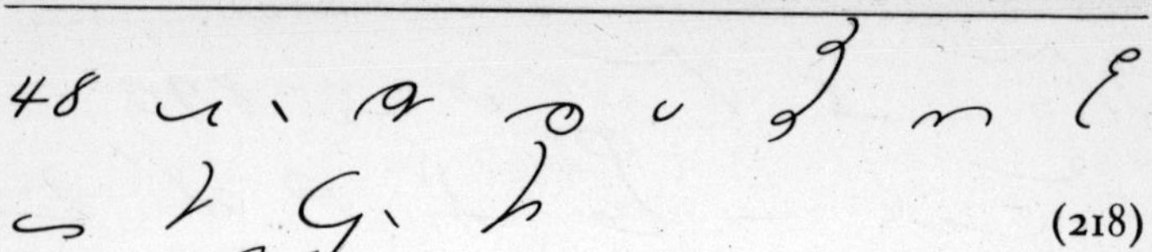

(218)

522.

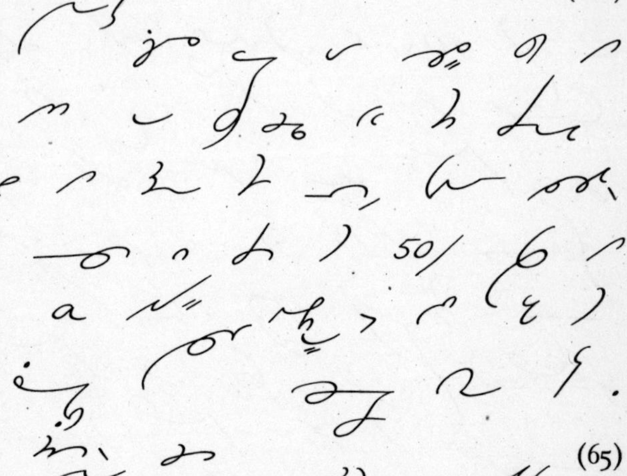

(65)

523.

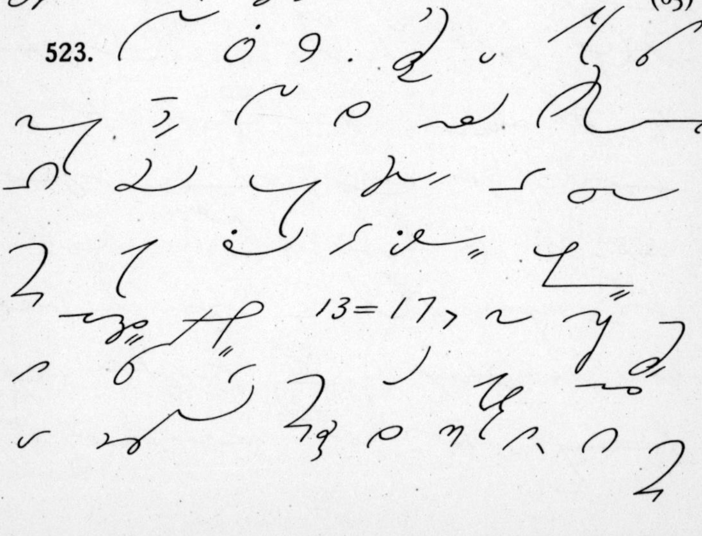

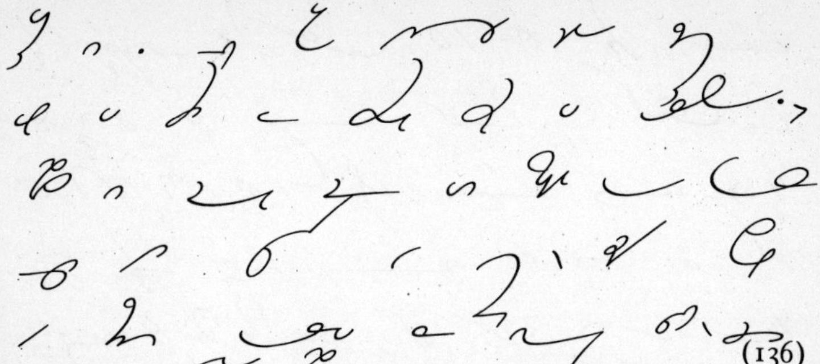

(136)

524.

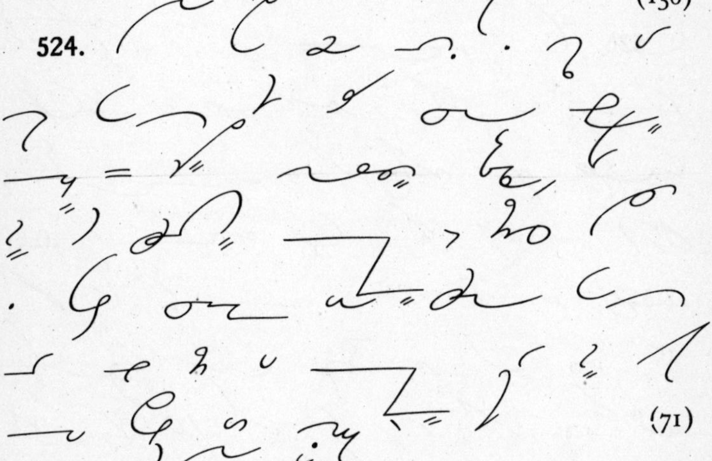

(71)

525.

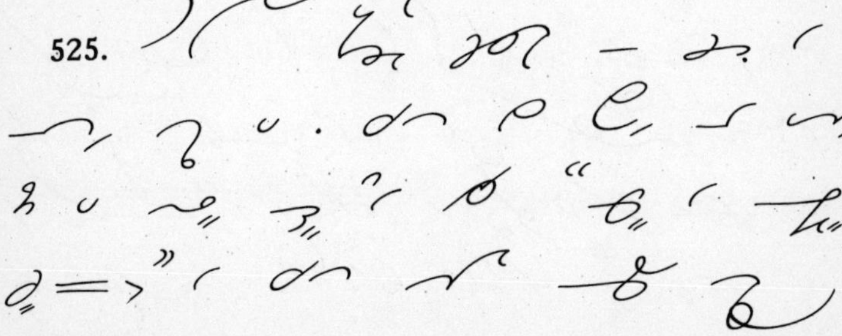

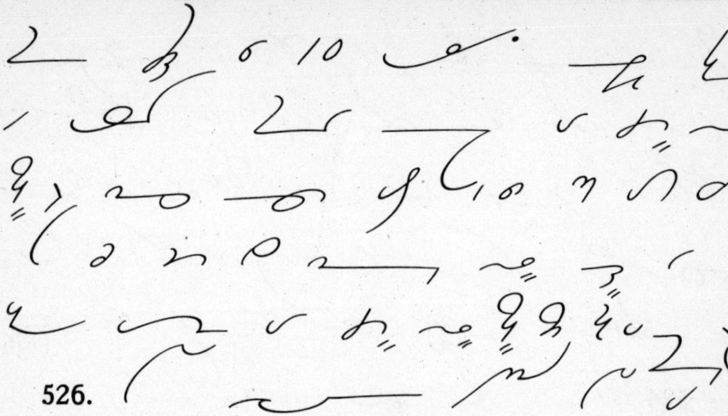

(103

526.

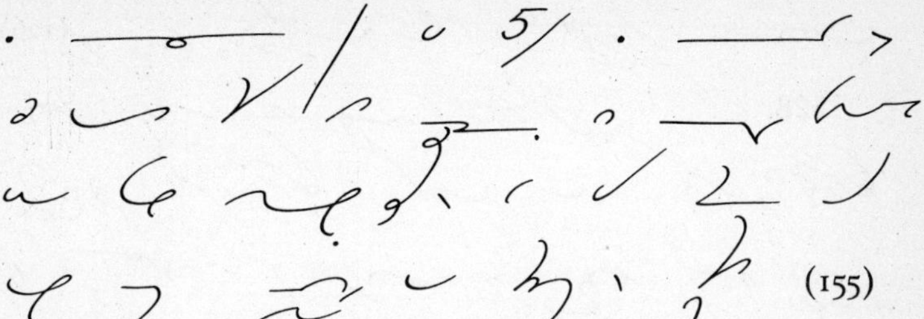

(155)

527.

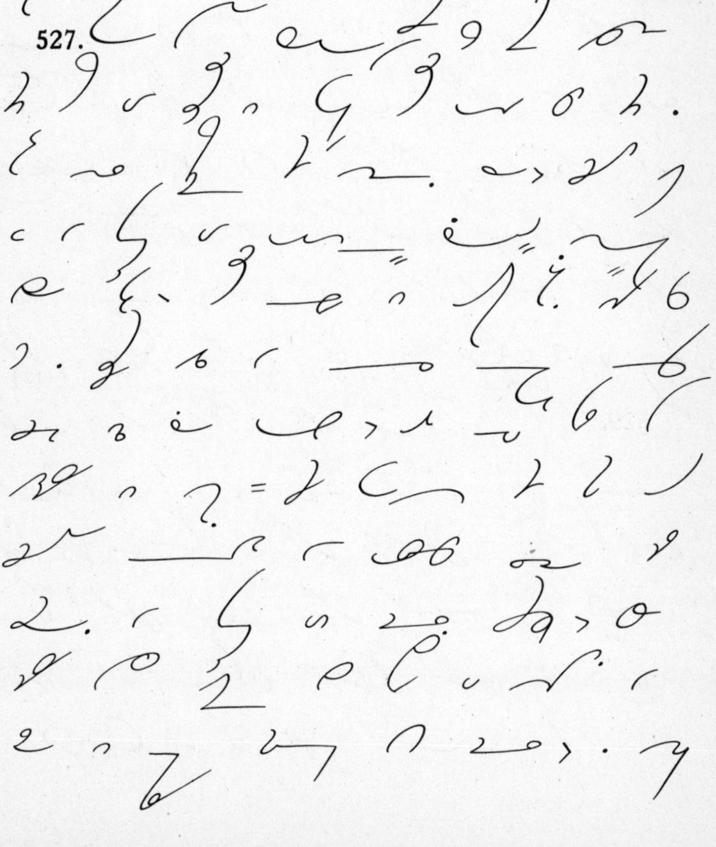

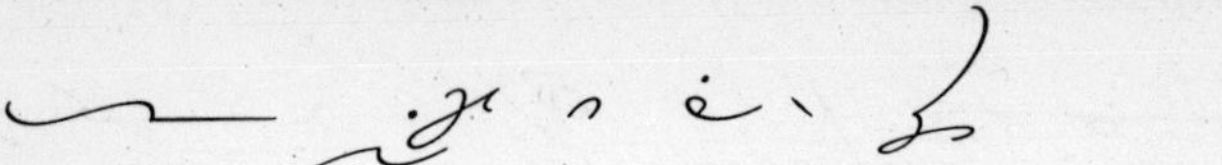

(126)

528.

(112)

529.

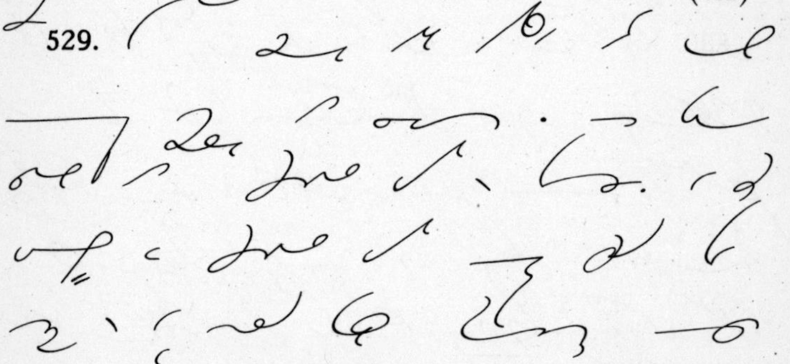

(156)

530.

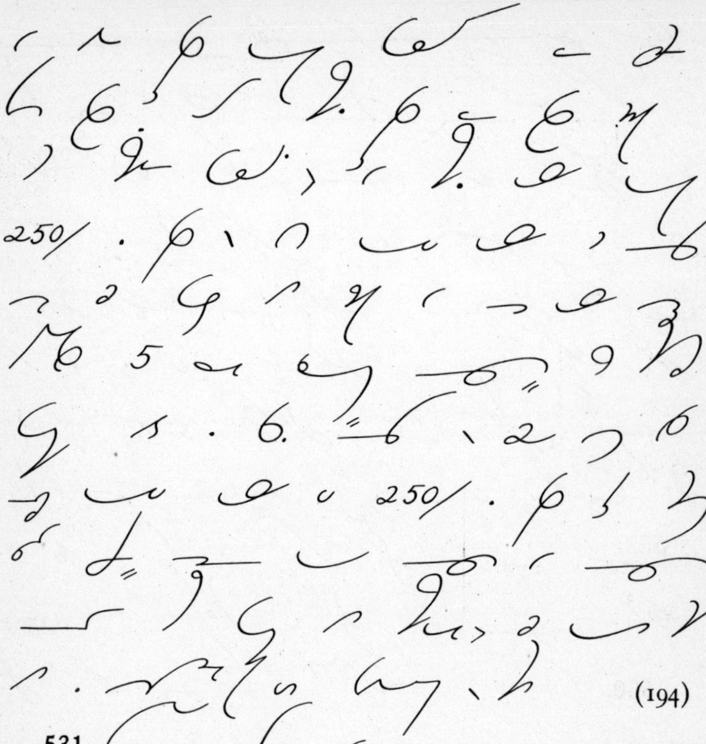

(194)

531.

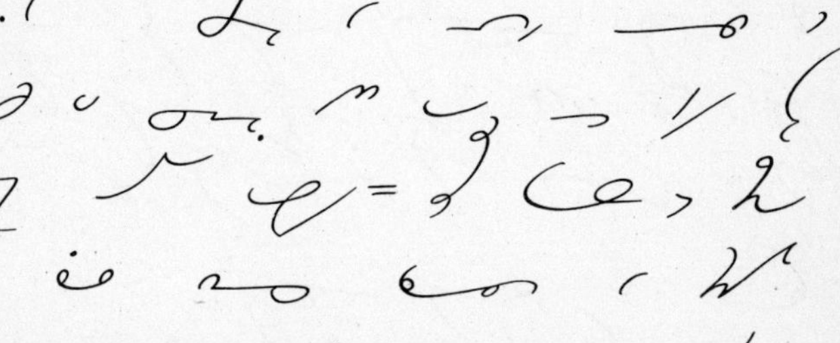

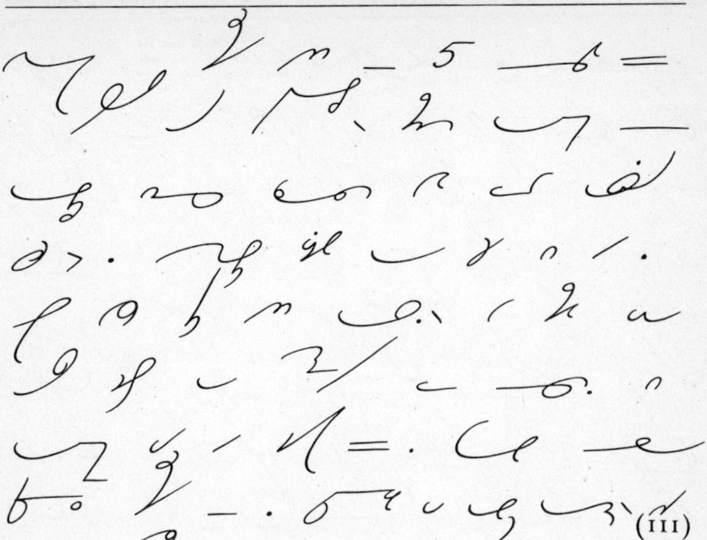

(111)

532.

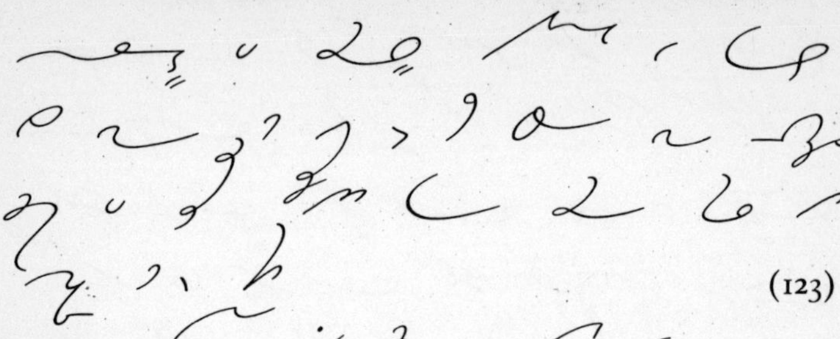

(123)

533.

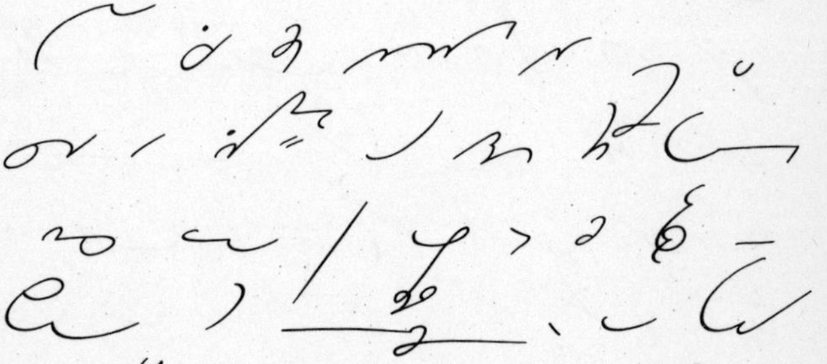

(98)

534.

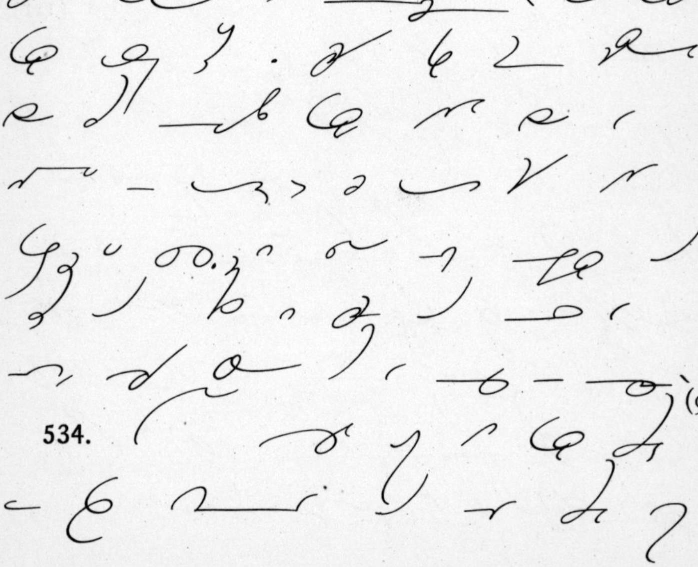

(193)

535.

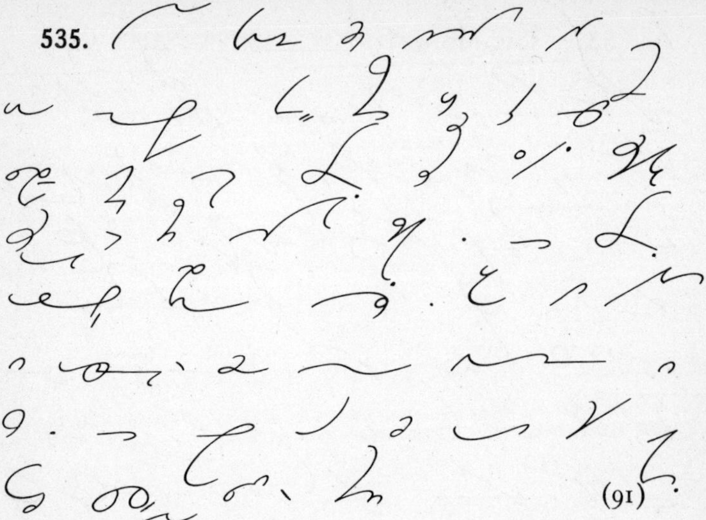

(91)

536.

(81)

537. The Monument in a City's Name

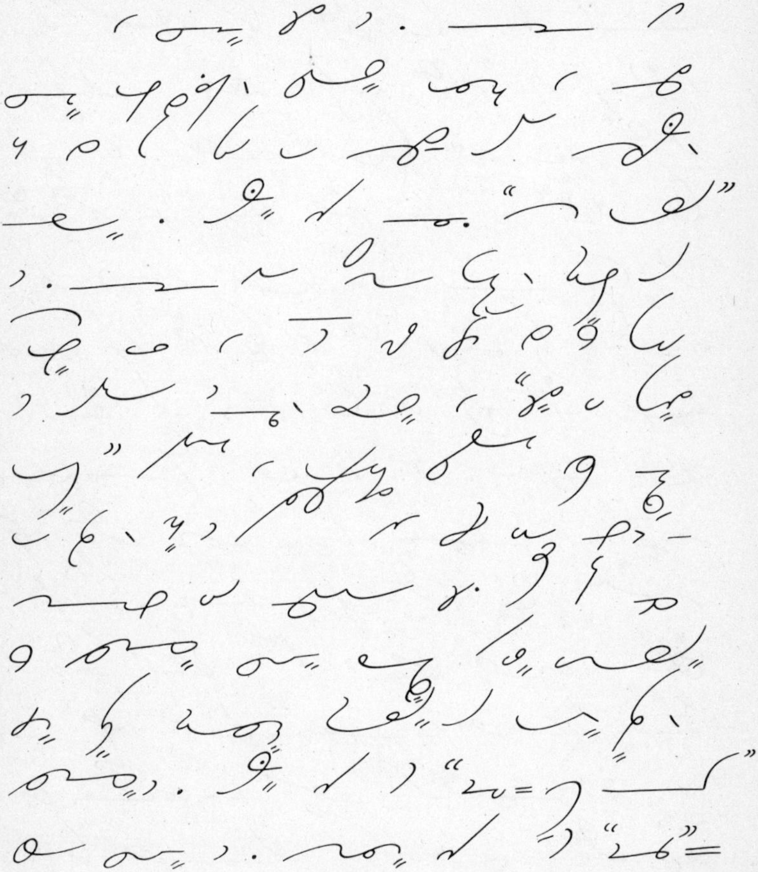

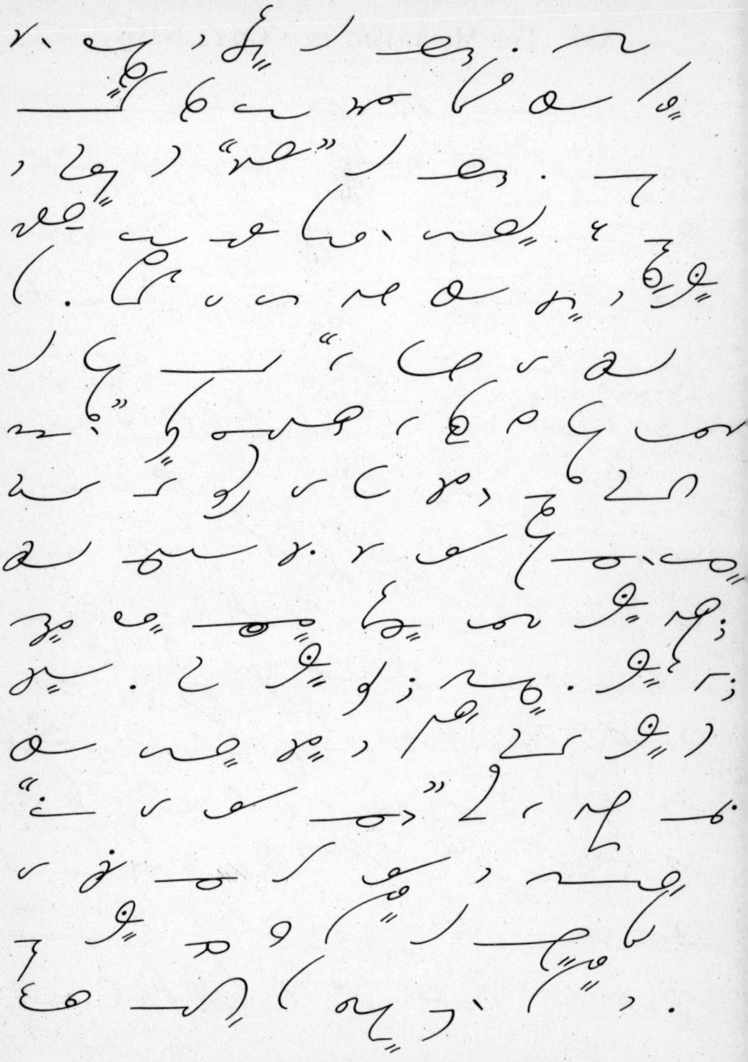

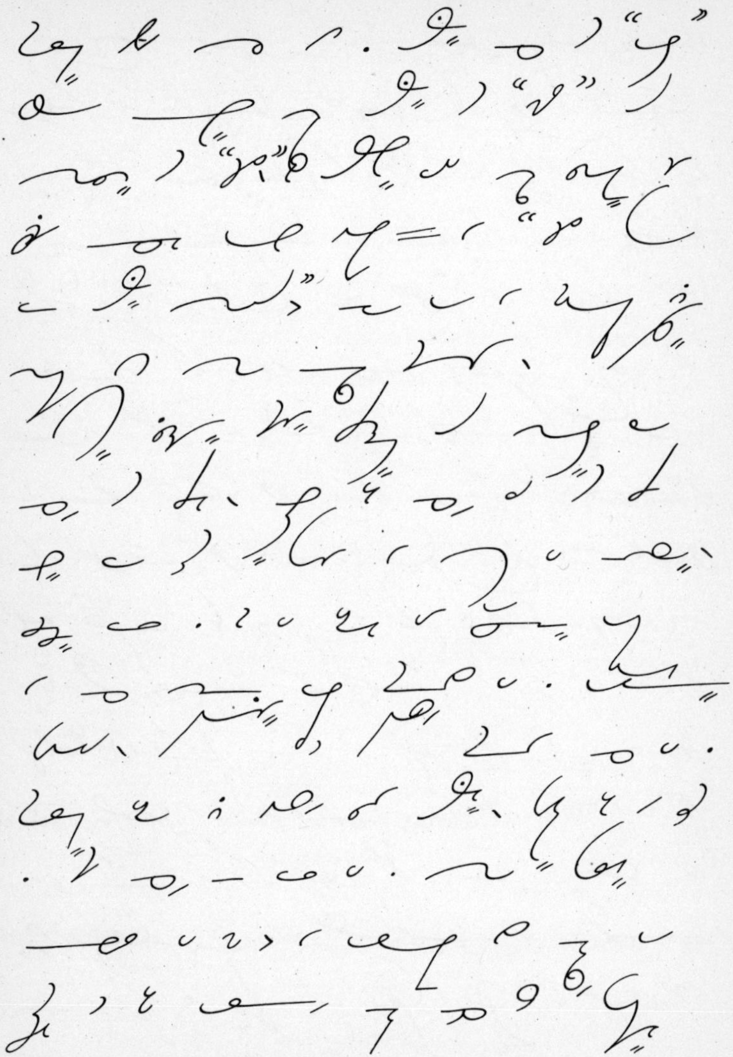

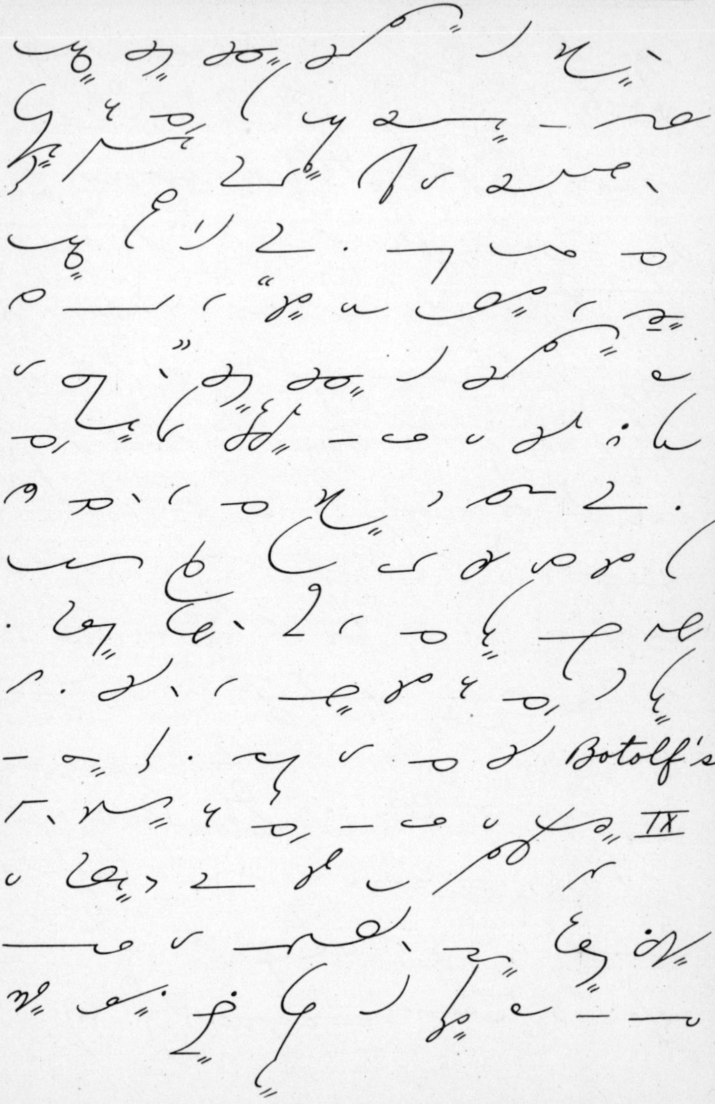
Botolf's
IX

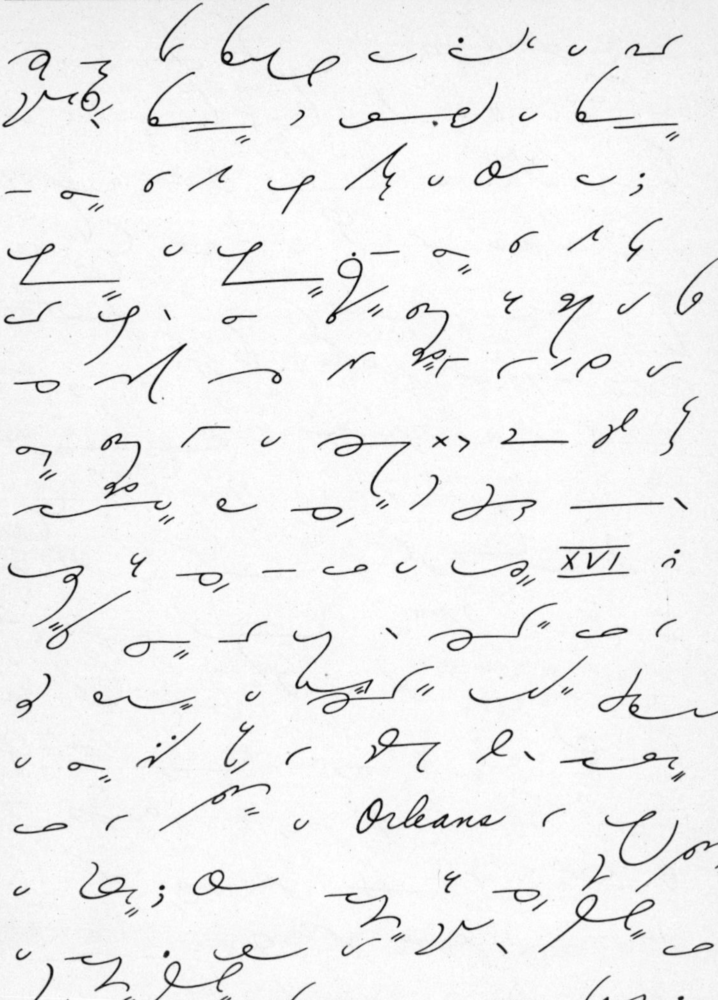
XVI
Orleans

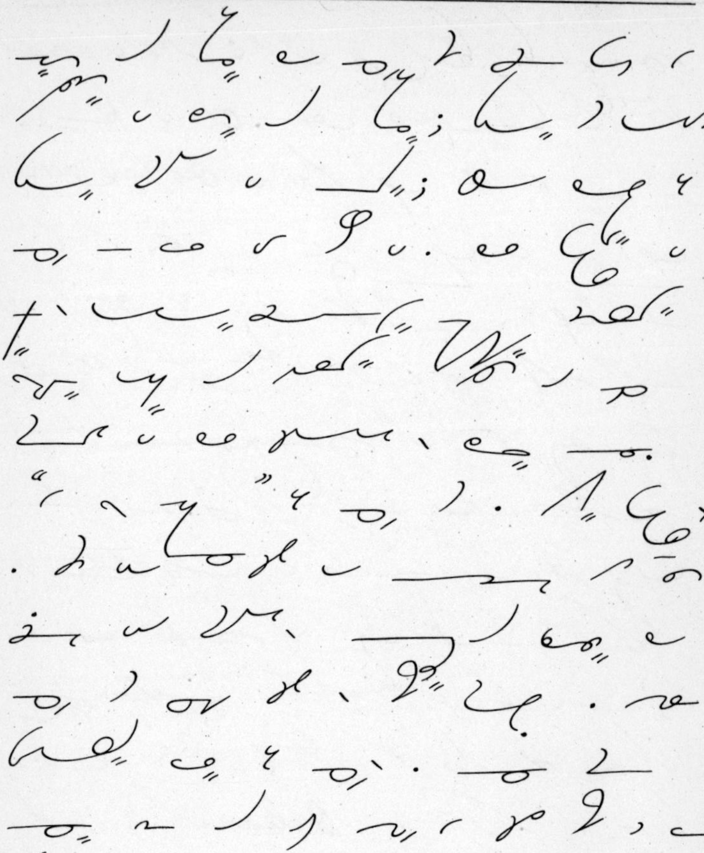

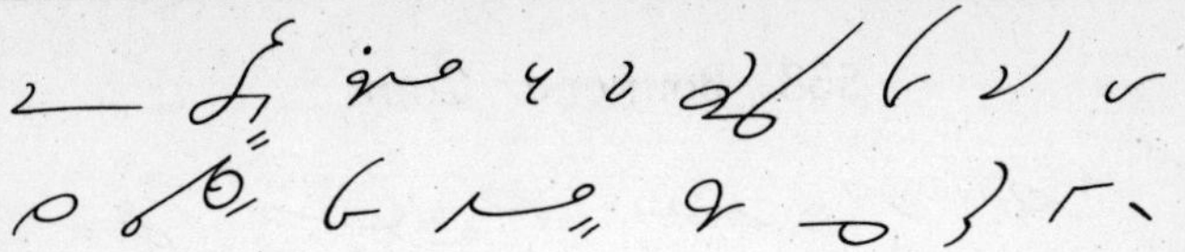

(988)

—*Lawrence David Brennan*

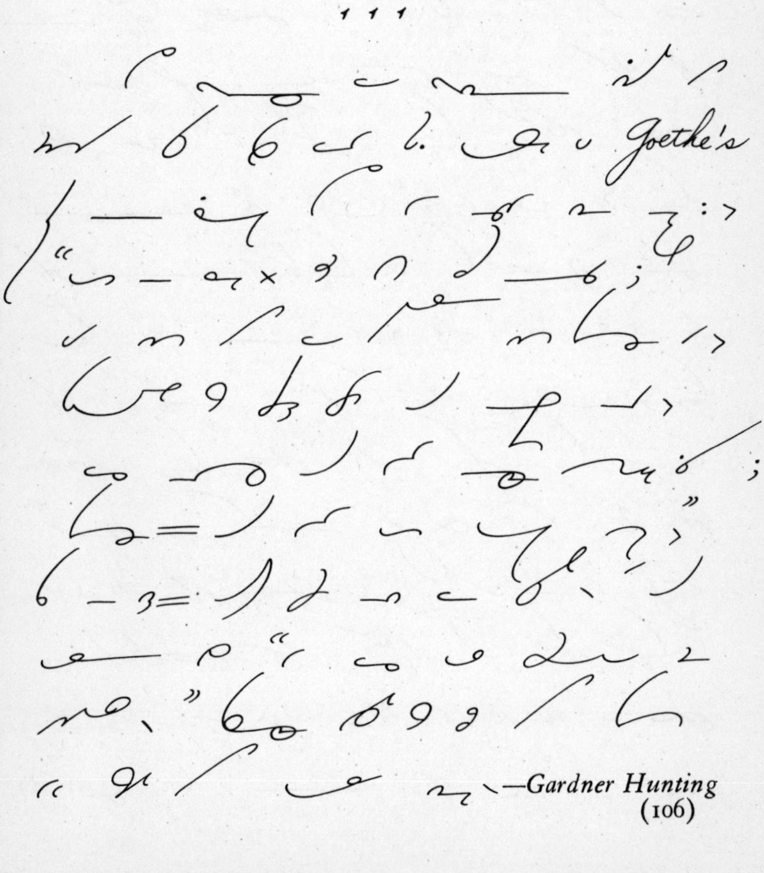

—*Gardner Hunting*
(106)

538. Bouncing Coins

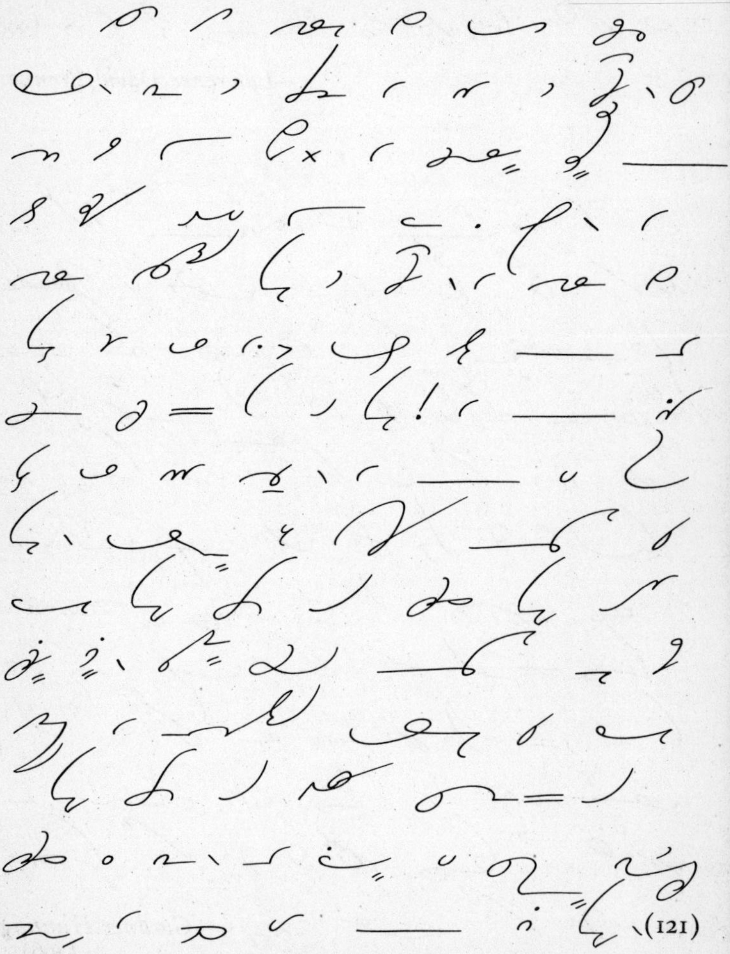

(121)